90 0891879 2

D1681072

EMOTIONAL BUREAUCRACY

EMOTIONAL BUREAUCRACY

Rupert Hodder

Transaction Publishers
New Brunswick (U.S.A.) and London (U.K.)

UNIVERSITY OF PLYMOUTH

9 008918792

Copyright © 2011 by Transaction Publishers, New Brunswick, New Jersey.

All rights reserved under International and Pan-American Copyright Conventions. No part of this book may be reproduced or transmitted in any form or by any means, electronic or mechanical, including photocopy, recording, or any information storage and retrieval system, without prior permission in writing from the publisher. All inquiries should be addressed to Transaction Publishers, Rutgers—The State University of New Jersey, 35 Berrue Circle, Piscataway, New Jersey 08854-8042. www.transactionpub.com

This book is printed on acid-free paper that meets the American National Standard for Permanence of Paper for Printed Library Materials.

Library of Congress Catalog Number: 2010051599
ISBN: 978-1-4128-1493-5
Printed in the United States of America

Library of Congress Cataloging-in-Publication Data

Hodder, Rupert.
    Emotional bureaucracy / Rupert Hodder.
        p. cm.
    Includes bibliographical references and index.
    ISBN 978-1-4128-1493-5 (alk. paper)
    1. Bureaucracy--Developing countries. 2. Bureaucracy--Psychological aspects. 3. Emotions--Political aspects. 4. Organizational sociology. 5. Developing countries--Politics and government. I. Title.

JF60.H63 2011
302.3'5--dc22

                                                          2010051599

Contents

List of Figures

List of Tables

List of Appendices

Acknowledgements

In the months spent treading the streets of Manila I was met only with kindness and candour. Yet in return all I can do—as I must do in a book of this type—is to be fair, and to extend my gratitude, to those who are named (and to those who remain anonymous) in the pages that follow. It is they who made this study possible. I am also indebted to Senator Miriam Defensor Santiago for her trust and invaluable support; to Sandy and Adel for their patience; and to Novelita for her memory, her files, and her shorthand. Special thanks, too, are owed: to Simeon Garcia, Girlie Amarillo, Willie Buenaventura, Mara, and Suharni for all their help and advice; to Neil Roberts and Richard Gibb who gave me the room to work on this; and to Tim, Jamie and Brian for their work on the tables and diagrams.

Preface

This book started out as an enquiry into the weakness of the Philippine civil service, but it quickly became an illustrative study of the importance of emotion in effective bureaucracy. Discussions with civil servants and politicians had begun to cast doubt on the Weberian distinction between emotion and a modern bureaucracy's impersonal and rational qualities, and led to quite another argument: that deepening emotion, a strengthened sense of the importance of social relationships, and informality are vital to the emergence of professional and stable organizations. Around this argument (which could not be particular to the Philippines) a still broader theme developed: that it is possible to account for social features with reference to actors' representations and practices.

Viewed through this perspective, actors' and scholars' representations (including notions of structure and culture) are necessarily of equal status, and interest is focused on the social world's "surface" features rather than on its putative deep or overarching structures (though the possibility that such phenomena exist is not ruled out). Implicit in this thinking is that the general is but a mental device—a way of arranging the particular; and that the world 'out there' must be extraordinarily fuzzy. Strings of representation and practice do form tangible opportunities and constraints; and there are ordered assemblies of strings. Shades of pattern and predictability arise from constant readjustments and compromise as actors seek a working fit with each other, aided by commonalities rooted in the human condition. These commonalities include, most fundamentally, an acute sense of self; a realization of the importance of interactions, relationships and community (upon which representations of self ultimately depend); and an understanding of the need to treat relationships, self, and others *as if* important in their own right. Yet these patterns of strings are poorly defined and are unable to reproduce themselves. They are better understood as congregations of everyday practicalities and commonalities rather than as closely integrated, large-scale, well-defined, and self-replicating arrangements in thought and behavior; and because they are dimensional, their subsequent influence (especially as constraints and opportunities) is ordinarily both uncertain and unpredictable.

Cast from this substance, bureaucracy is indefinite and ambiguous. Its weaknesses are as much about excessive formality as they are about personalistic behaviour, corruption, and political interference; and enmeshed around these features are other qualities—professionalism, technical competence, imagination, creativity, realistic compromise, commitment, and a willingness to take risks and suffer the consequences. Usually left unrecognised and undeveloped, these qualities—rooted in deepening emotion—keep the civil service and the organs of government working.

While these ideas are discussed in the context of the Philippines, they have much wider relevance to other states—especially, but not only, those whose bureaucracies are characterised as weak and personalistic. They suggest that these characteristics, and possible remedies, may need to be reconsidered: that it is through informality and emotion that more effective and stable organizations are built; and that excessive formalism may create the very problems that governments are trying to solve. The kernels—the means and qualities—around which bureaucracies might be strengthened are already "in-country" and need only be identified and encouraged.

Introduction

This study began with the simple, if ambitious, intention of understanding the weaknesses of Philippine bureaucracy. As it progressed, the study acquired two further levels of discussion. The first explores a model of bureaucracy—a model which, it is suggested, is peculiar neither to the Philippines nor to bureaucratic organizations. The second concerns ways of thinking about social features—ways that are more able to accommodate their dimensionality, less dependent upon the problem of structure, and less prone to their continuous bifurcation into classes (such as structure and agency, culture and structure, the political and economic, the formal and informal, the Western and non-Western, or even real and imagined). What emerges is an attempt to account for the social world and its attributes with reference to dimensional strings of representations (or understandings) and practices.

These discussions may be introduced through the matter of informality or, in other words, social relationships, emotion, and the unwritten norms and conventions that regulate them. Informality, it is often suggested, has an important place even in the most complex and formalized societies. It brings continuity despite alterations in the formal rules, processes, roles, and hierarchies of a society, and produces variation among societies with the same or very similar formal arrangements (North, 2004). And yet, as society becomes more sophisticated, formality is essential if predictability and stability are to be brought to organizations. Without it, organizations become weaker, interactions less efficient, and corruption more extensive. Informality and formality may lie along a continuum, but the two are quite distinct.

This distinction is sharpened by the suggestion that formality reflects a Weberian and, more generally, a Western cultural category. What is regarded as "informal" is, in fact, complex and different; and at the heart of this difference—and this is often thought to be especially true of Asia—is the primacy given to social relationships. Even corruption should not be seen in the narrow English sense of the word—with all its restrictive, provincial and puritan connotations—but rather as something more subtle, layered, and complex, like a "conversation, a ritual" (Haller and Shore, 2005: p. 3). In this respect, corruption is a form of exchange: a polysemus and multi-stranded relationship and part of the way in which individuals connect with the state (Haller and Shore: p. 7) Indeed, it is the ideal of formality and, more specifically, the rule of law and a legal-rational bureaucracy, which "gives rise to the concept of corruption in the first place" (ibid.).

This dichotomy between the formal (the legal-rational and the impersonal) and informal (the social and emotional) is questioned in this study on Philippine bureaucracy. Deepening emotion[1] or an "affective"[2] state—it is argued—is indispensable to the emergence of effective organizations. These terms describe the treatment of both emotion (as a general quality) and the understandings or representations[3] which actors form about (and in relation to) one another *as if* these matters are of importance in their own right. This requires the synchronous treatment of rules, processes, roles and hierarchies (and the organization itself)—the representations which inform the reconfiguration of emotion and relationships into a functioning corporation—*as if* significant in themselves. Synchronicity is necessary because without the treatment of these representations *as if* absolute, their mystique is lost, the true social nature of the corporation becomes evident, and the use of emotions and relationships for particular ends is laid bare. It also happens that, as a consequence, the corporation may become more unpredictable and unstable. It is in this way and for these reasons that emotion and social relationships (informal social practice) are translated everyday into official practice (formality).

Further, though more technical, qualities which may help to explain the efficacy of bureaucratic organizations are: the extent to which actors' understandings of their role within the organization, and of the organization's role within wider government and society, are aligned and integrated; and the circumstances or conditions (the prior matrix of understandings and practices) which account for the nature and alignment (or nonalignment) of current representations and practice. A matter that has a particular bearing on the case of the Philippines is the adoption of an American-style government with its heavy emphasis on the division of authority. Informed by these practices and representations, bureaucracy shatters and, within its shards, partial and partisan understandings of government evolve; authority is widely perceived to be misallocated; and, in an attempt to remedy the apparent situation, rules and process are circumvented.

This emotional perspective confronts a tendency to conflate emotion with either irrationality or personalism (the use of relationships to secure personal ends); and to equate the impersonal with the proper state of affairs, with following the rules, and with impartial, effective and clean government. In fact, this perspective goes further and suggests that a fetish with being impersonal and with absolute rules, roles, and processes (and so, with correct behavior, strict propriety and the repression of any sign of instrumentalism) may both encourage and shroud a return to strongly personalistic behavior. It is where Puritanism and orthopraxy are strongest (as in those countries described as Western) that corruption, well hidden at first, is likely to proliferate. Emotion, then, is placed at the core of an effective bureaucracy not because the Philippine civil service is "Asian" but because emotion and everyday social relationships are crucial to effective operation of any bureaucracy, East and West, North and South.

Strands of these arguments have appeared in the *Asian Journal of Social Science, Asian Studies Review, Environment and Planning C (Government and Policy)*, and *Geography Compass*, and in still earlier work (most especially on overseas Chinese and Filipino businesses). These publications are mentioned only because it helps to emphasize that this study was approached with various ideas in mind but with no framework intact. Indeed, as the work began in the field in Manila in 2007 it was clear that the application of any particular theoretical device would be rendered problematic by the comparative thinness of empirical and theoretical material on the civil service (whose analysis has been dominated by public administration perspective) and the wider political economy (in whose analysis patronage figures very strongly). Such a narrow base would only make it easier to accept, and more difficult to contradict, the motives and behavior assigned to politicians and civil servants through the application of one or another theoretical framework. For this reason, attention and energies were directed at gathering as many detailed (and triangulated) accounts and explanations of practice as possible from civil servants and politicians. As this material accumulated, however, it became clear that many possible and often contradictory frameworks (including many of those which have not been explored in the case of the Philippines) were capable of yielding intriguing and useful explanations for certain aspects of behavior but could not cope with others. The problem, then, is how to handle these dimensions?

The solution chosen is to accommodate civil servants' and politicians' accounts and explanations rather than to reject or re-interpret them in line with a preferred theoretical position. For these accounts, it is argued, trace interactions between "dimensional" practices and representations. That is to say, a given practice (such as the decision to rotate staff, or the influence exerted by a politician on an appointment in the civil service) or representation (such as the perceived misalllocation of authority over the national budget) lies at the intersection—and simultaneously forms part—of several different strings of representations and practices. It is these strings of meaning and events that together constitute, say, "division," "office," "rule," "process," "hierarchy," "agency," "legislature," or "government," each of which (in so far as their constituent strings interconnect) is fused with one another.

An important element of this argument is that "self," "others," "social structure," or "culture"—whether formed by scholar or bureaucrat—are also representations, and have a bearing on the social world only to the extent that they inform practice. In this sense they are no different from "government," "office," "process," or "rule." This point is of some importance because it refocuses attention on what might be called the surface features of the social world rather than on the "deep" structures of mind or society. There is, therefore, no compulsion to disentangle actors: either from the rules and principles which they create (and which, it is believed, are probably embedded at least partly in their genetic material and brain structures); or from those "external" regularized patterns of behavior which it is believed shape actors and which are, in turn, embodied and reproduced by them. In other words, it is assumed (*provisionally*) that understanding and explanation do not lie ultimately with something else (some kinds of biological or social structures) beyond practice and representation. Certainly, practice may impose very real limits and open up possibilities, so actors' representations of the social world may constitute what are, to them, tangible obstacles or incentives: together these strings of representations and practice comprise powerful constraints and opportunities. However, practices and representations are complex and dimensional, as are their antecedents[4] and their sequents.[5] Were it possible to step outside this matrix, then the patterns formed by these strings would appear to be extraordinarily fuzzy and indistinct. Representations of a world comprising sharply defined patterns may have a functional value in that they enable actors to operate and get by from day to day; and these representations may—to a limited extent, and more locally than over distance—find temporary and partial expression through practice. But, in the main, actors necessarily achieve a working fit with one another (and, therefore, a reasonable and practical degree of order and stability) through the constant readjustment of their representations and practice. This fit is achieved "necessarily" because fixed and coherent patterns of any great scale would breakdown more easily, while localized and constant adjustments are more flexible and durable. To this end, actors' representations of the general and distant social world are more functional rather than accurate. Thus, the fuzziness of the social world is perpetuated.

As the accounts of civil servants and politicians accumulated, a number of qualities in addition to their dimensionality began to emerge. Three of these are particularly significant. One is the common perception that, across government, authority is misallocated: that some branches, agencies and offices have too much authority while others have too little to carry out their functions and fulfil their duties properly. As already noted, the adoption of American-style government is one important reason for the emergence of insular and fragmented perspectives. But a marked difference among representations and practice, rather than sameness, is probably the default quality in a nation that is young, fragmented physically and linguistically, and a colonial manufacture. The prominence given to the market, and the efforts directed at economic growth both before and since independence, are also likely to produce different understandings of wealth, status, and purpose.

A second, and closely related, quality is widespread differences among officials both in their understandings (or representations) of the nature, function and behavior of other parts of government and other officials, and in the level of detail of their understandings. For instance, at the lower levels of the civil service, though not only at these levels, it is not unusual to find that officials have little sense of what it is that other officials, offices, agencies or branches of government do, or of how they should be integrated.

The third quality is the presence of affective and instrumental behavior in the same or very similar circumstances. It is suggested that deepening emotion forms part of three interlocking (rather than mutually exclusive) cycles at whose heart lies representations of "self" and "others." These cycles do not constitute external "forces." They are intended only as a means of describing strings of practice and representations whose abstraction, conceptually, from a fuzzy and dimensional matrix helps to account for particular features of the bureaucracy. Instrumentalism (it is argued) emerges with representations of self—representations which derive in part from the experience of awareness and the erroneous conclusion that self is the source of that awareness. But with awareness and the acquisition of a public language also comes the realization that "self" is rooted in, and dependent upon, interactions with other people and the natural world. The protection of relationships is therefore a powerful compulsion and a basic principle of practice. The first cycle begins when self, repeatedly challenged, tries to reassert its presence and qualities; and, as a consequence, instrumentalism and a sense of alienation strengthen. This downward spiral of alienation and instrumentalism (aided by over-conformity and authoritarianism as attempts are made to bring stability) prompts deepening emotion and then, in order to protect emotion, synchronous behavior within organizations. As effective organizations become prevalent and routine, there is a risk that an appreciation of the significance of deepening emotion will be dulled: and gradually and imperceptibly the distinction between relationships, emotion, rules, processes and organizations treated *as if* absolute and *as* absolute is lost. At first, in this puritanical atmosphere, any symptom of instrumentalism is prohibited. Self is at once idolized and hemmed in by an increasingly tight and complex mesh of orthopraxy. And once again, as this sense of repression and the desire to reassert self builds, a spiral of alienation and instrumentalism gathers pace.

The fundamental interdependency and interaction of these cycles may help describe other features, too. The significance of informality is overlooked when its translation is so much a part of everyday life and it is has become commonplace to accept the treatment of rules and process *as if* absolute; but it does become more noticeable when its reconfiguration into official practice is disrupted. When, in the case of the Philippines, relationships are used to circumvent and undermine rules and processes (such as those governing civil service appointments) for personal ends; when there are divergent representations of government, its functions and policies (and, therefore, sharp differences over which rules and processes are accepted and acceptable); when there is over-conformity (and, therefore, little or no possibility that rules and processes can evolve along with understandings about what civil servants believe to be important and needs to be done); and when authority is perceived to be misallocated such that divisions in authority conflict with the fulfilment of what are felt to be critical responsibilities and duties: under these circumstances, as existing sets of rules, processes and organizations lose psychological force, and as civil servants attempt to keep organizations functioning through their own devices, informality becomes increasingly obvious.

The features of Philippine bureaucracy, then, are multiple and dimensional, and blanket judgments are, more often than not, unhelpful. Rarely are organizations exclusively self-serving or corrupt, or professional and compassionate: they are, more usually, ambiguous.

Notes

1. Emotion is understood here to refer to a belief about, and a desire for (or in relation to), something.
2. Following Aron (1935), the term "affective" is used by Gerth and Wright Mills (1977, p.57) to describe a type of action that flows from emotion. In this present book, "affective" or "affect" are used as above: to describe the idealization of relationships (and emotion) or, in other words, their treatment *as if* important in their own right.
3. Understandings or representations are used to describe constructs or mental states about a thing that may exist or which may only imagined, but in either case may inform practice. Representations therefore encompass emotions as well as ideas, beliefs, and imaginings.
4. The strings of practice and representation that inform the current string.
5. The strings informed by current strings of representations and practices.

1

Toward a Model of Emotional Bureaucracy

Introduction

The Philippines' civil servants staff the country's executive agencies, the secretariats of the legislature, the five commissions, the judiciary, local government, the Autonomous Region of Muslim Mindanao (ARMM), and the corporations owned or controlled by the government. They aid politicians in the formulation of policy and they implement policies; they keep the legislature and its committees working and help legislators and their staff draw up laws; they gather, coordinate and transmit information; they collect revenue; and they provide direct to the citizenry services of one kind or another, from the administration of justice, to policing, education, and health. In spite of its faults, which are many, the civil service is essential to the life of the Philippines. Without it the organs of government, inefficient though they may often be, would cease to function.

The Civil Service Commission (CSC) provides the service with a rudimentary sense of identity. The commission is responsible for: establishing the policies, regulations, procedures, qualifications, standards, and codes of conduct that shape recruitment, discipline, and other personnel matters (such as training). It also rules on administrative—as distinct from criminal—cases; and it defends and fosters the service in such a way as to strengthen the overall administration of the Republic. The organization of the service into three levels—first (clerical), second (technical and professional), and third (managerial)—also works to bind the service by setting out a clear hierarchy of authority and a ladder for advancement.

Third-level staffs hold the rank of director or above, and it is at third level that the bulk of political appointments (in national government agencies) are made. Political appointees occupying the highest echelons are usually brought in from outside the civil service and are, by virtue of their appointment, classified as non-career civil servants. The terms "non-career" civil servants and "political appointees" are, therefore, widely and loosely used interchangeably by civil servants and politicians, and this convention is followed in these pages. However, this convention ignores two facts: not all non-career civil servants are political appointees (there are very large numbers of contractual and casual staff); and career civil servants may also serve as political appointees (especially, though not only, at director level).

1

The highest-ranking, civil servants (non-career and career) together with complements of other ranks are housed in an agency's or a department's "central office." Both these terms—department and agency—are used to refer to an entire organization, such as the Bureau of Customs or Department of Education or Civil Service Commission (CSC). In some cases these agencies, while discrete, comprise part of a much larger agency. Thus, the Bureau of Customs and the Bureau of Internal Revenue fall under the Department of Finance. "Office" (when it is not used in the official title of an agency, such as the Office of the President) refers to the main functional segments (such as budget or accounting or human resources) within an agency.

The terms given to the internal segments and hierarchies of an agency (led by a Secretary), vary from one agency to the next. For the sake of consistency, "group" (led by Undersecretaries and Assistant Secretaries) describes a set of offices (usually with related and mutually supporting roles); "offices" (led by various grades of Directors) are usually arranged into divisions (led by a Division Chief) which are split into sections (each led by a Section Chief). In the Commissions, Directors are subordinate to Assistant Commissioners, Deputy Commissioners and Commissioners. At the regional level, national-line agencies are usually organized as an Office and are led by a Director.

Basic statistics on the civil service (or bureaucracy) are unreliable. For instance, figures available for the numbers of civil servants are derived from a census conducted by the CSC every four or five years. At the time of writing, the most recent census, 2004, puts the total number of civil servants in central and local government (excluding contractual staffs) at 1.33 million (see table 1). This figure excludes contractual employees and elected officials who together bring the total number of government workers to 1.47 million (see appendix I). The majority (67 percent) of civil servants (career and non-career) work in agencies of the National Executive; a little over a fifth (21 percent) occupy the three layers of local governments (provincial, city and municipal) (see appendices II, III, IV); and some 6.6 percent work in corporations owned or controlled by the government. By far the largest agency—with nearly 498,000 civil servants—is the Department of Education (which excludes State Universities and Colleges). The vast majority (86.5 percent) of its civil servants are teachers. Similarly, within the second-largest agency (the Department of Interior and Local Government) most (91 percent) staffs are uniformed officers in the police, fire or penal services. Even so, DepEd remains the largest agency with some 66,000 non-teaching staffs.

Non-career civil servants (or political appointees) constitute only 1.4 percent of the total Service (see table 2). The proportion is a little higher in the Department of Public Works and Highways, the Department of Transport and Communications, the Department of Trade and Industry, the Department of Energy, local government (see appendices II, III), the Judiciary, and government corporations; and it is much higher (see appendices V and

Table 1
Civil Servants (Career and Non-Career)

Congress Of The Philippines	4826
National Executive Agencies	
Department Of Education	497767
Department Of Interior And Local Government	149234
State Universities And Colleges	54835
Department Of Health	26307
Department Of Environment And Natural Resources	20550
Department Of Finance	19075
Department Of Public Works And Highways	18140
Department Of Justice	16137
Other Executive Offices	15380
Department Of Agrarian Reform	13905
Department Of Transportation And Communications	12416
Department Of Agriculture	12043
Department Of National Defense	9082
Department Of Labor And Employment	7272
Department Of Science And Technology	4405
National Economic And Development Authority	4233
Department Of Trade And Industry	3191
Office Of The Press Secretary	2319
Department Of Social Welfare And Development	2263
Department Of Foreign Affairs	1881
Department Of Tourism	1322
Office Of The President	1084
Department Of Budget And Management	865
Department Of Energy	621
Office Of The Vice-President	89
Local Government Units	
Municipal Governments	114635
City Governments	88736
Provincial Governments	73622
Constitutional Offices	17255
The Judiciary	26878
Government Owned and Controlled Corporations	88923
Autonomous Regions In Muslim Mindanao	24961
TOTAL CAREER AND NON-CAREER	**1334252**

Source: compiled from materials provided by the CSC, 2007.

VI) in those agencies whose functions are essentially political—the Office of the President (26.5 percent), the Office of the Vice President (22.5 percent), and the legislature (the Senate [52 percent] and the House of Representatives or Lower House [54 percent]).

The agencies considered in this book include: DepEd; the Bureau of Customs (with nearly 5,000 staffs) and the Bureau of Internal Revenue (a little

Table 2
Political Appointees as a Percentage of the Civil Service

	PA	PA%
Congress Of The Philippines	2509	52.0
National Executive Agencies		
Department Of Education	973	0.2
Department Of Public Works And Highways	482	2.7
Other Executive Offices	348	2.3
Office Of The President	287	26.5
Department Of Transportation And Communications	265	2.1
Department Of Agriculture	176	1.5
State Universities And Colleges	171	0.3
Department Of Labor And Employment	116	1.6
Department Of Finance	114	0.6
Department Of Justice	100	0.6
Department Of Environment And Natural Resources	95	0.5
Department Of Trade And Industry	77	2.4
Department Of National Defense	67	0.7
Department Of Interior And Local Government	58	0.04
Department Of Agrarian Reform	40	0.3
Department Of Social Welfare And Development	32	1.4
Office Of The Vice-President	20	22.5
Department Of Energy	20	3.2
Department Of Science And Technology	20	0.5
Office Of The Press Secretary	17	0.7
Department Of Tourism	14	1.1
Department Of Foreign Affairs	13	0.7
National Economic And Development Authority	13	0.3
Department Of Health	10	0.04
Department Of Budget And Management	3	0.3
Local Government Units		
City Governments	2885	3.3
Municipal Governments	3694	3.2
Provincial Governments	1674	2.3
Constitutional Offices	251	1.5
The Judiciary	1144	4.3
Government-Owned And Government-Controlled Corporations	2254	2.5
Autonomous Regions In Muslim Mindanao	144	0.6
Total	**18086**	**1.4**

Explanatory note: These figures include personnel classified as 'non-career executives' and 'non-career service'. 'Non-career executive' refers to placements at the upper echelons of an agency (usually its head) made by the President with the agreement of the Commission on Appointments, or by another official body); and either they serve at the pleasure of the appointing authority, or their term in office is prescribed by law. 'Non-career service' refers to placements at lower ranks; and whose terms are, again, either coterminous with the President (or another appointing authority) or tied to the duration of a specific project for which purpose the appointment was made. These figures exclude personnel who are elected, or who are classed as contractual (employed for less than a year) or as casual or 'job orders' (employed for less than 6 months and usually paid by the hour).

Source: compiled from materials provided by the CSC, 2007.

over 11,000) both of which fall under the Department of Finance; the Civil Service Commission awith around 1,300 staffs; the Senate and the Lower House (with staffs of around 1,500 and nearly 3,000 respectivelya); Quezon City Government (or City Hall) with nearly 5,000 civil servants; and the Manila Metropolitan Development Authority (MMDA) with a little under 5,000 civil servants.

Finding Perspective

Although responsible for the day-to-day business of government—and despite its complexity and size—relatively little academic analysis has been directed at the Philippine civil service or bureaucracy. Empirical data and field studies are fragmented, poorly disseminated, and often remain unpublished. The conceptual basis of its study is also patchy. Very few models of the Philippine bureaucracy have been developed. Amongst the most notable contributions are those made by Varela (1990, 1995, 1996) and Cariño (1992). Varela directs attention at the distortion of a properly functioning bureaucracy by Filipino culture. De Guzman (2003), too, argues that what is formally prescribed by government may not in fact be practiced because of the administration's search for flexibility as external family, kinship, political and socioeconomic groups bring their influence to bear. Cariño, on the other hand, in her model of bureaucracy as "administrative development," argues that the Philippine bureaucracy is shaped: by a constant struggle with the executive (a struggle which reaches its peak during legitimate and illegitimate change of executives); and by the behavior of a range of other actors within and outside government.

There have also been only few attempts to explore the relevance and potential value of those theoretical approaches which—though formulated with reference to bureaucracies in other developing societies as well as in "the West"—appear to lend themselves to the study of the Philippine civil service. For the most part its study has been dominated by just one approach—public administration. This directs interest at the processes, content and implementation of policies and programs of government, and at the delivery of services to the people through "cooperative human action" (De Guzman, 2003, p. 4) whether in the public bureaucracy, in the private sector, in non-governmental organizations, or in society more generally. Thus, Philippine bureaucracy tends to be viewed as only one amongst many sets of activities and organizations (public, private, and voluntary) that are the proper subject of study.

These studies comprise a number of fields: the management, leadership, and re-engineering of political, economic, bureaucratic and voluntary organizations and their interactions; the participation of private and voluntary organizations in the public sector; the privatization of public organizations; the direct participation of citizens in planning, implementing, and delivering public services to the people; fiscal and monetary policy; local government and finance; technology's contribution to effective government; administrative accountability; and the strengthening of values conducive to effective administration. Many of these studies necessarily touch upon the bureaucracy, but relatively few concentrate wholly or largely on the civil service. Those that do, tend cluster within three of these fields. In the first (reorganization, management, and leadership), efforts focus primarily on the bureaucracy's historical evolution,[1] on its infiltration by what are held to be cultural features (including patronage), on its technical adjustment (including adjustments to pay, incentives, grades, and performance management systems), and on the failure the draw a clear line between the civil service and the polity.[2] In the second and third fields—administrative accountability, and the propagation of correct values—interest is directed mainly at corruption's effects, causes, and solutions.[3]

Underlying many of these studies is Weber's notion of rational bureaucracy which, in its ideal form, is both technically superior to any other kind of organization (Gerth and Wright Mills [eds. and trans.] 1977 [hereafter referred to as "Weber"], p. 214), and the most highly developed means of power ("Weber," p. 232). These qualities, Weber believed, owe much to a type of rational action described as instrumental or end-rational. This refers to an interest in means, rather than in the given ends or wants to which those means are directed. In contrast, value-rational action refers to the primacy of an interest and belief in particular values for their own sake rather than in the means by which they may be lived out. Both these types of rational action are contrasted with less rational or irrational types of motivated action—"affectual" action (motivated by sentiment or emotion) and "traditional" action (motivated by unreflective habit). Understood in this way, rational bureaucracy possesses a number of other important and related features. First, it separates the bureaucrats' private life from their official life. Secondly, the bureaucracy, as it develops, becomes increasingly mechanistic and depersonalized. Business is discharged according to calculable rules and without regard to persons. And the more it is dehumanized—and the more completely it succeeds in eliminating from official business "love, hatred, and all purely personal, irrational, and emotional elements which escape calculation"—the closer it moves towards perfection ("Weber," p. 216). Thirdly, the bureaucracy is based upon the leveling of economic and social differences, and, once established, works to level those differences still further. Indeed, bureaucracy inevitably accompanies mass democracy. "This results from the characteristic principle of democracy: the abstract regularity of the execution of authority which is the result of the demand for 'equality before the law' in the personal and functional sense—hence, of the horror of 'privilege' and the principled rejection of doing business 'from case to case'" ("Weber," p. 224). Fourthly, the bureaucracy takes on a permanent character. It is "*the* means of carrying 'community action' over into rationally ordered 'societal action'"[4] which, if methodically ordered and led, "is superior to every resistance of 'mass' or even of 'communal action.' And once the bureaucratization of administration has been completely carried through, a form of power relation is established that is practically unshatterable" ("Weber," p. 228). Rational bureaucracy, then, destroys those structures of domination (such as patrimonialism and patriarchy) which have no rational characteristics ("Weber," p. 244). But its march is relentless: the individual bureaucrat "cannot squirm out of the apparatus in which he is harnessed....the professional bureaucrat is chained to his activity by his entire material and ideal existence. In the great majority of cases, he is only a single cog in an ever-moving mechanism which prescribes to him as essentially fixed route..." ("Weber," p. 228). As the bureaucracy expands, as the fate of the masses is made dependent upon it, and as all are ushered into the machine, creativity, honor, charisma, and the individual are eroded; and humanity is condemned to a dull, repetitive existence.

Weber's influence is not always made explicit in studies of the Philippine civil service,[5] even though the service either aspires to or exhibits (though by no means either consistently or perfectly) all of the specific characteristics possessed by a bureaucracy as understood by Weber: fixed and official jurisdictions; principles of office hierarchy and levels of graded authority; the creation and preservation of files; officials imbued with special technical learning of the organizations' rules and through training in the specific aspect of their job; officials who are appointed on merit (and who are not considered the personal servant of the ruler), who are tenured, who earn a fixed salary, who are presented with a clear career structure, and who are held in high esteem. However, Weber's work does appear to speak more easily to studies of the Philippine polity. And it is from these studies that some of the most influential commentaries on the Philippines have emerged over the last sixty years. Of particular significance has been the work of Carl Lande who, when he began his work in the Philippines in the 1950s, was struck by the fact that in every province it was members of the wealthier classes or their representatives who led the two major political parties, and who benefited from government policy and action. How did they manage to win the votes of the poor? An important part of the answer, Lande argued, was the system of patron-client relationships or political clientelism: "the upwards flow of votes from ordinary voters to wealthy candidates ... and in return, the downward distribution of public and private funds and other favors to individual leaders and their followers among voters. Hoping to share in this distribution of benefits, poor voters could not afford to vote their class interests by supporting candidates of the left" (Lande, 2002: 120). During the years of martial law under Marcos, the two-party system collapsed and was replaced by competing presidential candidates all of whom were heavily dependent on their home regions for support, and treated political parties as transitory electoral vehicles. Philippine politics certainly changed over the years, but "personalism and clientelism remain an important element of electoral politics" in the rural areas at least (2002: 122).

In more recent years the conceptual base for analysis has broadened as variations on this theme or new models of polity have evolved (see, for instance, Landé, 1965, McCoy, A.W. (ed.) 1993, Hutchcroft, 1998; Putzel 1999; Sidel, 1999; Thompson, 1995; Wurfel, 1988). For while the patron-client framework is deservedly influential, there is a need, as Kerkvliet (1995) argued, to move beyond it and develop a more textured view of the Philippine polity. Yet Weber's influence remains strong as in Hutchcroft's patrimonial analysis. He argues that the Spanish failure to engage in state building provided room both for the emergence of strong British, American, and Chinese trading houses, and for the entrenchment of a Chinese-mestizo landed élite. This decentralization of power was reinforced by the Philippines' American rulers, who concerned themselves mainly with the construction of representative institutions while leaving outside those institutions oligarchs with their own strong economic and social bases. After independence, these oligarchs, both directly or through their proxies, moved in and out of those institutions at will and, as they did so, continued to maintain and build up their own external social and economic power bases. Local patrons in the provinces, through their personal relationships with the center, drew money, materials, and authority, towards themselves. Family businesses, faced with hostile and unpredictable circumstances, established complex and aggressive networks of relationships through which they could influence the political economy to their own advantage and to the disadvantage of their enemies and competitors. The center was rendered weak, and the state was left vulnerable to influence from powerful individuals and factionalized groups operating outside its institutions. Thus, the Philippines lies some distance from a strong, regularized, formal, impartial, legal-rational economy and polity of the kind described by Weber as a bureaucratic administration. In particular, argues Hutchcroft, the Philippines lacks calculation in the administrative and legal sphere; and family and business are not clearly separated. The essential question facing the Philippines is how it might transform itself from its present condition into a regularized, legal-rational, and bureaucratic state? Sidel, too, focuses in on broad historical and structural conditions. He argues that local bosses—in municipalities, congressional districts, and provinces—emerge and become entrenched under certain structural conditions. Widespread poverty and economic insecurity greatly accentuate the significance of state resources and provide those with control over those resources and state regulatory powers with the means to accumulate private capital. The actions of the Philippines' American rulers—who "subordinated a weakly insulated state to officials elected locally and under ... restricted suffrage" (2002:133), and superimposed this system upon an economy at such an early stage of capitalist development—was bound to produce "bossism." Since access to resources is the overriding priority, and since that access is controlled by locally elected politicians, then the provision of public goods and services is very likely to be dependent upon the discretion of those local politicians (2002: 136-37).

While often quite open—as in the case of, say, Hutchcroft's patrimonial analysis, Sidel's references to charismatic authority in his interpretation of bossism, or Thompson's exploration of sultanism[6] in his analysis of the anti-Marcos struggle—Weber's influence may also take on an amorphous quality and in this sense permeates a good deal more thought on the Philippine polity. For instance, the personalistic or particularistic behavior that is felt so often to characterize political and bureaucratic life in the Philippines, resonates with Weber's view that modern bureaucracies are more the exception than the rule: "even in large political structures such as those of the ancient Orient, the Germanic and Mongolian empires of conquest, or of many feudal structures of state. In all these cases, the ruler executes the most important measures through personal trustees, table-companions, or court-servants. Their commissions and authority are not precisely defined and are temporarily called into being for each case" ("Weber," 196-97).

This affinity between, on the one hand, Weber's rational bureaucracy and, on the other hand, studies of the Philippine polity (and the relative marginalization of the Philippine civil service in academic analysis) probably has much to do with the general and creeping bureaucratization of life in the West[7] and what is perceived to be the comparative weakness of that process in the Philippines today. It is, in other words, Weber's apparent foresight (see, for instance, Ritzer 2006, 2004), and the failure of the Philippines to bureaucratize as deeply and effectively as many Western societies, that charges Weber's work with analytical power: comparing "what should be" with "what is" provides a frame with which to construct possible explanations for the actual state of affairs in the Philippines today. Another, and perhaps more important, reason for the comparatively modest attention given to the Philippine civil service, and for the redirection of Weber's model to the study of the political economy, is the view that the bureaucracy is severely weakened, distorted, and corrupted by external political and business interests. It is with these interests that real power and influence lies, and on which it is more profitable to focus analysis. This is a view that also harmonizes with the public administration approach. Certainly, as Carino (1992) points out, a general conclusion of its study is that the bureaucracy is a tool for politicians as they pursue economic and political objectives either for their own benefit or on behalf of—and frequently in collusion with—particularistic and private interests rooted outside state agencies. To these ends, politicians will distribute the resources they control and the many favors that lie within their gift. In so far as it is ever made a focus for analysis, then, the Philippine bureaucracy is treated as part and parcel of a political economy that is inefficient, ineffective, and corrupt.

It is, therefore, understandable why the Philippine political economy should have attracted so much more attention, and why its analysis should be framed so strongly in terms of its departure from the Weberian ideal. It is surprising, however, to note that analyses of the Philippine civil service tend to be somewhat insulated (though not exclusively so[8]) from an extensive range of other international and theoretical perspectives on government and bureaucracy (and especially on bad government and bureaucracy). Of these, five perspectives seem to be especially relevant to the Philippines. These intersect with each other and with the debate on the Philippine polity referred to above.

1. The first perspective is as much concerned with behavior within bureaucratic organizations as with the wider political, economic and social context in which those organizations sit. It includes a range of approaches from, say, Weber's rational bureaucracy to public choice and bureau-shaping models,[9] and other still more generic theories of organizations and society. These perspectives also vary in the extent to which the explanatory burden is shared by "structure" and "individuals." Of particular interest are: the concept of organizations as social—rather than as purely, economic, political, or technical—processes (a quality emphasized by role of informal social relationships in undermining the official); and the view that organizations are social systems which interact with other social systems. A society's economy and polity (and so the organizations from which it is constituted), Parsons argued, are synonymous with "adaptive" and goals attainment systems; and conformity to a "patterns" or a shared system of value-oriented structures (rooted in a cultural system) brought a degree of stability to society. A failure to socialize actors through education initiated methods of coordination and control or "integration." Differentiation in these systems produces a constant process of splitting and re-integration of society into more complex forms. Other writers, while acknowledging the constraints within which actors must operate, allow them a little more room. Indeed, many go further, taking the view that organizations comprise human beings who, as they interact and attempt to give meanings to the wider world and self (which is shaped by interactions with other people[10]) produce streams of activities in constant change. A more recent and highly influential "take" on organizations is new institutionalism. While this returns more emphasis to structure, it also recognized the complex (as opposed to the purely economic) understandings of human behavior, and is willing to accommodate actors' representations of their world and, again, the importance of informality. For North (2004), institutional change is the result of interactions amongst formal constraints (conventions, codes of behavior and other socially transmitted information)

and formal constraints (such as rules) and organizations. Formal and informal constraints constitute the rules of the game; organizations are the players of the game. Interactions among these formal and informal constraints and organizations produce change in one another.

Although much of this work has tended to concentrate on America and Europe, approaches have been modified and applied to the study of bureaucracies in non-western societies on which there is now, as a result, a substantial literature. In his case study of elite politics in Sierra Leone, Cohen argues that when "interests and functions cannot be advanced by formal association"—when, say, the particularistic interests of an elite group are incompatible with the formal constitution of society—they must find ways of pursuing both particularistic and universal interests through informal or communal relationships such as kinship, friendship, godparenthood, and a host of other primary relationships"; and "if these relationships do not already exist, they are soon developed" (Cohen, 1981, p. xvi-xvii). The analysis of these communal relationships and communal organizations, Cohen believes, is "essential to understanding the power structure of any state" (p. xvii). Thus, processes which shape the organization of the elite in Sierra Leone "operate in all countries, developed or developing, liberal or autocratic, communist or capitalist (p. xiii). For example, there are striking parallels between Sierra Leone, Hausa trading communities, and the British Treasury where close personal relationships among officials made it possible to dispense the bulk of public money through informal dealings (Heclo and Wildavsky, 1974, p. xiv-xv):

> The distinguishing feature of Treasury Men who deal with public spending is not their intellect or their ideas but their emotions. Their supreme skill lies in personal relations....When we speak of family life in the Treasury or village life in Whitehall we are ... speaking of people whose common kinship and culture separates them from outsiders.... Life at the top in Britain may not be warm hearted chumminess, but it does demonstrate a coherence and continuity unknown in the United States.... Everyone who is anyone has got to have extensive personal contacts.[11]

Haque (2007), on the other hand, discerns a number of bureaucratic models operating in Southeast Asia: the colonial-bureaucratic, the post-colonial developmental, and the New Public Management (NPM) models (see, also, Fritzen, 2007). The first of these is described by the "formal" principles of the Western bureaucratic model (again strongly Weberian) from which, in practice, territories commonly diverged (most especially with respect to political neutrality). This is explained: by the dual roles of Western administrators in these territories; by departures from the ideals of the model even within Western countries; and by paternalism, kingship, ascription and kinship in traditional society. The challenges (such as one-party dominance and military rule) which these territories faced after independence made those bureaucratic ideals still more slippery. The post-colonial developmental model emphasizes the adoption of state-led economic plans and progress. It is related to, but remains distinct from, the notion of the developmental state, in that its concerns lie with the more technical and micro-administrative components of bureaucracy. The NPM model describes strongly market-centered administration: a small public sector with internal, market-like competition; flexible and more autonomous managers; an emphasis on performance targets and assessment; and a customer-oriented ethos. Whilst Southeast Asian countries follow both these models closely enough to allow their forms to be identified, they also deviate from the ideal: the emphasis on development, decentralization, and participation which characterize the post-colonial model, and the switch from state to market management demanded by the NPM model, are difficult to realise and sustain in practice. In an earlier work (which focuses more on developing countries in other parts of the world), Haque (1997) identified another model—an overdeveloped bureaucracy. This describes a bureaucracy that is so strong, and has so much control over scarce resources and economic activities, that politics decays and social divisions widen between a bureaucratic elite and the populace.

2. A second perspective is concerned primarily with the immediate political, economic and social context within which bureaucracy sits, and with the relationships among organizations in these various spheres of activity. This is often entangled with a debate on the nature and significance of informality. The term is easily stretched to cover "social networks," "values," "norms," "trust," and, therefore, "social capital"—a term which, as Partha Dasgupta (2000: 325) argues, is "a peg on which to hang all those informal engagements which we like, care for, or approve of."[12] In this case, informality may be understood as, say, the lubricant that makes any group or organization run more effectively (Fukuyama, 1999); as the bonds that keep society together; and as a means through which to secure economic, political and social advantage (see, for example, Bourdieu, 1990, 1980; Granovetter, 1995; Putnam, 1995, 2000). Low levels of social capital combined with a weak civic culture and unfavorable historical circumstances are, therefore, more likely to produce weak organizations.

In East and Southeast Asia—where economic progress over the last half-century has been remarkable and where, it is said, the emphasis on social relationships is especially strong—the economic significance of informality has a particular resonance. While the increasing formality of economic organizations Pacific Asia is often noted, informality is regarded less as a supplement and support, and more as a defining characteristic and the dominant modus operandi of these organizations. Indeed, informality is commonly thought to be crucial to any understanding of the general process of economic development in East Asia. Here, bureaucracies are not too far removed from the ideal developmental state—a state that is strong and intimately embedded in wider society (Evans, 1989, 1995; Weiss, 1998; Wade 1990). They are, in other words, closely tied to business and other social groups, and yet insulated from vested interests, and clearly focused on the good of the whole society. John Shuhe Li (2003: 670) goes a little further, arguing that there is nothing peculiarly "Asian" in these arrangements:

> ...economic development is fundamentally a process of establishing relationship-based government and subsequently making a transition to rule-based governance. This view is consistent with the historical facts.... Before rule-based governance was established, European business people during the pre-modern period made agreements, to a large degree, outside the legal system. Transition away from personal reputation in the United States occurred only between 1840 and 1920. During this transition period, relationships banking played an important role in monitoring firms. It was the Glass-Steagal Act, the Securities Act, and other regulations after the Great Depression that essentially ended relationship-based finance in the US. Therefore, there is little difference between East and West or between North and South other than they are at different stages of development.

Seen from this perspective, the Asian crisis is understood as a product of attempts to move too far too quickly to a rules-based Western-style regulatory state, rather than as a failure of informality.

There is, however, no shortage of more critical appraisals of informality: it may close down, as well as open up, opportunities; it may suppress, as well as invigorate, motivation, drive, and ambition; it may discourage, as well as encourage, freedom and creativity; it may sustain, as well as overthrow, poverty and "bad equilibrium"; and it may inhibit and distort, as well as facilitate, the communication of information, ideas, and decisions. And while informality may be cost-effective initially, it becomes increasingly less so as markets expand, the division of labour deepens, and the sheer number, scale and complexity of transactions increase.[13] Nor would it be unusual to view informality with still more skepticism as the means through which industrial and liberalization policies are "captured," and money and materials are diverted away from productive uses and into the pockets of crony capitalists (Haggard, 2000; Jomo, 2000) While collusive networks between government, business and financial organizations are more obvious in ASEAN states, they became more apparent during the 1997 Asian financial crisis for which they were, in large part, held responsible.

Nor is the argument that informality carries advantage for economic organizations transferred easily to analyses of political and bureaucratic organizations. Informality may, in certain circumstances, benefit political and bureaucratic organizations even if it is equated with corruption.[14] But for many commentators and practitioners, democracy, transparency, and accountability do not sit comfortably with informality as anything more than a supplement and lubricant. Even in the context of Pacific Asia, informality in political and bureaucratic organizations is commonly viewed with a deal of ambiguity. Such organizations may be tied into society intimately through informal connexions, but these must benefit society as a whole if the economy is to be managed successfully. Peeling away the formal and legalistic layers in Korea takes the analyst closer to politics on the ground; and an understanding of the actual workings of Korean politics is crucial to understanding of Korea's economic development. Informality freed the formulation and implementation of economic policy from a cumbersome legislative framework; but it also led to inequality, corruption and insularity, casting a shadow over democratic transformation (Hwang, 1996: 306, 307). In Japan, too, Edward Keehan (1990) notes that bureaucratic informality and discretion are crucial to the functioning and performance of bureaucracy and government, decisively influencing the scope and content of political action and leadership, "determining what gets done in the Diet, how issues are looked at, and how they are dealt with." Yet informality also ensures that policy and legislative problems are colored by bureaucratic and client interest, potentially restricting "opportunities for broader visions of national and international good that political or public leadership could impose through guided coordination of powerful ministerial interests" (Keehan: 1036-1037)[15].

The present crisis in America and Europe will, no doubt, complicate still further the debate on informality by lending support to the view that Asia's crisis more than a decade ago was indeed rooted in too much Western-style deregulation. Depending upon how Pacific Asian, American, and European economies handle the current difficulties, the credibility of the Asian model may be fully rehabilitated. And the tendency for analysis to concern itself with the extent to which the polity and bureaucracy are undergoing informal-formal transformation may become even more vulnerable to the criticism that it reflects an ethnocentric and rationalist bias.[16]

3. A third perspective concentrates more on the pattern and nature of political and bureaucratic organizations. Peters (1995), for instance, in his examination of American bureaucracy, argues that the separation of powers and further divisions of authority within the branches of government produces an administrative system in which the exercise of control is a major issue: "The use of numerous political appointees in decision-making positions, the need for executive agencies to service Congress as well as the

President, and the openness of the system to a variety of societal pressures point to the importance of control, and the number of actors involved in the struggle over who really runs government." (Peters, op. cit.:35). There are, however, unifying forces at work including: constitutionalism and legalism; an esprit de corps, at least among upper level bureaucrats; the centralized recruitment, placement and regulation of civil servants; and whilst there may be differences over the means and immediate ends, there is a common desire to put national interests first. Consequently, while civil servants are not trained in the "big picture" of government, they do their best for their agency (and country) and leave it up to Congress and the President to bring coherence.

4. A fourth perspective focuses a little more narrowly on the electoral goals of politicians. One example is Golden's (2003) constituency service model. This is shaped around the Italian case, but derived from Fiorina's and Noll's (1978) attempt to explain the U.S. political system. Under the terms of Golden's model, political patronage and bad government is rooted in an electoral system that enable voters to designate those specific individuals they want to represent them. Once elected, legislators must service their constituencies through two available mechanisms. The first of these—pork-barrel legislation—enables politicians to author and introduce their own bills (and these often pass through committee without having to return to the floor to the House). The second—the distribution of jobs in the bureaucracy (and public sector more widely)—requires the evasion of civil service laws and regulations by: limiting the scope of merit; appointing the "right guys"; and manipulating the selection and movement of personnel. As a consequence of these arrangements, legislation is made excessive—in numbers, detail and verbosity—and, with little *ex post* monitoring, the discretion of bureaucrats and the opportunities for corruption are increased. This, in turn, strengthens both the bureaucrats' loyalty to those politicians who turn a blind eye to their corruption, and the need of citizens for help from their representatives to navigate or circumvent the bureaucracy in return for support at elections. In short, politicians deliberately contribute to the growth of inefficient and cumbersome bureaucracy in order to improve their chances of reelection.

Opening Up

When set against this more generic literature, the relative thinness of the debate on the Philippine civil service, and its comparatively limited engagement with that literature, is very marked, as is the need for more critical attention to be directed at the problems facing the service. In particular, the certainty and ease with which the service is presented as a mere appendage of a polity distorted by, say, patron-client relations, patrimonialism or boss-ism, and its informal qualities are viewed rather negatively, seem to deserve closer scrutiny. Such doubts are not absent from existing studies on Philippine civil service,[17] but there is a good deal more scope, and much need, for more exploration and questioning.

It was, then, with these debates and questions in mind that work on the weaknesses and strengths of the Philippine civil service began. This work (which took place during 2007) focused on the central offices[18] of a small, but important, number of agencies: the Civil Service Commission (CSC), the Department of Education (DepEd), The Bureau of Customs (BOC), the Bureau of Internal Revenue (BIR), The Metropolitan Manila Development Association (MMDA), Quezon City Hall, the Lower House, and the Senate. A particular difficulty, however, was immediately apparent: the relative paucity of substantial empirical material which helps to make the Philippines an especially interesting case, also renders the development and application of models, and any interpretations they yield, problematic and less open to contradiction. One way forward is to explore civil servants' and politicians' accounts of their own and each other's practices and motivations—accounts gathered through multiple and triangulated interviews.

This emphasis on the accounts of civil servants and politicians as a means of enriching the empirical base also happened to bring out the dimensionality and intricacy of the bureaucracy. For instance, there is no doubt that patronage (and a sense of obligation) is important to an understanding of the bureaucracy and its features: but it is only one aspect of those features; and it is, perhaps, less of an explanatory structure than it is, for actors, a means to an end. Thus, political interference is as much about doing the right thing as it is about serving one's own narrow interests. It is about getting round a system in order to help constituents and country; it is about acting to good form and meeting other people's expectations; it is about survival; and it is about ambition, power and personal advance. As a consequence, officials may become more supine, or defensive, or conformist, or independent and bold; or adopt informal modes of resistance, such that it is difficult to equate informal behavior with negative and pernicious behavior. Methods of interference, too, are dimensional and multiple. Due process (in the form of, say, the legislature's committee meetings), humiliation, and fear are often associated with specific attempts in and around hearings to influence civil servants' decisions on appointments, discipline, and other matters.

Both these qualities—the intricacy and dimensionality—of the civil service challenge the explanatory power of existing perspectives. Indeed, whilst any one of the perspectives already mentioned (and many others that have not been referred to) would be able to forward and explanation for some or many of the bureaucracy's features, there are always divergent and confounding data. A few examples will help illustrate this remark. Viewed through the work of Mosca, Michels, and Marx, political interference in appointments in the Philippine civil service are symptomatic of a bureaucracy that is little more than a pool of secure jobs for the middle class and a conduit through which the politically dominant class maintains it hold on power. But then how are the varied and often strongly contrasting motivations present among civil servants and politicians to be understood? The case could be made, perhaps, that a useful analytical tool is already provided by Weber as, say, Hutchcroft's work demonstrates. The blurring of public and private spheres; the dominance of irrational and affectual action; the absence of calculable rules; the failure to eliminate from official business all purely emotional and personal elements which escape calculation; and the failure to discharge business without regard to persons: all this may go some way to explain the qualities of the Philippine bureaucracy—a bureaucracy that is in a state of transition between the traditional and emotional, the modern and rational. Yet, it is clear from the accounts and practices that the impersonal and mechanical are not synonymous with effective organization, and that emotion and explicitly social relationships are the very stuff from which the "official" organization is shaped.

A public administration perspective also provides a useful take on the civil service: the problems faced by the bureaucrat—which, ideally should be concerned only with the technical administration of functions agreed upon by the community—are those of inadequate education, training, technical competence, and political restraint. De Guzman's suggestion that external influences distort what is formally prescribed by government may well elucidate aspects of bureaucratic and political behavior; but, then again, why is more positive and committed behavior as well as a large measure of technical competence to be found in the service? Carino's model of a more robust and less supine bureaucracy in constant struggle with the executive might provide a better framework within which to consider these more favorable aspects as well as the tensions and conflicts among civil servants, political appointees, and politicians. Yet the battle lines are not clear cut: there are sympathies and alliances as well differences and disputes among the branches of government and within the civil service; and not all the features of the civil service are elucidated by, or *only* by, these struggles.

Models of public choice might afford sharper and more forensic understandings of particular aspects of behavior in the civil service. Many civil servants are concerned to defend and expand their budgets, and many are driven by both self-interest and altruism. Downs' (1967) explanation of the duplication and proliferation of agencies (as a consequence of the need to overcome resistance within inter-organizational hierarchies designed to coordinate and monitor agencies) may also have much to add. Meanwhile, other bureaucrats appear to follow more closely Dunleavy's (1991) bureau-shaping patterns of behavior. Quite apart from the political fallout that would follow attempts by the CSC to grow the organization, take on more powers and oversight functions, and become more assertive, there is also a very real concern that such actions would undermine the Commission's moral authority, encourage lower standards and more widespread abuses within the organization, and erode the Commission's informal influence over the heads of other agencies. Then again, it is often the case that civil servants attempt neither to expand their departments (or agencies) nor demonstrate bureau-shaping behavior: many are more concerned simply to keep the organization running and to manage the politicians as best they can; while others, in order to advance their own careers, will give in to external pressure. Nor are the advantages (such as monopoly power and the fragmentation of sponsors) handed by Niskasen (1971) to bureaucrats negotiating their budget easy to find the case of the Philippines. And whilst the proliferation of agencies may in part be understood, when viewed from the center, as a way of overcoming resistance to coordination and supervision, this feature also owes much to, say, the legislators' belief that existing agencies will not deliver enough to their constituents in their districts; and to a layering of political appointees with short political lives, little knowledge of the agencies they run, and a long list of populist initiatives to drive through.

Perhaps a less narrow framework is provided by Blau (1973) who suggests that important functions within a bureaucratic organization may also produce dysfunctions, stimulating the emergence of new practices that drive spontaneous and informal change. For these kinds of changes to occur, various prerequisites must be met. These include: minimum employment security; a professional orientation to duties; cohesive work groups; the absence of conflicts between workers and management; and a need for change that is "disturbing" or, in other words, necessary. Is it, perhaps, an absence of such prerequisites (or, at least, their presence to an extent and intensity insufficient to initiate change) which may help to account for certain problems in the Philippines? Political interference, mobbing, insecurity, and defensiveness are (despite tenure) enough to produce rigidity or over-conformity; restricted opportunities for promotion, the perceived need for political backing to ensure promotion, and tensions between career and non-career civil servants are bound to produce dysfunctional work groups; and frail professional orientation gives too much room for private maladjustments. Yet, in the Philippine case, quite the opposite is often true (as chapter 4 shows): constructive informality, innovation and change are common responses to the *absence* of those prerequisites and the *presence* of political interference, insecurity, poor cohesion, and conflicts.

Nor, though, does Cohen's view—that elites will pursue their interests through communal relationships when the formal means to do so are unavailable—seem to ring true on all occasions in the Philippine context. Yes, there are times when it does seem to be of direct relevance: when, say, it is *believed* that interests cannot be advanced through formal routes or that those routes cannot be trusted. Yet it is also the case that communal relationships are mobilized because there is excessive formality, or to counter what is perceived to be negative informality, or to circumvent, breach or undermine formal rules, roles, hierarchies, processes and organizations. Furthermore, this behavior is exhibited by politicians and civil servants from very different backgrounds and at very different levels of government and throughout its different branches: if there is a clearly defined elite (for there is considerable movement in and out of the multiple groups of politicians, civil servants, and businesses among whom exist intricate and shifting alliances and divisions), then the use of communal relationships is associated not only with that elite. And whereas informality comes across in Cohen's analysis as something different and distinct from the formal and official, it is clear that in the Philippine civil service informality is the material from which the formal or official is moulded.

Might this kind of complexity be handled more effectively if the civil service is thought of and analyzed as streams of social relationships and interactions? Perhaps so, but it goes without saying that politicians and civil servants come up against, respond to, and feel themselves to be constrained and conditioned by expectations, values, culture, history and large-scale patterns of authority (not the least of which is an American-style system of government). The problem is an old one and goes right to the heart of social science: how are "individual" and "society" to be reconciled if at all? Perhaps streams of relationships are, as Stryker (1962, 1980) argues, best analyzed when set within broad structures though, if so, it appears that those patterned structures, their meanings and their implications, as well as responses to those patterns, may vary or differ greatly from one politician or civil servant to the next. Or are frameworks rooted firmly and unambiguously in structure more helpful after all? Golden's (2003) constituency service model (synthesized from studies of Italy and the U.S.) describes and accounts for a number of practices very similar to those found in the case of the Philippines. The Philippine electoral system, as under the terms of the model, encourages support and votes for individuals, not political parties. The legislature's committees in the Philippines are not as strong as the model allows; but legislators author and introduce their own bills, and this practice is not only associated with pork-barrel allocations. Politicians do influence appointments. The scope of merit in the civil service is limited. For instance, laws against nepotism do not cover schools, nor do qualifications and standards apply to non-career appointments at third level. There is manipulation of the selection process and personnel movements. There is a deal of wordy legislation. Politicians protect corrupt bureaucrats. And ordinary citizens do need to look to their representatives and to their contacts within bureaucratic organizations to navigate and circumvent the bureaucracy. And yet the desire (assumed by the model) to perpetuate an inefficient bureaucracy (in order to offer routes through it and thereby attract votes for re-election) does not seem to figure much, if at all, in the case of Filipino politicians. The perspective offered by Peters, too, has much to give but does not explain why, in those circumstances it describes, behavior among civil servants should be more self-interested or more selfless and professional. North's (op. cit.) account also has evident strengths. In the case of the Philippines, divisions in authority, over-conformity, negative informality, and divergent representations may be described as the product of these interactions, part of the context of existing rules and, therefore, part of current interactions and processes of change. As organizations (the agencies of government) pursue their objectives and compete with each other, they may insist on strict observance of formal rules of the game (such as legislation, or the civil service's codes of conduct and its manual of standards and qualifications). Or they may urge change to those formal rules (as in the case the CSC's attempts persuade Congress to introduce legislation restricting to 50 percent the proportion of third-level positions filled by political appointees). Or they may attempt to bring about or prevent change by mobilizing informal constraints. For instance, civil servants may build up informal political resistance by playing to an organization's esprit de corps and common resentments; while the Office of the President works to forestall restrictions on its authority to appoint by calling on past favors, friendships, or kinship with legislators, or by appealing to their belief that an unelected civil service should not be insulated from elected politicians. But, again, does this kind of framework capture the nature and importance of informality in Philippine bureaucracy? So often, informality appears to take on fundamental significance as the material from which new practices emerge and around which the organization is formed, reformed, and improved.

Recognizing Dimensionality

Recognition of the importance of the dimensionality of Philippine politics is certainly nothing new, though it has not received the emphasis that it deserves. This is certainly true of one debate which has brought home the significance of the polity's and bureaucracy's dimensionality in a very direct, immediate, and emotional sense, and in this respect is of greater consequence than the coverage it has received since its publication would suggest. In a series of lectures and publications, Ileto (1999) argued that by "essentializing" Philippine political behavior and presenting the Philippines as a negative "other," American scholars idealized American democracy and justified American colonialism. The work of two scholars in particular—Lande and Sidel—figure prominently in his critique.

Not surprisingly, Ileto's criticisms stimulated lively and often acerbic counter-criticism, particularly, though not exclusively, from those American scholars who were the subject of his initial attacks. From Lande's point of view there is very little to connect his studies with the assertion that his portrayal of the Filipino political system provided a useful backdrop against which to highlight the advanced nature of American democracy. Lande acknowledges that he made mention of clientelist parties in the southern United States and in eighteenth-century England. But he is a specialist in the study of comparative politics, and he made no binary distinction between East and West: "Rather I was interested in the process of modernization. Whether [Ileto] likes it or not, modernization, however one defines it, did come earliest in the West and has led, in much of the West, to changes in social, economic, and political institutions that are widely admired in other regions of the world, including the Philippines" (2002: 123). And far from presuming that Philippine culture and behavior are fixed, it was his argument "that clientelism is a function of the economic dependency of the poor, and will become less widespread as the economy becomes more productive and the poor become less dependent on personal or governmental patrons" (2002:124).

Lande goes on to pick up and develop what appears to be his central concern: that his conscious and subconscious motives are the subject of extensive and incorrect speculation.

> [Ileto] suspects me of being more than a passive observer of Philippine politics, in part because it is the product of decades of American tutelage. He wonders if my work is not in fact an attempt to shore up a construction of a "normal" Philippine politics that is already under threat by a mainly Marxist-nationalist challenge to the postwar construction of history and politics. He thinks that I fear that the American-style party system will end up not being the sole vehicle of politics. He says that I think that the kind of politics offered by totalitarian rivals is un-Filipino. In fact I think that totalitarianism is bad for any society. He says that despite my criticism of the party system and my hope that it would change, I still favor constitutional democracy. Of course I do. And I hoped, then as now, that Philippine democracy, while remaining constitutional, will become more truly democratic by becoming more participatory and more equal. (2002:124)

As for Ileto's claim that the use of words such as "moods," "unpredictable," even "fluid" to describe party switching by Filipino politicians is indicative of Lande's desire to feminize Philippine politics, is quite simply "nonsensical.... I chose the words to describe reality, not to feminize Filipinos." In reply to Ileto's suggestion that Lande's research may be colored by his friendship with senators and congressmen, as well as by his race and gender, Lande asks, "how it is possible to study the tactics of politicians without getting to know them? And why my gender?" And in response to Ileto's attempt to impute to Lande the Hobbesian view that personal relations are basically founded on domination and fear, Lande states unequivocally, "That is not my view, nor that of other political scientists" (2002:126-127).

21

Lande further argues that Ileto's inaccurate speculations are the product of Ileto's method of criticism:

> The weakness of any ideologically driven, politically engaged approach, such as Critical Theory or Postcolonial Theory, is that it commits the true believer to finding what his theory expects to find and thus may lead him to misunderstand or distort reality. It can also lead him to assume a malign intent, where there was none. That is why Ileto's critique of American scholarship on the Philippines may please other postcolonial theorists, but will leave mainstream scholars, who judge a work by its factual accuracy and analytical persuasiveness, not by the nationality or gender of its author, unimpressed. (2002:127)

At the core of Sidel's rebuttal, too, are his objections to the motivations wrongly attributed to him by Ileto. Sidel, however, begins by distancing his own views from Lande and the patron-client framework. Whilst, like Carl Lande, Sidel was trained as an American political scientist, Sidel's research, unlike Lande, "was undertaken many years after the political science literature on patron-client relations had lost its original appeal and momentum, and at a time, "when it was abundantly clear from local accounts that coerces pressures played a much more important role in social relations and political competition in the country that had previously been acknowledged by scholars" (p. 130). Indeed, Sidel's exploration of Philippine politics was based on fundamentally different premises:

> I rejected the assumption that the Philippine political system reflected and reproduced the preferences and proclivities of Filipinos, that Filipinos got the government they wanted (and, implicitly, deserved). Politicians, in other words, did not simply respond to the demands of their constituents: they, and the political system in which they were embedded, in considerable measure determined, disaggregated, and diffused these demands. The perpetrators, not the victims, were to be identified and blamed. (p. 130-31)

Not only was the foundation of Sidel's work different from Lande's, but so was his motivation. Sidel's aim, from the start, was:

> to provide insight, evidence, and ammunition to those forces in the Philippines who were working to deepen the process of democratization ... and to expose and undermine those forms of local authoritarianism that seem to be thriving and conditions of formal democracy in the country.
>
> I was thus especially gratified when my own research proved to be useful to Filipino investigative journalists and political activists, and on more than one occasion I involved myself in efforts to

assist people who were clearly victimized by the local bosses who form the focus of my research. Here the advantage of being a foreigner—perhaps of being an American in particular—was not the supposed analytical clarity in comparative perspective that is said to come with distance, but my relative "untouchability" as a well-connected "*Kano* poking around in dangerous waters without fear of getting hurt." (2002:131-32)

Sidel, though, was careful to put distance between himself and American "muckrakers" for whom the Philippines did not measure up to the standards and ideals of American democracy. Indeed, he was at pains "to reverse this logic" (2002:132). He was keen to show that bossism was the product of American colonialism and owed very little to indigenous Filipino political culture. The "big men" or "men of prowess"—the pre-colonial counterparts of modern bosses—were no less the product of structural conditions. Pre-colonial political organization, leadership, and legitimation corresponded to particular "conditions of land abundance, dispersed settlement, and shifting cultivation, with kinship reckoned cognatically, and lineage ineffective in regulating succession to political leadership. Under these circumstances, it is suggested, power rested—in large part by default—on what Max Weber described as charismatic authority" (2002: 135). Today's bosses may be understood as latter-day "big men" only insofar as underlying structural conditions have remained close to those obtaining in the pre-colonial era (2002: 136).

In the light of this record, Ileto's argument that Sidel has set up the Philippines as a negative pole against which to compare real American democracy, or believes that Spanish friars and American constables (by suppressing the emergence of bosses) saved the natives from themselves, amounts to little more than a crude and unconstructive caricature. Nowhere in his work does Sidel suggest that American democracy should be idealized or that pre-colonial big-men reflect distinctive Filipino cultural values. To the contrary: "All my writings on local bosses in the Philippines have shown that local forms of authoritarianism flourish under conditions of liberal democracy, not because of the passive acquiescence of Filipinos, but because of the weight of colonial history and the dull compulsion of economic relations, in which American colonialism and global capitalism are clearly both deeply implicated" (2002: 138).

It is too soon to say whether or not Ileto's arguments will have a lasting effect on the study of the Philippine political economy. All that can be said at the moment is that the distance of the Philippines from a Weberian-style rational bureaucracy - and the problems of personalism, impropriety and corruption - remain uppermost in the minds of many politicians, civil servants and academics in the Philippines. Nevertheless, the debate is important, and this is so in three respects.

First, Ileto's arguments are infused with a concern to explain the dimensionality of his subjects—whether politicians or constituents—in the field. Arguably this concern is not contingent upon his decision to interpret studies of the Philippine political economy through "orientalism" although, for Ileto at least, the two do seem to go hand-in-hand. The emphasis on this concern is made especially clear during his (2002) counter-response to Sidel in which he endorses Resil Mojares' determination to explore the complex and dimensional relationships among politicians and constituents rather than to identify victims and predators and to apportion blame. It is this kind of attention to detail, to possibility, to variation, and to dimension, that Ileto would like to bring to the study of politics. Yes, conditions in towns such as Tiaong, Dolores, and Candelari have fostered predatory and local despotism; but there also exist among the towns' elites expressions of common good, a sense of community, justice and fairness. Moreover, "these sentiments are not just the effects of recent democratizing experiences, the birth of the radical movement, or ... modern education since the American-era tutelage. These were already present in those "backward" and "crime-ridden" towns from the 1860s in a form that was, of course, suited to those times or to the structural conditions prevailing then" (2002: 173). Yes, municipal governments could be dominated by a boss-mayor, but not always nor as often as is sometime thought. Bossism can be understood, argues Ileto, only if it is set "within a field of possible responses to structural conditions, and if we recognize that its materialization also spawned the elements that would critique and possibly subvert it" (ibid.)

Second, the debate initiated by Ileto illustrates the sensitivity surrounding motive and so, in a very intimate and personal way, the relevance and significance of dimensionality. Ileto's criticisms sting, partly because the very nature of the motives are galling; and partly because the structural and cultural conditions in which the scholars are said to be entangled makes their escape from the motives ascribed to them quite impossible. No matter how well scholars may think they know their own minds, they are being told by Ileto that they are mistaken. There is of course a delightful irony here, for it is under the terms of their own models of the Philippine political economy that American scholars confidently impute motives to Filipino politicians, civil servant, business leaders, and constituents. Sidel's and Lande's frustration with the intentions attributed to them by Ileto is probably equalled by some Filipino scholars' exasperation at the ease with which American scholarship mistakenly attributes motives to other Filipinos, and exceeded by the irritation of those politicians and civil servants to whom American scholars attribute those motives. In this regard, the remarks of one legislative officer in the Philippine Senate are telling. Despite the many and obvious faults with the country's political and bureaucratic organizations, there is much that is good and much that works; and there is, in his mind, no question that there are many politicians and civil servants who have the best interests of the country at heart. And yet, instead of recognizing and encouraging these strengths, "We always see things in terms of what's the problem ... we're so negative. It's gone so negative.... *Kawawà naman ang mga pinoy* [poor old Filipinos!]: we think we are so corrupt, we're so bad, we're so dumb."[19] This chronic self-doubt is rooted in part with the lack of closure on so many questions surrounding political leaders from Rizal, Bonifacio and Aguinaldo at the birth of the country, to Roxas and Laurel families during World War II, and to Marcos, Ninoy Aquino, Corrie Aquino, Ramos and Estrada... "There is always this feeling of...sweeping dirt under the rug—the dirt is still there. There wasn't really an effort to take out the dirt and throw it in the trash and start again."[20] But part of the explanation also lies with "the idea that the westerner knows more than we do.... We've survived, we've copied the western style.... We've been under the old west...and the new one and we're adapting to it. We [have had] barely 100 years.... You guys were worse than us.... You had despots and dictators and ... the popes [have] killed so many people.... And [yet] now they all say [disparagingly] "democracy here" [in the Philippines]"[21]

The scholars criticized by Ileto are undoubtedly aware that their models do not always capture the dimensionality of their subjects. This is clear in their original works, and in their responses. Lande (2002: 122) acknowledges that American scholars have often missed or downplayed both the patriotic motives of members of the elite, and the fact that reciprocity is the essence of clientelism. Sidel, too, acknowledges that while he was careful not to explain away the legitimating claims of local bosses as expressions of a instrumentalism, or to rely only on macro-economic conditions, his analysis, for better and for worse, did give more emphasis to more objective considerations (2002: 133-134). But if there is in these admissions the sense that shaving away dimensions is an acceptable and even necessary part of analysis, then it leaves the reader wondering why scholars admit for themselves dimensionality and self-determination over motives, and yet so often deny these qualities to their subjects. Just how reliable, then, are the scholars' models and the motives imputed under their terms?

Third, the debate sparked by Ileto appears to illustrate a general feature common to the models developed by American scholars and to Ileto's critique. American scholars may be quick to assign motives blanket-fashion, but so too is Ileto. The motives he ascribes to American scholarship are intended to be read not as an expression of his sense of irony, but as a product of the structural and cultural conditions shaping scholarship and, indeed, American society more generally. The dimensions of his subjects, too, may be questioned, for these are derived from Ileto's interpretation of historical texts and also reflect his take on what he holds to be the prevailing structural conditions of the period.

One interpretation of this common tendency to limit dimensions (and impute motives) is that it isa necessary quality: thought-anchors are needed if the analyst is to make sense of the world even though as a consequence certain of its aspects are flattened or excised. Another interpretation is that it is a product of the *realpolitik*, practicalities and privilege of academe. Azurin, a Filipino writer who is highly critical of Ileto, puts this case with a deal of energy:

> Foreign researchers usually proceed from a departmental perspec-
> tive or "school of thought." Also, they bring with them to the field
> site a carefully chosen set of books to convince themselves of the
> validity of their research entry point, objective and methodology.
> Among those of us who have mostly stayed at home, there is this
> longstanding…joke—that any archaeologist from Michigan doing
> fieldwork in the Philippines will sooner or later unearth the remains
> of "chiefdoms." Why so? Principally because this notion of settlement
> structure and dynamic is what their mentors had primed them to
> discover…. Consider, too, that their research time and budget is not
> infinite, nor are [they] gifted with infinite knowledge or patience to
> explicate the diverse and confounding data. (2002: 144)

Consequently, the researcher must spotlight: that is, they must concentrate efforts "on the particular issue being 'problematised'…[while] blurring the 'peripheral' concerns and factors intertwined with the multifaceted reality" (2002: 145).

The limits imposed by departmental perspective and spotlighting—reinforced by publish-or-perish, finish-or-fail demands of universities characterized by a culture of careerism among students and staff, and a utilitarian attitude to education and research—compel the scholar to play it safe. The result is publications comprising a mix of risk-averse analysis and advocacy, empirical field data and institutional bias. (2002: 145, 146). The problems which beset western studies of the Philippines are to be explained not by "orientalism" but by "scholastic academicism—an institutional process of resonating or elaborating on a regimen of knowledge as perpetuated by a "school of thought" or by the "masters of discipline" (2002: 147).

Accommodating Dimensionality: Representation and Practice

The dimensionality of the Philippine polity and bureaucracy may be widely recognized, but it is probably fair to say that Filipino writers and their subjects understand the meaning and significance of that dimensionality with greater immediacy. It also appears that scholarship finds it difficult to give primacy to this quality. The question that now arises is how a more unified theory capable of accommodating dimensionality might be developed? How might analysts deal with the complexity and dimensionality that confronts them every day? One answer might be to continue with the adjustment and application of existing models. Each study limits itself to a particular dimension of the political economy; but as long as the analytical framework chosen and its underlying assumptions are not transformed into absolutes, nor made a vehicle for careerism, then these efforts may, in aggregate, yield a rounded and dimensional account of the Philippine political economy, most especially if married with the kind of thick description and critical and reflexive analysis pursued by Ileto. Another way of accommodating dimensionality is to become conceptually footloose. This point is well made by Kerkvliet (1995) who argues that models—particularly if they are held to explain large swathes of society—are very likely to be totalizing and prescriptive. It is more productive to scrutinize the Philippine political economy while keeping in mind all or as many available interpretations and approaches as possible and remain open to being surprised by findings that do not fit any of them" (p. 417).

A further and quite specific approach, however, is to continue with gathering and layering the accounts of civil servants and politicians and to shift emphasis firmly towards *their* understandings of the world and their place within it. This brings analyst face to face with a number of questions. What are the actors' representations of the circumstances, constraints, and opportunities *they* face? What are *their* versions of "structure" and "culture"? How, and to what extent, do *their* representations inform subsequent action? How, and to what extent, are *their* actions portrayed in subsequent representations? And how are these representations and practices to be elicited?

Mental and social representations. The term representation is commonly associated with the notion of "mental representations" or "representational theory"—the argument that we perceive things (ideas and objects) in the real world through mental representations of those things and, therefore, that we see the real world only indirectly. The term is used in also used more generally in sociology to refer to images and texts which, through their portrayal of objects and phenomena, influence practice and understanding such that those objects and phenomena are subsequently altered. Just as art imitates life, so life imitates art.

The term "social representations" is most closely associated with social psychology, and especially with the work of Moscovici. In this branch of knowledge, social representations are commonly understood as a system of values, ideas and practices with a twofold function. The first is to establish consensual order among phenomena. The second is to provide a code for social exchange and thereby enable communication among members of a community (Moscovici, 1973). Social representations are also produced socially: that is, they are produced collectively and remain the property of groups.

Indeed, argue Duveen and Lloyd (1993), they exist prior to the individual: they are internalized by individuals and used as a framework through which they may interpret the world and place themselves within a community. Put another way, social representations are the elaboration of social objects by a community for the purpose of behaving and communicating. The belief that individual thought exists in isolation and that the individual can be considered as the basic unit of analysis is, therefore, entirely misconceived.

The genesis of social representations is understood with reference to two ideas: anchoring and objectification. Anchoring describes the reduction of strange ideas into familiar categories and images, and their positioning within existing systems of thought. And because representations are social, anchoring draws the individual into the cultural traditions of the group. The second concept, objectification, also works to make the unfamiliar more familiar, but in ways that are more "active": it turns the unfamiliar into the very essence of reality, transforming abstractions into concrete experiences. In the modern world this takes place in particular in the form of science (Moscovici, 1984, 1982).

These ideas require scholars to acknowledge that they analyze through the medium of representations. For instance, an insistence that psychology is a branch of the natural sciences, and that psychologists must conduct their research in a laboratory and follow its experimental protocols, betrays the influence of particular representations of the social and natural world current within the field of psychology. The notion of social representations also requires us to acknowledge that western social scientists, and their western subjects, are heavily influenced by a particular representation—individualism. Given this, and given the reality that our representations are social, then in our studies we must sample communities rather than individuals. We are also required to undertake research on "non-reactive" materials or, in other words, to build up an understanding of the representations carried by archive materials (such as books, magazines and newspapers). This is important partly because these representations are "frozen" whereas the psychologists' subjects, once they know that they are being studied, will alter their responses; and partly because those who study, and those who are being studied, are influenced by these representations. For these and other reasons, a variety of analytical and methodological techniques is advisable. Chief among them are, for some writers, participant observation and unstructured interviews during which attempts are made to elicit representations from subjects through negotiation and the introduction of contrasting representations.

Understood as reflexive images and texts, or as a guide or map for action, representations are treated as a specific category of thought with specific roles or even as something that has its own independent existence. These assumptions are common and established within an approach that is broadly phenomenological and whose aim is, as Johnston (1992, pp. 63-64) puts it, to understand "human action through the study of meanings allocated to the elements of the individual's life-world"—meanings that are rooted in the mind. Husserl's interest may have been to uncover an individual's inner mental states by "bracketing" more and more of the physical world (and, eventually, even the empirical self) until the pure essence of consciousness is left exposed; but other writers preferred to look outside themselves and into the social world. Schutz (1932), for example, rather than cycle down into consciousness, was determined: to examine how subjects build up typical constructs—types—of things (objects and knowledge) and people; and to build a second-order model of that world in order to understand how real people might act in the real world. In this task, he argued, sociologists must identify, separate and examine representations scientifically. Berger and Luckman (1966) went even further: representations are not only open to scientific scrutiny, but also possess their own independent and objective quality—. In other words, representations are real structures. This recalls Durkheim's view that collective representations (a term used to refer to ideas that help to create and make sense of the world) emerge from groups, but then take on an autonomous existence. These representations, Durkheim believed, are the structures of society and cannot be reduced to the individual.

A slightly different route to understanding mind has been to stress practice (the actions and behavior of actors), though here again the structural qualities of practice was brought to the fore[22] partly in reaction to the criticism that symbolic interactionists were too concerned with particular instances. Practice reflects the deep structures of the mind *and* has its own independent significance. "The structures of languages," writes Perinbanayagam (1985, p. 58),

> ...are viewed as features shared, wholly or partly by a community, that enable humans to create ongoing communicative relationships. These shared structures allow actors to take the role of the other insofar as the other articulates signifying acts that are subject to the logic of the structures and equally allow the other to take the role of the self insofar as he is able to articulate gestures arranged in the same logic. Such a structural logic may be founded on language itself, but when translated into other instruments of communication (nonverbal items) they too become ways in which interactions and selves are created and sustained. In this way, by interpreting the gestures around us according to a discipline and articulating our gestures according to the same discipline, it is possible to acquire, if not the "knowledge of other minds" (Malcolm, 1966), at least what it is that the "other mind" wants us to take to be in his mind at the moment and to proceed to the next step.... One does not really have to know all that is in the other mind, only enough to be able to respond to the other mind and continue lines of action ... or initiate

lines of action that will continue into at least the immediate future. The structures submit communication to a discipline and enable interactions, relationships, and social organizations to emerge and be sustained. Hence one must concede that interactions are not only symbolic but also structural.'

Structures of the mind and the structure of practice reflect one another, but society (and practice) is prior to Mead's "social emergents"—the individual and mind.

Intentionality. "Representation" may also be understood as "intentionality"—a conceptualization or construct of a thing (or, more accurately, the direction of mental states at something) which may exist or which may only be imagined but which, in either case, informs actions. In other words, a representation is a mental state encompassing ideas, objects, beliefs, imaginings, desires, and emotions. The aim of analysis, therefore, is to understand the world as it is perceived and those perceptions acted upon. This "take" treats a "mental state" as more than a picture or map or structure and, as such, it is closer the usage of the term "representation" in these pages.

Here, representations are held to be states of mind about things—whether objects, practice, natural processes, or other representations. They may be reasonably accurate and provide a serviceable description of reality, or they may be inaccurate or entirely imagined. Either way they inform subsequent practice and the subsequent interpretation of practice. As states of mind, representations are necessarily *experienced* and, therefore, cannot exist independently of mind.[23] Representations, then, are not artifacts to be picked over and examined scientifically.[24] Written words (such as those now being read), conversations, sounds, movements and pictures do not constitute a recording or facsimile of states of mind, let alone a representation. Rather, they prompt others to form particular states of mind and, for the most part, achieve this reasonably effectively. As states of mind, representations are also dimensional—that is, they have multiple meanings and implications that are revealed and altered by changes in the broader perceived context of representations and practices.

Practices are not representations; but practices encourage particular states of mind. This is achieved either by design or as a consequence of attempts to set up, avoid, take advantage of and close down constraints and opportunities through actions that are tangible and powerful especially if repeated, made routine and executed with physical force. Practices, then, inform and are informed by representations and in turn inform representations. Indeed, representations—including those of 'self', 'others', 'world' and 'self in world'—emerge and are sustained only through constant interaction with other people and with the natural world.

Of particular significance, therefore, are relationships or, in other words, representations of how "you," "I," "we" and "they" feel about, think about, and behave towards each other. They are of signal importance because they color all subsequent interactions upon which the stimulus and development of all representations depend. Relationships, then, are not so much a category of representation and practice as they are an aspect of all representations and practice.

In this view, then, the social world comprises strings of practice and representation—of dimensional events, meanings and understandings such that each practice or representation simultaneously forms points on many intersecting strings. No distinction is made between actors' and scholars' representations (including those of structure, self, and others): they are necessarily treated equally, and they intersect.[25] This willingness to treat scholars' notions of structure and culture on a par with actors' representations, shifts the focus of interest and analysis to what might be called the surface features of the social world —features which are to be understood in their own terms (that is, with reference to the strings from which they are shaped) rather than with reference to "deep" or overarching structures, though the possibility that strings of representation and practice may reflect such forces is left open.[26]

Eliciting Representations and Practice

The words of the civil servants and politicians, while loosely described as representations, do not (for reasons already set out) provide a frozen and precise record of their states of mind. Their words may help to encourage similar states of minds in others, and inherent in this is distortion and inaccuracy. This is especially so when past states of mind are being recounted or when one actor is reporting what is believed to be another's state of mind. Civil servants will, more often than not, make explicit a distinction between what they have witnessed and what they have only heard or they believe or surmised, and resist a temptation to attribute motivation and actions to others. But it is not possible to rule out deliberate attempts to mislead for no matter how benign the intention of the study, it is difficult to know how a question might be interpreted or whether the answers given are self-seeking or those which the subject believes the analyst expects or prefers, or produced simply because it is felt that some kind of answer should be given to someone who has taken the trouble to come all this way to find out something. Nevertheless, their accounts provide a glass through which, despite its many flaws, it is possible for all practical purposes to *appreciate* their states of mind.

The confidence with which these accounts may be accepted is strengthened by a two simple measures. One is to ask questions in different forms, and to avoid establishing an atmosphere or context that might convey the impression that certain answers are expected. Another, which has already been mentioned, is to triangulate interviews[27] such that a certain practice, problem, or person (and even the same instance or event) may be viewed from different angles. This is more likely reveal whether particular accounts of practice are isolated and possibly invented; or widely held and probably accurate; or widely held and, even if somewhat inaccurate or imagined, still likely to have a significant bearing on subsequent practice. It also helps to avoid the tendency to impute to civil servants and politicians motivations and behavior convenient for the analyst. And it provides—in addition to those that are already present (such as the atmosphere of caution and over-conformity in which civil servants often work, and the reasons for which will be discussed later)—another way to filter out deliberate attempts to mislead.

Triangulation required interviews to be conducted in as many sub-units as possible (groups within agencies, offices within groups, divisions within office, and sections within divisions[28]and with as many officials as possible, including the highest-ranking official, in each of those sub-units (section, division, office, and group). In addition, officials mentioned during earlier interviews were followed up when possible. Thus, an interview with the superior official at each level in the hierarchy (division, office, and group) requires further interviews: with at least one other official of the same rank within the same sub-unit; and with at least one subordinate at the next level down within that sub-unit, such that at least two officials at each level in the hierarchy within the same sub-unit are interviewed (such as two under-secretaries, two directors and two division chiefs—all from within the same group). When only one official occupies a certain level within a sub-unit (such as an undersecretary leading a group, or director leading an office), then at least two of that official's immediate subordinates within the sub-unit should be interviewed, and another official at the same level in another sub-unit should be interviewed. This other sub-unit should, if possible, lie within the same superior unit (for instance, two offices should lie within the same group, or two groups should have closely related functions). In this way, every interview within each sub-unit is triangulated: either with *at least* one superior, one subordinate and one equal; or with *at least* one equal and two subordinates; or with *at least* one equal and two superiors. In practice, the numbers of officials interviewed at each level were considerably more than this formula requires, and so each interview was triangulated by more than two other interviews. In addition, and as noted in the main text, other officials mentioned during the course of earlier conversations were also interviewed, wherever this was possible.

Although interviews and other materials provided detail on practices and an appreciation of actors' representations, there arose the question of whether it is possible to assess—on a larger scale than discursive interviews permit-ted—the extent to which politicians and civil servants within an agency are "personalistic"? That is to say, is there a way to estimate the extent to which they regard social relationships, obligations, loyalties, and groups (often centered around kernels of association such as kinship, university, or place of origin) as a means to pursue their own private benefits irrespective of whether such behavior is at odds with the interests of their agencies and the wider public? Some kind of attempt seemed necessary, or at least desirable, for two reasons. First, interviews with civil servants and politicians revealed many instances of behavior that did not seem to fit with the characterization of Philippine political and bureaucratic life as personalistic, as well as many that did. Secondly, an indication of the breadth and depth of this quality within organizations would provide a useful background against which to set specific representations or instances of behavior. But how could this be done? Any attempt would necessarily be experimental: although personalism colors so many existing understandings of Philippine political behavior, there has been no effort to assess its intensity within agencies. In the light of the model that was beginning to emerge, one method that suggested itself was to measure the strength of qualities held to be indicative of more or less instrumental (and, therefore, personalistic) states of mind and for which off-the-shelf tests already existed. These qualities are: the extent to which relationships are viewed as a means to an end; the regard with which others, self and organizations are held; a sense of alienation, and a tendency toward authoritarianism. And the tests selected and used in the field were: Christie's and Geis' (1970) Machiavellianism or "Mach" Scale; Berger's (1952) scale for self and others; McClosky's and Schaar's (1965) anomy scale; authoritarianism Levinson's and Huffman's (1955) abbreviated test for authoritarianism (or, more accurately, for traditional family ideology)[29]; and Kelly's (1934) scale for attitudes towards institutions. If these tests were fairly reliable,[30] and if the association among the qualities they are intended to measure are not too far removed from those understandings of behavior emerging with the layering of interviews, then certain correlations might be expected. Strengthening instrumentalism would be accompanied by increasingly negative representations of self and others, while a sense of alienation would sharpen. The association among these qualities, authoritarianism, and the regard with which organizations are held, are likely to be even more complex. This is so because actors' representations of the organization and of the need for authoritarianism would be colored by their own take on relationships, by their feelings of alienation, by their own day-to-day experience of political and bureaucratic practice, and by what they hear from colleagues or learn from the media.

A number of objections may be leveled at these tests. They were intended to measure attitudes which, at the time they were formulated, were understood as orientations towards, say, other people, situations, events, organizations and ideas. And since attitudes were held to be indicative of wider values and beliefs, then it could be assumed that they predisposed individuals to behave in fairly predictable ways. But is it the case that actors hold clear and well-formed attitudes? And how reliable is the assumption that stated attitudes reflect underlying values or beliefs and that there exists a causal connexion between those attitudes and subsequent actions? The suggestion that attitudes is inferred only from actual behavior does not remove this doubt. A further criticism is that a study of attitudes is, in effect, a study of representations—but one that attempts to reveal and emphasize differences among the social representations held by actors and groups. This is quite simply to misunderstand the truly collective and social nature of representations. Even if one treats these as representations, to what extent do they really inform subsequent behavior? All these problems are compounded by what are held to be cultural differences in the meaning of attitudes and indeed surveys. There is also the fact that the tests were formulated in the U.S. in the middle of the twentieth century; and surely language and culture is bound to distort also the meaning of the questions contained in the tests and, indeed, the very purpose and significance of surveys?

There are, however, various responses to these objections. First, the standard of English among officials is, on the whole, very good; and Tagalog[31] versions trialled in the *barangays* produced very similar results. Second, these tests were not used across countries. If returns were distorted by "culture," then these distortions are fairly consistent. Third, different tests were applied simultaneously—each official responding to a battery of tests. If reasonably effective, and if associations do exist, then fairly consistent patterns among the test scores should emerge. Fourth, while there can be no certainty that the civil servants' representations (which, it is argued, may be appreciated through their accounts) have a direct bearing on subsequent practice, they have the potential to do so. Fifth, while it is possible that civil servants will provide answers which they believe are expected (rather than those that they honestly believe in), these contrived answers are nevertheless revealing. It would seem plausible to suggest that responses which indicate a high degree of instrumentalism and are critical of self, others, and government organizations are more likely to reflect norms shared among an actor's colleagues than they are to constitute fabrications. On the other hand, if scores for instrumentalism and alienation are low while scores for self and others are high, then either these are genuine responses or they indicate that an official is acutely sensitive to what colleagues would regard as positive and likeable actions and statements, well able to deliver a low scores for mach and alienation along with and high scores for self and others, and certainly capable of being highly manipulative. Sixth, this attempt to gather a sense of the extent and depth of personalism is experimental. The notion—implied in the tests and the associations identified among the scores—that there exist discrete qualities (such as alienation and authoritarianism, and particular attitudes to self and others) which behave as discrete variables interacting in rather mechanical ways and generating well-defined patterns of behavior is not, I believe, an accurate portrayal of the nature of representation and practice (as the remainder of this chapter and subsequent chapters make plain). However, the tests (which present actors with a series of statements about the world and themselves to select from) do, for some reason, indicate associations between the sets of statements chosen—associations that do not run against the lines of argument pursued in these pages and seem to deserve explanation. And the mere fact that statements are being selected also allows some appreciation of the states of mind of a larger number of actors than would otherwise be the case. Theoretical objections to this experiment should be treated not as reasons to forestall it but as reasons to press ahead with it.

The materials that emerge from these test papers[32] are presented in the appendices, but the salient features of what is a complex picture are set out below.

1. The returns from each agency, and from the *barangays*, range from high levels of instrumentalism and alienation and low scores for self and others[33] (describing a parabola when plotted on a graph), to low scores for instrumentalism and alienation and high scores for self and others (describing an inverse parabola). A parabola is taken to indicate a personalistic state of mind, while an inverse parabola is held to be indicative of a more affective state of mind. The complexity of these returns is illustrated in appendix VIII which plots all returns from the Civil Service Commission.

2. The data do not provide a view of change through time. However, each official's profile (the set of scores returned on their tests) may be placed into one of the sixteen possible categories which emerge when scores for each of the four indicators (instrumentalism, self, others, and alienation) are placed either above or below the agency's mean scores for those same indicators. If it is assumed that each profile is a snapshot of a moment in transition between more affective and personalistic states of mind, and that each profile is a common stage in that transition, then it becomes possible arrange them into sequences which, when plotted on a graph, describe shifts between a parabola and an inverted parabola. Four strong patterns or sequences emerge; and in each of these there is a strong and consistent association among scores for mach, self, others and alienation. There are positive associations between scores for mach and alienation, and between scores for self and others; but between these two sets the association is negative. That is to say, as scores for instrumentalism and alienation increase, scores for self and others tend to fall. These associations hold true for most of the shifts (1-4) within with each agency (see appendices IX—XII) and also for each shift (see table 3) when data from each agency is aggregated.[34]

Table 3
Correlations Amongst Scores for Machiavellianism, Self, Others and Alienation (all agencies)

Shift 1 n567	mach	self	others	alienation
mach	1	-.628**	-.552**	.477**
self	-.628**	1	.760**	-.613**
others	-.552**	.760**	1	-.502**
alienation	.477**	-.613**	-.502**	1

Shift 2 n581	mach	self	others	alienation
mach	1	-.596**	-.550**	.703**
self	-.596**	1	.719**	-.618**
others	-.550**	.719**	1	-.520**
alienation	.703**	-.618**	-.520**	1

Shift 3 n 657	mach	self	others	alienation
mach	1	-.647**	-.592**	.527**
self	-.647**	1	.758**	-.646**
others	-.592**	.758**	1	-.556**
alienation	.527**	-.646**	-.556**	1

Shift 4 n560	mach	self	others	alienation
mach	1	-.690**	-.607**	.723**
self	-.690**	1	.748**	-.674**
others	-.607**	.748**	1	-.540**
alienation	.723**	-.674**	-.540**	1

Source: compiled from surveys conducted by the author in 2007.
Note: **Correlation is significant at the 0.01 level (2-tailed).

3. The meanings of the scores for instrumentalism, alienation, self and others, and the meaning of their association remain complex even in the absence of attempts by officials to dissemble or contrive. High mach scores do not equate with greater hostility, viciousness or vindictiveness (Robinson and Shaver, 1973, p. 592). Nor should it be assumed in this study of bureaucracy that high mach scores are *necessarily* indicative of personalistic behaviour. It is conceivable that high scores for mach, self, and others, together with low scores for alienation, might indicate a benign or positive and constructive use of relationships for the benefit of colleagues and agency; and that altruistic behavior may sometimes be quite consistent with high scores for mach and

alienation and low scores for self and others. It is also worth noting Christie's and Geis' hypothesis that high mach scores are less likely to be found in "traditional" societies where individuals "operate most effectively in unstructured situations" (Robinson and Shaver, 1973, p. 592). This recalls Polanyi's view that traditional societies are less manipulative. The neutral point of 100 on Christie's and Geis' Mach scale was determined at a time when it was believed that generational differences in the scores indicated that Americans were becoming more manipulative. The mean for selected agencies in the Philippines today is a little under 100, while the mean score for the selected *barangays* (where few of the people surveyed have had any experience of working in large organizations) is a little higher than 100. To suggest from such results that the Philippines is in "transition" from a traditional past to a modern future populated by manipulative beings would seem to require a very great leap of faith. A more reasonable interpretation is that these scores do not run against suggestions that the experience of working in large and often somewhat rigid and authoritarian organizations encourages an affective state of mind, and that agencies are not morbidly personalistic.

4. The associations between these scores (for instrumentalism, self, others and alienation) and those for authoritarianism and politicians' and civil servants' judgments of the quality of government organizations are still more complex. The developing model suggested that a more affective state of mind and high levels of instrumentalism are consistent both with high levels of authoritarianism (as attempts are made to bring order) and with moderate or low levels of authoritarianism. This suggestion is not contradicted by scores returned from the surveys, and is illustrated by the lack of association between instrumentalism and authoritarianism in appendix XIII.

5. The association between actors' representations of the quality of government organizations is also complex. The developing model suggested that somewhat more negative portrayals of organizations would be associated with higher levels of instrumentalism and deepening alienation (and with lower scores for self and others), though much would depend upon the organization in question, the immediate experiences of the official, and the stories and rumors already in circulation. The returns from the tests provide no strong statistical correlation between any of the other indicators and actors' judgments about the quality of government organizations, although there do appear to be concentrations of more positive representations of government organization when mach scores are low, and of more negative understandings when mach scores are high (appendix XIV).

This material should be treated with caution, but it runs against neither the complex, dimensional, constructive and imaginative behavior revealed and detailed through interviews with civil servants and politicians, nor the suggestion that any characterization of Philippine bureaucracy as strongly and hopelessly personalistic needs to be re-visited.

A Model of Bureaucracy

Interviews and surveys, then, provide comparatively simple and practical ways through which one may begin to gain an appreciation of the representations and practices of civil servants and politicians. But once harvested, how are their accounts and tests to be ordered—the proxies with which it should be possible to unzip and make intelligible the bundles of strings that comprise the bureaucracy and its features? The answer is not to impose a particular framework and interpretation upon these accounts but to allow a model to emerge from them—a model through which those same accounts may then be re-staged such that the dimensions of bureaucracy are revealed yet made comprehensible. This model is set out below in two parts.

A Fragmented Bureaucracy

The first part of the model is particular, but not exclusive, to the Philippines. It describes the "circumstances" or "conditions"—or, in other words, the matrix of prior strings of understandings and practice—that help to explain civil servants' and politicians' current representations and practices and, therefore, certain features of bureaucracy. Fundamental divisions in authority were guided by technical representations imported from America into the Philippines where representations and practices which may help to unify and coordinate were either less strong or absent (for instance, civil service recruitment and placement is not centralized). These multiple divisions of authority (geographical, center-region-locality, branch, agency, group, office, division, and section), fostered a cellular framework of administration within which civil servants' and politicians' subsequent understandings and practices evolved: understandings—of what bureaucracy is about, what it does or should do, what its problems and strengths are, and what the civil servants' and politicians' own roles are—that were poorly integrated and that together make up some of the dimensions of political interference.

A number of conditions, then, are proposed for the dimensionality of the bureaucracy. The first is the imposition of a political system that emphasizes local representation (most politicians, with the possible exception of Senators, are tied to their local constituencies) and the division of authority; and an emerging repertoire of historical experiences (of the Marcos era in particular) which counsels against concentration of authority. Second is the emergence of suspicion within government and bureaucratic agencies against the accumulation of authority in any other branch or agency. Third is the tendency to accept as a default position the proliferation of agencies, and the devolution of authority to various layers of local governments (*barangay*, municipal, city hall, provincial, congressional district). Fourth—and running against the diffusion of authority—is the practical necessity (most especially in a poor country) for central government to assume more authority over resources in order to coordinate the delivery of those resources to local governments. This accumulation of authority exacerbates tensions, suspicion and competition amongst the executive, legislature, center, and locality. Fifth is the further intensification of these tensions as a consequence of the dependency of government revenues upon a relatively small number of private businesses that are, for the most part, centered in Manila.

Under these conditions it is highly likely that there will develop—across the country, across bureaucracy and government, and within strongly hierarchical and segmented agencies—varied, particularistic, insular and partisan understandings of bureaucracy and government (local and central) formed largely around personal experience. This is especially so given that bureaucrats receive little or no training prior to appointment; the probationary period before tenure is awarded is only six months; there is no centralized recruitment or placement; the enforcement of civil service regulations (most especially in regions and local government) depends upon the referral of cases to the CSC; and there is a general reluctance to rotate staff either within an agency or around the country. As their respective and insular understandings develop, so much of the behavior they witness or hear about will, from their viewpoint, appear to damage or frustrate their own interests or those of the bureaucracy or country as a whole.

The alignment, integration and coordination of these highly varied understandings and practice is extremely difficult. Three further problems soon appear. First, the circumvention of organizations, procedures and rules increases as politicians and civil servants navigate through a system which, as they understand it, works against them and against what, in their view, would be a better system. Second—and this is in response to misalignment and circumvention—legislation thickens and over-conformity in the application of rules and procedures deepens, as politicians and bureaucrats attempt to align practice and thereby bring greater predictability and stability to political and bureaucratic life. The systems and patterns of authority and process ossified by the authors of this legislation and by those who monitor and enforce regulations and procedures, rarely conform to the systems and patterns envisaged or preferred by many other civil servants and politicians. Consequently, thickening legislation and increasing over-conformity are met with further circumvention. Third, the emphasis on local representation, decentralization and the division of authority intensifies more out of a desire to follow the path of least resistance, and less out of a concern for democratic principles.

An Emotional Bureaucracy

Fragmentation of understandings encourages fragmentation in practice and a host of other, related problems, and in turn breeds fragmented, poorly aligned representations. But whilst fragmentation may *help* to account for certain dimensions of bureaucracy's weaknesses and strengths, it does not explain why circumventions of process and breaches in rules for selfish ends (together with personalistic behavior and corruption more generally) are to be found alongside positive informal behavior, innovation, a genuine interest in the wider good, and loyalty to organizations and their core goals and functions. The second part of the model, then, is intended to deal with this question and describes three interlocking cycles of behavior. The first cycle (of instrumentalism and authoritarianism within organizations) stimulates the second cycle (comprising a deepening affective[35] [or emotional] sphere outside organizations and growing professionalism within organizations). The strengthening of the second cycle leads to weakening of the first cycle; but, as the second cycle becomes prevalent, it is more likely that a third cycle (of Puritanism and instrumentalism) will emerge. During this third cycle, the pressures which build up under the repression of self and any symptom of instrumentalism threaten a sudden return to a state in which instrumentalism becomes pervasive and the first cycle may be initiated once again. These interlocking cycles do not describe stages of development, nor are they particular to bureaucratic organizations. It is assumed that they are constantly at work and are to be found within any unit of analysis (such as economic[36] or bureaucratic organization, or bureaucracy or society), though the accent on one or other cycle varies from unit to unit and from time to time. Underlying these cycles are six sets of assumptions and arguments. These are outlined below.

Cycle 1: instrumentalism and authoritarianism

1. Social relationships describe: the behavior of individuals towards—or their treatment of—one another; and, therefore, the mental constructs or representations—such as "self," "you," "they," "community," "society," and "world"—which inform that behavior. It is with participation in existing relationships, and from interactions with the physical environment, that language and representations emerge in the young; and it is with constant participation in relationships that language and representations are sustained and developed. In other words, language and representations depend upon, as well as inform, the practice of relationships. Implicit in this interaction is a fundamental demand to protect and preserve relationships: that is, to avoid instrumentalism and, therefore, to prevent alienation, the death of relationships and, consequently, the disintegration of "self," "community" and other constructs. However, this demand tends to elicit recognition, and a response, only during periods of intense instrumentalism and alienation when it is felt intimately.

2. Social relationships are, therefore, the substance of any form of corporate body, including the bureaucratic organization. However, the emerging self is inherently self-centered and, left to its own devices, will manipulate relationships and objects to its own advantage. The heavy imposition of defined roles, rules, procedures, routines, hierarchies and divisions of authority, and, therefore, the emergence of more predictable action, may be understood as a response both to the uncertainty produced as individuals and groups pursue their own personal interests, and to a need for more stable, effective and focused organizations.

3. Whilst strongly authoritarian, the organization is not impersonal nor is it dehumanized. Authoritarianism may compel a reshaping of relationships (of constructs and behavior), but these remain the substance of the organization. To eradicate social relationships is to eradicate the organization. However, the reshaping of relationships, and the instrumentalism which first prompted that reshaping, create a sense of alienation. Constructs of "self," "you" and "they," and their place in "community" and "society," are no longer what they were, and behavior has altered. The crucible of relationships is now being re-ordered dramatically; and as the organization is driven towards a particular objective, its members find that their own understandings and sense of self are shaken, and that they are drawn into a gyre of instrumentalism and authoritarianism.

Cycle 2: the deepening of the affective and the professional spheres

4. It is in response to these twin challenges—instrumentalism and authoritarianism—that, outside the organization, a sanctuary is created in which relationships are idealized, initiating a second cycle. There is, in particular, a strengthening sense that relationships and constructs of "self," "you," "they," "community," and "society" are important in their own right and, therefore, should not be manipulated for particular ends. There is a deepening interest in these constructs, in the behavior shown to one another, and, therefore, in the quality of emotion. And an increasingly deliberate and focused contemplation of these matters finds voice through music, art, literature, and dance.

5. This response—the idealization of relationships—is driven by the understanding that is from relationships that constructs and language emerge, and, therefore, that descent into a state of alienation in which "others" are transformed into mere instruments must be prevented (see [1.] above).

6. The idealization of relationships outside the organization is not equated with the treatment of relationships as absolute or independent facts. Rather, the idealization of relationships (this deepening interest in the affective) is understood as the treatment of relationships (and constructs) *as if* abso-

lute—*as if* important in their own right. This distinction between the treatment of relationships as absolutes and their treatment *as if* absolute implies the *choice* and, therefore, the admission that relationships are not necessarily important in themselves in all circumstances. Choice, then, is vital to the protection of relationships in two respects. First, without it, relationships are transformed, conceptually, into facts or absolutes which *must* be thought of and treated as important in their own right. An intimate or felt appreciation of their significance is now lost; and, as appeals are made to these absolutes, relationships may be turned more easily into instruments. Secondly, choice allows for the possibility that there may be circumstances in which, in order to preserve relationships, it is necessary to treat relationships as instruments or absolutes.[37]

7. The deepening of the affective sphere *outside* the organization is paralleled by changes *within* the organization. The sense that relationships should not be manipulated is flatly contradicted by experience: within the organization relationships are plainly re-shaped, re-directed and used for ulterior purposes. It is, therefore, essential: that rules, roles, procedures, hierarchies, and divisions of authority are treated *as if* absolute or, in other words, *as if* important in themselves and, therefore, distanced *conceptually* from their true social quality; and that choice is sustained.

(a) This emotional professionalism (or, in other words, the treatment of the organization's rules, roles, hierarchies, routines, discipline, divisions of authority, and its functions and objectives, *as if* absolute, and their conceptual "distancing" from relationships) is necessary to protect the affective sphere. Were the true social nature of the organization to be recognised explicitly and openly, then the use of relationships for ulterior purposes in the form of the organization would have been exposed. That is, in open and general recognition both of the use of relationships and, therefore, of the instrumental potential of relationships, it is now easy to conceive of their use for whatever purpose and more likely that their instrumental potential will be realised. The affective sphere is now compromised and its quality as a distinct sphere and sanctuary is lost.

(b) Emotional professionalism is also necessary to protect the organization. Were the true social nature of the organization to be recognized explicitly, then the mystique of "the organization" and its frameworks (that is, its rules, roles, procedures, hierarchies, and divisions of authority, and its functions and objectives) would be damaged, and the organization would risk dissolution into competing sets of relationships. And were the organization's frameworks to be treated as facts (and their social content denied), they would be transformed into inflexible demands—absolutes to which those seeking to manipulate others would appeal, and over whose creation they would attempt to wrest authority. Constant monitoring and readjustments (centrally controlled) become necessary as attempts are made mitigate inflexibility while countering private attempts to circumvent rigidities or to distort and control these absolutes. Put another way, the treatment of the organization and its frameworks *as if* absolute describes a common and voluntary agreement on—and a shared and "felt" appreciation of—their significance. In this there is less threat of dissolution or circumvention; and it is less likely that the organization and its frameworks will be co-opted and manipulated by private cliques.

(c) The deepening of emotional professionalism also happens to be conducive to the development of a more effective organization. This is so for a number of reasons. First, there is less need for supervision and policing; and the organization becomes less authoritarian. Secondly, there is growing technical professionalism. That is, the treatment of the organization and its frameworks *as if* absolute (and their conceptual distancing from relationships) brings regularity, predictability, focus and reliability to practice.

(d) As emotional professionalism continues to deepen, and as confidence in this perspective grows, it becomes possible to admit within the organization: the emergence of relationships which are explicitly social (and treated *as if* important in their own right); and, therefore, compassion. That is, the affective sphere begins to intrude into the organization but in ways that are beneficial for the organization. This is so in two respects. First, the admission of explicitly social relationships within the organization helps emphasize the conceptual distinction between those relationships and organization's frameworks, and thereby ensures that the true social quality of the organization's frameworks remains unspoken. Second, with the admission of social relationships and compassion, comes recognition that competency, abilities, contributions, and failings are changeable, ambiguous, intimately entangled, and often dependent upon context. In this way, greater tolerance and, therefore, more room for creativity and flexibility are brought to the organization.

In short, the deepening of the affect outside the organization, and increasing emotional and technical professionalism within the organization, prompt and reinforce the other. The emergence, development, and maintenance of the organization and the affective sphere are interdependent.

Cycle 3: Puritanism and instrumentalism

8. Whilst the affective sphere grows because of its value to the operation of the organization, a personalistic or instrumental outlook remains of critical importance: the *choice* (rather than the demand) to eschew instrumentalism presumes the presence of such an outlook.

9. However, as the affective sphere grows, there is the risk that it will become, conceptually, entirely distinct and separate from the organization,

such that the social quality of the organization is no longer recognised, and instrumentalism (because of its potential threat to relationships) is taken to be synonymous with moral degeneration. Relationships and organizations, correctly formed, are treated as symbols of moral purity; and there is increasing pressure to eradicate any symptom of instrumentalism. There is an attempt to prescribe not only correct action but also correct thought and, therefore, possible future action. Correct rules, roles, procedures, hierarchies, functions and objectives (in the professional sphere), and correct social relationships, constructs and emotions (in the affective sphere) are presented as facts; and a felt and intimate appreciation of their importance and meaning is lost.

10. There is now, within the affective sphere, an unfelt acceptance of the importance of social relationships; while, in the professional sphere, the conceptual separation of the organization's rules, roles, procedures, hierarchies, functions and objectives from social relationships is so complete that their rigorous application in all circumstances becomes imperative. Instrumentalism and other expressions of self exhibited by non-conformists only prompt a further strengthening of this Puritanism.

11. It is now no longer enough to follow the rules (as in an authoritarian organization) or to choose to treat those rules *as if* absolute (as in a professional organization): rules within the organization, and relationships outside the organization, must be treated as absolutes; and behavior must be correctly motivated, and performed without discretion. The organization becomes less and less flexible; and self is marginalized by increasingly stringent orthopraxy. The repression of self generates intense frustration; at the same time it becomes possible, even laudable, to demand that others should endure misery simply in order to satisfy the puritan's sense of the importance of absolutes.[38] However, as a sense of rebellion mounts against this complete repression, and as resentments build against the Puritan's growing callousness and officiousness, there are likely to be swings, possibly sudden and violent, towards personal interests and open instrumentalism. Sporadic at first, these swings become more and more frequent; relationships become more unstable as uncertainty over their significance and meaning deepens; organizations become weaker and less effective; and the affective sphere thins out and begins to fray. And, as instrumentalism becomes prevalent, conditions are now formed in which the first cycle may be initiated once again.

Implications. These interlocking cycles collapse a number of apparent dichotomies present in Weberian conceptions of bureaucracy. First, an effective, professional or "modern" bureaucracy is not impersonal nor dehumanized: the distancing of relationships from the professional sphere is conceptual, not factual. Second, emotion is not a symptom of, nor is it equated with, irrationality. To the contrary, emotion is central to a professional bureaucracy. Third, doubts are raised over the distinction between forms of rationality—end-rational (means) and value-rational (ends). The emphasis shifts from whether actions are a means or ends, to whether they are treated *as if* absolute. The treatment of what are held to ends or means as absolute, makes instruments of them; while the treatment of what are held to be means or ends *as if* important in their own right endows them greater practical importance. Fourth, questions are also raised over the distinction between the formal and proper and the informal (and improper). Just as formal may reflect either a reaction to instrumentalism or a tool, so informality may reflect aspects of professionalism and, in a very real and practical sense, hold the civil service together. Fifth, the distinction between individual and society—and the notion that either or both are the prime unit of analysis—are brought into question. Both individual and society are constructs which emerge from existing relationships and inform the subsequent practice of relationships. The collapse of these dichotomies raises all kinds of interesting conceptual and methodological issues. In particular, if, as if often the case, most of these dichotomies are equated with western (rational, impersonal, formal, individualistic) and non-Western (irrational, emotional, personalistic, social, informal, collective), then their collapse suggests that the putative "Western" or "modern" is, fundamentally, "non-Western" and "traditional." It is the collapse of these dichotomies which also enable these cycles to accommodate the dimensionality of their subjects, such as the agency that at once exhibits strong currents of technical professionalism and bouts of authoritarianism, factionalism, and impropriety.

Conclusions

Layering civil servants' and politicians' accounts in order to augment the empirical base for this study happens to reveal the dimensionality the bureaucracy. This dimensionality speaks to a social world whose features comprise strings of representations and practice. And from this idea of the social world a model arises—one capable of restaging the accounts of actors in a way that retains coherence while allowing something of the complexity and dimensionality of political and bureaucratic practice to come through.

Although terms such as "cycle" and "framework" used to set out the model convey a sense of inevitability, they are better understood to describe commonalities and likelihoods in thought and action—congregations of common and recurring strings of practice and representations. These strings (and their congregations) make up very real constraints and opportunities. Their influence, though "soft" (in that they comprise actors' representations of "self," "others," and "world") as well as tangible (in that they comprise the practices effected by actors), is substantive. They are also interdependent such that the intensification of one encourages the other. (For instance, so rooted is the sense of self in its interactions and relationships with the natural world and other minds that its strengthening, and the feeling of alienation this generates, prompts a deepening sense of the importance of social relationships and "community"). But these strings are dimensional; and they are passive in their nature (in that they block, restrain, guide, and encourage) rather than active (deterministic). That is to say, they have an important yet uncertain bearing on subsequent events. They are also uncertain in the sense that strings have only the potential to congregate.

The substantive but uncertain and passive quality of these strings and their congregation reflects their key features. First, the influence of any prior matrix of practices and representations is mediated though actors' representations of that matrix; and these representations are experienced (and are therefore varied) rather than replicated. Given this, and given that each point on a string of representations and practice intersects with other strings, there is no guarantee that the strings formed subsequently by actors (even when faced with what may appear to be very similar circumstances) will be similar enough to be recognizable as a congregation. In other words, strings and congregations are not prefigured nor are they deterministic. Second, strings and congregations emerge from communication, practical compromise, deliberate alignment, and common reasoning in the light of circumstances—including, most fundamentally, qualities of being (such as a strong sense of self, and recognition of the significance of a public language and the need to protect relationships)—that are shared or are perceived to be so. Third, strings and their congregations occur simultaneously at different scales and over different periods of time. Cycles therefore conflict with, as well as complement and depend upon, each other. For instance, as the second cycle deepens, instrumentalism, over-conformity and other features associated with the first cycle disrupt translation of the social into the official and thereby impede innovation and flexibility, though at the same time positive informality now becomes more obvious.

"Cycles" and "frameworks" and other similar terms, then, do not describe prefigured, concretized patterns capable of determining subsequent patterns (as if actors serve merely as temporary custodians of those patterns). Rather, they describe thoughts and actions whose own immediate qualities (as opposed to "deep" or overarching structures) account for a social world that is at once fuzzy and yet also exhibits recurrent (though still imprecise and temporary) regularities—congregations of thought and practice whose simple commonality brings a measure of order and predictability. The social world's fuzziness is rooted in the variation and dimensionality of representation and practice; and in compromise and adjustment as actors attempt to achieve a working fit. Moreover, while representations bring a degree of order and clarity locally, this is not necessarily realized in ways that those representations describe. Representations function to integrate practice, but may often manage this by portraying a world that is more sharply and clearly defined than is in fact the case and, in doing so, contribute to a world that is in fact more blurred, complex, and dimensional than any representation is able to convey. The social world's uncertain and temporary patterns, meanwhile, derive from shared qualities of being and ultimately, therefore, from human interaction.

Notes

1. Possibly as a consequence of the rather limited number of studies and comparatively narrow approaches, historical representations of the bureaucracy are those of bureaucracy that has had, and is continuing, to struggle against its pre-modern qualities. Under Spanish rule, government (and especially public revenue and expenditure) was managed by a privileged class of bureaucrats, mostly Spanish, whose posts were either bought or distributed as political favours. Under the first, and short-lived, Philippine Republic of 1898, a distinction was made between appointed and competitive posts. The Americans then added new departments ,and introduced new systems of accounting for public resources. The ideals of merit and political neutrality (at least as far as competitive positions were concerned) continued after independence and, under advice from America's Bell Mission, an institute of public administration at the University of the Philippines was established in 1952. From 1972 until 1986, the bureaucracy "was construed to have lost its political neutrality" (Rebullida and Serrano, 2006, p. 233). After the fall of Marcos, the civil service was purged and its commitment to its essentially Weberian bureaucratic ideals was restored. Since then, periodic attempts have been made to introduce modern practices. These reforms focussed on: reducing the number of civil servants; improvements in training; greater transparency; strengthening ethics and the ethos of public service; and client satisfaction.

2. See, for instance, Abueva, 1965, 1970; Araral, 2005; Arce and Poblador, 1981, 1977; Brilliantes and Mangahas, 2006; Brilliantes and Panchii, 1988; Cariño, 1986, 1990; Chew, 1993, Corpuz, 1957, 1989; Dans, 1977; Department of Budget and Management, 1995; Endriga, 1985, 2001; Francisco, 1960; Guthrie, 1968, 1981; Heady, 1957; Mangahas, 1993; Masa, 1976; Reyes, 1994, 1990, 1999; Sta. Ana, F. 1996; Sto Tomas, P.A., 1995; Tapales, 1984; Thompson, J. 1995; Valdeavilla, 1995; Varela, 1992; Veneracion, 1988; Yang, D. 2008.

3. See, for instance, Alfiler, 1979, 1985; Abueva, 1970; Bautista, 1982; Briones, 1979; Cariño, 1979, 1975, 1985, 1986, 1992, and 1994; Cariño and de Guzman, 1979; Corpuz, 1989, 1957; de Guzman, 1979; Endriga 1979; Reyes 1982; Tapales, Enriquez and Trinidad, 1995; Varela, 1995; Veneracion 1988.

4. "Society," "association" and "community" correspond clearly with types of action—the rationally expedient (instrumental), "affective" (the affectual or emotional) and traditional (or habitual) ("Weber"); Aron, R. 1935.

5. Cf. Rebullida and Serrano, 2006

6. See also: Linz and Chehabi (1990), cited in Thompson (1995).

7. Indeed, Weber writes: "Today, it is primarily the capitalist market economy which demands that the official business of the administration be dis-

charged precisely, unambiguously, continuously, and with as much speed as possible. Normally, the very large, modern capitalist enterprises are themselves unequalled models of strict bureaucratic organization" ("Weber," p. 215).

8. See, for example: Wui and Lopez, 1997; Rebullida, 2003.
9. See, for example, Mosca, 1939; Weber, 1997; "Weber"; Blau, 1973; von Mises, 1944; Michels, 1962; Katz and Kahn, 1967; Downs, 1967; Niskasen, 1971; Dunleavy, 1991.
10. See, for instance, Cooley, C.H. 1964 and 1962.
11. Cited in Cohen, 1974, p. 223-4.
12. Cited in Quibria, 2003. There is also a literature that deals explicitly with the positive as well as negative) aspects of emotions in bureaucracy. This often describes emotions as 'bounded' and tends to understand them as qualities to be manipulated for a particular end or tapped into (enabling civil servants to, say, connect with clients in a welfare state). Bounded emotions might also encourage a sense of well-being amongst the members of an organization and their families, though whether this is for the good of employees or provides a more effective way of manipulating and controlling those employees is debated. See, for instance, Goffman, 1956a and 1956b; Bailey, 1983; Hochschild, 1983; Stencross and Kleinman, 1989; Mumby and Putnam, 1992; Fineman, 1993; James, 1993; Graham, 2003.
13. See, for instance, Balogh, 1966; Bardhan, 2002; Bauer and Yamey, 1957; Hayami, 1998; 1989; Li, op.cit.; Olson, 1982; Sobel, 2002.
14. See, for instance, Bayley, 1966; Huntington, 1970; Klitgaard, 1991; Leff, 1964; McMullan, 1961; Nye, 1967.
15. For a fascinating debate on formal and informal politics in China, see: Nathan and Tsai, 1995; Dittmer, L. 1995; Pye, L. 1995.
16. See: Haller and Shore (op. cit.).
17. See, especially, Cariño (1992).
18. The central offices number anything from a few hundred employees (in the case of the CSC) to around 2,000 (as in the case of the BIR).
19. Pawid, L. , Legislative Staff Officer, Office of Senator Gordon, The Philippine Senate, Pasay City, September 17, 2007.
20. Ibid.
21. Ibid.
22. See, in particular, Stryker, (op. cit.).
23. This suggestion would seem to imply that *only* mental states are intentional (that only in the mind can reference be made to something that may not exist) and, therefore, that mental states (and mind) are distinct from, and cannot be explained in terms of, the physical world. Yet if it is conceded that mental states are indeed physical processes, then physical processes *can* be intentional. Surely, then, representations can exist independently of mind in some form (preserved in, say, books, recordings and practice)? This question, however, may be a distraction. If it is accepted that mental states are a quality of the human body and, further, that mind is a representation, then the question is not whether representations are physical, but whether or not they are, in their nature and details, different from the artefacts and symbols formed and arranged to encourage their emergence in others. A book might encourage in a reader particular states of mind

desired by the writer. But the physical nature of the book is not that of the reader; nor do the details of representations encouraged in the reader reproduce precisely those of the writer. Even if it were possible in some way to copy exactly representations from the writer into the reader, these copies would be altered by the reader's experience of them. That is to say, whilst "mind" and "self" may be representations, they are nevertheless experienced acutely, immediately and without doubt *as if* they are more than representations: it is *as if* there is a distinct someone who is not the writer. Thus any representation—such as a representation of culture and structure—copied from writer to reader would, on a sudden, become a representation of culture and structure that is being considered and written about by this detailed and distinct "someone." Mental states, then, cannot exist independently of body because they are of the body, and because they are altered instantly by the experience of them.

24. As Perinbanayagam (1985, p. 28) observes, structure (understood as sets of ideas, objects and symbolizing phenomena with similar properties) "cannot...be taken as given by nature, though they may be found in it. They themselves are human constructions, albeit constructions from the past achieved by interpretations and classifications which in turn lead to their embodiment or "concretization," to use an image from Levi-Strauss (1963), in linguistically sound and publicly sharable entities, to wit, paradigmatic/syntagmatic structures." However, the suggestion that once "concretized," acts and their meanings "may become schedules and achieve both stability and order" and may become patterned roles that provide "a certain continuity and obduracy to society" (Perinbanayagam, 1985, p. 5), is to harden only *conceptually* representations designed by scholars to help explain, order and make sense. Representations have a bearing on practice but only insofar as they inform the scholars' or actors' practice.

25. If there is something else at work then it is likely to be found by way of features which cannot be explained with reference to strings of representations and practice. For instance it is claimed by Brown (1991) that from early infancy there exists "an ability to identify items that are known by one sense with the same items perceived in another sense, and see the world as a unity, not as different worlds imposed by our different sense modalities." If this is so, and it is not the case that prior constructs of a unity have emerged as a consequence of the infant's earlier interactions, then it does suggest that unity or at least the ability to construct unity from different senses is "hard-wired." On the other hand, a boy's possessiveness towards his mother may be better understood with reference to emerging representations of self and his place in the world (most especially in relation to the person that has figured so strongly in his interactions from which his representations of self, others and world have emerged) rather than by appeals to genetic or evolutionary-inspired absolutes or to the operation of social structures.

26. A further implication of this emphasis on surface features is that knowing the meaning of things—knowing the rules which enable actors to make sense of language, actions, pictures, and sounds—are neither innate nor are they imprinted by external structures. Rather, they are being settled upon constantly through trial, error and negotiation. And since these

settlements are multiple, functional and temporary, it is unlikely that any one actor will be aware of, or understand, all their dimensions.

27.   The numbers of officials interviewed in each agency's central offices amounted to around 2-5 percent of those offices' staff, and to much higher share (from around a fifth to a third or so) of those offices' third-level staffs. In the case of the Senate and the House, interviews were conducted with legislators and their staff, and with members of the secretariat. The total number of interviews conducted amounted to more than 200. In most cases, the sources (interviewees) used here are cited. However, there are instances where either the author makes a judgment that the source should remain anonymous, or interviewees have requested anonymity.

28.   These units describe the hierarchy found within most government agencies. The terms for these units are also used frequently in government agencies. There are variations, however, and, on occasions, terms commonly used to describe one level in the hierarchy are also applied to quite another level.

29.   Levinson and Huffman (1955) claim that family ideology overlap with ideological views of other social institutions (along a democratic-autocratic continuum). Might it, therefore, provide a more rounded view of an actor's authoritarian or puritanical leanings?

30.   McClosky and Schaar's (1965) anomy scale is "one of the most thorough investigations of attitude states in the literature" (Robinson and Shaver, 1973, p. 5). Berger's scale for self and others, too, is "the most carefully developed scale to measure attitudes towards self that we found in the literature. Evidence of validity is more extensive than for most scales in this book" (Shaw, 1967, p. 433). Levinson and Huffman's scale is somewhat dated, but "remains a comprehensive scale for this area" (Robinson, Shaver and Wrightsman, 1991, p. 510); and, given the emphasis on the family that is supposed to characterise Filipino society, may have particular relevance to the Philippines. The content validity of most of the items used in Kelley's scale is sufficient to allow it to be used to measure attitude toward any organization (Shaw and Wright 1967, p. 553). "The strongest component" of Christie's and Geis' (1970) mach scale "taps a respondent's feelings about whether other people can be manipulated so as to achieve (usually the respondent's) desired ends" (Robinson and Shaver, 1973, p. 587) and "has achieved very interesting results in field studies" (ibid). The scale has "the most demonstrable substantive rationale" for scales on interpersonal trust and attitudes toward human nature." (Robinson, Shaver and Wrightsman, 1991, p. 374).

31.   Some of these tests (such as Christie's and Gies' mach scale) have already been translated into Chinese and Swedish among other languages.

32.   The tests were distributed as randomly as possible to between about 4 percent and 20 percent of all staffs in each agency, and to 3 percent of constituents within a single contiguous area that cuts across three *barangays* (in Quezon).

33.   Higher levels of instrumentalism, alienation and authoritarianism are described by higher test scores, while more positive representations of self, others and institution (organization) are indicated by higher test scores.

34.   Data for *barangays* are excluded. Data from the MMDA are also excluded because only a local branch office of this agency was surveyed.

35. Following Aron (1935), the term "affective" is used by Gerth and Wright Mills (1977, p. 57) in their introduction of "Weber" to describe a type of action which flows from emotion (see above, note 4). In this present book, "affective" is used here to describe the idealization of relationships (and aspects of emotion) or, in other words, their treatment *as if* important in their own right see above (Introduction, note 2).

36. Indeed, certain ideas which have now come to form some elements of these cycles first evolved in analyses of Filipino, Chinese, Korean, European and American businesses in the Philippines and China (Hodder, 1996, 2006).

37. There is in this argument something of what Weber termed the "ethic of responsibility" (trying to do the best for all concerned) as opposed to the "ethic of absolute ends" (adherence to morally pure actions regardless of the consequences [see following note]). For Weber these two types of ethics had a particular political relevance. But while the terms are Weber's, the tension they describe, and the problems they pose, form part of much older and broader debates. The more important aspect of the argument set out above in the main text—the emphasis on the importance of relationships in their own right—to some extent mirrors Kant's categorical imperative, though it is understood less as a moral imperative derived from reason alone, and more as a necessity in view of its psychological and practical ramifications.

38. This state of mind might also, perhaps, be described as "ethic of absolute ends" or "ethic of attitude" (see previous note).

2

Political Interference

Introduction

The core problems afflicting the civil service are rooted in administrative principles and arrangements introduced under American rule. Inherent in this system as it evolved in the Philippines is an emphasis on the division of authority amongst branches and agencies of government; a suspicion of authority concentrated in any other branch or agency; and, consequently, a tendency to view the proliferation of agencies and the devolution of authority as a default setting. The sentiments attached to these representations and practices were strengthened by reactions against what was, from the perspective of central government in a poor country, the need to centralize control over the collection and distribution of resources, and the dependency of government revenues on a small number of private businesses centered largely in Manila.

From this prior context of representations and practice emerged today's highly varied, insular, and partisan understandings of bureaucracy and government. Bureaucratic and governmental practice has become strongly cellular, and representations and practice are misaligned. Viewed through the eyes of many politicians and civil servants, authority is either too diffuse or too centralized: they seem to have more than enough influence over matters which they see as peripheral, and far too little say over those that are central, to their interests; while too much authority, they feel, is concentrated in other agencies and branches of government. This perceived misallocation of authority creates a deal of irritation, prompting them to take whatever means necessary (formal and informal, proper and improper) to perform what they hold to be their necessary functions and duties and meet their interests.[1]

Whatever the analyst might think about the notion that authority is misallocated (for it implies an optimum distribution), actors sense it keenly enough to construct elaborate models to account for it and for the "misunderstanding and mistrust and frustration"[2] that it generates. One such explanation (and it is one from which this study partly draws) is that the American system of government (with its emphasis on the separation of authority among its branches and agencies) works reasonably well, but does not always suit the realities faced on the ground by Filipinos, nor do Filipinos always understand that system. The difficulties created by this mismatch, and by a lack of understanding, were exacerbated by a tendency to deal with those difficulties through piecemeal legislation, and through reform "really driven by survival: we reform because we have to, not because we want to."[3] Thus, politicians and bureaucrats unwittingly built around themselves a system whose internal mechanisms are poorly integrated and frequently grind against each other. A further consideration which helps to explain civil servants and politicians' poor or partial understanding of the system and its uncoordinated evolution, is that their view of it is limited to their own experiences:

> ...you have a lot of agencies who say "why does Congress have to poke around [in] our funds, not understanding that ... Congress is elected to make sure that there is no taxation without representation.... So the bureaucracy doesn't understand Congress. Congress, on the other hand, is stuck in the past and doesn't understand the bureaucracy. There are few people who really study, who try to understand, who try to reform ... because of the lack of reading and knowledge, most of our conclusions are based on experience. [4]

As civil servants and politicians take matters into their own hands, there soon follow attempts by competing actors within the organization to circumvent or manipulate or exert influence over the creation and enforcement of rules, procedures, roles, and hierarchies—the frameworks through which relationships and actions are ordered, divisions of authority are maintained, and the everyday business of government is coordinated. Circumvention, however, produces unpredictability and a loss of focus, and prompts a more absolutist treatment of those frameworks. This very practical response is countered by further efforts to circumvent, manipulate, and control absolutes which, in turn, become increasingly specific, detailed, layered, and rigid. Authoritarianism, then, refers more to the absolute quality of rules, procedures, roles and hierarchies than it does to periods of centralized personal rule. Indeed, it is the experience of martial law, and a desire to prevent the country from slipping once again into the arms of a strongman, that now counsels the strict application of those frameworks and energizes that tendency to meet circumvention with further divisions in authority, usually in a piecemeal fashion rather than in accordance with a coherent vision.

Thus, sections of the bureaucracy swing unpredictably between states of ossification and fluidity, and there emerges an officialdom whose members lament the "harsh" structure of rules, regulations, and laws within which they must operate while complaining about the predilection of so many of their colleagues to ignore or circumvent that structure. As far as the bureaucracy is concerned, the most significant manifestations of this first cycle are divisions of authority over appointments, promotions, and discipline within the civil service; and political interference.

Political Interference

As with many areas of political and bureaucratic life, the authority to make appointments is diffuse. The Office of the President has legitimate authority to make appointments to the upper (or third) level of the bureaucracy (secretaries, undersecretaries, assistant secretaries, and directors) and at more junior levels in some agencies (as in the Department of Education). Appointments to directorships commonly draw from the permanent service, while appointments to higher ranks are more often than not brought in from outside the service. Legislators (members of the Senate and the Lower House) may also legitimately influence appointments—and at the highest level—through the Commission on Appointments. It is the civil service itself, however, which has authority to make appointments to first and second levels, and to determine the eligibility of career civil servants for third level positions. Each agency is entitled to make its own appointments, but it must do so according to the qualifications, standards, rules, codes and procedures set out by the Civil Service Commission. Precisely where the limits of authority over appointments lie, however, are unclear; there is "no law yet which clearly defines how much percent should be devoted to political appointees"[5] while the proportion of positions in which may be placed those career civil servants deemed to be eligible is similarly undefined. In practice, the number of political appointees follows precedent and what the other branches of government will allow the president to get away with; and those probably well placed to know, put the figure at some 5,000-6,000[6]—a figure that is close to numbers estimated in recent academic research (Brillantes and Mangahas, 2006). The total number of political appointees (more broadly defined) is put by the civil service at some 18,000 (see table 1.2)—a number that includes all agencies, government corporations, and local government. Here in local government the appointing authorities (particularly mayors) are "respected ... especially if *on paper* the processes are regular."[7] Indeed, local government is so politicized that the Civil Service Commission "does not have permanent HRMD positions in LGUs ... Head of agencies [mayors and provincial governors] change HRMD [personnel] as quickly as they like and put their own people in."[8]

The authority to discipline civil servants is similarly diffuse. The Commission, through its Office for Legal Affairs, has authority over administrative cases involving civil servants. The bulk of these cases are classified as "conduct prejudicial to the best interests of the service"—an umbrella phrase that includes offences such as "grave misconduct" and "dishonesty." Decisions are issued in the form of resolutions which either exonerate a respondent or find them guilty. If guilty, penalties range from a reprimand to suspension or, as the ultimate sanction, dismissal from the service. The Commission's authority, however, is limited. First, each agency has original jurisdiction over the bulk of its own staffs though, again, it is expected to comply with the rules and procedures set out by the Commission. For example, original cases involving third-level employees must be filed directly with the CSC; and the CSC has discretion to take on cases which it regards as novel or important or which it feels might otherwise receive little more than a whitewash. But the CSC has no jurisdiction over elected officials or political appointees. In practice, then, most cases (between about 70 percent and 90 percent) involving permanent civil servants only (at all levels) are heard by the CSC on appeal. Second, no reports on the type or number of original cases filed and disposed of within agencies are made to the Commission. Nor does the CSC vet or examine disciplinary procedures within agencies. And whilst it may instruct heads of agency (political appointees) to provide information and documents, it has no authority to compel them to do so: "Let's put it this way: discipline is essentially the prerogative of management. So if she is your staff and commits an infraction and you don't want to discipline her, that's your prerogative."[9] Nor is the fact that managers may overlook an offence regarded as complicity: "Under Philippine jurisprudence we cannot find any liability on the part of the agency head except—probably because there are too many bad eggs in the organization—that would reflect on the kind of performance that the agency would have. But the only consequence, probably, is that the agency head will be booted out of the service and changed by a higher authority. But none the less I have to see the situation where the higher authority really reprimands the head of the agency for not disciplining people."[10] The Commission is also limited in that it "can only get into the picture once somebody complains. If the agency head does not want to discipline [a subordinate] but somebody will complain about the infraction and the behavior, then we can take cognizance. But we have to have a complainant." [11] It is possible for a complainant to remain anonymous if there is an obvious truth to the allegations or if there is complete documentary evidence available, but in general, "anonymous complaints must be dismissed."[12]

There is, as a consequence of these restrictions, the very real danger that offenses committed in agencies are not picked up or dealt with. Matters are further complicated by the fact that the Ombudsman has concurrent jurisdiction over administrative cases. Clients may, therefore, file a case either with the civil service or with the Office of the Ombudsman or with both, "hoping that they will get favorable decision from one of the agencies. So ... if we discover that there is another administrative case filed with the Ombudsman—and it was filed first with the Ombudsman—then we dismiss the case here..." In response, the Commission now requires [a] certificate of "non-fora shopping"—to be submitted along with a complaint. This comprises an affidavit attached to a complaint in which complainants attest that they have not filed a similar (or the same) case in any other regional office or court. Despite this measure, however, "unscrupulous complainants ... do file with other agencies; and if we discover that in bad faith he or she filed the same case elsewhere, then that certificate of non-fora shopping ... can be used to file an action ... probably perjury ... against that person."[13]

The diffusion and lack of clarity over appointments and discipline reflects sensitivity over these matters. It is difficult to find at any level within the Commission those who would like to assume more authority over administrative cases "because then you would be intruding into the jurisdiction of the agency heads. It is like saying that these agency heads are not to be trusted. If I [were] the agency head I [would] be insulted."[14] Matters would be made worse in other ways, too, if the CSC were

> ...to shortcut and centralize and say "I know what I'm doing".... You have to try to mature the bureaucracy in the final analyses. You have to look at what kind of a system we should have, and I believe that the more decentralized or down-to-the-grassroots we get, where you are not centralizing power but decentralizing [and] localizing power, is ultimately the best way to manage. It cannot be perfectly done now [but] I don't think the answer is to get it all back and to say "I will show you how to do it" because that will never happen. It is like saying that this democracy does not work, so we'll be a dictator first and show them. So you try to get things to work, to make the policies that provide the guidelines, but do not take over. You will find abuses, [and] you can deal with abuses, with indirect contempt and all these things; but you do not solve the problem by taking the power back.... The power of influence and power of shame [are the key], not the power to instruct...the Philippines has been short-circuiting everything all these years. It sounds crazy, but you have to have faith that we will learn our lessons. It will be slow, but you won't learn unless you learn the lessons yourself.[15]

But whilst indicative of a strongly held belief in the separation of powers, the reluctance within the CSC to take on more authority is also a concomitant of the perceived necessity for curtailing the concentration of authority in the Office of the President. "...I tell you, [it's] back to politics.... Again, it is the power of appointments.... I have had experience in the past. I wanted the following people under my watch and the president would say: "But I have already agreed with the congressmen that his nephew would be doing this or that there." So you go back to the power of appointments.... Even when we ... recommend the most qualified people, up to the last minute, you do not know what is going to come out."[16]

Meanwhile, within the executive and legislature there are many who believe that their respective branch of government has insufficient authority over appointments and discipline, while the other branch, and the civil service itself, have too much say over such matters. This is especially true of the Office of the President and the political appointees who staff the upper echelons of departments. Commonly, they are of the view that the bureaucracy is, or should be, the means through which policies are implemented and services delivered and, therefore, should serve as the executive's technical arm. A comment which typifies responses by members of the legislature and executive to the complaint that civil servants are not sufficiently insulated from politicians is that "the bureaucracy is there to deliver basic services from the executive who are elected by the people ... [civil servants] are supposed to be professionals...why should [they] be insulated?"[17] Pawid went on to express his view in a more forceful and still more revealing form of words: "[the civil service] is like an animal ... sorry for the comparison ... you pet it, you order it, you feed it, or you raise a whip or something to make it move and go your way, because that is something that needs to be done."[18]

In the face of views such as these, Constantino-David's assessment that "basically the bureaucracy has always been taken for granted ... as simply an extension of whoever is in power"[19] is both measured and accurate. Yet, in practice, the assessment is often challenged: by the fact that, from its point of view, the Office of the President must vie with the legislature (through the Commission on Appointments) to place candidates in many of the most important posts in the Republic; and by a bureaucracy whose members often seem (to the politician) to act either in their own interest or as a non-governmental pressure group.

In local government, too, there is a strong belief that it should have more authority than other branches and agencies (especially at the center) probably expect them to have; and in some vital areas, such as Education, particular understandings of various legal arrangements are drawn on as a pretext to bolster that belief. For instance, under the local government code superintendents have the authority to appoint principals but are expected to consult with a district's Congressional representative and other local politicians on the appointment. Politicians, however, frequently read "consult" as "compel" and, in practice, "if you don't get the recommendation of the politician concerned ... you are in hot water..."[20] for it is they who control local funds. Of particular importance is the Special Education Fund whose Chairman is the Mayor and whose pro-chairman is the superintendent. The fund comprises 1 percent of the real property tax. Whilst the fund's reserves are small in poorer areas, they are substantial in wealthier parts of the country. The fund is used "supposedly for the construction of buildings *et cetera*—but usually they will utilize this for their travel, they will ask for the schoolteachers to come here to Manila, to attend programmes, to attend seminars, or sports activities. They will ask the Mayor for money and it will be charged against this [the special education fund]."[21] This gives local political leaders much sway over appointments in schools.

Methods of Influence

It is not hard to appreciate, then, why both the Office of the President and the legislature also exert informal influence at national, regional and local government levels. The Office of the President may simply override legal provisions which are supposed to fix the number of upper-level posts (filled either by career civil servants or by political appointees) and create a new position.

> For example, we have for an agency [X]: the law will say [it is permitted] two undersecretaries.... I don't want to say that she [the President] did it with malice, but she would appoint a third undersecretary—an undersecretary for "special external affairs".... When that undersecretary is appointed, the DBM [the Department of Budget and Management] will scramble to find money to pay that guy ... they will scramble to pay the people that this guy will have—a secretary, a driver, at least one technical person. And that person will eventually retire as undersecretary...[22]

The President may also exert influence through existing placements in the career service and through political appointees, most especially heads of agencies who exercise considerable discretion over the appointment of career staff to career positions at all levels (first, second, and third). Following a ritual of advertisements and selection procedures, the agency's own selection board furnishes the agency's head (the Secretary or Commissioner) with a list of suitable[23] candidates from which to choose. Such influence is not confined to the President. In Customs, for example, "...apart from political appointments coming from the president ... there are other influential people [legislators and members of the Cabinet] who call on the Commissioner to appoint this, this, this, this. So even if we want to be very strict in the assessment of our applicants (and we have a lot of them actually) sometimes we have to bend a little..."[24] Heads of local governments are granted similar latitude. For instance, mayors can appoint who they want from at any point in a long list of qualified candidates. The normalcy of this practice is illustrated by the problems with which the assistant head of one department in Quezon City Hall must grapple. Finding work for the placements routed through the mayor, "would be easy if the person is highly qualified. However, if the person is not, that's a different matter—it's very difficult. You have to look for a job for her or him which really fits his qualification."[25] Indeed, "we can even go so far as saying that you cannot be appointed in local government if you do not know the appointing authority or, at least, if you do not have any [political] recommendation..."[26] And even once in place, the civil servant's position is not secure: "If you look at local governments which are fast growing in influence, usually the department heads are career. But when the new mayor [comes], he just tell them I'll file [a case] against you, or resign. And it's such a widespread practice and nothing really happens in the court."[27] The CSC is aware of large number of such instances, and the hard fact is that "in local government units, where politics is very powerful, if the respondent happens not to be a supporter of the incumbent, and very vocal against the incumbent, and [even if] the Commission sees that, well, we can say that that person may not get justice in that agency."[28]

The exercise of influence through various forms of intimidation is not restricted to local government. Civil servants in the regions and at the center know that a Senator or member of the House may have a constituent lodge a formal complaint with the Ombudsman against them; or (by virtue of the legislature's oversight functions and its constitutional authority over ratification of the General Appropriations Act) legislators may openly threaten to launch an investigation against a department or reduce its funding. Pressure is sometimes applied directly. Undersecretaries, assistant secretaries, commissioners, assistant commissioners, and more junior officials whose duties bring them into contact with legislators, are approached (within and outside committee meetings) by politicians with the intention of shaping decisions either on disciplinary cases, promotions, appointments and other personnel matters, or on the direction of spending and programmes. The legislators' threats may be based on sound knowledge, and they may have the power to back up those threats; but often they simply fish and bluff and rely on the civil servants' desire to avoid entanglements even if they have no skeletons hidden in their closets. "You have to ask questions, you have to be enquiring about so many things, sensitive matters, of a particular agency like the DPWH [Department of Public Works and Highways], or the Department of Health, or the DepEd [Department of Education], if you want to be noticed, so they will approach you and say 'here are some projects'..."[29] And, indeed, it is in order to forestall difficult or embarrassing questions in public, that civil servants will try to pre-empt the legislators' wishes:

> You know that Filipino game, the trumpet?... Whenever there is a budget hearing in Congress, I go from one congressman to another—there are more than 200 congressman—just to ask them "What are your problems, do you have cases, do you have follow-ups?" Because if you don't do that, [then] during the hearing proper or the deliberation proper you will leave questions [on] a lot of things that will embarrass your head of agency. So you better do that before things like that happen. And, you know, while these deliberations are going on, you can see a lot of them [in groups] talking to one another; sometimes there are eight congressmen around; sometimes in the middle of the deliberation there will be 14.... I don't like that kind of sight, you know.'[30]

Pressure is also applied through the Office of the President via intermediaries in the House including, for instance, legislative-executive liaison officers, party leaders, the Speaker, relatives of the President, and other members who have the ear of the President. This indirect route through the Palace often reflects the quid pro quo that is part of the manoeuvring between legislators and President; and on occasions a legislator's hand may be strong enough to persuade even the President to create a third-level post within a Department and against the wishes of its Secretary.

> So we had three undersecretaries in the Department. And right when the President had just taken over from Estrada (and we were very new) there was a lady from Mindanao who wanted to be the fourth [undersecretary], and it did not exist—there was no such position. And she came with letters from her cousin who was the congressmen of X.... And for a Secretary like my boss at that time, who was keen on professionalizing her office, you really come across as a dodgy character. Because if you're good, you don't ask [for] a position to be created on your behalf, and you don't go around flashing congressmen's letters in their faces. So initially ... we said, "No, we only have three positions, we would have to create a new office for you." So she was frustrated and went straight to the Palace; and they created the position for her; and we had a fourth undersecretary. The President ... had a party to take care of, a Congress majority to maintain...she had a rather fragile hold on Congress at that time because *Erap* [Estrada] still had some of his people there. So she wasn't sure ... she succumbs to this political pressure and, because of that, appoints people in the bureaucracy and she basically screws up the structure: some of budget of the Department will have to go to that new position ... it's taken away from other programs.'[31]

A reduction (for whatever reason) in an agency's budget may also work to the legislators' advantage. For while they may feel compelled to surrender a larger portion of their pork barrel as departmental programmes are scaled back, the urge to ensure remaining programs go in the direction of their constituencies and the direct influence which they wield through their share of the "pork" also strengthen:[32]

> There is one ... I won't mention the region.... Congressman [who] want[ed] ... a retiring [civil servant].... This person [civil servant] has a cataract and he said that "I'm going to retire this December" ... that's barely three months [away]. [But] here [comes] the congressmen [and] says "You have to put him in the division where I am, in my district, otherwise I'll pull out my [pork].... I'll stop putting in resources. But if you put in this fellow, and I'm happy about it, then I'll increase the assistance that I'm giving." So you see.... [But] I would like to believe that not many politicians do that.[33]

Legislators, however, do not hold all the cards—far from it. Complaints may also be filed against politicians; and investigations by legislators depend upon a department and its executive masters being forthcoming with information and some measure of cooperation. The threat to cut central funding, too, may also be more apparent than real: this, at least, is a view commonly adumbrated by legislators.

> In the constitution it says that Congress has the power of the purse. When Marcos was president, he passed a presidential decree—presidential decree number 1177, it gave the president plenary powers over the budget and rendered nil the powers of Congress over the purse. How? It gave the president the power of impoundment.... Meaning to say, if we allocate one million pesos for a particular road, that law gave the president the power to impound as much as 30 percent for logical reasons: "Well, we cannot foresee what will happen in the course of a year, and natural calamity might arise. We might not have the funds to address these problems. So we will impound these funds." But if, at the end of the year, a calamity has not occurred, she has no obligation to bring it back: she can reallocate and realign [the funds] somewhere else. The second big power it gave the president, was the power to choose which items to fund and which items not to fund, given a deficit. This is an awesome power, because even if it is now in the budget, the president can decide "Well, we have a deficit. Revenues are low. So we will only fund it to the extent of 50 percent or I won't fund this item or fund that item." And since we have 382 billion pesos worth of unfunded laws, she can decide to find one of those instead.... The third power which it gave the president and government was to automatically appropriate the unfunded laws—meaning to say that it doesn't even go through Congress any more. It is automatically appropriated. It does not go through...debate, it does not even [appear] in the budget document: if it is a law that we have to pay, it will be paid.
>
> The Lower House, and even the Senate to a certain degree, even the pork barrel of the congressmen, are dependent upon that bill and that law. Now they complain, against that presidential decree (1177). Congress would never pass such a law, that is why it was enacted through a presidential decree when Marcos still had lawmaking powers (under an amendment ... of the 1973 constitution). Then, when Corrie Aquino assumed power, they were rallying the streets against that particular law (1177). But not only did she not repeal it, she reenacted it in the administrative code of 1987—the last law she passed under her own law-making powers.... which therefore perpetuated that system up to now. Congressmen have a fixed constituency, Senators don't—we are elected at large. We can get away with not having any pork barrel. In the House, [members] will find it difficult to get re-elected without a barrel. That is why, ever since

that law was passed, the president always controls a majority in the House of Representatives. Always.[34]

In short, whilst the Lower House must ratify the General Appropriations Act, it is the executive which is seen to control the release of funds and has at its disposal numerous powers to withhold, reallocate and transfer subventions including the pork barrel.[35] And if the House should refuse to pass the budget, then the previous year's act is reinstated, handing to the President considerable freedom to reallocate and spend as she wishes.

A member of the House may, therefore, *threaten* to reduce an agency's funding, "especially Senator Enrile, who can give you a one-pesos budget for the whole year."[36] But unless that threat can be backed up with connexions in the Office of the President or with the support of coalitions in House and Senate, it amounts to no more than bluster: "Even if you tell them I am not going to give your budget unless you tell me [what I want to know], the President will just tell them 'Don't appear!... It doesn't matter if you don't have a budget—we'll find a way through.'"[37] Such threats also assume that an agency's budget has not already been cut to the bone. And the more determined the heads of agency, the less dependent they are upon a large budget, or the more bureau-shaping their ambitions, the less willing they will be to play the role expected of them in what is

> theatre more than anything else. The one time I was threatened with a one-peso budget, I said "Thank you!" Because I knew that within the rules, after the budget is passed, the budget secretary will simply restore that budget. It's not as though it will all come out and you will have nothing to operate with. In fact, from 2001 up to the present, I have refused to ask for an increase. I don't need it. I am able to give ... bonuses [every] year without having to ask for more money. So this entire budgetary process, "You're not going to get this, and you're not going to get that," is all stupidity.... At the beginning [of my tenure] most people were so scared that we would get into trouble, because I was too outspoken, because I didn't know how to compromise. "They might cut our budget!" But I said "No. Let them try." They did try once—the only time that I ever had any problem with the usual budget hearings. I said, "Look at it the other way: these people, if they know they can get away with murder, then they will murder. When they know that they can't get away with it, they won't try ... ultimately they will realise this is off-limits. And I have hardly had any problems.[38]

It is, then, through the more nuanced play of existing placements that influence on appointments and discipline is mostly worked. Often the atmosphere surrounding relationships between politicians and civil servants can be described as convivial: both sides understand that political interference is, in many agencies, a daily reality, and that a compromise needs to be reached.

They cannot just push and say, "You have to put this person in." No, because we have some standards that have been in place quite some time. And if we allow ourselves to be influenced [on every occasion], especially if that person is really not qualified, we are surely going to demoralize a lot of people. We do write to politicians ... sometimes if ... the person they are endorsing is not really qualified we categorically say "Thank you for your interest. However, after screening the person we notice that he not qualified. Perhaps you could refer him to another office where he would be more useful. We have matrices, we have criteria, and there are issuances of the Bureau." And we use all this as our fallback.... So we are very, very, very careful with that. Perhaps if that politician will still insist on having that person, perhaps you can have them in but only in the position that he is qualified for.[39]

As a former Commissioner of the BIR turned House representative puts it, some way has to be found of balancing

...who would be the people that are going to be promoted and who can be ... hired without really offending any politicians. Like, during my time, it would be the speaker of the House ... de Venecia.... Whenever we would see each other he would say, "Hello, Commissioner. You have not yet accommodated me on the people that I have sent to you." And I said, " Sir, how many are they, anyway? There are so many, *you've* lost track of them all!" Anyway—just laugh. You know. That would be the way to do it I guess. You can only accommodate so much. If you accommodate everyone it would unsettle the entire bureaucracy.[40]

But the effect of the unrelenting pressure brought to bear through intimidation should not be underestimated, and the atmosphere can easily turn. The meetings which take place around the budget and oversight hearings, as well as the hearings themselves, provide legislators with opportunities to get what they can through bluff and force of personality. With the hope that the official will prefer to capitulate rather than suffer, legislators will intimate that the official's career is on the line, and that she will have to bear the blame for cuts to the department. In these and other ways, legislators will bully, embarrass and humiliate civil servants, enough to leave them shaking at the end of an encounter. In one such Committee hearing—called to examine the fall-out from a strike by a group of government employees after the revelation that their head of agency had been giving away turkeys at Christmas to Senators and House representatives—a member of the Civil Service Commission suddenly found herself in a very awkward position.

There were a bunch of congressmen there, and one congressmen (from a party list on Labour) ... was not doing a very good job at defending these people.... I made the mistake of opening my mouth.... I said, "On the behalf of the Civil Service Commission, we are just concerned about the fact that some employees in government service can be unilaterally transferred or removed from office or suspended for something that we feel is our duty as public servants—to tell things how things are." And the guy got so angry and said, "Are you the Commissioner of the Civil Service?"

I said, "No."

He said, "Are you authorised to be here?"

"Yes."

He said, "Shut up! You have no right to take anybody's side on this."

I said, "Can I answer that, Sir? I do not take sides, I didn't take a side. I'm just here to tell you that, as the central personnel agency, the welfare of the employees is our concern, and you can tell us if we're not doing our job right." And so he threatened me with a lot of things. A lot of congressmen were there. Everybody was shocked, and he was screaming. Apparently, he was friends with the head of agency who was giving away turkeys, and who was married to a congresswoman. After he was done with me, he picked a fight with the Committee's secretary who was taking notes, saying that the notes were not accurate and this and that...[41]

Thus, gradually, departmental priorities are "dictated by who has a bigger voice, who has connections to Malacañang, who would have more information about certain officials, and who can make life difficult for them: those are the things that go into the workings of the bureaucracy."

Motivation

The misallocation of authority over appointments and discipline may provide the immediate rationalization or justification for political interference. But, as already noted, the desire to have a hand in appointments also derives in part from a deep frustration with many other divisions in authority which, from the point of view of those concerned, appear to be too rigid and excessive.

One matter of particular sensitivity is control of the budget. Members of the House are faced with the fact that much of their authority over the budget has, in practice, been ceded to the Office of the President. Opponents of the President and (over some issues) her allies will, therefore, want to find ways of strengthening their hand. This they may try to do either by establishing alliances with local government leaders (especially mayors and their networks of *barangay* captains) through which they can promise to withhold or deliver votes, or by tightening their grip over locally generated funds. Or they may form voting blocs across the legislature and, more especially, the House where members coalesce around geographical areas: "like, congressmen from

Region II or congressmen from Mindanao, or [from] one of the regions in Mindanao, and so on ... they cut across the party lines ... because ... a lot of the things they want are parochial in the sense that it is for their area ... what would benefit their specific districts, their specific areas."[43] Another and more important strategy is to secure membership or, even better, the chair of one of the legislature's oversight committees.

> If you ... look at membership of committees you will see that there will be committees that are *so* overloaded.... Appropriations has ... I think, 150— ... half of Congress will be there.... That would be one. Ways and Means would be another one. Then you would have the committees for regular departments—agriculture, trade, and industry.... [And] if you hear what each member of Congress wanting to be part of that committee ... talk about—it really comes down to "What do I get out of this government agency?" Like the Department of Agrarian Reform,—there are certain things [to be had] in terms of farm-to-market roads, things like this.[44]

Thus, the Office of the President may find that it is forced, if only on occasions, to bargain and compromise with a House whose members are (from the perspective of the executive) primarily interested in their geographically defined districts, and with a Senate occupied by would-be presidents.

But the efficacy of the legislators' ploys to create leverage is uncertain; and the executive may forestall or undo those compromises and bargains by filling the bureaucracy with its own people such that members of the House, if they are not entirely reliant upon the Office of the President for funding, are made dependent upon the Office indirectly for the implementation of projects, programs, and legislation. The executive's control of the bureaucracy helps in other ways both to secure leverage over the House and to deny the House possible leverage over the executive: the bureaucracy is a vital source of information without which it becomes very difficult to draw up sensible laws, or to challenge legislation sensibly, or to use effectively the legislature's oversight functions against the executive. Senators may also be left with the sense that they are dependent upon what is (from their perspective) a partisan bureaucracy for implementation and for information. The power of the Senate is considerable: they number only twenty-four (the House is ten times larger); they have their own oversight committees, they have a national constituency, and their assent is required if the Executive and House are to have their legislation (national and local bills) passed and funded. Nevertheless, Senators must secure the support of the House and the cooperation of the bureaucracy if their legislation is to be passed and implemented; the Palace is equally willing to ignore the authority of its oversight committees; they are, in common with the House, reliant upon the bureaucracy for information; and they, too, have election expenses to meet (every six years).

Legislators, then, "don't really have any hold over policies or projects or decisions made, except at the level that you propose laws or conduct investigations."[45] For instance, "...my boss's committee is public order and illegal drugs. If I need to get information from the PNP [Philippine National Police] on anything that requires non-public disclosure, they usually have this thing called a 'command conference.' Then we go there; my boss asks questions; and they answer. But no media—it is just them and him."[46] But "in the general functioning of an agency, legislators have nothing to do with it." Even the authority of Senators in their own right, or as Chair of a committee, extends only in so far as the Palace—"the one agency that has the capacity to draw information from just about any other agency"[47]—does not order an embargo. For a Senator identified with the opposition, "it's very difficult for us to get any information from these agencies. 'Are you done building this road? How much did you spend?' And they take forever to write back."[48] For members of the Lower House, too, "it's really hard to increase the amount of spending in your district. What you would have to rely on is your relationship with the administration, and your relationship with the secretary.... If you are blacklisted by the Palace, [then] no matter ... what he stands for, and how he projects himself to his constituencies, he'll lose [the election]."[49]

It is understandable, then, why legislators should feel a deal of frustration with what they perceive to be the misallocation of authority and an unresponsive and self-serving bureaucracy. Civil servants, they feel, are concerned largely with their own career and disinterested in "what their role is, what they are supposed to do.... [They] just time in, time out; they don't know the importance of their work.... 'I'm here to earn a living,' and that's it..."[50] They are also duplicitous:

> ...they have to go through us, they need our approval, for their budget. And we see that they have so much ... lump-sum funds in their budget, like maybe they have one billion for computers or so. We look at it and say, "Hey, we need computers back home. Why don't you give us some?' And they say, "Yeah, we'll give you." And some give it after two years; and some don't give at all. That's the reason for the frustration.... They are willing to talk, but, like I said, in my experience, maybe 60 percent of these guys, when you speak to them personally, you go to their offices, you take time out to see them—you tell them, "this is what we need ... we'd like [this] ... we like to [do that].."—to be candid with them. And they say: "Okay, we'll see what we can do." But nothing happens.... So most of the money in government goes to these guys [the civil servants].[51]

Legislators are well aware that civil servants are no less irritated with politicians: "I understand, on the other hand, if they are frustrated with us, because ... they say, "These guys are so demanding,'" and there are some congressmen who demand the moon and the stars ... something that they [the civil servants] can't deliver. In that case I would understand why they would promise [but not deliver]".[52] But representatives must find *some* way to compensate for their lack of authority over the budget, to weaken the grip of the President on the bureaucracy and, more generally, to redress what the feel to be the imbalance of power between the executive and legislature if they are to survive elections and fulfil their duty to deliver material benefits to their constituents. They must ensure that their share of the Priority Assistance Development Fund (the notorious "pork barrel") is released, that a proportion of national-line agencies' and local government funds is spent in their district; and that projects and programs (whatever the source of funding) are indeed implemented. The bare truth is that "congressmen, I think, have only one goal: it is to get as much as they can from that government agency for their district."[53] One very obvious, tactic—used in addition to securing membership on House and Senate Committees, and to forming alliances with the centre and local governments—is to switch parties in favor of the President, and this is very common after elections. Another is to infiltrate the bureaucracy to establish "a network, especially of those [civil servants] who are vying for higher positions. 'I have someone there, I can contact him. He'll help us get this or that.'"[54] For instance, "if you have someone in there, in the DPWH, and they are building something, they would become motivated. You have someone inside."[55] Placements are also "one way of putting a check on the agency ... because [an] appointee who is an ally of the congressmen can look into the manoeuvre and workings inside the agency..."[56] And this is especially useful if the intention is to elicit information from the Palace: "That's where friends come in.... Only as far as we have friends [can we obtain information]. Otherwise we are just like any other person: they will just give us the official line."[57] The hard fact is that "the only way these people [the bureaucrats] will ... notice us, is when we make it difficult for them. In other words, [political interference in appointments is] being used as a leverage."[58] Indeed, in these circumstances, political interference is "totally legitimate ... I mean, it's better than asking for an appointment for personal aggrandizement; because there may be provinces that are off the radar—structurally ignored. Actually, my province is one of them."[59]

A related, but more direct and raw, motive for political interference is money. The politicians' election expenses are not met by the state; and so the staff and running costs of their offices (usually two or more) must be financed from of their own pockets. One solution for legislators is to dip into their pork barrel:

> ...In my first term in Congress, I asked the older guys: "Why don't we just give our [office staff] enough funds. We are given six staff, and the minimal amount for everything else; and we're supposed to know the whole bureaucracy; and that six staff includes secretary and our driver. Not even district staff is included there".... So I told

the other guys that an ordinary director would get a car, 12 people in his office, a conference room, and he's just dealing with one [office]. We are dealing with everything [the whole bureaucracy]. The older guys said "Get it out of your pork barrel." I said, "But that's precisely what is wrong with the pork barrel system..." But they said, "But how do you answer to the media?" And I said, "Be honest." So there is also a generational thing.[60]

Another solution, for all politicians, "is to make sure that you have people in sensitive agencies."[61] In the BIR ... the politicians have their people—these people that they take care of ... they have their ... *kadalang bata* or their *kanang manok*—their chicken ... they get their *manok* in the *sabong* ... that's their fighting cock ... partly because they feel, or they know, they are able to raise funds for politicians, for elections, for other activities—so it's part of their fundraising activity."[62] Indeed, agencies across government are infiltrated for very similar reasons:

> I can tell you that I was not happy last Friday when I went this meeting [in Quezon city], this discussion, of the third level positions ... the government executives. They were meeting, and they were talking for hours, and they were [talking about] recruitment, retention, the rewards, and retirement.... It was appalling to hear that many of the civil service rules are not fully observed. They are observed, but they are not fully observed by many of the politicians who head the agencies.... Because politicians, to be able to join the government, have to spend; and so they may ... feel that the government owes them also.... It's appalling to hear that in many of the government agencies it's very difficult to implement most of these rules, recruitment rules.[63]

Placements are also made out of a sense of obligation. This may derive from the fact that the appointee is a politician's relative: it was noted above that relatives of members of the House who are close to the President (or have struck some deal with her) may secure valued, high-level posts. Or it may be rooted in the fact that than an applicant is either from the same place as the politician or his constituent or both: "Like [Senator X] ... comes from X province. So if somebody from X province asks for a recommendation he gives it to him even if he doesn't know him from Adam. But if he is from X, he must be good, right?! So I write him a recommendation!"[64] Or a placement may be offered as a reward for a political favor: "...maybe this [person] had helped them [the politicians] in a past election, or just a recent election, so now it's payback time. Get me in a juicier spot, because that juicier spot will translate to something personal for that person [the placement]."[65] These repayments may also be made to beneficiaries' children or wider family without thought of their suitability or qualities: "'Since I owe your father a favor and

69

his son wants to go into this agency ... I will write a recommendation', not even thinking that the father may be good but the son is a jerk."[66]

The return of favors may sometimes be made without harbouring ulterior motives, and certainly "I don't think anybody thinks ... this is a way for your policies to be pursued..."[67] Yet, for others politicians, there is no question that "it's really more for their political ends: [it] is not only "pay-back time" but "a time when they can collect also"[68]; and it may help to keep supporters onside. For instance, placements worked by the Palace on behalf of mayors are often intended to "make sure that the mayor .... remains loyal. So appoint his ... daughter as Assistant Secretary. It's straight horse-trading and that's so disgusting.... They have used the career bureaucracy as a playground."[69] By the same token, political appointees, non-career and career, may find themselves dismissed and career appointees transferred precisely because they are highly effective and acutely aware of what is going on within a Department.

Political interference is also motivated by a desire to protect existing placements. Here again, a sense of obligation plays its part together with a desire to avoid the back-draft which might follow if placements should feel they have been abandoned and hung out to dry:

> I've seen with my own eyes that there are some people who get away with a lot of things because of the favors they have given in the past. They are protected ... not only because of money, but because of ... .*utang nalo'ob*..... My boss was complaining one time that "When you owe somebody that *utang nalo'ob* ... there are some people who tend to think that ... since I have helped you, you owe me your life till you die." As my boss would say... "There are people who think they have proprietor rights over you just because at one point in their life [they] helped [you]...." So there are people who get away with a lot of things, because they helped somebody rise. They did something [for] you at the lowest point in your life.[70]

For all these reasons there is a deal of interest from politicians in disciplinary cases within the civil service. The extent of this interest and intervention is difficult to assess. The dispersal of authority over disciplinary matters discussed earlier in this chapter means that heads of agencies (political appointees) are most likely to feel the pressure brought to bear by politicians intent on influencing decisions; and the CSC is likely to experience this only in so far as cases reach the appeal stage, or involve third-level career staffs, or are regarded as especially important or sensitive. The proportion of cases which reach the CSC on appeal and, indeed, how many and what kind of original cases are filed in the first place, are therefore unknown. However, the fact that no appeals have emanated from Customs over recent years may provide one indication of the depth of interest from politicians. And it is worth nothing that whilst heads of many other agencies are probably more susceptible to influence than the CSC,[71] the Commission is by no means immune:

> Technically, the president has no power over us. But again it depends...it's, like.... There is one very celebrated case, where the president fired the undersecretary at the Department of Education, and he came to us. Unfortunately, the president got to my two commissioners. So I became a dissenting opinion.... One commissioner had not yet been confirmed and ... went to pieces: "You are not going to be reappointed if you don't toe the line." The other commissioner was in his last two months of his term and was promised another appointment.[72]

Interest in administrative cases handled by the CSC is especially intense when approval for the Commission's budget is being sought.[73]

> ...They will ask us a lot of follow-ups of their constituents, the cases of their constituents. If they have constituents who have cases here—they will follow up, [and] at worst they will not allow us to present our budget unless [these cases are] finished. [There are] a lot of cases ... administrative cases.... One of the congressmen told me:
>   "What you do is finish it! I don't care what's the result, as long as you finish it!"
>   "Okay [placatory]." We went to our lawyers here ... and then when it's already done he [the Congressmen] shouted at us..."Why is this the result like this"!? He wants the result in his favor. Then ... I told him, "You know sir, you just have to read all the pages," because he just read the dispositive portion. Sometimes they are like that. We have not much problem in the Senate, but ... in the Congress we have that kind of problem because they have their constituents who [they] are following up for."[74]

Political interference (in placements and in disciplinary and administrative cases) is also encouraged, or even driven, by career civil servants who can be just as animated by self-interest. On the one hand they will close ranks and use (or circumvent) qualifications, standards and selection procedures both to keep out those who may threaten their interests, and to set aside posts. Posts in the BIR, for instance, may be reserved for the relatives (often the children) of officials due for retirement. Or career civil servants will turn a blind eye to political interference: "You can't do a thing about it ... it's beyond your control.... There are norms ... just do what you want to do, and don't mind the people around you or the people beside you—do what you have to do." And you have to play [to] the norms ... if you want to fit in, if you want to stay here.... There's nothing wrong with accepting it, or there is nothing wrong if you don't accept it.... You do what you have to do—you just go straight."[75] On the other hand,

> ...the career people are also the ones that make it [political inter-ference] happen. Because they want to ensure that *they* get the position. Congressmen, and Senators for that matter, will not really know what's out there unless somebody approaches them.... The congressmen or Senators ... get involved only if someone initiates it with them.... Let's say for a principal position in the Department of Education, in a school. They will ask [me] "Can you recommend me to the Secretary for Education so that the item can be given to me?" Of course I will say "Are you the only one qualified for the job? Or are there others who are qualified? Because if you're the only one, and you're the one next in rank, then I don't see any problem. But if you're not the one next in rank, and there are other people quali-fied, then I wouldn't want to cause trouble within the bureaucracy by bypassing certain people." But it has happened. And sometimes, in order to avoid that situation when there are [several] who are qualified for the position, I recommend all of them. So it will boil down now to the qualification of the person.[76]

One consideration informing these machinations is career advancement; another is financial gain, for "there is a lot of money people *think* they can make being employed in ... sensitive ... agencies"[77] of which the most "sensi-tive" are BOC, the BIR, DPWH, and the Bureau of Immigration. And judging by the openness with which admissions are made, even the most self-serving motives appear to be acceptable in some quarters of some agencies. One young lawyer in Customs was quite clear that her ambition is

> ...Well ... to earn money.... This is the Bureau of Customs and you cannot deny the fact that, well, that there are a lot of corrupt people here; and I think that morality in anything pertaining to money is not a big deal here.... In the Bureau of Customs ... I cannot put it in exact words ... it's like ... I notice that the culture here is, like, that you don't care about the policies once you have money ... about the existing laws or policies, as long as there is money involved...[78]

Requests from career civil servants for political support, then, are com-mon; and common enough to have made such requests expected:

> My father ... has got some friends who have been telling [me] "Can I have your CV because I will give it to the national league presi-dent—[the] Mayor's league—who is the uncle of the president, if you want to get appointed [to another agency] when you leave the CSC." Unfortunately this is still a mindset of a lot of people especially if you go down to the municipal level. You need the support of a politician

to get appointed. It happened to me right after college wherein we had to seek written support from our local executive for the prospect of getting employed in a government bank. It is still happening. It's unfortunate because it destroys the merit system.[79]

While for those who are concerned to appear less ambitious, the politicians' threats to their department's budget is a convenient a screen behind which they may accept preferment or avoid transfers.

What happens is some local congressman pressures the regional director. The public propaganda is that we will hit you with a budget. No, the real thing is appointments. The real thing is: "I don't want that regional director." He goes up either to the Cabinet Secretary or to the President to say: "I want that person out." And that's your life; so you give in. Even if you're not going to be taken out, you know that you've made an enemy, and so when you're up promotion, you might not get it.[80]

Effects

Politicians interfere in civil service appointments and promotions, and in their decisions on disciplinary matters and in policy and in day-to-day operational matters. They do so—it has been noted in these pages—largely in response to the frameworks through which authority is (as the politicians so often see it) misallocated—a response motivated by the sense that these divisions block their personal interests and ambitions. For their own advantage, politicians will place within the bureaucracy insiders through whom: information is hidden or extracted; decisions (on, say, policy, spending, and the implementation of projects and programmes) shaped or determined; opponents undermined or stonewalled; and funds siphoned off to meet election expenses and pay for running of their offices. They also interfere in order to line their pockets and to protect existing placements; to repay favors. And they will interfere out of a sense of expectation from—and obligation to—friends, family, and constituents; and with the possibility in mind that these networks of civil servants may be useful to them in the future. Politicians secure placements and influence other decisions by simply creating new posts or through their relationships with existing placements. They also do so through intimidation (sometimes backed up with effective action) and through bluster. Meanwhile, civil servants intent on furthering their own careers or making money will, for their part, solicit political support, or turn a blind eye to political interference, or give in to the demands of the politicians while claiming that this is the only way to preserve their department's budget. This interference, and the civil servants' occasional complicity in it, is damaging in a number of respects.

1. First, policy decisions and the allocation of personnel and abilities are distorted. Most obviously, the wrong people find themselves in the wrong jobs: "You get the impression that a few political appointees for ambassadorial positions and high positions are really quite good appointees of the president. But aside from that you get negative feedback because of the disappointments. And this is true in many government agencies. In most cases I would say the impression or feedback is not good ... the people who are appointed, the political appointees, are just there to enjoy the perks, not do anything; and possibly [are] even corrupt ... I mean not possibly ... they just do that..."[81]

Even the better political appointees in the best organizations may cause problems by confusing policy with management: "...It's always a difficult issue: what's the demarcation between management and governance, policy and management?... There's no problem on the part of management because they act within a certain level, within a certain limit; but then for the political appointees, are we intruding into management or not? And in [the] planning sessions we have had, in very carefully worded language of course, management has called the attention of some of those on top: they should observe such demarcations"[82]

At more junior levels, too, political interference creates distortions, as in the Department of Education: "...if the teacher is the relative for a friend of the mayor operating in that particular region ... you will obviously experience a recommendation coming from the mayor and sometimes, even though we have a strict policy of hiring, you cannot do anything but just ... accept.... This stifles the smooth operation of the Department..."[83] From the perspective of central office, these distortions have been exacerbated by the devolution of authority over the appointment of teachers to principals whose own appointments are influenced by politicians.

> Normally, in the past, the situation was it's the total discretion of the superintendent—the superintendent has the power to hire and fire. The ranking is done [at] the level of the division. It was criticized: undemocratic and not transparent; inflexible.... They were saying that guys at the division office were hiring the wrong kind of teachers, that they are not the teachers we need. So what happened was we devolved it. There is now a system wherein the school itself will do the ranking. The rationale being [that] the school would know [its own] needs. Do they need a maths teacher? a physics teacher? a social studies teacher? But in the process of devolving to the schools, the principals ... [are] being criticised..[for] ... appointing their relatives.... One of the problems here, which I really want to do something about, [is that] the Department is not governed by the nepotism rule. That means I can have my son and my daughter, my mother or my children in positions of which I am the appointing

authority. That is a clear conflict of interest. If there are 20 people applying for this teacher [post] ... in this specific school, and you would appoint your relative, that becomes a problem. And [then] here comes this criticism that the principals are now selling the teacher items for 20,000[or] 30,000 [pesos].[84]

2. A second problem is the layering of political appointees and politically aligned career staffs over time: ...past sins have become carried over. When a new president sits, it's very unpopular for her to remove employees from government. They can't remove the people who are already there, and she wants to put her own people in as well.... This has been carried out and carried on over so many administrations."[85] The legislature, too, forms its own layers "during budget time ... [when] it's possible that a member of the appropriations committee [will say,] "Okay, I'll approve your proposal for a new office, but I hope two positions there will be reserved for me".... These are not recorded ... so we just get in people who may not be deserving, and then who ... may be resisting your authority inside the organization because he has a powerful backer. So it affects the organization."[86] For example, "even though you are civil service and civil service eligible you cannot enter Customs without political backing; you *cannot* enter, you cannot, *definitely* ...without political backing—there are many X protégés here, and Y protégés..."[87]

3. Political interference also undermines the authority of organizations. The Civil Service Commission finds that its writ does not always extend much beyond its own front door.

> the Chair ... and the other commissioners frankly tell [the politicians] why these people are not qualified and this is against the law.... But at times it doesn't work ... the Congressmen would [still] be insisting on the appointment.... We see that [also] in local government units. An example would be a mayor ... appointing someone who is loyal to him or her, but the appointee, based on CSC scrutiny, is not qualified; so we had to disapprove the appointment; but [this]is not followed by the mayor.[88]

Nor will politicians and political appointees running agencies necessarily take any notice of demands to reinstate those who the Commission finds have been removed unjustly:

> ...if he or she was removed from office, they will come to the Civil Service Commission. And then the Civil Service Commission says, "You're right, you are not supposed to be fired, that's a bad thing that your boss did, we are going to reinstate you." So we hand down a resolution, [and] reinstate this employee. And what we're doing now is checking whether the agencies actually do it, or whether we just hand it down and it dies. So we found out that there are

heads of offices who don't reappoint their people, and the people there are languishing asking if they have to file another document. So we have the power to bring cases, but we don't have the power of contempt—to bring cases against these people, these heads of agencies, who do not follow the directive.[89]

3. The uncertain (and often very short) life expectancy of political appointees brings to departments instability, discontinuity, and a short-term outlook. There are ways of working round the frequent changes in politically-appointed leadership. For instance, it is possible to tailor existing policies and programmes to fit new initiatives: "Usually ... the Secretary doesn't take a look at the specific things that we are doing, so we continue with the old projects we are doing.... With the [new] Secretary there is a new thrust ... [so we] ... develop the [old] project actually to the thrust of the [new] Secretary..."[90] But, viewed in the round, programmes are fragmented more than would otherwise be the case. "At the Department of Agriculture ... it is very frustrating: there's a new secretary every so many years, and with every new secretary there is a change in direction, there's no continuity.... The Department of Education ... [too] ... has switched secretary so often.... It's a problem of continuity: every time a new secretary is appointed, then the whole top shelf of management is thrown out of the window, [and] priorities change."[91] As a consequence, there is loss of focus, and a braiding and thinning of energy, funds, and materials.

4. Much stress is created, especially among third-level career civil servants who are asked by political appointees to alter decisions improperly; or who—given the complexity of regulations, laws, and memorandums, and the speed at which interpretations and decisions must often be made—are not entirely sure if they are being asked to do anything improper or illegal; or who know or suspect that their decisions are being overturned by their superiors. Even in the Civil Service Commission, "there are decisions made by the higher management which you know would have been different if the management was ... and sometimes you have to know when to keep quiet and not tell anything about what you know just so everything will sail smoothly.... You have to keep things to yourself."[92] "Let's say I have a case, I research it, I have Supreme Court cases to back my decisions, my findings; and then when it goes down to the Commission ... they have a different way of deciding it.... And that's where political influence comes in.... Later you find out the one of the Commission is close to the party involved in the case."[93]

5. An atmosphere of cynicism develops in which just about every appointment or promotion quickly attracts suspicion and, eventually, both allegation and investigation.

I was investigated and suspended by the ombudsman ... the ombudsman was misinformed ... and you know I sued [my] team.... [It was] politically motivated ... envy ... envy ... what concerns most in Customs here now is envy.... My item is only a messenger, but I do technical work: I draft memorandums for the office of the director ... [and] if you are close to the chief ... if you're always talking to somebody ... [it is assumed that] you are cooking something.... The problem here is that too much is political ... too much ... too much...[94]

6. Strong resentments also build up amongst permanent civil servants against political appointees. "Let's say a presidential appointee doesn't have the necessary qualifications and he gets appointed. Well, of course ...that fuels the bad sentiments of those belonging to lower-level positions, because instead of choosing the right appointee, they choose the one who gets closer to the gods."[95] And the nearer career civil servants are to opportunities that are closed down, the deeper their resentments are likely to be:

> ...This guy, our OIC, is one of those people who would not have got into the service ... you know? [had it not been for the Commissioner's support] ... I don't know if it's a good or not; but to me, because I think I can tackle any job in the bureau, it was a bad thing. But where there are guys who feel that they need the expertise of these people who were brought into the bureau, it's a good thing for them. But overall I think that it lessens the opportunity for those already here.... For me, I am a salary grade 21 employee. My boss is salary grade 28. He has been here for around five years. I have been with the bureau eighteen years. So what does that tell you? For sure there are grudges, especially in the higher level. The thing is most of these things get noticed because it's really a pyramid: at the lower level, because there are plenty of positions, you can jockey yourselves and everybody can be accommodated; as you progress in your career it becomes a little narrow, so only one person can go in at the top. So it becomes highlighted.... But it's really bad, you know, really bad.
>
> The worst thing is that I've experienced is that I had a Customs guard when I was deputy collector for operations in Cebu. This guard is around salary grade 8. And it was election time. He was one of my *guards*. Fortunately he told me "Boss. I'm not feeling well, I don't want to be assigned on board [ships]." "No problem. You stay there and get whatever job you can." I was good to him. The following May his brother won as congressman.... You know what happened? He became chief of division! So all those guys badmouthing him, treating him bad, suddenly they were aware that he was the new boss ... even of us. So it's really that bad.[96]

6. The belief that so many other civil servants have their political backers, and that every politician is interfering in the service, heightens the incentive for politicians to interfere, and for civil servants to seek political support. And

this, in turn, strengthens the belief that most decisions made in the Service are influenced by politicians. For those who are more circumspect—and especially for those whose experience and position affords them a broader vision—the extent and nature of political influence appears to be far more complex and varied. Even in Customs where there is a deal of political interest at third level, interference at entry level is weaker "although some people have this false impression that if you have a senator or congressman backing you up you can enter the Bureau of Customs."[97] Yet for many others, there is little or no doubt in their mind: *they* may have survived or progressed without political support; but the same cannot be said of most of their colleagues.

> I think in all government departments [political influence] is the reality. In my case ... I applied ... directly to the mayor, and my papers went down here to the department. I had no backup, I have nobody here influential that I know of. But normally, in normal cases, people get in if they have endorsements...[98]

Certainly a familiar view amongst staff in the lower ranks is that getting into the civil service, and getting on within it, is solely or very largely about politics. In local government the simple truth is that: "There's a lot of politics, and that's how it is, that's the reality, you have to live with it.... The civil service has this merit system, but I don't think it ... applies..."[99] Similar representations prevails in Customs' central office: "Well, this is only my own opinion, this is not backed by evidence, this is just an observation, [but] I think that political influence here is a *huge* activity..."[100] Indeed, a common understanding of government more generally, and what is believed by some to be "a fact that I have come to accept when it comes to government agencies ... [is] that you cannot move around, or you cannot move up, without [political support]. It's a reality I have to accept."[101] From the upper levels, too, when viewed across the piece, this kind of broad-brushed, black-and-white representation is pervasive. "Recently ... in support of the career executive officers' convention—it is a gathering nationwide of government executives and managers from all over the country from all offices ... we ...[surveyed] them and [asked] them about the state of professionalization in the Philippines. And we were responsible for consolidating that report; and ... one of the ... many issues ... is ... the influence of the Office of the President in the appointments at third level which really is very demoralizing. That's affected the operations of government."[102]

Circumventing Process

A further effect of political interference is to weaken procedure more generally within the civil service. The appointments procedure is affected most directly as politicians attempt to place civil servants and influence discipline (with all that this means for the Service). But the sense that process of any kind doesn't really matter that much is also encouraged; and the ramifications of this, too, for the service are far-reaching. In the atmosphere of unpredictability and uncertainty that emerges, civil servants may well decide to follow the politicians' example and put their own personal interests before those of agency and process, most especially when pay is low.

Appointments

Formulated by the CSC, the central elements of the appointments process are intended to be binding upon those government agencies that employ permanent civil servants; and it is the Commission in the selection of its own staffs that provides the best model of this process. For those who are already in the service—or who have already passed the national exams and are therefore eligible to be considered for posts—the selection procedure begins with the publication of vacancies in print and electronic media, and with the distribution of adverts in government agencies and throughout the Commission's own field offices. Selected applicants must then submit themselves to a series of tests under the scrutiny of four assessors. These tests include group discussions (in which candidates are given a problem to solve) and essay writing. As noted earlier, the watchwords for the selection and assessment of candidates are qualifications, seniority, training and experience; and the details of requirements for every post and grade are set out in the Qualifications and Standards Manual. Other less tangible qualities (such as integrity) are also regarded as important and, while less susceptible to codification and enumeration, are nevertheless assessed through various personality and psychometric tests. Candidates are also interviewed by the PSB (Personnel Selection Board). This comprises: three members of staff from the third level (one at Director III and two at Director IV and one of whom serves as the chair); and two members from second and first levels (one of whom is a union representative), though both are dropped from the Board when candidates are being considered for a third-level position. Interviews are generally polite affairs (in which candidates are given the opportunity to set out their accomplishments) though on occasions they can be Socratic in style and, even if not designed to do so, may nettle candidates and exploit their sensitivities:

> ...They asked me to choose a position.... I felt that [the question] is not called for. When I was occupying the Director II position, I applied for a higher position.... Since the vacancies open were Directors III and IV, my understanding is that I [am also] qualified to be screened or assessed for Director IV.... But I deliberately did not indicate [on the application form] which one—Director III or Director IV—because my understanding is I can be [considered] for both positions. They asked me, they *asked* me, they made me *choose*, which position! To me it's disheartening because that puts

79

on you a certain block or ceiling. So it's kind of offensive; and that happened not only to me, but [to] another applicant for a director position.... They made me choose ... whether I'll be applying for a Director III or Director IV position.... [This was] ... unnecessary ... because if you say ... you're applying for a higher director position, then that means...I could either go to a Director IV or a Director III.... So if they see me as not fit ... for a Director IV position, they can just put me to a Director III. So it's up to them. I felt, then, it was up to the Commission proper to decide, and not for the selection committee to give me a certain block.... So for me it is somehow disheartening...[103]

CSC staffs also conduct "background investigations": these include a consideration of references, and interviews with a candidate's present or former superiors. A recommendation is then made to the PSB, sometimes in the teeth of opposition from a candidate's superiors.

...In the Bureau of Treasury.... when I interviewed him [a candidate's immediate superior] he bragged about a lot of things.... [in order] to despise the subordinate ... [who] is the subject of my conversation. He thought that he is not giving much [effort] so he doesn't deserve the eligibility that is supposed to be granted to the person. But I told him that "Well, I've interviewed four of the staff of that person and ... they overwhelmingly rated him as outstanding; and now you're telling me that he is not doing well. Well, I'm sorry I cannot follow your [recommendation] ... you are one against four." At the end he told me that he's not really against giving that person eligibility, he is just trying to emphasise he's not doing as expected.... As a manager he is not doing well as expected of that person. In the end the person was granted eligibility because of my recommendation; but you know he [the applicant's superior] bragged about a lot of things...[104]

The job of the PSB, too, is to advise and recommend: the authority to appoint lies with the Commission itself (The Chair and two commissioners). The PSB therefore provides a list of suitable candidates ranked in order of the Board's preference. The Commission is not compelled to agree with the Board and may select a name from at any point on the list, though within the CSC, and certainly for third level appointments: "...whoever topped the screening test would be the one appointed first.... So I've never had the experience, or even in my observation among my peers here in the office, that ... you'll get appointed because you're big-time to management.... I have not had that experience."[105] It must be said that there are undoubtedly occasions when representatives of clerical and technical staffs on the Board are unclear about the reasoning for the final selection of new appointees:

"...Some are questioning their capacity or capability because the ones who are bringing them in is our Chairman. It is within her jurisdiction and you cannot question it.... Sometimes they have the qualifications, but they don't know her mind—what's the point? We follow the policy of making a new roster of candidates, and rank them according to their assessment, though usually the Chairman takes the one that she wants..."[106] But the problem is far more pronounced in other agencies such as Education where "the head of appointing office can do *deep* selection as long as the entry qualifications are met... it is not always the next in rank..."[107] And, more especially in Customs where "...even if the candidate is in the number one [position]—because we rank them according to points, from highest to lowest, so even if you're number one, if the commissioner doesn't want you, he can select to others [lower in the Board's rankings] for the position."[108]

Adherence to process in the recruitment of its own staff is essential for the CSC if its attempts to monitor and to ensure compliance in other agencies are to have any credibility. The CSC, through its field offices, keeps watch over some two-thirds of government agencies. Monitoring relies partly on the examination of appointment papers and attachments, and partly on the complaints received by the Commission. Were candidates properly qualified for the post to which they have been appointed? Did their appointment follow correct procedure? And, more especially, were candidates scrutinized and ranked by a properly constituted PSB? However, the monitoring process—already made burdensome by the sheer number of appointments, agencies, steps in selection, and fulsome documentary requirements—is made still more complex by the fact that the appointments process within agencies is at once dispersed and centralized. It is dispersed in that selection is often made locally, and centralized in that decisions must be reviewed and approved by Central Office's PSB and head of agency. Thus, in Customs,

> We publish our vacant positions—that's [required] by the civil service rules.... So once these are published, we announce it to all those [within the agency] who are interested. Those who are next in rank are no longer required to apply for the position because they are next in rank [and are considered automatically].... And even if they are not next in rank—and they think they meet the qualifications, the requirements—they can [also] apply for the position.... So once we announce the vacant position [and applications are received], the local selection board of the port where the position is vacant will evaluate the candidates for the position; they will prepare a line-up for the position; and then they will submit this line-up of candidates for the vacant position....The HRMD, as the secretariat, will review the line-up submitted by the local selection board and, if all the rules and regulations are complied with, they [check] that all the candidates for the position are qualified.... We [then] schedule

81

the deliberation for the vacant position by the central selection board here [at Central Office]. This is headed by the Deputy Commissioner for internal administration—he is the chairman of the central selection board.[109]

The Department of Education's regional offices also replicate the appointments process of their central office; though here, in Education, candidates for certain local posts such as assistant superintendents and superintendents, together with candidates for directorships at regional and central office, are scrutinized by the Department's National Search Committee.[110]

There are, then, variations in the implementation of the recruitment process as set out by the CSC. Another example of these variations, again from the Department of Education, is that the PSB is chaired and co-chaired by Undersecretaries or Assistant Secretaries. This formally introduces a second layer of political appointees into the recruitment of permanent staff. There are also considerable variations in the qualities which candidates are expected to exhibit and according to which they are judged. In an office in Quezon City Hall, a candidate should, first and foremost, "....be able to sell herself. And secondly, I have some ways of determining whether he is straightforward … I just re-phrase my questions and, so far, I can tell whether he or she is telling a lie or not."[111] In the Central Bank, too, where technical competence and potential is a given, "I put a premium on integrity. Of course it's difficult to judge whether the person has integrity or not because this is the first time that you see him; but there's a way, you know, when you talk to people—you can judge whether there is integrity in what they're saying. You look at their bio-data and ask them, 'Why did you leave this office?'... You don't have to explain it … you know whether a person has that kind of first-rate [grade] of integrity…. Of course, both intellectual or intelligence quotient and emotional quotient, to me, are also very important."[112] In the Department of Education, a quality held to be essential is, inevitably, "academic background. For instance, if it's a director in our bureaux that handle elementary and secondary education … the academic preparation of the candidates, and of course their professional experiences … are very important considerations. But for … people working in the field offices—since they have a lot of interaction with local officials and local politicians—we also look at their interpersonal skills and their ability to relate with different types of people…[13] Even in the CSC, where there is a tendency to adhere closely to the four prescribed criteria—qualifications, seniority, training, and experience—there is room for individual preferences:

> …For me the only important thing is track record—performance. If, for example, an employee or an applicant who is due for promotion … has, based on performance, a bad record—like, [only] gets "satisfactory" ratings—these applicants should not be given the chance.

But we're looking at different things, like experience ... or seniority. [These are] not a good gauge of efficiency and effectiveness. We are probably looking at different things, and not really looking at what's important. Performance—that is my bias.[114]

Still another layer of complexity is added by the fact that "other government agencies ... are not precluded from developing their own internal systems to support what we [in the CSC] set as standards and that means becoming more stringent...like a more thorough interview by the director; and [their] internal exam ... may have higher standards in terms of the passing rate.... Agencies are at liberty to set up their own mechanisms ... as long as these mechanisms support the existing ones."[115] Thus, while some offices are content merely to make their preferences for an appointment known, others have established their own selection panels to examine applications and interview candidates in parallel with the agency's central PSB. In one division in Education

...I requested for filling up of positions of accountant, because we need accountants and we have vacant positions [for] accountants. Then we advertise it. Then applications arrive. Then afterwards we evaluate. I have a group ... I created a group—a committee, a promotions and selections board [in addition to and separate from the Department of Education's central PSB]—a group of accountants. I was recruiting for an accountant II: a group of accountants III, headed by an accountant III who is designated as chairman, ... study and evaluate the applications. [They] evaluate the [candidate's] personal discretion ... they verify the applications ... [and] ... with a representative from the personnel division, interview the applicants.[116]

In the Central Bank the review of candidates by the particular office recruiting or promoting staff is now fairly standardized, though a strong central lead is also provided by head of group: "...the departments ... do the first screening. They coordinate with the HRDD [Human Resources Development Department]. Of course I give them guidelines. You know: you should get only people from these of schools [and] at least a *cum laude* or with high honors, with experience, good communication skills. Ask them to write essays on the economy or the financial system—those things." [117]

As a consequence of this layering of process and the sheer quantity and complexity of the work involved in approving and disapproving appointments—and in order to avoid the impression that the Commission is merely acting as a rubber stamp—an accreditation program has been devised and applied to about a third of government agencies nationally. This concentrates the Commission's efforts on the validation of an agency's appointment procedure rather than on individual appointments and leaves the agency with the "final action" on appointments (though each month the agency must still submit information on its decisions to the CSC).[118] But the fact that procedures governing recruitment into the career service (and promotions within it) are, if properly applied, lengthy and thorough only sharpens the mockery that political interference makes of it all. Matters are not helped by certain features of the appointments procedure (other than its length and complexity) that may both encourage political interference and, possibly, exaggerate its true extent.

1. First, political appointees already involved in the selection of permanent civil servants: heads of agencies can indulge in "deep selection"; and, as in the Department of Education, political appointees may serve on the Personnel Selection Board. This blurs still further the divisions of authority to make appointments.

2. Secondly, the tendency to attach equal importance to qualifications and seniority, and to emphasize these criteria over performance and experience, produces a very large number of candidates for an ever-diminishing number of higher-level posts. Thus, "there are times that in the vacant position there are several or may be a hundred candidates for the position. Like, for example, the position is customs operations officer V, there are several incumbents who are next in rank to the position, the next in rank is customs operations officer III, customs operations officer IV... in one port only."[119] Among the disappointed and increasingly disaffected masses the belief that any appointment is political and the incentive to seek political backers intensify.

3. These pressures may also help to account for what appear to be limits on the dissemination of advertisements for posts, as serving bureaucrats work to protect their own interests.

> ...All vacancies should be posted in a "newspaper of general circulation"... [so] that it reaches the far corners of this country.... So how are you going to preserve these positions for qualified staff who have been in the Service over the past decade. Agencies comply ... by publishing in some secondary or tertiary newspaper of general circulation, so you have few eyes looking at the newspaper and few of those interested in the job reading it; and ... when one does get to apply for the supposed vacancies you will then automatically get a letter saying that "We are undergoing—all kinds of alibis—reorganization or rationalization" or that "the positions have been posted for manpower planning purposes only"—very generic and standard replies.... You have all these alibis. Now the thing was posted here [with this] 'publication' or with a regional office, [so] people who don't know a thing about the way the government works wouldn't know that there are vacancies.... There are a lot of organizations out there and you don't know about them.... They have good jobs,

[but] the only time the people get to know about them or about vacancies [is when] they happen to be passing through the regional office of the Civil Service Commission and chance on the vacancies posted. The reality is that … .people … want to limit the number of applicants…. I almost didn't make this job; [and]…. looking back it's quite an honor…. The only impetus for me to apply here was because my friend asked me to do so. I know that there are other qualified people out there who could take on existing positions here, especially those who have had training abroad in management; but they didn't have the same opportunity that I had to apply because they didn't know [about the post]. [120]

4. Fourthly, the recruitment process—with its emphasis on qualifications and on the kind of work associated with different levels (first, second and third)—is often accompanied by a rather condescending attitude to subordinates. For instance, first and level representatives are excluded from PSB when positions for third level are being considered "because we don't expect second level [to] ask questions."[121] Nor is "a lowly clerk … expected to be so calm during stressful situations compared to a division chief who is supposed to cover everything."[122] These kinds of views and practices suggest that those who already hold first and second-level posts are by definition unsuitable for promotion; and, again, the sense that political support is pre-condition for an appointment is strengthened.

5. Fifthly, the Commission's monitoring of the appointments made by other agencies relies very heavily upon its scrutiny of paperwork and its review of appeals and complaints—all of which originate from the organizations being monitored. Nor have the means been established by which agencies are to be monitored once they receive accreditation. Without greater certainty on these matters, suspicions over the extent of political interference are bound to flourish.

6. Sixthly, the freedom given to individual offices and agencies to develop their own additional procedures for recruitment may leave those prescribed by the CSC looking redundant. In Quezon City Hall, for example, the need for qualifications is often overlooked (hence, in lieu of a "mandatory" degree, emphasis is placed on the ability of candidates to communicate well); and the PSB is often replaced by interviews with the mayor or with the head or the assistant head of an office. The staffs who conduct these interviews may be quite capable of picking very good candidates, but circumvention of process adds to the impression that local governments have indeed established their own kingdoms; that political interference is rife; and that the writ of the CSC does not run very far. Moreover, circumvention does away with the checks and balances that would be necessary if those who are able to select competent and effective candidates were to be replaced by those who are less perceptive or do not have the best interests of the organization at heart.

7. The inclusion of political appointees and (in the case of City Hall) politicians in the appointment process for permanent civil servants; the criteria for appointments; the pressure on promotions (and attempts to relieve that pressure); attitudes to subordinates; the uncertainty surrounding monitoring and accreditation; and variations permitted in the appointment process: all this fosters an atmosphere of suspicion, and feeds representations of a civil service in which political interference is commonplace. Further incentives for politicians to interfere, and grounds for suspicion, are laid by the separation of authority to create and fund posts from the authority to make appointments. While authority to appoint (at least to the permanent service) lies, on the whole, with heads of agencies (subject to the approval of the Civil Service Commission) [123], salary structure, compensation, position classification, and the release of funds, are determined (wholly or partly) by the Department of Budget and Management. One consequence of the difficulties which the DBM and CSC have had in coordinating their roles is to throw into confusion the criteria for selection laid down in the Qualification and Standards Manual.

> When I was in the field, there was this move by the Department of Budget and Management to change the position titles of mostly those in the administrative sector to a more generic position title. So now we don't have a plumber [or] carpenter—you have a generic position such as administrative assistant. So that created a problem for the CSC because the qualification standards for each one were a bit different.... There should have been a prior coordination before the Department of Budget and Management would release that ... order or circular...[124]

Another effect has been to encourage politicians to seek influence (directly or through the Palace) over the decisions of the DBM and persuade it either to create openings for "ghosts" or, as they are sometimes known, "15-30" employees[125]; or to appoint contract workers who, as such, lie outside the jurisdiction of the Commission. To all intents and purposes these "ghosts" and contract workers are grace and favor appointees. The problem is most acute in local governments where it is possible—at least, for the wealthier municipalities and cities—to bypass the CSC, the DBM, and even the Palace, by tapping into local funds (derived from the real-property tax and the Internal Revenue Allotment). Thus, local governments

> ...operate now like corporations. The thing now that limits their operations is the budget that they get from their internal revenue allotment and the money they generate from the property tax. At times we see that phenomenon of a lot of government employees not doing anything—this is in local governments which have surpluses.

They can afford to have people who are not doing anything. It's also a matter for concern especially when there are lots of people applying at local governments and they are often frustrated, especially the young ones. We have in the DILG ... an oversight bureau for the operations of local governments, even the financing aspect; but there is a need to tie up the efforts of these agencies ... with the personnel complement of these agencies. It is very difficult even at our level—it's difficult for my division to solicit a report ... from the regional office that there *are* incidences of ghost employees in their jurisdictions [even] when everyone knows that that happens. We were pressured to issue directives to the regional offices ... I think coming from Malacañang ... because the Palace wanted to find out if there were incidences of ghost employees.... The thing was—I don't know if the regional directors formed a group or caucus or something—that nobody ... report[ed] any incidences of ghost employees.... I think that is already a failure of this organisation that we weren't able to report such incidences unless of course something breaks out into the media and the institution is forced to investigate and either confirm or deny that such incidences occur. Most of the time the reality is that [they are] political appointees...[126]

As a method of political interference, the motivations underlying "ghosts" and contract labor are similar to those discussed earlier:

There is a limit to the projects that they [local governments] can engage in. For example, even though a local government would want to improve, let's say, their existing road infrastructure and have the money, they can't do it because improving that section of the highway is already considered a national government project and it is for the DPWH [Department of Public Works and Highways] to implement it on a national level and establish a project management office in that area. There is some frustration with regard to other similar undertakings. Let's say putting more significant infrastructure up for water, for sanitation ... the local government unit is reluctant to deal with the national-line agency that it has to deal with it. There are two schools of thought here: they are reluctant to deal with national-line agency because the national government agencies are more professional—there won't be any leakages, so they want to keep the project themselves and make sure all the leakages leak into their pockets. Also Filipino culture is reactive—there is no initiative coming from the national-line agencies. The thing ... with surplus money [in] local government is that the only time this surplus money gets disbursed is when an election is near—[only] then [are] all these projects ... visible' [127]

The suspicion that ghost employees and contractual workers are, therefore, more numerous—and that meddling by politicians is more extensive than it appears to be—is deepened by the sheer lack of data. The precise number of ghost employees is not known by the CSC (nor anyone else). Nor does the CSC know the precise number of contractual or non-permanent posts or permanent posts, for this information is not always forthcoming:

> ...it's a struggle to get consensus on directions of this project. For instance, I have to convince the Commission that we can do it this way, or that we can do the data cleaning on our own using certain program parameters..... and one stumbling block is that we don't yet have the data we need from the DBM.... They say they haven't revised their standards for office position titles, or that they are still staring at the 2002 index of government positions.[128]

Tenure

Informed by representations of a bureaucracy in which political inter-ference is extensive, it is not surprising that civil servants should find it acceptable, even necessary, to circumvent other procedures that are of direct and personal interest. Two matters of particular importance are tenure and rotation.

On paper at least, security of tenure has been linked to performance since 1992. Very simply, bureaucrats who receive an "unsatisfactory" rating for two consecutive semesters (each semester being a period of six months), or who receive one "poor" rating at the end of one semester, can be dismissed from the Service. By the same token, a "very satisfactory" rating will earn a bonus. In practice, however, the tendency to treat security of tenure as a given (and to put to one side the condition of reasonable performance) is widespread throughout the service. This undoubtedly breeds, in some career civil servants, a degree of complacency which is, at times, expressed quite openly: "I observed that ... security of tenure tends to make staff ... unproductive.... I really heard some of them say that, 'after all, they will not be terminated' because they have that security of tenure."[129] This attitude—enhanced by a frequent and regular turnover of third-level political appointees, and by a certain amount of *schadenfreude* in their fate—sparks a deal of annoyance among political appointees who view it as another expression of the unhelpful division of authority in favor of the permanent service: "They always have this concept of security of tenure—that's the main reason [why] ... no matter how mad you are at the way they perform, they can always stay in. They always keep on saying 'I can stay here as long as I want; but you are an appointed position—you can come and go.'"[130] Political appointees who are more sympathetic to the permanent service are no less dissatisfied with security of tenure as understood and practiced by permanent staff:

> The Commission, which basically has been charged with this, has closed its eyes all these years to the fact that performance ratings

and performance evaluations are just not really based on performance: it doesn't really matter whether you perform or not, people will say "Well, but he has seven children." The other side of this is more demoralization among those who really perform, because if you get the same ratings—so what?[131]

The sentiment is shared by those—whether political appointees or career civil servants—with long experience in the private sector:

> Our reputation is very important. The economy in a way depends on the reputation of the Central Bank. We may have political problems, we may have corruption issues in other government agencies being discussed in the papers. But when we deal with financial institutions or with other institutions from outside the country, we can stand up and can give them some comfort and confidence in that there *are* responsible institutions in this country which we can rely on; and we can continue doing business with them.... [But] we have [a] handicap in government.... In so far as people-handling is concerned, in that under the civil service law the employees are adequately—or more than adequately—protected. It's very hard to discipline; it's very hard to dismiss people here. In the private sector it's easier to discipline, it easier to institute changes, because you can carry a big stick which you may not have here. You have some tools here—performance rating; but it's very difficult; and there are cases where supervisors are being sued by their subordinates—we have seen that. That ... rarely happens in the private sector. If a cash teller here misappropriated money, it will be fast if that teller can be dismissed in six months. So it affects morale: "Why is she here? Is she receiving pay? Yes she is, and yet she's dishonest." And, of course, you do not give her work; and then the government employs her twice over because you cannot dismiss her, and yet she is still earning for six months; and that's fast—six months.... In the private [sector] if that teller takes out money, on that day we have a blank form to be issued by the branch manager: "Please explain why you should not be dismissed?" In the meantime you are preventively suspended—so she's out of work. You are given 48 hours. You may ask for another 48 hours. But if the evidence is clear, on the fifth day she's out—she's dismissed. So you can instil more discipline among personnel in that manner. And...in terms of incentive, [in the private sector] there can be a more direct relationship between performance and rewards. In a very broad organization like this you may all do the best work ... but the reward may come one or two years later.... Private organizations have more flexibility in giving recognition, not necessarily monetary; [so] it's essential that these victories [here in the Bank] are immediately celebrated.[132]

And even among those whose life has been spent in career service, there is frustration with some their colleagues' willingness to take tenure for granted, and with the effect this has on the Service:

> The ... performance system needs to be interdependent such that you cannot isolate the work of individuals from the output of the office and the leadership of that office and division.... A supervisor told me:
>
> "But Ma'am, there is a constitutional provision for security of tenure."
>
> "Well, yes: security unless there is cause. You cannot be removed unless there is cause. If you perform really badly, is that not a cause of separation?"
>
> There are some people who have been supervisors for 20 or 30 years and now—it's only now—that they have the CSC director who tells them to their face: "There is no such thing as security of tenure. If you don't do your job well, you should be separated..." And the tool that will take care of that is the performance management system. [Yet] we have bad workers, [and] how do we deal with them?... Until you're 65, until you retire or die—that's the only time we stopped seeing the face of these people. You have a tool, but you're not implementing it. You [should] give a person a poor rating and [have] that person automatically dropped from the rolls; but that person has been there for 10 years and that person is even ... promoted. Why? It's not that individual that has that problem—- it is *you* [the supervisor], because every rating period *you* give them a very satisfactory rating, and you don't give feedback that that person is doing badly. And so, for the last 10 or 20 years, we've been fooling each other and *now* you complain? And now this poor person doesn't know what she's doing, how she stands, because each time you've given that person a good rating. She doesn't know she's working badly.
>
> But what supervisors then reply is: "For humanitarian reasons. We give them a 'very satisfactory' rating.... We give them a 'very satisfactory' rating, because if you are a 'very satisfactory' performer, you get 2000 pesos."
>
> "Yes, we know that [you] sacrificed everything—the goal, the mission of your office, the integrity, and the motivation of the rest of the people in your office—for one cell-card load[133] costing 500 pesos."[134]

It is, however, more a sense of insecurity among career staff that pervades these agencies. Tenure provides some peace of mind when political interference is thought to invade so much of the service and to account for so many curious decisions, disappointments and problems; and it provides some protection against the vagaries of political intimidation. It thereby transforms pay that is comparatively[135] low, into regular and secure pay. As one Division Chief put it, "in the government, at least your consolation is security of tenure. Not unless you do something wrong, you can stay up to the time that you retire."[136] With the loss of tenure, then, there is much to lose, especially in a society in which there is no welfare net to speak of. Indeed, security of tenure is so often seen not merely as a substitute for better pay, but as preferable to higher pay without tenure. From this viewpoint, it is easy to understand why there is resistance among first and second level staff to measures designed to bring an edge to tenure, such as performance evaluation and rotation. Nor is it difficult to appreciate why third-level permanent staff are sympathetic to the problems which their subordinates face in their everyday lives, and why they reach the conclusion that the benefits attending a more rigorous application of those measures would not outweigh the disruption and ill-feeling this would generate, and who as a consequence are often unwilling to implement these measures too stringently. [137]

> I think we in government are a very kind lot.... We have that rule, that probationary period, that if you don't make good, then either you shape up or you'll be shipped out.... But I would say that because ... government people tend to be very kind towards government people, their colleagues.... That's why I'm not really certain about whether ... we have a very, potentially, [effective] management tool in weeding out the non-performers. If a person gets an unsatisfactory rating for two consecutive rating periods, then she is a candidate for dropping from the rolls ... every six months. If you get two consecutive unsatisfactory ratings in one year ... you can be dropped from the rolls: that's non-disciplinary, meaning that you can still go back to the service if somebody will take you.... But mind you, I have not heard [of this happening], well, at least in the Commission there's none. In other agencies...—there are so many agencies—I'm not certain if you can even find 3 percent of our people being dropped from the rolls for non-performance. And the norm—if you take a look at the performance ratings in government—the norm is still 'very satisfactory'. It's very rare that you see people getting poor unless the director is really very mad at them.... So, that's how kind [we are]...[138]

A new set of appraisal procedures introduced by the CSC does not appear to have fared much better. Piloted in the Commission and a number of other agencies, it is intended to inject new life into performance evaluations. By "emphasizing outputs and quantifiable points," it becomes possible, it is hoped, "to eliminate the process of being subjective in the way that you praise your subordinates,"[139] identify "dead wood" and "rid the service of inefficient employees."[140] In practice, however, the new system "is not being strictly implemented"[141] and everybody gets a very satisfactory rating. This still is happening, it is amazing—even to us, HRD, implementing the new performance evaluation system. When I meet with ... the members of the different divisions (we get representatives from these divisions to sit with me as their chair, to discuss about the ratings of the individuals), if you ask the division chiefs, for example, who are members of the [performance evaluation committee] ... and this is fairly recent, nobody except one would rate their staff satisfactory—all of them are VS [very satisfactory]. And since I'm very hands on and I would know the performance of individual staff, you get amazed and surprised listening to what they are saying ... and this is even CSC. How much more [difficult it must be] to implement [the new procedures] in other agencies where performance is not treated seriously!?[142]

After all, any set of evaluation procedures, if properly implemented, will be understood to disregard the pact between security of tenure and low pay that exists in the minds of so civil servants. This fundamental objection is compounded by a number of others.

First, the notion that any system is objective can only be viewed skeptically when it is believed that political interference in the bureaucracy and the circumvention or distortion of its processes is widespread. This response to the new evaluation system from lower ranks at the coal-face is fairly typical: "I don't know how it's going to work ... but it's easy to get away with those things if you really know how..."[143] The view from a little higher up is not so different: "...they can always manipulate performance targets. It'll be okay—I'll do better next time."[144]

Secondly, the new procedures—despite the work of "calibration committees"—does not appear to those concerned to take into account the nature of the work in which they are engaged. "We had some discussions on the point system. At first most of us in the office we were not amenable to the points system, because of the nature of the job of lawyers in actual offices. We believe that it could not be measured by points that easily.... We have adjusted to that system, but we are still trying to figure out how we can accomplish the requirements. The points required for us are not that attainable right now."[145] For example "a disciplinary case gets 29 points only. But the time it took! It took almost 1 month [to deal with one case]. And since 'the number of points you get for each item of work is low ... we only got to 61 percent [of the quota] which [was classed as] "unacceptable."'[146] The sense that points and tasks are poorly connected is widely shared by many of those whose involvement in more complex tasks produces no immediately obvious results: "...if the nature of the work is on development areas like policies or if you are developing or designing conceptualizing research policies, it's very difficult to get points."[147] Nor does it favor those involved in services:

What's ... disheartening is that ... well, in my division we are five: I am the head, I have two technical people, and two on [the] front-line, and they do not earn any points. Here in the Commission when you entertain 'phone calls, you hear clients crying about inefficiency over their pensions, retirement—so you entertain them for one hour or 30 minutes. You don't get points for that. Here at the front line they serve people, but they don't get any points. And for a particular division, say, for example, for every person like me, I have to come up with 972 points in a year, times the number of personnel in our division.... We are five in the division, so we have to come up with 4,800 points. Only three of our technical people—me and my two technical staff—are the ones earning the points: [from] letters, papers. When you attend meetings outside the Commission, you lose time, but you don't get any points. So what we do is we work double hard, in order to come up with these points that these two people should be earning.... Yet the two people in front are doing their job pretty well. But they don't get any points.[148]

Thirdly, given the difficulty of defining tasks and what is being measured, it does not do away with the need to be subjective. Nor, indeed, do the new procedures measure what it is believed that any evaluation should be measuring—"helping and learning from each other."[149] This is especially so when those tasks being measured, such as tax investigations, are collective, complex, and require staff to evolve new techniques continuously over many years.

...For me it is hard to determine how much ... to give ... to those persons, because in their work.... there is no monitoring of what they are doing.... I am not asking them to give me an accomplish-ment report daily, because.... we used to implement that when I was still an assistant.... my former boss used to be like that. But ... we stopped it, because it was less productive: instead of finishing their work, they had to do the accomplishment report. When the [new] evaluation comes around, we find it hard ... it's only the perception, we base our evaluation on perception, on how we see the person, how he works ... and [on] attendance of course, because we have an attendance [record]....[150]

Fourthly, by encouraging competition between offices, the points system works against alignment and encourages territoriality:

Each office ... is trying to outdo each other.... So if there is one project that would best be done if either two or three offices work together.... I would like to see that done collectively rather than independently. [But] because of this point system, where each office seems to outdo the other, they are competing with each other. So what happens is that instead of asking for cooperation ... you won't give me good cooperation because you will see it as something from which you can earn points: *I* want to be the one who is earning the points.... It's one of the things that keep people from co-operating. If you work as a collective, you don't look any more at the points that you earn—you look at what benefits the entire organisation.'[151]

Fifthly, the new system generates unnecessary work and formality as staffs look for easily performed, and easily quantifiable, jobs:

So what we do is, like, if you receive a phone call ... a request for assistance ... we entertain you [the caller] for 30 minutes [but] we have no points. [So] then we [the technical staff] write—we send a letter to the agency. So, for example, she's complaining about the SSS [the Social Security System] about non-receipt of pension benefits. We write the SSS that we received a 'phone call complaining.... We earn two points for every letter. So... we find ways to multiply the points; and we have this list.... The Chair ... well, she's a bright person ... she came up with this list of...assigned activities ... points [for activities] that will apply to all offices. Some points ... are solely for this office [for very specific activities].... But, in general ... when you write a memo, all memos ... regardless of what office they came from ... will get two points. So what we do is ... we multiply.... After we receive a 'phone call we write a letter, and we do a follow up ... another letter...[152]

Rotation

Those within the civil service (most especially at third level) who have sought and come to value their own periodic rotation among offices within an agency and between centre and regions are convinced it should be practiced more widely. "I have been to legal, [though] I'm not a lawyer. I have been to Information Systems, though I am not a computer expert. I have been to the operations group.... So I have been around.... It broadens me. In fact, the first time I attended the budget hearing—it [the rotation] helps [me] to understand."[153] For some, too, moving from the centre to the province at least carries a sense of freedom because here "you don't have a boss except yourself, and you're treated differently in the regions—I don't know why. You could move more freely, you could do things mostly on your own, because of the non-hierarchical setup that we have wherein you can just move, do things as you please." [154] And for those who are being groomed for promotion to third level in the BIR, "it is expected of you—to be job rotated, to be reassigned elsewhere in the country. It is part of the risks that you take when you accept the position, and it is part of the process." This is so "because when you go [among the offices] you will have a feel of how it is to be there. And [later] when you write directives, or write letters, when you review papers coming from certain offices, you have an idea of what they are saying: it's not just words, it's not just an abstract explanation, but you have a feeling of how the people are doing their work on the ground."[155]

Generally speaking, however, policies on rotation are the business of individual agencies and are rarely adhered to. Consequently, its practice across and within agencies is inconsistent. In the CSC, the rotation of directors among different offices within central office occurs every three to five years, and recently this has been extended to include division chiefs. But the rotation of lower level staff is practiced little, though subordinates may request transfers and it is expected that managers should recommend transfers when staffs have been in their posts for seven to ten years. Within regional offices, too, where authority to make rotations has been devolved to regional directors, rotation at lower levels is infrequent. The BIR's revenue district officers are supposed to be rotated every two years "to minimize familiarity with the taxpayers"[156]; while for those working in tax collection and assessment in central office "there is a provision that if you are three years in that position you can move—that is to avoid familiarization..."[157] In practice, however, officials exercise their own discretion: "I think that moving people is less productive. If we can just trust, just trust, people.... Let's take that out—familiarization.... It's more productive.... Usually I don't want to move people because of their specialization—this one already knows this [the job] ... it's more productive. But ... if I see someone in a section who has potential and can be more productive [if moved] ... then I initiate and ask if he would want to transfer."[158] A willingness to circumvent or ignore policies on rotation also stems from credentialism and a concern with status (reinforced by the Qualification and Standards Manual): to become an examiner one must be a qualified CPA or "at least an accounting graduate ... we have to have that education standard."[159] A further concern is a reluctance to break the compact between low pay and being left in settled, familiar, and secure surroundings, particularly given a context of what is believed to be widespread political interference. Any insistence on rotation is, therefore, usually taken to suggest that something is badly wrong: "...job rotation, it's really part ...—it *should* be part—of human resource development. However ... I think it is viewed ... with some connotations like ... maybe he or she transferred because there is a problem. Generally that's the feeling."[160] Indeed, "in some organizations, such as CSC, to be job rotated or reassigned to other offices which are seen as not favored or not doing anything, looks like a punishment."[161] On the whole, then, "most people, I think ... *most* people, don't like the idea."[162]

There is particular disquiet over the rotation of staff among regions or between regional and central offices. Grafting oneself onto existing networks among relationships shaped around place, language, kinship, friendship, educational background, and shared experiences can be very hard work when moving between different towns, cities and provinces[163]; and there are matters of status to be thought about, especially if an official is moved to the rural areas, to the provinces or, worst of all, to "the mountains." There is also the fact that rotation takes the official away from their families unless they, too, are prepared for the move and all that it entails. Either way, they will receive no re-location expenses, no help to sell and buy homes, and no help with schools. A two-day family visit, once a month, and inclusive of travel times, is the most an official is entitled to.

Pay

Circumvention of key processes—such as recruitment, conditions of tenure and rotation—within the civil service is informed in part by the practice and representation of political interference. Another stimulus is low pay and its acceptance by civil servants in lieu of an observance of procedures which they feel would constrain their interests.

Various considerations work to keep salaries meagre throughout the civil service: the generally poor economic and financial health of the Philippines; competing priorities; political interference; the uneven reputation of the civil service; a tendency to think of civil servants as inefficient at best or, at worst, deliberately obstructive; and the lack of certainty that increases in pay would do much to improve matters. As a consequence, the civil service "attracts people who really just a have nowhere else to go.... The Cambodian finance minister—he was here in November or October. He was saying that in Cambodia they get paid so little that you can't ask them not to be corrupt. They just don't get enough to live on. While they get paid better here in the Philippines than in Cambodia ... attracting people who are committed and capable is a problem."[164] The view from the top of the civil service is little different: "...low compensation means essentially that from the period of recruitment you no longer get the good people, because even if an entry salary is not bad, people know that ...you go up with an almost 0° slope whereas your counterparts vary drastically go up. So if your recruitment base especially at the professional level is weak because you have a poor choice, then necessarily the people who go up it in the career path are not as good."[165]

Attracting enough people of the right stuff, however, is not just a matter of pay. The uncertainties and blocks (such as the restricted dissemination of information on vacancies) set up by the recruitment process deters applicants, as does the widespread perception that the problems of the civil service—such a political interference and a "tendency to do things which are not in accordance with the usual procedures and just hope that nobody finds out"[166]—smother opportunities to advance one's career:

> Well I've heard ... there are times that people get promotions for humanitarian reasons because they are about to retire and it is assumed the last pay will be equivalent, or have an effect on, your

pension. I've seen that in organizations I've worked in before. But I heard this story from someone that the qualified person was by-passed because of a person was about to retire [who got the job in the CSC]. I told the person that's okay _... he's about to retire. But once he has retired it should be understood that the person who was bypassed and really qualified should automatically be put into that position. Looking at how I tried to explain it, it appeared that it didn't work out that way. The question is how you retain the younger staff especially if they feel that they are not rewarded accordingly? They can always leave and that is the reason why the staffs here have been skewed towards 40 and above.[167]

There is, then, also the problem of retaining staff:

My concern was to look at what are those jobs and positions that we are losing people. The process, the figures, are alarming ... there are more people going out than coming in. There are a few reasons here. One is that agencies are downsizing. So there are more people going out but they cannot take in people. I also have to [mention] age: it is understandable if the person exits when he's 40 or 50 years old; but some are leaving because they are disgusted ... you don't see many people in their 20s.[168]

Retaining high quality professional staffs is especially difficult: "You have doctors and nurses leaving their positions almost every quarter"[169]; and indeed for some, such as qualified lawyers and accountants, short-term entry into the service is part of long-term career strategy. A stint in government service until they achieve a respectable position will stand them in good stead: a lawyer or an accountant—who knows how, say, the BIR works—will not find it difficult to pick up a very well-paid job in the private sector. In the CSC, too,

...the one thing that motivates people to enter ... is ... the high integrity of the Civil Service Commission; and they know that they will be able gain good experience by joining the Civil Service Commission. But retaining them is a very big problem ... [The turnover is] ... very fast: most will last only a year.... We have retained a few, but we expect very few retentions and that the majority will leave.... Afterwards they go and get good jobs because of the credential that they have come from the Civil Service Commission.[170]

From the perspective of many of those concerned with day-to-day operations there are, as a consequence of these recruitment problems, insufficient personnel of sufficient calibre to keep offices functioning properly; and those that remain are overworked. The problem is evident in Education where "every year we are requesting for 10,000 teachers ... and that is based on catch up with enrolment which is increasing at about 2 percent a year which means we need another 10,000 teachers.... So, on a regular basis we request for 10,000 teachers every year."[171] And those teachers who have been pushed onto the schools by politicians only create an additional burden: "you really have to take them, and it's up to you to train them ... they are already in the system....We have to train them ... during [the] vacation ... March to May."[172] A still more pressing problem is leadership within schools: "...It's not just a question of funding: in some of the poorer areas in the northern provinces they have some of the highest levels of achievement.... Right now we lack principals ... the right people ... we don't have principals ... good principals, who know how to motivate."[173] In the BIR, too,

> ...we have many vacant positions for collectors, examiners, but we cannot fill up these positions because we don't have the budget. We have to get approval from the Department of Budget [and Management], and they have to list the money for that particular position. So the situation now is that people are retiring but we are not filling up.... The commissioner ... can transfer more people to [our] office. That would be a welcome move. Actually, we have now pending requests for more personnel. Before I joined this office, last July, we only had 70 examiners. I was able to request 30 more. So we have a hundred now. You have to understand they had 70 before covering almost 700 [large] taxpayers, so that's 10 to one. So with the additional examiners we were able to reduce the ratio from one examiner [to ten taxpayers], to one examiner to six [large] taxpayers...[174]

The problem is worse in some districts: "...South Makati ... (the second biggest district in the whole country) ... has 6,000 corporate taxpayers—small ones and medium-sized corporations. We only had, before, around and 40-plus examiners and supervisors, so actually [it was] grossly undermanned."[175] Indeed a widely and strongly held view is that the Bureau in general is "struggling":

> To give you a better perspective ... of the need for more resources. In 1995 I was technical assistant to the Deputy Commissioner. I would go over the data [and] the goal then was around 330 billion for the whole year. And we had around 13,000 people for the whole of the Bureau of Internal Revenue. Now, for this year we are supposed to collect 760 billion, that's more than double, and we have only around less than 11,000 personnel. So the organisation is shrinking, but the goal is going up. The bottom [line] is [that] to improve collection I need more people. I ... need more people.[176]

What is perceived to be the problem of too few people of sufficient quality is compounded by the poor allocation of personnel. At a national scale, low compensation, combined with higher living costs and a greater concentration of private businesses in the capital, means that: "In the regions we have *much* better people ... but they are hampered in terms of [career advance]. [This is] because, first, the powers that be never see them. Secondly, the 50 percent who are women generally will not leave if they have already settled families there. (The men, they can leave their families). Third... the career path in the regions is stopped at a lower level whereas in Metro Manila it's higher."[177] There are also circumstances that work in the opposite direction, preventing the movement of good staff from Manila to the provinces. One set of considerations (alluded to earlier) is the challenge of leaving or moving one's family and having to deal with new languages, new networks of relationships, and the stigma of being posted to "the provinces." Another impediment is the salary structure. The difficulty which the CSC experienced in filling positions at the level of director II—who head field offices—is a case in point. There were simply not enough staff at central office with third-level eligibility, and those who were eligible and who were next in rank—division chiefs—did not want to accept the promotion. Once they reached the eighth increment within their post, their salary was "much higher" than the first increment for director II: a promotion would mean a cut in salary.[178] Personnel are also poorly allocated among agencies and within agencies: "there are instances where we have duplication of work and ... there are people in [some] agencies who are not doing anything while in other agencies people are overworked. We need to put positions in agencies where they're needed and take them away from agencies where they're not."[179] In the Central Office of the Department of Education, at least, "...there are still many in the central office—more people than I think we need ... in other countries the central offices are lean, very lean, and the people are the right people and the salary is good."[180]

Again political interference and the separation of authority to fund civil service posts from authority to appoint contribute to these problems:

> ...any office is fixed to its *plantilla* positions. They cannot just create their positions—they have to put the request for a position for funding ... from the Department of Budget and Management before it gets approved. Most of the time it doesn't ... DBM looks at your budget and when it comes back to you there are several items that are not there, and [several other items] that are there ... even though you didn't have any plans for them. So at the end of the year you're not going to use this money and you're going to have to hand it back to DBM or you have to go through the hoopla of securing approval for reallocating this money [to] another item.[181]

Training

A pejorative view of civil servants so often found among politicians, the bureaucrats themselves, and the public at large is given a deal of credence by circumvention of process, political interference, low pay, and the poor allocation of staff. It also finds succour in the fact that little or nothing is done to establish among civil servants common representations of officials and government agencies and their roles, functions, methods, techniques, and interactions. Civil servants so often appear to know only their own very small "patch" and seem unconcerned about whatever else—proper or improper—that goes on around them and in the outside world. Moves are underway to establish a national academy, but training has been and remains very much in the hands of

> ...the human resource division of each regional office. And really there's not much scope for taking a look at whether, you know, are the programs standard? Or [has] the training has attained the objectives? Well, we have a Human Resource Development Office, but HRDO handle so many things: coming up with policies on local scholarships, doing some modules.... [And] because there are many constraints, [they] cannot focus on training or ... development intervention. Here at central office you will find a lot of directors who are very good trainers but, because they are saddled with their office functions, it's really quite difficult to pull [them] out ... [to] do the training. We are currently doing two things here that require directors to be fielded and to train other organizations—I'm talking about a gender sensitivity seminars and performance management systems. So we have trained people, most of them are directors, to help shepherd agencies in terms of setting up their performance management systems. [But] it's very difficult because they really have to spare some time to do that alongside their own functions.[182]

Consequently, there is much variation in the intensity, nature and objectives of training. The Central Bank, for example, has put together an extensive regime. The BIR, too, has, in more recent years, introduced "a decent training programme."[183] "We have the General Course for Revenue Officers..."[184]; and "those who are considered experts are asked to help in disseminating their knowledge down the ladder.[185] We are recipients of training scholarships—we maximise that by sending people there."[186] The purpose of this training is also clear: it "will make a big difference, because now that you have a common understanding, a common approach, unlike when you don't have the training, it is subject to individual interpretation."[187] Customs, on the other hand, provides only a very short orientation course in which new entrants are briefed on "the history of the bureau, the organisational setup, the officials—some basic information regarding administration, like civil service rules and regulations."[188] Nor is there any great sense of purpose and direction. After all, officials "are not required to have that kind of training.... What is required of ours is, yes, we have to meet the qualifications—the qualification requirements of the position."[189] Officials must learn on the job.

For the most part, then, civil servants

> ...are not equipped with updated, relevant and important data to enable them to perform their functions and to plan properly.... Civil servants are qualified, but they haven't got updated training. And they find it very difficult to get money for training whether to be sent abroad or to attend a seminar or convention. There is no funding for that.... The Philippines, unlike other South-East Asian countries, whenever the economy is bad, the first item we cut from the budget is R and D [and] training and education for our own civil service—that has been going on the last 20 years.... So they are basing most of the things they are doing on guesswork, at best.... So what you have is a bureaucracy that is not only bloated but not well compensated and ill-trained for the job they are supposed to do.[190]

Poor training is to be explained only in part by inadequate funding. There are other influences at work, too. From the point of view of many civil servants, the essential substance with which they must work is people; and the reality which must be faced is the need to defend one's position and livelihood. Provided one has the necessary credentials, then seniority (experience and sheer length of service) should count for everything when it comes to promotions and apportioning authority. Training is another consideration in these decisions, but it is a low priority and is measured somewhat mechanically in hours (and usually takes the form of seminars, lectures, and workshops). There are, indeed, certain technical matters and procedures that one must know. But these are only technical matters and can be learnt through experience. This outlook, combined with funding scarcity of money, is associated with a number of problems.

First, personnel offices are small and their staffs are themselves poorly trained. Changes are underway in many of these offices; but programs are, more often than not, fragmented and treated by those who participate in them as a relief from everyday routines, as a means of lengthening their curriculum vitae, and as another box ticked against the long list of requirements they must meet if they are to be considered for promotion.

Secondly, whilst learning on the job has much to commend it (and in some areas of work it may be the only effective way to learn), the absence of training means that so much experience is lost when older staff leave, retire, or die, and much time and effort is wasted reinventing the wheel. At Customs, for example, civil servants responsible for post-entry audits build up their own extensive knowledge of methods and informants over a decade or more.[191] This information and experience is particular to each of them and is not recorded; nor are these officials involved in training younger colleagues.

Thirdly, members of staff—especially if they do little reading in their everyday lives (as is usually the case)—are limited to their own personal experience and knowledge.

Fourthly, members in different parts of the organization have a poor sense of what is going on in the rest of the organization; of how they and the various components of the organization fit together; and of how the organization fits into government. There is, in other words, poor alignment and poor coordination.[192]

Fifthly, there are wide variations in interpretations of rules, regulations, processes, procedures, and methodologies. This creates confusion within the organization and in the minds of those outside the organization with whom its officials deal.

Finally, in the absence of training (and the alignment of representations), much space is left to be filled by lurid, exaggerated, or wildly inaccurate accounts of conspiracies and practices within the agency and in government more generally. New entrants are inculcated with these stories and may feel they have to buy into them if they are to be accepted by their colleagues. It is they who are also more likely to feel compelled to accept, participate in or turn and blind eye, to illicit practices. Civil servants whose duty it is (day in and day out) to handle administrative and criminal cases, often make the point that bureaucrats who commit these offences are well aware that what they are doing is wrong, but feel either that since everyone else is trying to get what they can out of the system for themselves, there is no reason why they should not also try to do so; and that their unwillingness to participate will mark them out as possible whistleblowers.[193]

Supplementing Income

Representations of a civil service in which political interference is rife, and wonly the worst remain, only weaken morale. Demoralization is especially evident among first and second level staffs for whom advance within a narrow hierarchy is restricted further by political placements. And, to cap it all, "Some superiors cannot understand our situation. For example, if we are absent because of health problems with our children.... Salaries are poor."[194] These circumstances—in which many civil servants believe themselves to be caught—prompt the emergence of methods to supplement to income.

1. There exists, in addition to salaries, a range of official allowances. These include, for example, a personal economic resource allowance, additional compensation allowance, a clothing allowance, a rice allowance, a 13th-month salary (divided into two payments, one made in June and the other in December), and a Christmas bonus that is to all intents and purposes mandatory (though said to be conditional upon good performance). Division chiefs and third level staffs may also claim representation and travel allowances. Medical benefits (funded by contributions from members) usually protect only contributors, though some benefits also cover a small proportion of certain costs incurred by their immediate family. Vacation and sick leave

earned by civil servants are worth a small amount each month, and may be taken either as leave without pay or as the equivalent cash sum. Second jobs, often teaching or legal work, also help supplement incomes, and may be taken on provided these are performed out of hours and permission has been granted by the agency. And loans are available from a variety of government and private lenders. These include, as in the Department of Education, a loan association set up by retired members of the Department. Interests rates vary from around 6 percent to 16 percent per annum.

2. There also exists an array of unofficial (but largely tolerated) supplements. Of particular interest are informal loan arrangements—rotating credit associations—formed among staff usually from the same office or from a set of closely grouped offices. For instance, in one office in Education each member of the association buys into shares which are lent out on the fifteenth and thirtieth day of each month. After ten months, the capital is returned to the shareholders, and the interest made on the loan is paid to them two months later—in December. Similar arrangements can be found in an office of the CSC: "We call it *paluwagan* ... every month you choose how many shares you want. One share is 400 pesos. So if you want two shares you pay every month 800 pesos. We lend that money at 5 percent interest per month. At the end of the year, the capital and the profit goes to you."[195] Repayment is (as far as can be expected) guaranteed: ..."because we have their [the lender's] ATM [card].... We have, like, a liaison officer who ... takes it [the cash] out.... If you borrow, you give her your ATM card. And on payday [she] withdraws it [the loan repayment] ... and returns the card." [196]

3. A further source of income, and one that appears to have been tolerated widely (at last until recently), is a cash advance. Ostensibly for travel on official business and to attend seminars, these advances are either never reconciled or "liquidated" only after several months or years. These payments are, in truth, regarded as

> ...entitlements. These people! They always believe that they are entitled to travel ... to all the benefits; but.... I look at it as a performance incentive for them. They could only travel if they have achieved [a certain] objective at work.... You can't just travel every now and then, to assist in programmes here and there, unless you have achieved a certain level of expertise. But ... these things ... are written into the contract of work, so if you don't approve their travel they will go to the union and then the union will ... say things against me.... As I said, there [are too many cliques] in the organisation.... They always think they are entitled to that.'[197]

4. Mention must also be made of various liberties granted in lieu of money. It has already been noted that security of tenure and resistance among civil servants to measures—such as performance ratings, disciplinary procedures,

and rotation—designed to bring an edge to tenure, are often seen as a substitute for (and indeed, preferable to) higher pay. To these allowances may be added late arrivals in the morning, early departures in the afternoon, and long and lavish lunch breaks, such that many offices either close down or are left with a skeleton staff who, with their pillows, are to found stretched out on sofas and desks from around late morning until 1.00 PM or 2.00 PM. There is, then, a general understanding that government service is, or should be, less stressful and offer flexibility and time.

> People get comfortable.... Some here have the thinking that "We're not getting paid much, but we are also not getting that much pressure, we have a little more time." Because right at five o'clock they can get out of the office. Actually, in some other agencies they're out before five o'clock! But here, at five o'clock they can go home. But of course that doesn't work for the bosses; but for other staff, yes, they are out of here at five.... And they are comfortable, actually, they are comfortable with that; but once you try to change that, then I think there will be some opposition.[198]

Many staffs are quite open about this: the pay may be better in the private sector 'but the problem is parents can't go on leave.... In the government you are entitled to sick leave, vacation leave."[199] This room to balance family and work life is undoubtedly an important attraction: "One of the reasons why I am working for the government is that it is not giving me that big pressure, unlike when I was working for a [private] organisation. I have two kids and I'm separated, so I have to consider my time with them and time away from them. That is why I'm working for government—because the pressure is much less here."[200] The view from third level is similar, but a little more mixed:

> [In] the private sector ... you have a more frantic pace there. Of course it's profit driven, so there is always pressure to perform, and there is always the threat of either demotion or removal from work ... or a threat that you will not get a huge bonus like the others.... So there is more pressure or, at least, that is what I feel. Or it's a different kind of pressure, because I can't say that there is no pressure [in government]—there is also a lot of pressure. But in the private sector they are more ... demanding of their employees simply because they are the ones who are really providing the sense that they are spending for your time and so you should perform. Here [in government] ... the top management cannot say that they are the ones providing the employment, because they are not the ones signing the pay cheques. So I think the pressure to perform is not that high. One part of the reason is, I think, the recognition that people are not getting paid well.... In the private sector you know that they are getting paid for their time, so they should produce commensurate to

their compensation. But here, I think, the top management is more lenient because people are, well, they are not getting paid well. To put pressure on them—they already have pressure in their personal [life]—is not seen as something fair.... So there's not that much of that kind of pressure.[201]

The effect of these permitted or tolerated supplements is damaging in a number of respects. First, the patchwork of allowances and bonuses is expensive to administer, it dilutes salaries, and its effectiveness is blunted by a raft of deductions—tax, contributions and most especially loan repayments. "I can see from the people around—those who are really trying to make an honest living, living within their means—you can see from their pay slips that they almost do not have [anything to take home]. Because they loan ... there are so many loans ... [and] ... it's eaten up by all the loans, all the deductions.... It happens very often."[202]

Second, variations in allowances among agencies, most especially between third and lower levels, cause a deal of resentment at first and second level, and a concern among third-level staffs to temper that resentment with gifts in cash or kind. These gifts are usually made to subordinates at Christmas; but they are also distributed at other times of the year, through other means, and in other forms. One example is the use representation allowances to pay for subordinates' lunches, and at the BIR these are both regular and often sumptuous affairs.

Third, these supplements, both the official and the unofficial-but-tolerated, look very bad and they can, and do, open the civil service to ridicule. They also run the risk of creating a general sense of indiscipline such that there is, at times, a complete breakdown of routine within the office: children run around; traders are allowed in to sell their food and other wares; and a hum of general conversation soon dominates. All this adds to an atmosphere in which the distinctions between the improper, gray, officially tolerated, and the proper are easily lost.

Conclusions

It has been argued that political interference may be understood in large part (though not entirely) as a remedy for what actors perceive to be a misallocation of authority. Other expressions of circumvention—such as waiving conditions of tenure or failing to reconcile of cash advances—may be viewed in similar terms: either as direct responses to the misallocation of authority; or as avoidance of processes and rules which, in the context of what is felt to be widespread political interference, mask politically motivated actions (such as the manipulation of performance indicators or use of rotation to remove the uncooperative) inimical to the interests of civil servants; or as an attempt to mitigate the difficulties (such as low pay or limited prospects for promotion) which owe at least something to the actions of politicians.

Partly as a consequence of circumvention there build up in offices close-knit groups of staff, some of whom may have political connexions, many of whom have known each other for most of their careers, and among whom there is a general understanding that the boat should not be rocked. It is upon these networks of relationships and their informal conventions that the operation of the office grows more dependent as its casing of formal rules and processes wears thin and becomes less convincing. This is, perhaps, most common and noticeable in local government. In Quezon City Hall's Budget Office, the management of staff is "difficult ... basically because [of] their attitude: 'I'm in government,' they think, 'Government is the one paying my salary, so I can relax.' It is not as strict as the private sector ... they have security of tenure, they don't work so much, they don't work at improving themselves..."[203] The problem is mitigated to some extent by the sheer number of staffs available: "in the private sector you have few people to rely on, [but] in government you have a lot of people to rely on ... so if some of them were not working too hard you go to those who are good ... who are dependable..."[204] Thus the bulk of operations within the office is shouldered by a small clique, and rules and processes are "modified": "it's not really 100 percent [compliance]— it's 60 percent or 70 percent ... and if they deliver then it's okay."[205] And if "when we budget for a particular expense ... some people influence our [decisions, and tell us] ... just expend that expense on another thing ... we have to adjust..."[206] then that's a simple political reality. The camaraderie bred under these conditions is a solace for the stress and drudgery of the job. Equally, however, these groupings dull or inhibit new ideas and practices; and, by making indiscipline seem everyday and tolerable, they camouflage another dimension to these forms of circumvention—corruption.

Notes

1. Cayetano, A. P., Senator, the Philippine Senate, Pasay City, December 19, 2007.
2. Ibid.
3. Ibid.
4. Ibid.
5. Tabino, A., Director, Civil Service Commission, Quezon City, December 18, 2007.
6. All kinds of figures are given which often vary greatly on either side of this estimate. These are probably more symbolic of what is felt to be excessive interference, especially from the Palace. Thus "the president is appointing too much, appointing so many positions, or the appointing power of the president extends even to—I would say—so many, many, many positions. I think she appoints at least a minimum of 2000 positions." (dela Fuente, C., Director, Civil Service Commission, Quezon City, December 4, 2007). Others provide numbers that are five times higher: "I've read a few research papers that say there is way too much discretion in the president to appoint ... she appoints something like 10,000 employees [civil servants] at

the start of his or her term, and I'm referring to GMA [Gloria Macapagal Arroyo] in particular" (Angara, S., Congressman, House of Representatives, Constitution Hill, Quezon City, November 21, 2007).

7. Tabino, A., Director, Civil Service Commission, Quezon City, December 18, 2007.
8. Porio, F., Director, Civil Service Commission, Quezon City, November 21, 2007
9. Tabino, A., Director, Civil Service Commission, Quezon City, December 18, 2007.
10. Ibid.
11. Ibid.
12. Pablo, R.V., Atty. VI, Civil Service Commission, Quezon City, December 17, 2007. The office responsible for passing incoming communications to the Chair puts the number of allegations received directly by the CSC around 25 a year. 'They are [usually] complaining about some employees [who] are not working but [have] a salary; complaining that there is... an arrogant employee; ... that employees are disobedient; that [a boyfriend or husband] has left her for another woman who is already married; or [that] the wife is asking help for benefits ... because these are being given to another woman ... [while] the man also complains that [his] wife is with some other guy who has a higher salary [and yet she is claiming benefits] ... [There are] also complaints about the custody of children... (Cajucom, F., Data Controller IV, Civil Service Commission, Quezon City, November 29, 2007.)
13. Pablo, R.V., Atty. VI, Civil Service Commission, Quezon City, December 17, 2007.
14. Tabino, A., Director, Civil Service Commission, Quezon City, December 18, 2007.
15. Constantino-David, K., Chair, Civil Service Commission, Quezon City, December 27, 2007.
16. Ibid.
17. Pawid, L., Legislative Staff Officer, Office of Senator Gordon, the Philippine Senate, Pasay City, September 17, 2007.
18. Ibid.
19. Constantino-David, K., Chair, Civil Service Commission, Quezon City, December 27, 2007.
20. Source (CSC) requests anonymity.
21. Source requests anonymity, Department of Education.
22. Source (CSC) requests anonymity.
23. The criteria for suitability are qualifications, experience, and training.
24. Source (BOC) requests anonymity.
25. Dela Cruz, G. R. F., OIC [Officer in Charge] (Administrative Division), Environmental Protection and Waste Management Department, Quezon City Hall, Quezon, May 3, 2007.
26. Pablo, R.V., Atty. VI, Civil Service Commission, Quezon City, December 17, 2007.
27. Cayetano, A. P., Senator, the Philippine Senate, Pasay City, December 19, 2007.
28. Pablo, R.V., Atty. VI, Civil Service Commission, Quezon City, December 17, 2007. All that can be done, in the view of some, is to minimize political

interference and its effects: "it cannot be removed." Taroy, C.B., Director, Civil Service Commission, Quezon City, November 29, 2007.

29. Vinzons-Chato, L., Congresswoman, House of Representatives, Constitution Hill, Quezon City, November 27, 2007.

30. de la Fuente, C., Director, Civil Service Commission, Quezon City, December 4, 2007.

31. Abad, J., Chief of Staff, Senator Aquino, B., the Philippine Senate, Pasay City, December 19, 2007. A very similar point is made by officials of the Secretariat of the CSC who prepare and check the papers for the Commission's weekly board meetings. "In ... law, an agency should have, [say], only two undersecretary's—but the president appoints three more, and that creates a dysfunction in the organization because the three political appointees would have to create staff for each of them and that [requires] more resources... " (Fernandez, M.T.C., Director, Civil Service Commission, Quezon City, November 22, 2007).

32. Galvan, J.G., Assistant Secretary, Department of Education, Pasig City, October 8, 2007.

33. Joson, L.G., OIC (HRMD [Human Resources and Management Department], Planning), Department of Education, Pasig City, September 10, 2007.

34. Escudero, F., Senator, the Philippine Senate, Pasay City, 19 December 2007.

35. For example, "opposition congressmen who voted for the impeachment of the president in the 13th Congress ... didn't have any development assistance fund released to them.... Even the regular budgets for those districts were not released. So if you have no development in your district, you worry about where you're going to get the funds. But I know that some of the opposition congressmen had access to overseas development assistance funds, so they tapped them; [and] NGOs had the funds available, they could undertake projects in their district—[these] were the source of their projects" (Vinzons-Chato, L., Congresswoman, House of Representatives, Constitution Hill, Quezon City, November 27, 2007).

36. Urquiola, P., Chief of Staff, Senator Honasan, G., the Philippine Senate, Pasay City, 12 December 2007.

37. Ibid.

38. Constantino-David, K., Chair, Civil Service Commission, Quezon City, December 27, 2007.

39. Villalon-Rodgers, L., Atty., Assistant Commissioner, Bureau of Internal Revenue, Quezon City, October 3, 2007.

40. Vinzons-Chato, L., Congresswoman, House of Representatives, Constitution Hill, Quezon City, November 27, 2007.

41. Umbac, S., Chief (Legislative Liaison), Civil Service Commission, Quezon City, December 7, 2007.

42. Vinzons-Chato, L., Congresswoman, House of Representatives, Constitution Hill, Quezon City, November 27, 2007.

43. Inocentes, A., Undersecretary, Department of Education, Pasig City, October 1, 2007.

44. Vinzons-Chato, L., Congresswoman , House of Representatives, Constitution Hill, Quezon City, November 27, 2007.

45. Abad, J., Chief of Staff, Senator Aquino, B., the Philippine Senate, Pasay City, December 19, 2007.
46. Urquiola, P., Chief of Staff, Senator Honasan, G., the Philippine Senate, Pasay City, 12 December, 2007.
47. Ibid.
48. Abad, J., Chief of Staff, Senator Aquino, B., the Philippine Senate, Pasay City, December 19, 2007.
49. Tanada III, L.R., Congressman, House of Representatives, Constitution Hill, Quezon City, November 27, 2007.
50. Ibid.
51. Angara, S., Congressman, House of Representatives, Constitution Hill, Quezon City, November 21, 2007.
52. Ibid.
53. Rodriguez-Zaldarriaga, A., Congresswoman, House of Representatives, Constitution Hill, Quezon City, December 4, 2007.
54. Urquiola, P., Chief of Staff, Senator Honasan, G., the Philippine Senate, Pasay City, 12 December, 2007.
55. Abad, J., Chief of Staff, Senator Aquino, B., the Philippine Senate, Pasay City, December 19, 2007.
56. Sarmiento, J., Personnel Specialist II, Civil Service Commission, Quezon City, November 22, 2007.
57. Urquiola, P., Chief of Staff, Senator Honasan, G., the Philippine Senate, Pasay City, 12 December 2007.
58. Rodriguez-Zaldarriaga, A., Congresswoman, House of Representatives, Constitution Hill, Quezon City, December 4, 2007.
59. Angara, S., Congressman, House of Representatives, Constitution Hill, Quezon City, November 21, 2007.
60. Cayetano, A. P., Senator, the Philippine Senate, Pasay City, December 19, 2007.
61. Vinzons-Chato, L., Congresswoman, House of Representatives, Constitution Hill, Quezon City, November 27, 2007.
62. Roldan, J., Assistant Commissioner, Bureau of Internal Revenue, Quezon City, October 9, 2007.
63. Dulce, V.H., Deputy Director, *Bangko Sentral Ng Pilipinas* (Central Bank of the Philippines), Malate, September 18, 2007.
64. Urquiola, P., Chief of Staff, Senator Honasan, G., the Philippine Senate, Pasay City, 12 December 2007.
65. Roldan, J., Assistant Commissioner, Bureau of Internal Revenue, Quezon City, October 9, 2007.
66. Urquiola, P., Chief of Staff, Senator Honasan, G., the Philippine Senate, Pasay City, 12 December 2007.
67. Ibid.
68. Vinzons-Chato, L., Congresswoman, House of Representatives, Constitution Hill, Quezon City, November 27, 2007. A time to "collect" refers partly to "votes, votes, votes. I took care of you, I gave you jobs—that's what they'll tell them at election time. I gave you jobs" (Fernandez, M.T.C., Director, Civil Service Commission, Quezon City, November 22, 2007); and partly to other kinds of favors such as money, information, and an influence over decisions and spending which "these people cannot refuse them, because

they already got the favor from them [the politician]." Sarmiento, J., Personnel Specialist II, Civil Service Commission, Quezon City, November 22, 2007.

69. Constantino-David, K., Chair, Civil Service Commission, Quezon City, December 27, 2007.

70. Urquiola, P., Chief of Staff, Senator Honasan, G., the Philippine Senate, Pasay City, 12 December 2007.

71. At least this was so under Chair Constantino-David.

72. Constantino-David, K., Chair, Civil Service Commission, Quezon City, December 27, 2007

73. The Ombudsman, however, is often the preferred instrument for investigation and prosecution. The reasons for this are set out later in this chapter.

74. de la Fuente, C., Director, Civil Service Commission, Quezon City, December 4, 2007.

75. Source (Clerk II, Quezon City) requests anonymity.

76. Source (Lower House) requests anonymity.

77. Vinzons-Chato, L., Congresswoman, House of Representatives, Constitution Hill, Quezon City, November 27, 2007.

78. Source (BOC) requests anonymity.

79. Porio, F., Director, Civil Service Commission, Quezon City, November 21, 2007.

80. Constantino-David, K., Chair, Civil Service Commission, Quezon City, December 27, 2007.

81. Porio, F., Director, Civil Service Commission, Quezon City, November 21, 2007.

82. de Zuniga, J., Assistant Governor, *Bangko Sentral Ng Pilipinas*, Malate, September 21, 2007.

83. Galvan, J.G., Assistant Secretary, Department of Education, Pasig City, October 8, 2007.

84. Malaya, J., Assistant Secretary, Department of Education, Pasig City, September 27, 2007.

85. Escudero, F., Senator, the Philippine Senate, Pasay City, 19 December 2007.

86. de Zuniga, J., Assistant Governor, *Bangko Sentral Ng Pilipinas*, Malate, September 21, 2007.

87. Source (BOC) requests anonymity.

88. Porio, F. Director, Civil Service Commission, Quezon City, November 21, 2007.

89. Umbac, S., Chief (Legislative Liaison Division), Civil Service Commission, Quezon City, December 7, 2007.

90. Quijano, Y., Director, Department of Education, Pasig City, September 25, 2007.

91. Angara, S., Congressman, House of Representatives, Constitution Hill, Quezon City, November 21, 2007. These frequent changes also mean that among the Secretary and third-level staffs "the trust would be different … then you would have to explain…" and justify plans and programs all over again (Benito, N.V., Director, Department of Education, Pasig City, September 24, 2007).

92. Source (CSC) requests anonymity.
93. Source (CSC) requests anonymity.
94. Source (BOC) requests anonymity.
95. Costes, V.C., Chief Personnel Specialist, Civil Service Commission, Quezon City, November 22, 2007.
96. Source (BOC) requests anonymity.
97. Anquilan, R., Director, Bureau of Customs, Manila, September 7, 2007.
98. Source (Quezon City Hall) requests anonymity. This kind of mantra is commonly repeated in the central offices of national government agencies and at the higher levels: "For myself, I have not gotten any endorsement. But I think that it would be a very great help if you really have endorsements; and in my experience right now I find it very difficult to be promoted to the next highest ... position; it would be very hard for us to get a deputy commissioner because ... I don't know if it's just *chizmiz* [gossip] ... but we really need to have an endorsement coming from influential political persons to get a promotion. Because, in my experience, I didn't really have any endorsement, it's always based on merit, and it has always been my immediate superiors who have pushed for my promotion. But there are a lot of people, really, who have been depending upon political endorsements" (King, C., Atty., Assistant Commissioner, Bureau of Internal Revenue, Quezon City, October 4, 2007).
99. Source (Quezon City Hall) requests anonymity.
100. Source (BOC) requests anonymity.
101. Source (CSC) requests anonymity.
102. Porio, F., Director, Civil Service Commission, Quezon City, November 21, 2007.
103. Porio, M. T. A., Director, Civil Service Commission, Quezon City, 28 November, 2007.
104. de la Fuente, C., Director, Civil Service Commission, Quezon City, December 4, 2007.
105. Ibid.
106. De Lumen , B.R., Administrative Assistant II, Civil Service Commission, November 27, 2007.
107. Inciong, T., Assistant Secretary, Department of Education, Pasig City, September 25, 2007.
108. Lazaro, E., Chief, Bureau of Customs, Manila, May 4, 2007.
109. Ibid.
110. Bacani, R.C., Undersecretary, Department of Education, Pasig City, September 24, 2007.
111. Dela Cruz, G. R. F., OIC (Administrative Division), Environmental Protection and Waste Management Department, Quezon City Hall, Quezon, May 3, 2007.
112. Guinigundo, D., Deputy Governor, *Bangko Sentral Ng Pilipinas*, Malate, September 28, 2007.
113. Bacani, R.C. Undersecretary, Department of Education, Pasig City, September 24, 2007.
114. Porio, F., Director, Civil Service Commission, Quezon City, November 21, 2007.
115. Ibid.

116. San Pablo, O.M., Chief (Accounting), Department of Education, Pasig City, October 9, 2007.
117. Guinigundo, D., Deputy Governor, *Bangko Sentral Ng Pilipinas*, Malate, September 28., 2007.
118. Porio, F., Director, Civil Service Commission, Quezon City, November 21, 2007.
119. Lazaro, E., Chief, Bureau of Customs, Manila, May 4, 2007.
120. Source (CSC) requests anonymity.
121. Gocon-Gragasin, N., Director, Civil Service Commission, Quezon City, December 7, 2007.
122. Ibid. Combined with limited openings for advancement and routine duties, such an attitude nurtures much despondency among first and second-level staff: "I've been here [in the CSC] for more than 16 years.... Now I feel that my job has become very routine and that there is no hope for promotion. I am now a taking a Masters with the hope of getting a promotion ... Accounting ... is for me ... mostly routine.... [We are] confined to mostly processing claims and vouchers and completing reports....We are using an electronic accounting system so every transaction we have to encode into the system. So collections and disbursements use the system. Although there are some transactions that require us to be analytical, it has generally become less challenging to me. I hope that, with my Masters degree, I hope that I will be given the chance to be given tasks that are more challenging.... I was trying to persuade my directors to transfer me to another item [position]—to, say, the budget division, but what they did was ... transfer the general fund which I was handling ... to another person and gave me another fund to handle. [But] I want to be somebody who is no longer confined to working [on] papers or processing papers, financial papers. What I want to do is to encourage people, inspire people, to train people ... I enjoy doing that." Source (Administrative Officer, CSC) requests anonymity.
123. As noted at the beginning of section 2 of this chapter, the precise limits of authority to make appointments are often unclear.
124. Gocon-Gragasin, N., Director, Civil Service Commission, Quezon City, December 7, 2007.
125. These are employees without official designation and who appear only to collect their salaries on the fifteenth and thirtieth of the month.
126. Source (CSC) requests anonymity.
127. Source (CSC) requests anonymity.
128. Ibid.
129. Barba, M.C., Chief Personnel Specialist, Civil Service Commission, Quezon City, November 27, 2007.
130. Galvan, J.G., Assistant Secretary, Department of Education, Pasig City, October 8, 2007.
131. Constantino-David, K., Chair, Civil Service Commission, Quezon City, December 27, 2007.
132. de Zuniga, J., Assistant Governor, *Bangko Sentral Ng Pilipinas*, Malate, September 21, 2007.
133. The interviewee is referring to vouchers (commonly worth 300 and 500 pesos) bought to "re-load" pay-as-you-go mobile 'phone accounts.

134. Agamata, L., Director, Civil Service Commission, Quezon City, December 6, 2007.
135. That is to say, salaries seem low given the aspirations seeded by the emphasis on educational qualifications and by salaries in the private sector.
136. Source (Department of Education) requests anonymity.
137. Indeed, it is very rare for civil servants in any agency to receive a poor performance rating: two consecutive poor ratings are sufficient grounds to dismiss a tenured official.
138. Gocon-Gragasin, N., Director, Civil Service Commission, Quezon City, December 7, 2007.
139. Galvan, J.G., Assistant Secretary, Department of Education, Pasig City, October 8, 2007.
140. Porio, F., Director, Civil Service Commission, Quezon City, November 21, 2007.
141. Dino, M.T., Supervising Personnel Specialist, Civil Service Commission, Quezon City, November 21, 2007.
142. Porio, F., Director, Civil Service Commission, Quezon City, November 21, 2007. Disquiet at first and second level is indeed widespread in the CSC: "We meet once a month in the office with our directors to discuss what is going on, and we use this opportunity to say what we have in our minds, and ... there is an issue about the performance evaluation system. Because some members of our office are members of [the union], and they were asking not to have the system implemented.... We said we didn't understand the PMS [Performance Management System] and we were clamoring for its deferment; and the directors told us that the Chair was angry. We said that it is not that we are against its implementation, we are just asking for its deferment..." Source (Administrative Officer, CSC) requests anonymity.
143. Source (Quezon City Hall) requests anonymity.
144. Source (Budget Office, Quezon City Hall) requests anonymity.
145. Cuevas, A, Administrative Officer, Civil Service Commission, Quezon City, December 14, 2007.
146. Ibid.
147. Dinsay, Z.F., Chief Personnel Specialist, Civil Service Commission, Quezon City, December 10, 2007.
148. Lopez-Espejo, C., Supervising Personnel Specialist, Civil Service Commission, Quezon City, December 6, 2007.
149. Taron, R., Chief (Collection Enforcement), Bureau of Internal Revenue, Quezon City, October 5, 2007.
150. Ibid.
151. Barba, M.C., Chief Personnel Specialist, Civil Service Commission, Quezon City, November 27, 2007.
152. Lopez-Espejo, C., Supervising Personnel Specialist, Civil Service Commission, Quezon City, December 6, 2007.
153. Duncano, D., Deputy Commissioner, Bureau of Internal Revenue, Quezon City, October 9, 2007.
154. Porio, F., Director, Civil Service Commission, Quezon City, November 21, 2007.
155. Lim, C., Atty., Assistant Commissioner, Bureau of Internal Revenue, Quezon City, October 10, 2007.

156. Cosca, E., Head Revenue Executive Assistant to Assistant Commissioner, Bureau of Internal Revenue, Quezon City, October 2, 2007.

157. Taron, R., Chief (Collection Enforcement), Bureau of Internal Revenue, Quezon City, October 5, 2007.

158. Ibid.

159. Cosca, E., Head Revenue Executive Assistant to Assistant Commissioner, Bureau of Internal Revenue, Quezon City, October 2, 2007.

160. Silubrico, I.J.F., Supervising Personnel Specialist, Civil Service Commission, Quezon City, November 27, 2007.

161. Porio, F., Director, Civil Service Commission, Quezon City, November 21, 2007.

162. Duncano, D., Deputy Commissioner, Bureau of Internal Revenue, Quezon City, October 9, 2007.

163. It can be hard enough even when moving between offices within an agency: "When I first came into the civil service I was assigned to the international affairs office.... I had a close friend there because she is my seat neighbour, my office mate.... We get to talk a lot about relationships and the family and domestic concerns, and we had similar lives ... so we became close. But when we were reorganized, and I got to be transferred ... when I came in [to the Commission Secretariat] it was already later in my career ... people [had] already established their loyalties.... Some of my office mates [had] established personal relationships among their families because, like, when a female employer delivers [the baby] and she gets a friend [in the office] to become the godmother ... and that brings them closer, and then they exchange gifts during Christmas. But in my case when I came in I had already three kids and I had them baptized already, so there was no opportunity for me to get her [god]parents from among my office mates. So there are no longer intimate personal relationships [with my office mates]. Sarmiento, J., Personnel Specialist II, Civil Service Commission, Quezon City, November 22, 2007.

164. Abad, J., Chief of Staff, Senator Aquino, B., the Philippine Senate, Pasay City, December 19, 2007.

165. Constantino-David, K., Chair, Civil Service Commission, Quezon City, December 27, 2007.

166. Source (CSC) requests anonymity.

167. Ibid.

168. Source (CSC) requests anonymity.

169. Ibid.

170. Tabino, A., Director, Civil Service Commission, Quezon City, December 18, 2007.

171. Galvan, J.G., Assistant Secretary, Department of Education, Pasig City, October 8, 2007.

172. Ibid.

173. Ibid.

174. Lim, C., Atty., Assistant Commissioner, Bureau of Internal Revenue, Quezon City, October 10, 2007.

175. Ibid.

176. Ibid.

177. Constantino-David, K., Chair, Civil Service Commission, Quezon City, December 27, 2007.

178. Gocon-Gragasin, N., Director, Civil Service Commission, Quezon City, December 7, 2007.
179. Dino, M.T., Supervising Personnel Specialist, Civil Service Commission, Quezon City, November 21, 2007.
180. Quijano, Y., Director, Department of Education, Pasig City, September 25, 2007.
181. Naz, M.T.N., Chief (Research and Statistics Division), Civil Service Commission, Quezon City, December 19, 2007.
182. Gocon-Gragasin, N., Director, Civil Service Commission, Quezon City, December 7, 2007.
183. Roldan, J., Assistant Commissioner, Bureau of Internal Revenue, Quezon City, October 9, 2007.
184. Duncano, D., Deputy Commissioner, Bureau of Internal Revenue, Quezon City, October 9, 2007.
185. This includes the development of manuals by officers with long experience in complex field investigations. An example is the newly created Policy Cases Division, part of whose remit is the production of manuals to help guide the entire Bureau on the auditing of particular industries. Bongaling, N., Assistant Chief (Policy Cases Division), Bureau of Internal Revenue, Quezon City, October 4, 2007.
186. Roldan, J., Assistant Commissioner, Bureau of Internal Revenue, Quezon City, October 9, 2007.
187. Duncano, D., Deputy Commissioner, Bureau of Internal Revenue, Quezon City, October 9, 2007.
188. Lazaro, E., Chief, Bureau of Customs, Manila, May 4, 2007.
189. Ibid.
190. Escudero, F., Senator, the Philippine Senate, Pasay City, 19 December 2007.
191. Atty. Ligon, R., OIC (Post Entry Audit Group), Assistant Commissioner, Bureau of Customs, Manila, September 7, 2007. Very similar comments can also be made of practices in the BIR's collection and enforcement division.
192. Dulce, V., Assistant Director, *Bangko Sentral Ng Pilipinas*, Malate, September 18, 2007; De Zuniga, J. Assistant Governor, *Bangko Sentral Ng Pilipinas*, Malate, September 21, 2007; Guinegundo, D., Deputy Governor, *Bangko Sentral Ng Pilipinas*, Malate, September 28, 2007.
193. Tabino, A., Director, Civil Service Commission, Quezon City, December 18, 2007.
194. Source (CSC) requests anonymity.
195. Ibid.
196. Ibid.
197. Galvan, J.G., Assistant Secretary, Department of Education, Pasig City, October 8, 2007.
198. Roldan, J., Assistant Commissioner, Bureau of Internal Revenue, Quezon City, October 9, 2007.
199. Source (CSC) requests anonymity.
200. Source (Quezon City Hall) requests anonymity.
201. Source (Assistant Commissioner, Bureau of Internal Revenue) requests anonymity.

202. Lorenzo, M., Assistant Commissioner, Bureau of Internal Revenue, Quezon City, October 5, 2007.
203. Source (Budget Office, Quezon City Hall) requests anonymity.
204. Ibid.
205. Ibid.
206. Ibid.

3

Corruption and Over-Conformity

Introduction: Corruption

There is no question that, in practice, corruption within the bureaucracy is a problem of both substance and scale: civil servants' and politicians' accounts of political interference (which may often prepare the ground for corruption) and of other activities which are clearly synonymous with corruption (such as channeling public funds illicitly through placements for private ends), are too frequent and consistent to reasonably suggest otherwise. The cases which reach the courts—and which are referred to below—reinforce this point. Not surprisingly, then, representations of a polity and bureaucracy in which corruption is widespread and deep-rooted are pervasive throughout society; and civil servants are only too aware of this.

> Actually, even [for] the ordinary person who [isn't] really engaged in these corrupt activities—that's the majority—there is a sort of the stigma attached to working with the bureau [BIR]; because when ... let's say at a meeting in a school, you are asked to introduce yourself, where you work, when you say "I'm working at the bureau"... the first thing that comes into their minds [is]: "Oh God, this person must be rich!" I think you can see from the lifestyle, you can see [from] the way they dress, that there are really people who obviously, *obviously* [are] spending much more than they earn. So sometimes [colleagues] ... some of them—not me, I'm proud to say that I'm working in the bureau because of the fact that I could help them—but for many of them, they just say "Oh, I'm a government employee." Some would tend to say that."[1]

Critical understandings of government agencies are also commonplace among bureaucrats:

> We once had an exercise here [in the CSC] about trust—where items would be left out. But [we were told] don't touch items belonging to other groups. Only touch your items. [The items were then all mixed up]. We couldn't find our items: there were other items there but we didn't touch them. We did not because we don't do that. We

117

don't get other people's stuff and pass it off as our own. But ... .if this was the Bureau of Customs, or some other god-forsaken agency, we probably would have stolen from them.[2]

Pockets of professionalism are to be found but

I hate to say this ... it is more of an exception than the rule. This is how I would [describe] levels of corruption. There are the blatant ones; then there are those in the middle ground, who are corrupt a little, but not corrupt enough to give the department a bad name; and then there are those who are saints, and whatever you do they will be good; and there are more of those ... how shall I say this? ... who are corrupt through the heart. For example—a government project: if I'm a very honest guy I will not get a single cent in bribes; but ...you [the moderately corrupt civil servant] don't ask me [the businessman] but I give you 20 percent, because that is how business is done. They [the businessmen] are so used to the corruption [that] they have already set aside 10 percent or 20 percent of the project price for the guy who signs the paper. To them, it is no longer whether it is corrupt or not—it is part of business. So they give it to you ... the middle-corrupt guy: "He gave it to me? So he gave it to me! It's not going to affect the project.".... So I think, in my twenty-five years, there are accepted corrupt practices that don't really affect how things are run—they only affect your moral fiber. Because if this thing is okay with you as you grow older, your tolerance level goes up. So I was content with 1 percent now I want to 3 percent, 4 percent, 5 percent, and so on. So there are more [of those] in the middle. Unfortunately, it has become an accepted practice. Of course, there are still those who, whether you give them 1 or 2 or 20,000 pesos, they absolutely won't [take it]. I hate to say it, but they are the exceptions rather than the rule. [3]

Corruption is not only represented as being widespread, but also highly resistant, as in Customs:

...The ombudsman had its own project on integrity; the Presidential Anti-Graft Commission had its own project on integrity; and we are part of what we call the World Customs Organization—which is the organisation of all customs administrations all over the world, and they too have an integrity programme for customs organizations. So at the start we had to develop action plans for WCO, action plans for OMB, action plans for PAGC; but lately, a year ago, we ... consolidated everything because they taught us the same thing. So when I report to WCO I give the same report to OMB and to PAGC. So finally we were able to manage one anti-corruption plan, responding to the requirements of these three organizations.... Tackle individual integrity, then the systems, and then the interrelationship with the stakeholders outside the Bureau of Customs. It is important that these three are looked into all at the same time.... [But] integrity cannot be cured by an action plan.... When we come into the Bureau of Customs we already have our own levels of integrity, and we already have our own values which cannot be changed ... So, in that area of our integrity, [the] plan is just to ... it's not values formation ... it's just a tickling of their values.... So we have regular... values seminars for all personnel at different levels, wherein the discussions mainly focus on ... telling us that "We are from the Bureau of Customs," [that] "these are our responsibilities in so far as the economic development of the country is concerned," [that] "we have a very big role to play and if we do not so this, [then] this is what happens." Something like that. I don't know if this will be effective, because when the seminar is going on everybody claps, everybody's happy, everybody thinks that the seminar is good. But when they go back to their work environment I don't know whether they are still clapping.... But that is the only thing that we can do as far as individuals are concerned.... Of course, it's another thing during the hiring period: we should be able to really establish that that person already has the kind of integrity that we're looking for.... But [that] has already been tried before, many years ago, when a lot of customs personnel were purged ... [and] replaced by new people; [and] the new people who came in were much worse than the people they replaced.... Although the hiring process should be careful ... this we have not been able to do, actually, because a lot of our appointments are political in nature.'[4]

Yet it is also the case that civil servants' representations of corruption are often built from stories circulating among their colleagues and in the media, rather than from direct experience. The civil servant who says, "I don't really know the extent of corruption in these agencies but I know that there [is] corruption in those agencies"[5] is probably more reliable than the clever raconteur. Still more nuanced and complex representations of corruption are also to be found.

If you ask foreign businessmen what their number one complaint about the Philippines is, and why they don't want to do business in the Philippines, corruption would be number five. This is relatively low compared to other more significant concerns they have. Among them would be instability in the political climate and an absence of predictability with respect to the regime governing whatever business they have entered into. Number two would be interference in the courts. Number three would be lack of infrastructure. Number four would be the high cost of [energy]. Corruption would be number five on the list.... It's present in most countries—some tolerable and some intolerable. In the Philippines corruption per se is of course bad. [But] it is intolerable only when policy itself is dictated by corruption. When you talk about a secretary asking for 500 pesos so that she would type up your application form immediately—it's still bad and something the government must address, but it is something which is within tolerable limits in so far as any person doing business in any government agency is concerned; and ... [it] ... is present in most (except probably Singapore)—in most southeast Asian countries. So, to my mind, as far as corruption is concerned, as long as policy is not dictated by corruption, by corrupt motives.... I think it would be tolerable.... Of course it should be eliminated ... [but] it should not be an obsession.... There are other more important things in the general scheme of things that government should address."[6]

Distinctions are also made between officials who take money to keep the wolf from the door, and those who are greedy.

In the village where my mother lives, ten years ago they started paying security guards what lawyers or doctors would get if they start out. So they started paying security guards 15,000 to 20,000—ten years ago. First offence—you get a reprimand. Second offence—you get suspended. Third offence—you're out.... And what happened was—no corruption. Almost none. Everyone follows the law. My driver himself was caught speeding and he said, "What do I do?" I told him "I'll pay it"....I gave him 500. "The next time I'll take it out of your pay." So all of the questions [over corruption]....were all answered by giving them ... standards. One—where they are afraid to lose their job; two—a focus on the job; three—the dignity of working for a living. [These standards] were all put in place.... [But] talk about, for example, the police. Let's say that the lonely policeman basically gets money from traffic violations, [while those] higher up, get it from illegal gambling. Go a little bit higher, and a little bit more extreme—[they] get it from drug money, kidnapping, etc. The lower guys do not make enough to feed their family. They get basically 11,000 to 15,000. You rent in Metro Manila for a family of five for 4,000. Utilities: 1,000. You spend another 6,000 for food. So there is no money for medicine, no money for clothes. The problem is that those higher-ups know that they [the lower downs] get their money from traffic violations, so they can't complain about this guy getting money from illegal gambling. This guy [lower down] can't complain about higher-ups. It messes up the whole system.... So I look at it simplistically, but really.... I've seen staff here basically get sixteen months instead of thirteen months: they get good pay and so on, and you can see the discipline, you can see the pride and work, you can see the overtime without pay, and so on. So in my very simplistic view ... the whole system is messed up, because you take out the dignity in work by not paying them and making bureaucrats beggars and cheaters.... The problems of raising pay and corruption are twinned. The only question is do you stop corruption first and then give them higher pay, or the reverse?... We had a study, a study of the World Bank ... that for every one peso collected from the Philippine government, forty cents goes to corruption.... So 40 percent (500 billion pesos or a little more) of the budget. But there are other studies, or simple computations, that will show that for every pesos collected, two pesos is not collected. I will give you an example from Customs: if you are bringing a billion pesos worth of goods, and duties are 100 million, you won't tell me [the customs official] "I'll pay 80 million, here's 5 million," because [for] the 15 million savings I [the official] will hound you the rest of your life. So you probably pay 30 [to the government], give me [the official] 20, and save 50. So you, at least, save a pesos, [and] give a pesos to government. So really it's a twin problem of raising pay and corruption. [7]

To these distinctions between serious and petty corruption and the gritty matter of hand-to-mouth survival, a further distinction of some importance is added: "I think it would be ... wise to differentiate between corruption in the usual usage, which ... has to do with private gain, from abuse of power—because that's really just bad government. And I think that the problem is bad government rather than corruption per se.... I would say that 80 percent of the people in government are clean. They are, however, party to corruption, because they close their eyes to the 20 percent."[8] This understanding is of some interest because if Constantino-David is right and corruption *is* conflated with the abuse of power, and if the misallocation of authority is conflated with the abuse of power, then the extent of corruption may often be exaggerated. The focusing of corruption may also work to magnify its extent. "If you look at that [corrupt] 20 percent, you will find that the 20 percent are found in very specific vulnerable areas that have been allowed to exist for as long as the head of agency is not clean, or does not have any passion to fight against corruption. You have heads of agencies who are clean but don't care about corruption happening. So it will still go on."[9] Records from the courts seem to confirm these concentrations. It should be said that the materials available are by no means free of uncertainty. Cases are often transferred among the *Sandiganbayan* and other courts, and this is before any appeals are made (and these may end, ultimately, in the Supreme Court); records are fragmented among the various bodies; and spellings and other conventions used to encode data into electronic formats often vary from one official to the next. The politicization of corruption must also cast doubt over the reliability of the raw materials. But with these provisos in mind, records from the *Sandiganbayan* over some thirty years exhibit a number of interesting characteristics.

1. First, corruption (measured by the amount of funds extracted) is heavily concentrated in National Capital Region (figures 1 and 2). However, only 16 percent of the number of offences[10] committed originate in the NCR, some 47 percent are concentrated in Region VII (most especially in Cebu), and the remaining third or so are distributed throughout the rest of the archipelago. These concentrations of expropriated funds in the NCR, and of offences in the regions, may indicate that both public funds and the centre's authority are comparatively thin in the provinces; they also reflect the fact that only a relatively small number of cases are responsible for a disproportionately large share of the funds secured illegally.

Figure 1
Number of Offences and Amounts Involved: by region

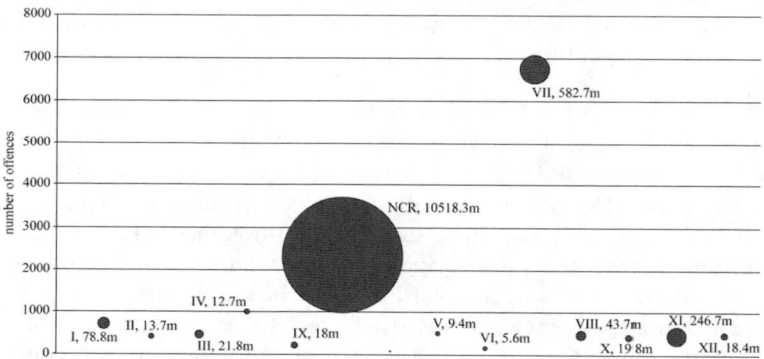

Source: compiled from material provided by the Sandiganbayan, 2007.

Figure 2
Number of Offences and Amounts Involved: by province

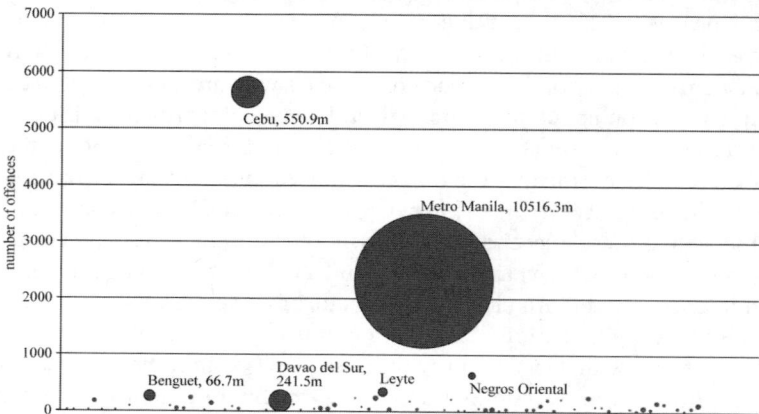

Source: compiled from materials provided by the Sandiganbayan, 2007.

2. This last point is emphasized in figure 3. By far the largest concentrations of corruption (as measured by the share of the total amount of expropriations) are in the private sector (37 percent) and the Office of the President (35 percent). The next largest concentrations are found in: government corporations (8 percent), DOF (6 percent—a figure that also covers the BIR and Customs), DPWH (4 percent), DECS[11] (3 percent), DOLE (Department of Labor and Employment) (2 percent), DENR (Department of Environment and Natural Resources) (2 percent), DILG (Department of the Interior and the Local Government) (1 percent) Constitutional Commissions (1 percent)[12] and DND (Department of National Defence) (1 percent). These agencies and the private sector are responsible for a large share (a little over 90 percent) of expropriated funds and for about 85 percent of offences. However, some 63 percent of all offences are concentrated in the DPWH (38 percent), the DOF (19 percent), the DILG (11 percent) and Constitutional Commissions (5 percent) who, together, account for only 12 percent of expropriated funds; whereas only 9 percent of offences and some 80 percent of expropriated funds are accounted for by the private sector, the Office of the President, and government corporations. Put another way, most government agencies (with the exception of the DPWH, DOF, DILG, Constitutional Commissions, government corporations and the Office of the President) are responsible for only a very modest share of offences and for the expropriation of a still smaller proportion of funds.

Figure 3
Number of Offences and Amounts Involved: by agency

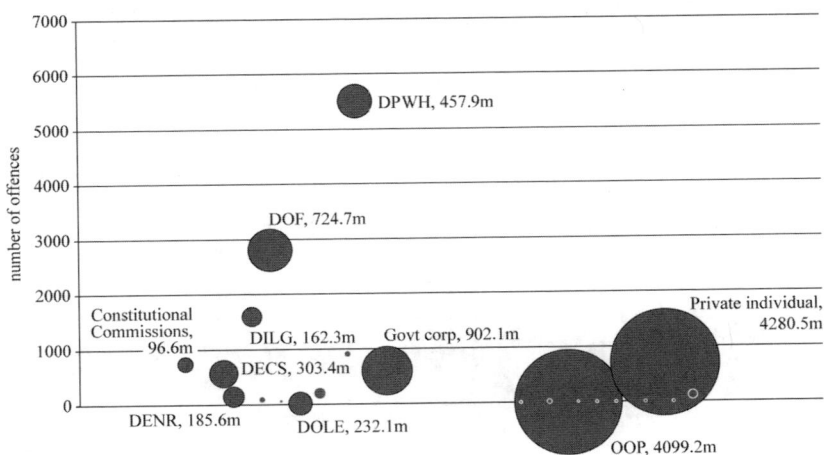

Source: compiled from materials provided by the Sandiganbayan, 2007.

3. The imbalance between the number of offences and share of expropriations is also reflected in figure 4. Only very few of the offences committed involve large—or, in some cases, huge—sums of money. Most offences involve only very small (if any) sums of money; most convicted officials are each responsible for only a small number of offences; and while some officials commit multiple offences, they are usually responsible for the expropriation of only a small proportion of funds. For example, in the DOF and DECS there is a clear concentration of expropriated funds in few hands, while other officials are responsible for a large number of cases involving only small or modest sums (Appendix XV and XVI). There are exceptions, as in the DPWH, where the reverse is broadly true: officials involved in large number of cases are also responsible of a large share of the funds. But in general, offences and expropriated funds are concentrated in the hands of relatively few officials; and these officials—those responsible for a large share of offences, and those responsible for a large share of expropriations—form quite separate groups.

4. Corruption (as measured by the number of offences) is also concentrated in certain posts within agencies: those which carry responsibility for financial management (accountants, audit, budgeting, treasury, collection, examiners), or for constant or frequent contact with public (such as principals and teachers), or for the implementation of projects funded by government but tendered out to private companies (Figure 4). And while it is those officials at the upper reaches of the bureaucratic and political hierarchy who extract the largest sums of money, some mid-level and lower-level officials have also amassed personal fortunes. This is especially clear in DECS (Appendix XV).

Figure 4
Number of Offences and Amounts Involved: by position

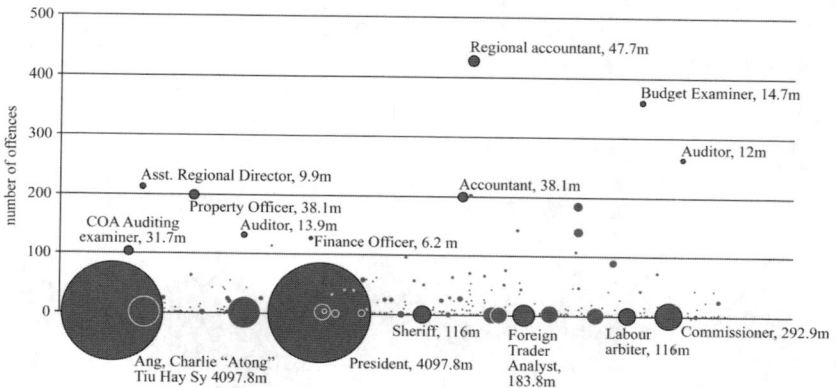

Source: compiled from materials provided by the Sandiganbayan, 2007.
Note: each bubble represents one official

Overall, then, corruption (as measured by the sums extracted) is concentrated geographically, and in the private sector and the Office of the President; while the number of offences are focused in a small number of agencies (most especially in the regions) staffed by civil servants. Throughout government more generally, most convicted civil servants are responsible for a small number of offences in which only small sums of money are involved.

It must be recognized that these figures are only indicative: the extent of corruption will be greater than they suggest. But it is also possible to see why, whatever its true extent, the prevalence of corruption may be greatly magnified. Officials responsible for large numbers of offences (usually involving the extraction of fairly small or modest sums of money) occupy sensitive positions which form a nexus of interactions either with other civil servants within an agency or with the citizenry. Most offices within an agency will have to deal with those officials handling budgets and disbursements; officials with technical expertise and engaged in projects which are government-funded but tendered out to private businesses, will have frequent dealings with those businesses; while officials in revenue-collecting agencies, and teaching and uniformed staffs in agencies delivering public services, will have still more regular contact with citizens. If only a few officials at these nexus commit multiple offences, news of their behavior will quickly spread, and the number of officials implicated will (in the minds of their colleagues and among citizens) quickly multiply.

> It's like this. We have institutionalised the taxpayer's assistance section—that is the office where we are most exposed to the public. When you get a tax identification number, [when] you need to ask something ... anything about taxation, [when] you just need to get forms, you go to that section of the district office. We have training for these people, the Officers of the Day.... [When I was revenue district officer] I regularly met these people: "So you're the Officer of the Day for this month (we have a schedule): Please be courteous to the taxpayers. If they shout at you don't respond in kind!" ... We really have that—that is why [you are Officer of the Day] only for one day, because you can't take two days of aggravation. Taxation—it is not easy to get money from people.... All I'm saying is that, on this front line we train them, we remind them ... to be courteous, compute the correct tax, do not do anything bad. But there are people who will try to do something that will benefit them: a taxpayer would ask for a computation, and [the taxpayer asks].... "What can you do to help me reduce this?"... And they may start talking about something for the benefit of the examiner. And what's bad is that from the very beginning...he should not pay the original amount—it was bloated by the examiner. And that happens all over.... I'm not saying that happens in *all* offices but it could happen in any office of the bureau. And we have ... offices all over the country ... and there are

365 days in one year. So the probability of that happening is large. So if it happens, every act [is] ... told as a story by this taxpayer to another person: it [the story] would travel all over. There is [now] a negative perception, and those people having dealt with the bureau personnel would have a negative perception: they would [say] "Next time we can do deals with some people in the bureau." That's fine if these are only individual taxpayers, because they don't have to go to the bureau [very often]. What's bad is if it has also become a practice with the tax practitioners—meaning accountants who handle accounts of businesses.... What if this accountant has this experience that he can reduce his taxes by just making deals with these people [in the bureau], with these examiners, and he [represents] a hundred taxpayers? What's the effect on the collection? It's really big. In fact ... if you multiply that a hundred times [because he represents a hundred taxpayers], and a hundred practitioners, that's 10,000 taxpayers.[13]

In local government, too, certain offices have extensive and frequent contact with the public, such that the corrupt practices of a small number of officials will quickly become common knowledge among citizens. That they seem so blasé about it all, and do not seem to care who finds out, makes their behavior seem all the more astonishing and exasperating: 'The Chair's own child said she went to see the division that gives permanent building permits—[a] section of an LGU in Quezon City. And the officer said, "I need 50,000 pesos," and he did not know that it is the Chair's son. So the Chair called up and said "What are you doing? You cannot deny this? It's my very own child who told me that you want 50,000 pesos."[14]

The damage done in this way by a comparatively small number of officials to the reputation of agency, bureaucracy, and government is exacerbated by those few civil servants who stockpile huge sums for themselves; by the politicization of corruption and a determination to make allegation and counter-allegation through the media; by attempts to compensate for the perceived misallocation of power; and by the formation of closed groups of civil servants with limited experience of government beyond their office and among whom speculation and suspicion of the world outside has taken hold. Thus the feeling that corruption is endemic, that it entangles most civil servants, and that it is a normal part of 'the system', deepens. Representations of corruption snowball as stories of all kinds of practices are conflated. Greed and the outright theft of public money and materials; bribery; the exercise of improper influence on decision-making within the civil service; attempts to breach divisions of authority; legitimate political pressure and bargaining; compromise; differences in interpretation; mistakes, inefficiency; ignorance; slowness to act; poor judgment; missed opportunities and unsuccessful competition: all are frequently amalgamated.

"Corruption the representation" may be at least as pernicious as "corruption the practice." First, corruption is now expected and is made the preferred explanation for any problem or fault or matter of disapproval. Secondly, it may erode civil servants' resistance to corruption: 'Most of the time—I think it is less a conscious perspective, you know—"I might as well be on the take myself" as people ... who are not ... part of the corruption are ridiculed in corruption-endemic agencies.... The pressure on them is so strong because everyone knows they may be the whistleblowers."[15] Thirdly, it re-focuses attention and energies on the search and prevention of corruption rather than on raising the general competency of governance and on identifying and propagating existing strengths.

Over-Conformity, Proliferation, and Layering

Through its various manifestations—including political interference, the avoidance of the appointments' procedures and conditions of tenure, limited rotation, poor training, low pay, attempts to supplement income, and corruption—the circumvention of rules, process and divisions of authority brings uncertainty and unpredictability to practice; it also helps to initiate or reinforce (and may, in return, draw energy from) other notable features of the bureaucracy—over-conformity, a proliferation of agencies, and the layering of rules and process.

Over-Conformity

It is partly in response to the perceived misallocation of authority and to the circumvention of processes through which authority is apportioned and other government business is conducted, that efforts are made to establish new rules. An example is the case of the Civil Service Commission's attempts (through sympathetic representatives in Congress) to introduce legislation to restrict to 50 percent the proportion of staff within an agency at third level who may be appointed by the Office of the President.

An alternative response is to apply existing frameworks more rigorously. For example, the Manual of Qualifications and Standards—which helps defend the authority of the civil service over appointments—is inordinately detailed and, all too often, treated as absolute. This is widely acknowledged, even by staffs who draw up the Manual and who advise agencies on its implementation and interpretation:

> ...In 2003 we came out with ... revised policies on qualification standards.... We opened our door to new ideas. [For example] division chief appointments: usually we will require a Masters degree; but ... we ... now consider that those holding third-level eligibility can be appointed to division chief positions even without Master's degree. But [there remains] ... rigidity. We are boxed. We are contained in this box: we have to look at basic and minimum requirements, such

127

as education and training, eligibility and experience.... Of course there are other areas to look into, for example, personality traits [and] performance.... But despite our [attempt to make] our policies [less] rigid, people still tend to look at it as being formatted.[16]

The appetite to counter the circumvention of rules and procedure is sharpened by the poor reputation of government and by what are felt by some politicians and civil servants (especially at third level) to be poor levels of competence and sophistication among bureaucrats in general. So often, when seen from its upper echelons or from Congress, a department's response appears to be either slow or haphazard or unexpected—for "there are times when they interpret [rules and procedures] for their own convenience."[17] The complaint is a common one:

> ...When you make policy, and the theory and the rationality behind it is perfectly clear, and it's issued and it is sent down to the divisions, even the manner of sending it down takes time.... Our project just got scattered. It was supposed to solve our manner of sending down decisions, memorandum orders, and circulars to the field. But our problem is [that] once it gets down to the field, it's rewritten [by civil servants] in their own form ... and the signature is changed to the superintendent's or regional director's; and I don't know why they do it! ... And then their implementation is sometimes different or totally different from the rationale or justification which came from above. That is a problem.[18]

Strict observance of rules and process, and severely restricted discretion, may not be ideal but it is—or so some believe—the best that *this* bureaucracy is able to achieve. It may be slow and awkward as a result, but at least it can be relied on. And this is generally true, even of Education. As one Under-secretary puts it, "...the strength of the organization lies in the fact that it is very hierarchical....You want certain things done, you can rely on this structure to help you implement these plans.... Teachers are very obedient in the sense that, because of their training and experience ... [and because of the] obedience they expect from their students ... you can get them to do certain things, you can rely on them to follow whatever you have instructed them to do."[19] After all, without compliance within the service more generally (and all the way down to local government) "...we wouldn't have existed for a hundred years.... There are deviants but on the whole things work more or less as they should work."[20]

Over-conformity is also, perversely, a concomitant of an emphasis on personal trust at the highest levels of government. There is much variation amongst heads of agency: there are those who are intensely loyal to the appointing authority; there are those who feel no obligation to the Office of the President or who, even if they do, will not allow the organization to be subverted by the Office; and then there are those who are compromise appointments, and those who the President may prefer were not there at all. But, for the most part, the general atmosphere will be one of expected obedience: heads of agencies are to deliver to the President who, they can be sure, will be looking over their shoulder: "...every president will have to have in his own men who sing the same tune ... in fact the President is very strong on that—if my Cabinet member does not sing the same tune then he is free to go."[21] At the same time, heads of agencies are faced with what are often huge departments in which there are—save the small group they gather around themselves—few people in whom they feel they can have much faith. There is, therefore, a deal of pressure to ensure that subordinates in the department will conform. The philosophy of executive government, then, is straightforward:

> Once you have ... a common agenda, you have too implemented strictly.... You get your own people to manage the departments, people you rely on and trust; and you effectively pursue what you have agreed to do. Let's say, the Senator, after inauguration, says "Okay, Luis. You are in charge of BIR. Here are the guidelines of what we are supposed to be doing...implement them."... You get your team, you get your talent in.... The bureaucracy is there to deliver basic services from the executive who is elected by the people. Following that line, they [civil servants] have their independence. It's based on the basic [assumption] that they are supposed to be professionals, they have to be qualified, you know—the basics. Once they have passed that part of the civil service exam. They are then the bureaucrat, the director. [But] a new government comes in: this is the platform we won on; you [the civil servant] implement it.
> ...You start it on day one ... you get a majority, and then you try to convince the rest [of the civil service] of the wisdom of your decision. You give them a voice, let them express themselves.... You give them something to do, and once they've achieved something, you give them a pat on the back. Here is the policy, what you think? There is a debate, there is discussion. We come to an agreement about what is to be done. If you don't agree? Sorry, it's up to you! You can help out or ... if you don't like it, you can resign. This is the policy, this is what we all agree, this is the majority. Don't stand in the way: we are a democracy.... We know that people in the country are hungry, so sometimes we get mad. You can't explain all the time, you sometimes just have to do. We can't persuade everyone that we have a mandate and we should deliver. That's how it is.[22]

The officer, then, must learn their place and keep to it. There is some room for debate without risking marginalization, dismissal, or transfer. But, "...as they say, freedom has always a cost. That, for me, is always at the back of my mind. So if my bosses don't agree with, or don't like, my ideas, they can either boot me out or put me in the freezer. So I think I am pretty much aware of those consequences...″[23] Deference and obedience is for the most part expected.... There is the boss, so [it] is only up to a certain extent that you can argue with him. You'd be lucky if you have a boss that asks your opinion, and I'm happy that our bosses are like that. There are some areas wherein he speaks with authority, and therefore we would rather not talk with him about it, because he would know.... When we talk about pushing a [piece of] legislation, if he says this he says that, I follow it. But ... I do my homework, I ... complete [the] staff work; everything is ready so all he has to do is approve it. So in a sense my influence on him is considerable. But when he says something, everybody should shut up.″[24] As for *his* subordinates:

> I try to listen as much as possible because no one has a monopoly of ideas. But there will be sometimes when I have to insist, because I notice that in this department we do have some activities that cost a lot of money but have no impact. So I always tell my staff if we are going to do a project it better have some impact.... Like ... culture—I'm handling culture.... We have this commemoration, Quezon day.... They [the department's officials] ... do the same activities over and over again, bringing twenty teachers, thirty teachers for a seminar. I feel this has no impact. It's a big bureaucracy, so what is the use of [it]?... Let the National Historical Institute do the wreath-laying and the flag-raising. Our role is to educate. So, for example, next month is consumer education month, and you know that consumer education is an important.... People ... should know how to buy, what products to buy, and what laws to follow when they buy stuff. So...I was telling them, "What is the use of having activities with 100 people or 200 people? Let's produce teaching manuals on consumer education." So I talked to the Department of Trade and Industry—they are the experts in consumer education. We talked together, we developed teaching materials. It's been validated in schools, and next year we will send copies to all teachers ... so they can teach consumer education. That I had to insist [on] because it had never crossed their minds. The people I talk to who have been doing all these things over and over again never even thought of producing teaching manuals on consumer education. Those are the times when I insist.′[25]

3. Rules and process, when strictly observed and treated as absolutes, may only encourage further rounds of evasive practice which may, in turn, be formalized. One example is an attempt, through executive order,[26] to sanctify what had become (certainly under the Arroyo administration) the convention and expectation (on the part of the Office of the President) that civil servants should not comply with any summons from the legislature to attend hearings in which they may be questioned on matters sensitive to the President. The anger and exasperation was palpable, even in the most serene:

We asked for the documents—they don't give them. We asked them to show up at investigations, and they don't show up. They only show up to ask for their budget and to give confirmation. Given that we are co-equal branches, it is really just rude. It is complete disrespect and disregard for the authority of a coequal branch, and it is just saying "We can get away with it, we don't want to go and participate." It is making the Senate into a weak institution, and that is not a good thing. And so you get this— I mean, even for non-controversial bills. We chaired the committee on local government, and we had a hearing on ... the depository banks of local government units and posting their sources of revenue in public places. You can't imagine anything less harmful than those two bills. Yet no one from the DILG came.... It is as if they don't want to have any relationship with the legislature.... I will say that between the Senate and the executive—it is a very tenuous relationship.... I mean, it is rude, it is as if they are saying the Senate does not matter. That is not how you should treat half of Congress.[27]

Absolutes may also be more prone to manipulation. An example is the use of the Ombudsman. It was noted earlier that this Office and the CSC have concurrent jurisdiction over administrative cases. The Ombudsman also handles criminal cases (which carry much stiffer penalties) and has greater powers. The Ombudsman can, for instance, file a case based on anonymous allegations laid against any civil servant (permanent or political) or elected official. Once a complaint is picked up, a docket is issued and the matter must be pursued to its conclusion: there is no fact-finding, no preliminary investigation to determine whether there is *prima facie* evidence before a case is filed. "And that is so unfair. It goes against everything with regard to due process, anybody can scribble down anything and it is given a docket number and you can't get clearance."[28] The period between the issuance of a docket and final decision can often be measured in years, during which time the official suffers a deal of anxiety. Officials with sensitive responsibilities are frequently placed in an invidious position:

> There was a complaint which ensued from the Office of the Ombudsman.... They usually address the subpoena to XX—so I was the one [to whom it was addressed] and my name was included there. And we verified it, and they said it's a complaint: my name, the commissioner, [and] the members of the selection board. So it's a complaint regarding those who [were] not selected for promotion to a position. I worry about it—because they think there was irregularity in the selection.... We are required to follow the process under the civil service rules, [but] if there is somebody who has political backing, then, well, that's beyond our control. Because if there is a candidate here who is being recommended by a certain politician, well, we can't control that.[29]

The nature of this process, and the authority handed to the Ombudsman, is such that if it is the intention to remove, undermine, unsettle and "harass…you will definitely file a case against them in the Ombudsman."[30] Officials, then, as they make decisions, especially in areas such as tax, customs, and appointments and promotions must bear in mind that mischievous allegation against them is a risk; and, in many agencies, it is common to find at any one time members of staff who have been, or are being, investigated by the Ombudsman.

> That is *always* here … .in fact, I have been a victim of more than one [investigation].… We have a lot of taxpayers … [and] some wackos out there…. There is one where I issued a very basic legal opinion and that person, who also works for government in another government agency, complained to the Supreme Court, [and] asked for my disbarment…. Of course, the Supreme Court cannot just sweep that away. They have to make it go through the process. So I am [now] going through the process of having that case dismissed. But it's clearly a wacko case. It's a waste of time, totally unnecessary…. The risk is always there. Aside from the wacko cases, you have the tax-payer who is being somewhat unreasonable…. There's an impatient taxpayer … he has a case that has complicated legal issues but he cannot wait and so he might file a complaint accusing the office of not acting or ignoring his case.[31]

The Ombudsman is also used in more focused and determined way. The present Ombudsman is closely allied to the President and her husband, and it is frequently alleged that their political opponents attract an inordinate amount of attention from the Ombudsman, while their supporters are left alone. [32]

> If you are with the opposition, and you're a political opponent—of course I'm generalizing, there are exceptions—[but] if you are in the political opposition and an opponent of the President, expect your case to run its ordinary course at the very least, if not hastened. If you are with the administration, expect your case to be either dismissed or given the run-around. Best example of which would be the comparison between Erap and a former secretary of the President—XX. Complete documents from the United States government, from Swiss banks, from the government of Switzerland: in so far as the money trail is concerned, the case was filed against him in March of 2001. The case was filed against Erap in May 2001. Erap's case was decided upon by the *Sandiganbayan* a few months ago, but the case against XX is still undergoing a preliminary investigation by the Office of the Ombudsman—up to today.[33]

Thus the President is able to breach divisions of authority, extend her arm across the branches of government, and even ignore the decisions of the Supreme Court. For example, "the Supreme Court voided a contract for automated accounting machines. They were worth billions of pesos, they voided the contract, they found officials guilty of malpractice (I don't know what the exact legal term is), and they recommended that the Ombudsman file cases against them [and] against COMELEC officials, and to this day there has been no action. So this is the Ombudsman completely disregarding an order from the Supreme Court."[34]

Clearly, there are good and pressing reasons why officials, especially those without political insulation, will demonstrate overtly their accountability and conformity, and studiously avoid behaving in ways that could be interpreted maliciously as improper. Pressure for over-conformity is particularly severe in those agencies responsible for revenue collections. "[There is] so much assessment. Then the taxpayer is asking: 'we would like to avail of this, or a compromise, and...reduce the tax.' [And] sometimes the law is not so clear, and then the bureau would say, 'Actually, it could have been done but the examiner ... is just an accountant, he's not a lawyer.' So [the examiner says] 'I can't do that, I might be charged before the Ombudsman. I will not reduce'.... It's ... fear of being charged before the anti-graft courts—that's the normal reaction among ... the bureau's examiners."[35] Consequently, "...by and large we follow [rules and procedure].... We have a resident ombudsman, and if we don't follow the procedures, and a taxpayer complains, they can go to the ombudsman and complain ... and here at our level we are exposed to possible complaints. So we are *very* careful to follow."[36]

Procurement, too, especially for big-spending agencies is a highly sensitive matter. From the perspective of those civil servants who find their day-to-day business slowed down by processes set out under the Procurement Law, the procurement service is "in the box ... that really needs to be immediately addressed."[37] But for those responsible for it, a deal of caution is essential: "...When you join government ... there are a lot of rules on ethical behavior, on graft and corruption, which are more stringent than the rules and regulations in the private sector. It is mostly generated in government. So coming from the private sector, I have only one [thing] in mind, [and that] is to implement and follow the laws; and especially in procurement, where the accountability and the processes are clear, there is no reason for you to deviate, so you only have to implement it, no matter what."[38]

Meticulous record keeping is, therefore, in so many areas of bureaucratic life necessary and often proves to be justified subsequently.

> There was a time, I think last week, there was a letter received from the Civil Service [Commission] from a wife of a customs officer here. In the letter she was saying that her husband has never been promoted since 1992, and her husband was very much qualified

for any promotion because he is a doctorate, he is a professor. She was also saying that in the selection for promotion there are employees who were not qualified for appointment, and there are some who have pending cases. But we answered the letter, and we showed them: here are the line-ups for the candidates for the certain positions in which her husband was included because he is next in rank for the position. It so happened that he was not selected by the Commissioner. Imagine! For two vacant positions, how many candidates are there? Maybe around 150 for selection by the Commissioner.[39]

The pressures for over-conformity, then, are very personal (in that a failure to acquiesce may damage or destroy careers and livelihoods and policy ambitions) and therefore very strong. The problems generated by over-conformity are also severe, closely entangled around each other, and mutually reinforcing.

1. First, the behavior of civil servants becomes extremely pernickety.

There is so much accountability in government. For example, when my secretary makes a call or calls another official I want to talk to ... they log everything.... I need to sign a form saying that that one minute or two minute call is official. And if calls are made to other offices here, and outside the Commission, and I'm not aware of it [I ask]: "What was that call about?" I should know because I am accountable.... It slows things up because you have to explain and discuss: "what happened here," "I wasn't informed," "you have to tell me," "you took the wrong move," "this costs money, "it should have been approved." And so people ... file cases against each other. You want to know everything and be in control—because of the accountability. You have to know everything that is happening in your office. For example, in this office, there are twenty and growing and I should know the official affairs and activities of each and every one.... When it's relatively low-key it is all right, but if it is something that requires a decision, some money, you need to buy something, they inform me.[40]

And when there is a matter in which the impartiality of the civil servant might be questioned the observance of protocol again seems almost obsessive, even to the official concerned. The appearance of a colleague from another agency bearing gifts is very likely to set alarm bells ringing in the minds of officials in the CSC: "a person comes in with a basket of fruits, and the first thing that comes to mind is that he may be bribing ... and [we say] we cannot accept that ... even if it is a small bar of candy ... sorry..."[41] Requests for the release of documents are also likely to put an official on edge:

The Commission on Higher Education's Deputy Executive Secretary X asked for documents on the appointment of the Executive Secretary ... this Deputy Executive Secretary happened to be my friend, a family friend. He's been coming here, two, three times.... Actually ... what he wanted was just a copy of official documents that are on file [concerning a complaint against the appointment of the Executive Secretary]. It is a public document—there is nothing secret about it. These are public documents—they may be released at any time to the proper authority, and he is an authority. I could have ... .released it in just five minutes. But in fact [it] took three-and-a-half days, because I wanted to be really objective.... Only when he ... submitted a formal letter and it passed through the Office of the Chair and [it arrived] on my table: then it was safe to release the documents ... I ... made a very careful letter and outlined all the documents so that nothing could be attached or detached. And then the Executive Director, who was the subject of the complaint, he also came around; and then an Assistant Commissioner wanted to talk to me. And then another—the Director [who had made the original complaint] from the same agency. They all wanted to come to this office. I wanted to be very safe in my actions.[42]

2. Second, over-conformity ossifies and chokes the conduct of day-to-day, run-of-the-mill business. The atmosphere in many offices throughout government is "very bureaucratic" and thick with "red tape ... so many procedures ... step A, step B ... [before a decision is made].... There are so many people to approve a particular [action]..."[43] And few agencies, it seems, "conduct studies on how a particular service has to be simplified. So there are times when they have to have particular documents signed by many, many, many, *many* officials when in fact they can do with just one or two signatures and [remain] accountable."[44]

This is felt especially by lower level staffs who must chase superiors for signatures. Indeed, from their perspective, in budget and accounting in the Department of Education, "most of the delays are due to absence—official absence of the signatories"[45] In the CSC too, "...sad to say, there are still employees in divisions in offices in the Commission where they are still very much dependent on, say, the Division Chief ... they cannot decide there and then what to do, when in fact they can [act] in their capacity of Assistant Division Chief."[46] The compulsion to refer decisions upwards or to other offices within an agency—a compulsion rooted in a defensive observance of procedures and rules—is to be found even in the Central Bank.

I have seen that from time to time ... a tendency to delay or a tendency to shift [responsibility] ...
"Oh, this is a legal problem"
"We don't see any legal [aspect to this]"

It's [an unwillingness to accept] accountability. I see that here. We should improve on that.[47]

Indeed, in some agencies decisions over some matters (especially financial), responsibility is sometimes shifted outside the agency altogether: "We always consult. If we cannot decide it at our level, we consult our immediate bosses, and if we really cannot solve at that level, we consult COA—they are always available, by e-mail, by cellphone."[48]

3. Third, over-conformity suppresses creativity in, say, formulating research policies or policies for career development. A new policy may be generated with a deal of enthusiasm and hope and hard work, but is then subjected to complex and hierarchical vetting procedures. "It will go to the Division Chief, and then from the Division Chief it will go to the Assistant Director and then the Assistant Director will submit it to the Director IV. From the Director it will go to the three top officials, before it can be approved by the Chair. It's a standard operating procedure—it has to go to 'the slayers'!"[49]

Discussions, too, are restricted and often directed to pre-determined outcomes. In the Department of Education "the problem is ... usually the things that are to be discussed ... the secretary has a position on that already.... So ... you don't want to have the Secretary embarrassed before for group..."[50] One ASEC puts it a little differently: "While I'm saying that we are consulted, there are issues they do on their own..." Yes I will consult but you are still below us.[51] The pressure to conform is also felt in set piece discussions involving directors: "Unfortunately the system works this way: the Executive Committee [Secretary, USECS and ASECs] comes first before the Management Committee [directors, including regional directors].... So initially we already have the decision aspect before it will be discussed ... [and, moreover] during the Management Committee, usually the first topics that will be discussed will be about the budget ... before we go to the concerns of the regions. By the time we go to the concerns of the regions it is already three o'clock [and] everybody is already tired and nobody is listening."[52]

A concomitant of this repression is that the development of subordinates is inhibited: 'Of course, we always tell them [staff] about the benefits of having trained people [subordinates], like they can go on travel, they can go on vacation, otherwise they just have to stay in their offices. And we always try to come out with some development interventions so that the bosses here will know that we have to train people otherwise we will also suffer. [Yet].... We know the areas where delegation is not practiced because ... we immediately find that decisions are centralized even for little or small matters."[53]

4. Fourth, when conformity of process and hierarchy for some matters is set alongside devolution of authority over related matters, the result is a dis-

connection. In Education this goes someway to explain both a dissatisfaction with school principals and a desire for political interference. Principals are at once given more latitude, yet the supply of funds and materials is either denied or delayed. This, from their perspective, forces them into actions which are easily construed as improper or even corrupt, and provides the excuse or justification for genuinely corrupt behavior.

> Our system works this way: it's a ladderized system. We have five levels. We have the national level, the secretary, the under-secretaries, the assistant secretaries here in the Central Office. And then from the national level [down] we have the regional level that is the regional directors. The third level that we have under our law is the division level, and here we have the super-intendents. Then from the superintendents [down] supposedly there is the district level. And then the fifth one is the school head. Now supposedly we are trying to implement school-based management.... In the high schools, they are receiving some MOOE—budget for their operations. In the elementary level, the problem is there is no MOOE.... The school heads ... they are not only instructional leaders. They have been made into an administrator [and] manager of all the funds, properties, and personnel... The problem with that [is that] they don't have funds. So everything ... is expected of them ... like, for example, the supplies.... [If] there is a need for chalk ... they will give the chalk etc. But there are no funds for that. By the time they will be able to ask for that from the Central Office funds, and [its] pass[ed] through the ... [system] ... it's already the end of the school year! So they have a problem. Even textbooks: like, for example, yesterday there were books that were delivered. Textbooks!? This is already September! So what happened to June, July, August? That's how delayed things are, and that is only in Tagaytay city. So the school-based management [system]—the problem with its implementation are, one, no funds. Another problem is that we gave a lot of authority to the principals and also a lot of problems.... So what he does is to collect from the schoolchildren money. But that is illegal, it is a violation, so usually there will be complaints against the principal. So [they are] always placed in hot water—so they call it a principal problem! [Or] for example, security guards: there is no item for security guard. So who will secure the premises? There will be a lot of theft if the properties are not secured. So they will ask, usually, from the Parents—Teachers Association.... So they are beholden to the Parents-Teachers Association. Even the test papers: every time there is an exam they will have to raise it [money for printing test papers] from the schoolchildren.[54]

The Proliferation of Offices, Agencies, and Functions

If—as a consequence of the uncertainty created by political interference and other forms of circumvention—there is no belief that an agency will fulfil its responsibilities or do so impartially, then there will be calls for the establishment of new agencies which *are* thought to attend to the politicians' agendas. A related consideration in some instances is "turf: if you know too much about what I'm doing here, you might end up being able to be the one doing it or earning from it, not me. Turf. There is an overzealous desire to protect one's jurisdiction and territory for corrupt motives."[55]

The desire to set up yet more agencies is heightened by the short life-expectancy of political appointees and their rather short-term outlook: "...there are, basically, mostly, political animals at the top of agencies. Political animals whose primary objectives [are]: one, to make a name as their investment or capital for other political activities; two, to keep the President happy. So the focus is on launching things and things of that sort.... They are not expected to do substantive work. They asked, they are expected, to be personalities."[56] Partly as a consequence,

> none of them really deal with the organisation itself. And when you are at the top and you don't deal with the organization and how it's structured and designed, the tendency is [that] for every project you launch [and for every] group that is created, a new office is created; and when the new ones [political appointees] come in ... they don't even know that there is such an office there. They just continue.... There are so many agencies that should be closed down. If you really want to have a bigger budget, close down all those stupid little agencies that are unnecessary."[57]

The layering of offices and agencies often takes place quietly behind the scenes. But it may also occur more noisily during periodic "rationalization" programs, driven by the Executive, when politicians sense the opportunity to replace old and recalcitrant agencies with new, more accommodating, ones. It is as such times when those civil servants in the CSC (together with those in the DBM) who are charged with the collapsing offices and putting together retirement and separation packages, find themselves working for what is, in practice, a proliferation of agencies.

> It's crazy. These are congressmen and they have, some of them, served in the Cabinet, and they think they know what's best. Or there are certain industries, like, if their field [of interest] is ... medicine, they would want something good for ... that industry. So that's what they do.... They come up with, or they create, [new agencies].... For example—they say that IT is a booming industry and that it will bring us out of our present situation: so they want

a Department of ICT—information and communication technology—separate from the Department of Transportation and Communications. They want to separate them.... The Muslims want a new office of Muslim Affairs.... There is an existing office [but] they want to remove that and put up a commission—a bigger and better one.... So we are supposed to go there and say "Yes, that would be good, but let's try not to bloat the bureaucracy." [But] it's already bloated. We are trying to trim it down and [yet here we are] creating offices..... They are saying that the Department of Agriculture should not have both land and water resources, [that] the Department of Agriculture [should be] focused on rice and everything that is planted on land. But how about aquaculture? So they want one for aquaculture.... They are saying that ... the Department of Trade and Industry, which is supposed to promote all the products of the Philippines, is favoring certain products ... so leaving behind some products.... So let's create an office to promote these. It's a bit desperate how we tried to find solutions for all our problems. I think they mean well, but in the end it's just so convoluted.... They even wanted to create a commission on reorganization: they would build a new office to take out all the old offices. Aren't we just adding to the problem? But you don't say that in polite conference ... you just say, "The Civil Service Commission has no objection, but we feel that you should look into how much money will we spend on this.... And if you appoint an officer ... there has to be staff and tables and chairs and..."[58]

The atmosphere which develops between agencies is often uncertain, suspicious, and secretive; and cooperation becomes difficult. Some functions and information are duplicated while others slip between fragmented and guarded agencies and are simply not done, so that again more legislation is needed. For instance,

...the media has been barking that we should pass a Right to Information Bill so that some confidential documents would be made available to the public after a number of years. I told them we can pass it any time: the problem is how [are] records being kept? [For example], confidential documents on the arrest of a person by the military: the question is ... where are the records? So we're passing a law on record-keeping and on information gathering and data gathering and ... mandating national and local government to keep records so that we can have [an] information build up. That [has] not [been] done. NEDA is supposed to be doing this [but] it was never done. It has never been done in the past, except for one time, when Habito was head of NEDA. And that's what I'm trying to do now. I've got the consent of the Secretaries ... [and] the directors of planning have all agreed to sit down and form an informal coffee group—with me paying for the coffee—just to exchange views, just to be able to ... know what's going on in the department ... [to bring it all] outside [into] the sunshine, [into] the light of politics, because these directors of planning are all civil servants.... NEDA should be doing that actually.[59]

The loopholes created up by the Banking Secrecy Law and by a failure to oversee the Customs' inspectorate have also been left open:

The only legal barricade towards releasing information is in relation to the BIR. That is the only agency that is not allowed to release information with respect to in to an individual taxpayer. The exceptions would be through the oversight committee and order of the President or a waiver of the taxpayer himself. But other than that, all agencies are supposed to ... share information, except for the BIR.... [And] even the Banking Secrecy Law, Republic Act 1405, has exceptions: an anti-graft case, if there is a pending case, [the] courts can order the opening up of the bank accounts; waiver of depositor; and, later on, there was an implicit amendment when we passed the money laundering law which requires banks ... to report to the and Anti Money Laundering Council transactions in excess of 500,000 or, even if it is less ... transactions which could give rise to suspicions that it is money laundering. So, in a way, it has been loosened.... [There should also be a] waiver of secrecy of bank deposits on the part of any government official or employee, together with her statement of assets and liabilities.... They should sign a waiver in so far as RA 1405 is concerned. We have also sat down with some World Bank officials and IT people on how to go about ... modernization computerization.... [For example], if the same importer goes through the same inspector more than three times in one quarter that [should raise] a red flag.... There must be a backup system either by a computer or an oversight team to check on that whether there is an actual anomaly or that it just so happens [it] went through the same inspector. They haven't done that, but they should do that.[60]

Proliferation, duplication and, as these last examples illustrate, poor cooperation also work to deepen mistrust and to stimulate a layering of monitoring or policing functions among and within agencies. But as each new layer proves itself to be, or is perceived to be, unreliable or partisan, a new layer is rolled out, further dividing powers and responsibilities, aggravating frustrations, and intensifying a desire to circumvent.

People keep changing the system, rather than developing it.... And they modify it and they do that [even] when there is no need. And because they are so scared that ... you [will] put [in] one person there ... not a good person ... they will [add] layers, and everybody gets their wings clipped.... But as you do so, you are also layering corruption. That is what happens if you keep layering to protect from corruption, [because] you don't think that the people you are layering it with are also corrupt.... With successive presidents you have to deal with more and more layers...[61]

The Accretion of Laws, Rules, and Processes.

Along with over-conformity and the layering of agencies come the accretion of laws, rules, roles, duties, and procedures, and the detailed proscription of what should and should not be. The framework for this orthopraxy is set out, in part, in legislative records, court rulings, published acts (including the Constitution and its amendments) and other forms of text. For many politicians and civil servants the law is an implacable absolute, and their resort to legislation marks an attempt: either to deal with circumvention (of earlier legislation or convention); or to legitimize and formalize routes around existing legislation (as in the case of EO464); or to establish alignment and some common sense of direction (rarely agreed upon by past or present-day legislators). It also demonstrates that the politician is doing something; it is a platform for re-election; it is eye-catching decoration; it is one of the few means through which the politician may be able to exert a genuinely benevolent, if limited and patchy, effect on society; and it is a symbol of virility—the greater the number of bills authored, supported, and preferably enacted and funded, the better.

The effects of this layering, however, are not always expected or desired. The point is made a little flippantly, but with evident frustration, by one Senator in connexion with widespread political interference in civil service in local government: "our laws are so complicated and so technical that really if you implement all of them only the newborn will not be jailed, and even they might be—we might even find something they did wrong."[62] Life is made still more difficult for the civil servant (and for politicians trying to understand the behavior of civil servants) by the orthopraxy detailed in handbooks, codes of conduct, and flow charts produced by agencies. Particularly troublesome are the issuances cascading from departments. They are intended to "institutionalize" policies, ensure the alignment of representations of practice, and improve the compliance of their officials. But their effect, especially when draped around legislation, is to produce a gimcrack and opaque framework which officials 'cannot get it in one sitting.... There are so many memorandums, orders, circulars ... you have to read, and understand ... [to] keep on reading ... [to] keep abreast of what is happening."[63] And there is, inevitably, "...a tendency really for reports ... administrative reports, data reports ... the requirements ... to pile up.... That has been a problem since I don't remember when—since a long time ago; and there have been many attempts to streamline it.... So there is no problem as to the dissemination of what's new, what you should comply with."[64]

If it is difficult for officials to get a sense of constant change in highly technical matters such as tax, it is still more difficult for the small business.

> Concerning the revenue issuances which govern the activities of taxpayers, it would be good to organize them because you have so many amendments you can't recall exactly which is the original regulation, what is the latest amendment ... unless you are a tax practitioner. Like, if you are a partner in the SGV tax group of course you will be updated. But if you are an ordinary taxpayer with a business it might be really hard for you ... to reduce it, to simplify it. It might be really difficult because we have such a large body of revenue issuances, it might be hard. [What] I would suggest would be to organize that ... to organize the body of revenue issuances that affect taxpayers.[65]

Variations among officials in their interpretations of changing regulations induce further confusion and suspicion:

> ...Taxpayers—especially if they are in nearby regional district offices, or neighbouring district offices...would tend to compare: "why is this district office more lax, and this one more strict?..." Some taxpayers would compare, really.... Sometimes they say that this [district office] is more lax because probably [it] is receiving something.... But if that's not so, if the only reason is that they have different interpretations, I think it is unfair for the other [taxpayers].[66]

Evermore harsh and byzantine, the frameworks produced through the accretion of legislation and internal orders provoke new rounds of circumvention and aggravate a number of other problems already set in train by political interference. Establishing a clear focus becomes still more difficult. There is a further shattering of information, policies, materials, and funds; and energies are necessarily funnelled into quick-fix, high-profile initiatives that look good and seem to offer immediate and widespread solutions. Broader visions and "plans" are created after the fact in order justify and promote the right image. Basic problems (whose cause and solution are often very plain to all) are left unattended because they would require complex political manoeuvring if legislation, funding and efforts were to be secured and sustained over long periods.[67] And creativity even in the use of memoranda is put to an end:

> ...Having memos all over the place is a fair indicator of how hierarchal still the bureaucracy is.... You can't even be creative in disseminating the information.... Like, we were discussing the gender

thing earlier this morning. I would have wanted for posters (this is very petty) to be posted around the CSC—[so that] the office memorandum [OM] [would] not *look* like an OM. Because we have this publication, [for which] we are supposed to get contributions for journal entries, and stories of success about women in the CSC. But it's written in OM form, so it's, like, the packaging is more of ... it's a bit boring, and I don't want them contributing stories just because this is an OM and the Chair says that [they are] supposed to be submitted on or before this date or that date. I would have wanted a poster but my boss said it is a waste of time and resources. So I think it's a lost cause!... Even if I told her that I would be using recycled paper anyway, she told me it would be a waste of time and resources.... So my creative juices are not that ... [stimulated].[68]

But while dissatisfaction with the accretion of a highly detailed and formalized framework may be strong, so is the perceived necessity for it. Attempts to reorganize, simplify, and clarify are, therefore, often matters of individual effort.

...I've been sent to Japan for training ... and I understand that in Japan they don't amend regulations ... piecemeal. I mean, [here, in the Philippines] you only amend a portion of that issuance, but then you have to leave the previous issuances.... What they do in Japan is whenever there are amendments, [they] deal entirely with ... the whole issuance, and issue a new one—consolidated.... I brought that up [with] the Commissioner.... In fact, before she assumed office, that was one of my suggestions to her: that to make it easier for the bureau to read issuances, we don't amend on a piecemeal basis but rather [as] a whole.... [But] because I don't want to... offend the people who are in charge of the promulgation of these issuances ... it's just between [me] and the Commissioner ... [though] ... in one of the meetings I attended ... she really made a pronouncement to update all issuances and consolidate [them] into one. On my part, in my small way ... there is one issuance [that] concerns withholding taxes that is so large that you get confused. So ... I consolidated all issuances about withholding taxes.[69]

And just as this last official took it upon himself to consolidate issuances on this one matter, another official in the Department of Education brought all memoranda together into 127 volumes. More commonly (and less ambitiously) officials will simply try to cope, as in the CSC where "on a day-to-day basis, our field directors (we have field directors stationed in different government agencies) ... communicate our policies to the agencies."[70] And "when there are new orders circulated, the Information Division will see to it that every [other] division and all the services are provided with copies.... Whenever I get hold of orders that affect us in personnel directly, then it is [passed on] to section chiefs to inform our staff. That is in personnel. I do not know in other offices. There are instances when [new orders] do not reach us."[71] The internet offers a possible solution but, more often than not, fast and mass communication merely increases the volume and speed of issuances and does little to harmonize interpretations. "Of course, the bureau has its own website and we publish all issuances there, so it really puts individual responsibility [on to] the employees to keep track [of] issuances as published on the website.... But I realize as an Internet user that sometimes you don't have the time to visit a lot of websites. I myself, in my individual way, I created my own group. It's a Yahoo group, I have members ... [and] I send to them, to their address, all issuances of the bureau. It's for free."[72]

Defensive Groups

Defensiveness is a dimension of many features of the bureaucracy discussed so far. One example is a heavy emphasis on qualifications as the gateway to appointment and promotion, and as a mark of status and ability. Another is a tendency for heads of agencies to keep out of the affairs of other offices if they are to maintain any semblance of cooperation. It is partly for this reason that the head of the CSC does not attempt—except on comparatively rare occasions when it may bring through the courts charges of indirect contempt against officials—to compel other heads of agencies to adhere to, say, procedures for appointment, promotion, or discipline. A third example is over-conformity; a fourth is resistance to conditional tenure.

The civil servants' defensive behavior is often informed by mental states concerning quite specific practices that are understood to be threatening. But it may also indicate a more generalized sense of uncertainty, suspicion, and hostility. This is marked among civil servants whose experience of government outside their office is limited and whose representations of wider government are, as a consequence, heavily dependent upon all manner of speculation and second or third-hand accounts circulating among colleagues and in the media. For many at first and second level—and even for many directors (especially in the regions)—their training has, for much of their career, been fairly limited; and what they know they will have learnt on the job. Outside the office, their world is one of family, friends and shopping malls, and they read very little. But they have a first degree, perhaps from a notable university; they might also have a postgraduate qualification or have ambitions to study for one; they have some kind of status as a civil servant; and they have such responsibilities as they have been given. They are at least a "professional" and their job is relatively secure. Their routine, the people they work with or see each day, and the people with whom they have occasional contact in other parts of government, are what keeps them and makes them who they are. Their knowledge, experience, qualifications, and the sheer number of years they have put in (their seniority) give them their status, livelihood and self-esteem. Beyond office and family the world may be quite vague. They might not be sure how the rest of the agency is arranged, nor what its various groups and divisions do, nor how the organization fits into the rest of government. This does not matter too much, they feel, because the agency is probably changing anyway, and they know what they need to know. They know the tasks to be performed, how to perform them, and who else is involved; and they know who to go to for a decision and who it is that will have to shoulder responsibility if what they have been given permission to do goes wrong or should not in fact have been done. The people in the agency "out there" and "up there" create a world in which there are few promotions, where there is political pressure to do what you would rather not do, and where you need political connexions to get on. Here at least, in their division and section, there is comparative safety and predictability.

It is, then, the office (and its divisions and sections) that are among the most important kernels around which defensive groups form. In part, this reflects opportunity:

> ...usually the friendship ... is developed here [in IAS] ... not so much [in other offices].... We have this service vehicle, so that's the time when I get to meet most of the people in other offices in the Commission: we talk, we tell stories, but it's not that deep. Unless [I] go out and audit other offices, or I get assigned to do something that relates to another office, unless you personally move through their offices ... unless there is an official matter I have to discuss with them ... I seldom see them ... and I don't really get to talk to them.[73]

It also reflects shared experience and interests, and shared representations of an uncertain and sometimes hostile bureaucracy riven by political interference and in which they must try to survive. The civil servants' sense of self, others and their place in the world evolve partly around the office. It is here that colleagues "grew up together." It is, therefore, the office far more than the agency that develops an *esprit de corps* and personality—a distinctive "us" thrown into sharp relief by "them." One example, to which reference has already been made, is the annex that lies one or two minutes walk from the Department of Education's Central Office:

> ...they're calling us the independent Republic of X.... We have a different work culture here ... they say that X is straight ... and the comment of the bosses there, like budget and accounting, whenever X submits its reports ... it's always in order, always neat, orderly, and untainted.... Basically ... people here are dynamic.... I would not say they [in Central Office] are very good in terms of performance.... We do our job more actively, more intently, more studiously, more

efficiently ... especially when it comes to money matters. You cannot play here.... I would say ... [you] cannot really play around with money here—the people on guard are very strict, very transparent. I don't know about Central office, but we hear things ... because it's very big, about 1000 plus...[74]

But the office is not the only kernel of association. Between an agency's central and regional offices, among its regional offices, and sometimes within its central office, it is not uncommon to find civil servants who are related to one another by blood or marriage. More often, though, kinship reaches across agencies. There is also a tendency for children to follow their parents or siblings into the service—often into the same agency or even the same office—once kin have moved on or retired. In the BIR this became an unwritten convention in the regions where: "it was really automatic more or less.... It still happens, but I don't think it's automatic.... But there are some cases."[75] And even in Central Office "I know of some people who have retired here and their children are here—some of their kids, for some reason or other."[76] The practice is not regarded as improper, nor as illegal, provided the parents have retired; and children will inherit their parents' surviving relationships within the Bureau such that a group, or part of it, renews itself. In the vast and sprawling Department of Education, too, and most especially within the schools where rules against nepotism do not apply, there are "strong binds among family members: so some people here in the Department ... are actually with the rest of their family members, their brothers and sisters, their sons.... If you make bad comments against one person, he will go to his family and they will all gang up against you."[77] Still more common are groupings established around year of entry into the service (sometimes described as "batch-mates") and those established around place of origin. This is more evident in regional offices "where there are...different 'tribes'.... [these] form the base of competing factions."[78]

Whether they exist prior to a perceived threat, or are formed only later (and perhaps in response to that threat), these groups and the various kernels (such as office, division, section, kinship or, say, year of entry or university) around which they gather provide the framework for defensive behavior. Threats to the group are threats to each member's sense of self as well as their livelihoods; and as each member draws upon every other member's anxieties to reaffirm their own fears, the ranks close. Any practice read as an attempt to encroach on another area of responsibility is met with suspicion and hostility; a reluctance to stray outside one's own theatre grows; and a concern on the part of superiors that they should know everything that goes on among their subordinates in the office becomes more entrenched. Thus, defensiveness brings sharper definition to the group and increases the density of its practices. A director who intends to bring in tougher performance evaluation procedures or more systematic rotation, or who intends to ensure that cash advances are reconciled, or who allows in an unpopular political appointee, is faced not with a few disparate and half-hearted objections but with solid bodies of resistance. These groups and the defensive behavior of civil servants more generally create or exacerbate a number of problems.

1. Hemmed in as much by their own understanding of the world as by the practices of others around them, there is a predilection for "turf-thinking" among civil servants; for "thinking always in their home group"; for focusing on "the box rather than on what it is that connects the box..."[79]; and for their interests and sense of responsibility to begin and end with their office or division and their specific functions. A common view from first and second levels, and expressed here by a Division Chief in the Department of Education, is that "we are confined to our particular tasks," and this seems to work: "so far—I can't see any complications that have arisen."[80] The perspective from the senior ranks, however, is very different. Tunnel vision and lack of empathy among their subordinates' groupings makes life difficult:

> ...If A is responsible for this kind of job, [the] others won't care any more. So there has to be a system where, within a division, they should know what is happening to the others. And sometimes ... they seem to forget ... to provide information to one another.... I think the anchor within the division is the Division Chief. So in a meeting I think you should be able to ask people to report, to update each other.... But sometimes [they] don't...I think part of our accountability is really to provide superiors with updates.... They don't have to write long reports—just [write]: "I have done this, I have done what you told me, and this is the result." I think here at the Civil Service Commission, there's really not much process of updating ... the Commission proper is composed of the Chair and the Commissioners. Among them I think they have discussed, in terms of executive functions, the day-to-day operations of the civil service. Documents pass through the Chair *alone*, and they need not pass through the [other two] Commissioners because I think most of their functions would deal with policy-making. But how would these Commissioners feel if at some point ... they would know [only] later that there is something happening in their environment, that the information is not that well timed, or they've not been updated? There's not much conscious effort [at] providing reports or updating; and that happens not just at the level of the Commissioners, it also happens within ... offices. For instance, here [in my office] we have three divisions, and the instructions or directives to the directors [are] that we ought to be active in terms of supervising the divisions within the office.... And they have asked us to [divide up] the labor or work. So in an office of three [divisions], two divisions are directly under the supervision of the Director IV, and one

under my supervision. So sometimes there are things that don't pass through me, especially those pertaining to the two divisions that I'm not really handling. And my sentiment is there's really [a] lack of updating on the part of the Division Chiefs. So I'm not complaining, I understand the process, but sometimes it slips [past] you. So what I do every time is to check … that [it's] been filed, talk to each division, and ask for updates.'[81]

2. Second, over-conformity may harden still further: the official adheres strictly to process not only to demonstrate their probity and put themselves beyond reproach, but also to defend their authority and their office. The performance of simple tasks is necessarily preceded by a deal of consultation and by the production of notifications and written authorizations. Subordinates are compelled to waste a good deal of time chasing after senior staff for signatures; superiors become heavily dependent upon memoranda without which their subordinates will not depart from their normal, established, and closely prescribed routines; and even the most basic requests and instructions may need to be made in writing[82]: 'There are people who would move even if it's just a phone call. Let's say, for instance, there is an emergency meeting or there is a last-minute short notice meeting … with congressmen, or the Secretary of Defence or whoever. Then we need this data, we need this data, we need this data. There are ten offices. [To] some of them [you] just say, "Oh we need a status report on this," and they would give it to you…. But … there are heads who won't move if there is no written order for them…. They would say "Where's the notice of the meeting? What's the agenda? What's the format?"[83] Thus communication between and even within offices become sclerotic and the speed of decision-making is reduced to a crawl.

3. Third, information is distorted by civil servants determined to avoid putting anything in writing which might present their office or unit in a bad light: "The culture of the department is don't embarrass your school. So if there is a problem the report is sanitised by the teacher; it goes to the principal; the principal further sanitises it and gives it to the supervisor; and then when it comes to Manila everything is pretty clean. So the manner of reporting and monitoring and implementation can sometimes be a big burden."[84] Consequently, problems build up such that "when I go to the field I get complaints on *everything and anything*. I was telling my staff if I will worry about all of these small things I would no longer be able to do my own work because they complain to me about their superintendent, they complain to me about their school…. And the problems are big."[85]

4. Fourth, the movement of personnel is restricted, for there is a strong sense that it is "better to appoint them from within rather than bring them from outside. And if external appointments have to be made then: 'We will have to scrutinize all the work that he is doing…. Unlike if he is already

there and just rose through the ranks and we already know him.... There is no hardship involved.'"[86]

5. Fifth, there is chronic resistance to change. Major reform is extremely difficult to contemplate. For instance, rearranging or removing segments and hierarchies in Department of Education's regional offices—which form, in the view of some, an unnecessary layer between central office and the school superintendence and schools[87]—is unthinkable. This is very understandable when tension is created among civil servants even by those everyday practical considerations which demand that colleagues breach one another's territory.

> They say "I won't do that because it's not my job."... They don't wish to do it just because there's no black-and-white restatement of their functions.... There is a line there [in the contract] "other duties and responsibilities"; but unless it's spelt out in specific provisions they won't accept it. Probably it is an evolving function which has not yet been written.... But sometimes there are instances when you have to ... when you're the one doing the other's job.... That's really very stressful.... Or when somebody does your job, when you're the one who's supposed to do it.... I wouldn't take that personally.... I look at it as the job has to be done. But probably that would leave a mark on some people: she refuses to take jobs which should really be her responsibility, so more or less she is a difficult person to deal with. So the next time ... if a similar job comes up you would anticipate that you would be the one to do it again.[88]

More substantial change, especially if it works against colleagues' personal interests, will generate still greater heat, stress, and self-doubt as in the case of this Director brought into central office from the regions.

> I was ordered to report to the Central Office and take up this position, against my will.... I'm asking myself if I could handle the pressure. First of all my idea of the central office is that I might not meet the expectations.... But because [it's] an order, I'm also afraid that I'll be charged [with] insubordination. So I have to follow.... The first impact on me [was] that I got a stroke, a mild stroke, because I couldn't sleep: I'm asking myself ... can I handle it ... the pressure, the outside pressure, the pressure in the office? Then, after the stroke.... I was included in [a] rally because of some changes [to] unliquidated cash advances that I had to impose.... Of course, the changes need the approval of the Secretary, but they are also changes which I firmly stand [by]. And that is one reason—that is the main reason—why I was rallied, because ... people [in the Department] ... don't like me, because.... I'm asking for liquidation of cash advances. But I'm very firm on that, because there are orders, there are memorandums. It is in the rules and regulations: ...if you get money from the government, you have to liquidate it...

...After that, because I'm very firm.... I am not expecting to stay long. I thought when the Secretary [is replaced] I will also be [out]. But before Secretary X ... stepped [down], I was already appointed as Y in this department. But still, at the back of my mind, "Can I handle this situation?" ... I keep asking myself. [Often, I am approached]: [they] might be lower than me, [they] might be the same level, [they] might be higher than me, but ... I do not answer right then and there, but I always [say] can you give me time to study? And afterwards, maybe tomorrow, or before Friday, I can give you my answer.... I'm studying the case—the form of appropriation. If I don't like [it], I will tell you I don't like [it]; and if you persist, then maybe that's the time I'll [put] it in writing:... I'm against [what is proposed] for the following reason. But I'm not ... closing my mind. If there are ways, [then] we will be doing it, we will use our flexibility. Of course, number one is [that] we should not be against the rules and regulations.... Maybe one of the reasons why I stay is because I am always very candid, very frank. When I say no, I mean no. When I say yes, we will do it right. If you ask me how can we do it, I'll give you some advice, but definitely we shall do it right.[89]

These features—turf thinking, over-conformity, restricted communications, distorted information, limited movements of staff, resistance to change, and the tensions generated by attempts at reform—conspire to weaken cooperation and alignment, and to stultify new ideas and practices. Nor, therefore, are subordinates given much room to experiment and develop: without the right qualifications and sufficient experience and seniority, a member of staff is automatically considered incapable of undertaking certain tasks. Robbed of initiative, then criticized for being without initiative,[90] subordinates are further demoralized. Thus, the popular reputation of civil servants for being slow, obstructive, lazy, unimaginative, bureaucratic, limited, and incompetent is reinforced.

Conclusions

Any portrait of Philippine bureaucracy and polity is bound to be limited in breadth and dimensions. Yet it is possible to capture something of its shifting and fuzzy colors and shapes. The introduction of American-style government encouraged the fragmentation of authority and agencies, and the emergence of varied and partial views of that polity and bureaucracy. Discontent with the arrangements of government (and especially with the distribution of authority) as perceived from its different branches, agencies, offices, and levels prompted the circumvention of rule, process, hierarchy and agency. This, in turn, stimulated attempts to block manoeuvring and, through over-conformity and layering, impose certainty and predictability. Thus, divisions in authority and the fragmentation of government intensified, and further circumvention ensued.

This cycle is described by a host of problems within the bureaucracy and wider polity: political interference in appointments, promotions and discipline; uncertain and politicized funding; the circumvention of vital processes governing appointments, tenure and performance; low pay; poor training and alignment; corruption and its politicization; a proliferation of agencies and their continuous re-organization; and thickening red-tape, increasing inflexibility and defensiveness. These practices inform, and are informed by, a complex of representations or understandings of bureaucracy, government, self, and others. They include a fragmented bureaucracy and polity in which authority is either too dispersed or too concentrated and, either way, is usually taken out of the hands of the right people and lodged with the wrong people; widespread procedural abuse and organizational weakness; a bureaucracy whose agencies are often working in different or contradictory directions; a slow, incompetent, and recalcitrant bureaucracy that is unsympathetic to the needs of politicians; and a legislature and executive populated by self-centered, arrogant, and domineering politicians. It is also understood as a bureaucracy in which political interference is rife, whose staffs are over-protected and complacent, and in which corruption is commonplace. It is also a bureaucracy which is felt to "box" its staffs into petty routines, such that if every rule and procedure were followed, little would happen and life for the civil servant would be intolerable. It is a refuge in a hostile and uncertain world. And it is a bureaucracy trapped by historical and economic structures and by culture. Thus, the closeness, the *esprit de corps*, and the defensiveness to be found in, say, many offices and divisions of the BIR or in Quezon City Hall, are to be explained partly by the fact that "...people ... have been ... around some time already," and partly by "the culture of Filipinos—to be friendly ... not to be adversarial in our actions."[91] It is, then, Asian culture that explains why, for example, "if I hate you but you are appointed secretary, I'm embarrassed not to confirm you"[92]; or why, "...you come to me, head-to-head, [and say] 'You know, X, I know you don't like me but I'm now Secretary,'" and offer "both the carrot and the stick....extending my hand of friendship, and at the same time [making it clear that] I am the Secretary."[93] It is Filipino culture that explains why, "if instructions are not clear, people tend to interpret them in their own way."[94] It is culture that explains "Filipino clannishness"—why "if I send the people [from] here to an international conference they would likely go together,"[95] and why, at any particular event, we are sitting together "...even though we have friends in [other] bureaux..."[96] It is "Filipino heart" and "the Filipino nature" that determine compassion should rule at the expense of efficiency and procedural rigor, and explain why, "when we see a bad performer, and that performer is sick or has many children or is old, we close our eyes and give a good rating."[97] It is Filipino culture that explains why, "if instructions are not clear, people tend to interpret them in their own way."[98] The authoritarian nature of government as a whole is also to be explained by the fact that: "we still have basically an Asian culture. But we love the West. So we adopted mostly American systems. But the problem is, we tinkered with it to favor the executive. So we liked the separation of powers but we don't like the check and balance."[99] Within agencies, too, "I would say the setup ... is ... very, very much Asian, and it is really authoritarian ... but we are trying to learn. It's still difficult to move about.... As I said, it's very much Asian ... but we are able to do things."[100] Unpredictability and unreliability, though, are Filipino traits that must look to their "...Spanish heritage. Some [Filipinos] are temperamental: the less educated the taxpayer, the more difficult it is to explain why he has to—why he or she—*has* to pay this kind of tax."[101] And both patronage and reciprocity are "...partly culture. If, for example, a mayor who gets elected got the support from minions, the tendency of a mayor is to reciprocate and, therefore, hire the son or the daughter or the relative of the supporter in the *municipality*—it is *quid pro quo*.... It may vary: some of the supporters may not need support [reciprocation], but it is also their way of getting influence, somehow, from those in authority which may be translated later on if they would be needing something..."[102] Similarly, within the civil service "the problem is our culture. Our culture is not Western, so you will have those bureaucrats who are permanent and who are capable, but they will give their loyalty not to the institutions but to the persons—that's a Filipino trait."[103]

It is not the intention here to downplay features such as patronage, obligation, violence, intimidation, corruption, and personalism, or to jettison existing explanatory devices such as patron-clientelism, patrimonialism, bossism, sultanism, administrative development or the more generic concepts of structure and culture. My suggestion is that these features constitute strings of representation and practice woven around and fused with other dimensional strings that together constitute polity, bureaucracy and, indeed, the wider social world; and that scholars' theoretical concepts through which attempts are made to explain these features should be seen as functioning strands of that compound—as representations which, alongside those created by actors, inform and are informed by practice. That is to say, scholars' representations (such patrimonialism or structure) are functioning constituents of the social world, and are best understood and treated as such rather than as privileged and authoritative prisms set apart from it.

Thought about in this way, scholars' and actors' representations are uncertain and unpredictable in significance and meaning. For instance, politicians and civil servants often turn, seemingly as a last resort, to the structures of patronage and the cultural predilections of "the Filipino" to explain why those who make contributions to their election campaigns, or who have in the past have done them some kind of favor, then behave as if they own the politician. Rarely, however, are these cultural and structural traits used to account for their own behavior; and while they are content to leave with those who have supported them a sense of prefigured obligation, they will quickly disabuse them of that feeling when it is in their interests to do so. Senators, in particular, seem very comfortable with these arrangements. Bureaucrats and politicians whose personality and authority is not quite so strong may find it more difficult to resist the pressures brought to bear through the notion of "obligation." Yet there is no question that many of them do resist these pressures when they arise, citing as their excuse legal, procedural, and regulatory proscriptions, or a simple lack of authority.[104] Meanwhile, "corruption the representation" may work to magnify "corruption the practice" by conflating corruption with all those acts which politician or civil servant disapproves of. "Patronage the representation" by emphasizing the instrumental quality of relationships and reciprocity allows for any political appointment or vote cast or favor given to be interpreted as debt repaid or obligation created for political advantage. And "misallocation of authority" may be transformed conceptually into a structural feature that blocks ambition and impedes the realization of what should be. Thus, scholarly and street representations exaggerate the bureaucracy's weaknesses, intensify the conviction that others are behaving improperly and for the worst of reasons, and provide actors with further justification (if any is needed) for their own actions.

Inherent in the discussion so far is the suggestion that so many of these political and bureaucratic features, and the cycle they describe, inform and are informed by a view of world and others that is self-centered and instrumental. Surrounded by visions of an uncertain, weak, and corrupt polity and bureaucracy—one that, as consequence, should be subject to the iron hand of the law or the strongman—civil servants and politicians are very likely to emphasize the personalistic aspects of each other's behavior; and the more this is so, the more entrenched those visions become. The idea that the civil service is incestuous and complacent; the emphasis on the accumulation of educational and professional qualifications for entry into the service and promotion within it; and constructions of patronage and deference to authority and status: all this (and more) create a potent mixture of representation and practice which seems to bar the vast majority from entry into the professions and into the civil service. The few remaining routes to political influence and wealth—such as the military, business, and acting—are now lit all the more brightly. Another is local politics, for while the absence of state funding makes life much harder for those without money and educational qualifications, it would not be easy to justify the exclusion of such people from holding public office in a democracy (though it is not difficult to find those even within Congress who would dearly like to try). Provided enough money of one's own can be generated, or funds can be secured from a collection of interest groups, then it is possible even for those from modest backgrounds to gain a foothold on the lower rungs and climb from *barangay* councillor to *barangay* captain, to city councillor, vice mayor, mayor, governor, congressman, senator, cabinet post, and perhaps even vice president or president. As one goes up it becomes easier to secure financial support, or tap into the state's coffers, and pay for elections and a growing entourage of advisors. Nevertheless, the path is strewn with difficulties. There are webs of rules, regulations, procedures and laws constraining what the politicians would like to do. And as they progress towards the summit, their frustrations only mount with their broadening vision—as they realize what they could have were it not for all these constraints. This drive and frustration produces a coarse and loose form of politics: rules and procedures are either ignored or circumvented or interpreted imaginatively; and such authority as they do possess is used to bargain with. Their primary concern is not economic or social or institutional development, but how funds, regulations, procedures, organizations, authority, and constraints can be used or disposed of in order to extend their reach. All energies are consumed by this instrumentalism: the ultimate goal of economic and social well-being (if it was ever present) is never quite realized in any sustained or coherent way, not even by the most well-meaning and honorable politicians. The style of politics carried from the *barangay* and local town up to the national arena is reinforced by a necessarily loose and familiar atmosphere to be found at the top of the executive and legislature. This quality—together with a deep mistrust in government, the division of authority and the frustration it breeds, and a willingness to play hard and fast with constraints—fuels a tendency to rely on those who are trusted confidants. The politician (President or Secretary, Senator or Congressman) looks to the experienced street fighter who has clawed his way up through local politics; or to the military man; or to those who were born into the business elite or have managed to break into it; to one's parents' allies and their offspring; or to old friends and their relatives. And then there are those with particular abilities and experience—the lawyer, administrator businessman, or accountant—who have been recommended by the politician's confidants. At the upper levels, then, the pool is very mixed and its quality depends very much on the politicians' judgment. But they have one thing in common: they are used to getting their way. Either this is because they were born into privilege, handed wealth and influence, educated, treated with considerable deference and, as a consequence, have acquired the feeling that things and people usually go their way (or at least ought to); or it is because they are experienced at working around or turning to advantage regulations and rules designed to constrain what they see to be their legitimate and richly deserved responsibilities and interests. At the top, surrounded by a deal of mistrust and by many unnecessary restrictions, it is easy to justify malpractice to one another and to oneself, so much so that malpractice becomes the norm or at least necessary and tolerable: it is how politics works.

But this vision of the polity and bureaucracy, aspects of which may find expression through practice, is only one vision. Despite evident weaknesses, and despite the strong and disturbing vein of personalism which runs through the bureaucracy and polity, there is implied in the accounts of politicians and civil servants—and in their frustration, their disappointments, their anger, their exasperation and their disgust—an aspiration for, and a vision of, something better. Indeed, implied in the simple fact of these accounts is the possibility that there also exists competence, integrity, open-mindedness, loyalty to the organization and its functions, and good intention. It is to these more positive and highly significant aspects of Philippine bureaucracy that chapter 4 now turns.

Notes

1. Lorenzo, M., Assistant Commissioner, Bureau of Internal Revenue, Quezon City, October 5, 2007.
2. Umbac, S., Chief (Legislative Liaison Division), Civil Service Commission, Quezon City, December 7, 2007.
3. Source (Senate) requests anonymity.
4. Source (Director, BOC) requests anonymity.
5. In this case a lawyer involved in the administration of discipline within the Service.
6. Escudero, F., Senator, the Philippine Senate, Pasay City, 19 December 2007.
7. Cayetano, A. P., Senator, the Philippine Senate, Pasay City, December 19, 2007.
8. Constantino-David, K., Chair, Civil Service Commission, Quezon City, December 27, 2007.
9. Ibid.
10. The total number of offences is a little under 14,500. This refers to convictions or guilty pleas only.
11. The Department of Education, Culture and Sports is the name previously given to the Department of Education. However, this category—DECS—includes recent figures for the Department after its change of name.
12. This figure refers primarily to the Commission on Audit.
13. Lim, C., Atty., Assistant Commissioner, Bureau of Internal Revenue, Quezon City, October 10, 2007.
14. Agamata, L., Director, Civil Service Commission, Quezon City, December 6, 2007.
15. Constantino-David, K., Chair, Civil Service Commission, Quezon City, December 27, 2007
16. Madrid, D.L, Supervising Personnel Specialist, Civil Service Commission, Quezon City, November 28, 2007.
17. Inciong, T., Assistant Secretary, Department of Education, Pasig City, September 25, 2007.
18. Malaya, J., Assistant Secretary, Department of Education, Pasig City, September 27, 2007.
19. Bacani, R.C., Undersecretary, Department of Education, Pasig City, September 24, 2007.

20. Tabino, A., Director, Civil Service Commission, Quezon City, December 18, 2007.
21. Inciong, T., Assistant Secretary, Department of Education, Pasig City, September 25, 2007.
22. Pawid, L., Legislative Staff Officer, Office of Senator Gordon, the Philippine Senate, Pasay City, September 17, 2007.
23. Mateo, J., OIC (Office of the Assistant Secretary, Educational Development Projects Implementing Taskforce), Department of Education, Pasig City, September 11, 2007.
24. Malaya, J., Assistant Secretary, Department of Education, Pasig City, September 27, 2007.
25. Ibid.
26. Executive Order 464 was subsequently declared unconstitutional by the Senate, rescinded by the Supreme Court, and re-issued as a memorandum order.
27. Abad, J., Chief of Staff, Senator Aquino, B., the Philippine Senate, Pasay City, December 19, 2007.
28. Constantino-David, K. Chair, Civil Service Commission, Quezon City, December 27, 2007.
29. Source (BOC) requests anonymity.
30. Dela Fuente, C., Director, Civil Service Commission, Quezon City, December 4, 2007.
31. Source (BIR) requests anonymity.
32. The problem is nothing new. A failure to realise closure on so many questions has been a long-standing feature of Philippine political life: "There is always this feeling of sweeping dirt under the rug.... The Ombudsman is there to prosecute wrongdoing ... Estrada got caught and was convicted, but since there was no closure in previous cases, people say Estrada was just stupid ... Marcos stole more, Ramos stole more, Corrie stole more, but they were not caught." (Pawid, L. , Legislative Staff Officer, Office of Senator Gordon, the Philippine Senate, Pasay City, September 17, 2007).
33. Escudero, F., Senator, the Philippine Senate, Pasay City, 19 December 2007.
34. Abad, J., Chief of Staff, Senator Aquino, B., the Philippine Senate, Pasay City, December 19, 2007.
35. Source (BIR) requests anonymity.
36. Source (BIR) requests anonymity. As noted earlier, pressure derives not only from fear of the Ombudsman and allegations by taxpayers who feel they have been treated unfairly, but also from the upper reaches of organizations: "the media is always following up ... and it is so easy to replace the top officials because they are political appointees.... The failure of staff is reflected as the failure of the commissioner, and the failure of the commissioner is reflected as the failure of the staff. So we have to support one another" (Escober, A., Atty., Bureau of Internal Revenue, Quezon City, October 4, 2007).
37. Joson, L.G., OIC (HRMD, Planning), Department of Education, Pasig City, September 10, 2007.
38. Carpentero, A., Director, Office of Procurement, Department of Education, Pasig City, October 8, 2007.

39. Source (BOC) requests anonymity.
40. Agamata, L., Director, Civil Service Commission, Quezon City, December 6, 2007.
41. Fernandez, M.T.C., Director, Civil Service Commission, Quezon City, November 22, 2007.
42. Ibid.
43. Galvan, J.G., Assistant Secretary, Department of Education, Pasig City, October 8, 2007.
44. Dino, M.T., Supervising Personnel Specialist, Civil Service Commission, Quezon City, November 21, 2007.
45. Sources (Department of Education) request anonymity.
46. Dino, M.T., Supervising Personnel Specialist, Civil Service Commission, Quezon City, November 21, 2007.
47. De Zuniga, J., Assistant Governor, *Bangko Sentral Ng Pilipinas*, Malate, September 21, 2007.
48. Roldan, J., Assistant Commissioner, Bureau of Internal Revenue, Quezon City, October 9, 2007.
49. Dinsay, Z. F., Chief Personnel Specialist, Civil Service Commission, Quezon City, December 10, 2007.
50. Sunga, F. C., Undersecretary, Department of Education, Pasig City, September 27, 2007.
51. Inciong, T., Assistant Secretary, Department of Education, Pasig City, September 25, 2007.
52. Ibid.
53. Dulce, V.H., Deputy Director, *Bangko Sentral Ng Pilipinas*, Malate, September 18, 2007.
54. Sunga, F.C., Undersecretary, Department of Education, Pasig City, September 27, 2007.
55. Escudero, F., Senator, the Philippine Senate, Pasay City, 19 December 2007.
56. Constantino-David, K., Chair, Civil Service Commission, Quezon City, December 27, 2007.
57. The interviewee mixes 'office' and 'agency' here, but her meaning is plain: offices and agencies are constantly being created in the pursuit of short-term and often superficial objectives and then left to wither on the vine.
58. Umbac, S., Chief (Legislative Liaison Division), Civil Service Commission, Quezon City, December 7, 2007.
59. Escudero, F., Senator, the Philippine Senate, Pasay City, 19 December 2007.
60. Ibid.
61. Urquiola, P., Chief of Staff, Senator Honasan, G., the Philippine Senate, Pasay City, December 12, 2007.
62. Cayetano, A. P., Senator, the Philippine Senate, Pasay City, December 19, 2007.
63. Source (Department of Education) requests anonymity.
64. Lorenzo, M., Assistant Commissioner, Bureau of Internal Revenue, Quezon City, October 5, 2007.
65. Lim, C., Atty., Assistant Commissioner, Bureau of Internal Revenue, Quezon City, October 10, 2007.

66. Lorenzo, M., Assistant Commissioner, Bureau of Internal Revenue, Quezon City, October 5, 2007.

67. Quijano, Y., Director, Department of Education, Pasig City, September 25, 2007; Inciong, T., Assistant Secretary, Department of Education, Pasig City, September 25, 2007.

68. Porio, M. T. A., Director, Civil Service Commission, Quezon City, 28 November 2007.

69. Duncano, D., Deputy Commissioner, Bureau of Internal Revenue, Quezon City, October 9, 2007.

70. Madrid, D.L, Supervising Personnel Specialist, Civil Service Commission, Quezon City, November 28, 2007.

71. Joson, L.G., OIC (HRMD, Planning), Department of Education, Pasig City, September 10, 2007.

72. Duncano, D., Deputy Commissioner, Bureau of Internal Revenue, Quezon City, October 9, 2007.

73. Source (Internal Audit, CSC) requests anonymity.

74. Source (Department of Education) requests anonymity.

75. Lorenzo, M., Assistant Commissioner, Bureau of Internal Revenue, Quezon City, October 5, 2007.

76. Ibid.

77. Source (Department of Education) requests anonymity.

78. Dino, M.T., Supervising Personnel Specialist, Civil Service Commission, Quezon City, November 21, 2007.

79. Galvan, J.G., Assistant Secretary, Department of Education, Pasig City, October 8, 2007.

80. Joson, L.G., OIC (HRMD, Planning), Department of Education, Pasig City, September 10, 2007.

81. Gocon-Gragasin, N., Director, Civil Service Commission, Quezon City, December 7, 2007.

82. These features are strengthened by a number of other considerations. One is a performance management system which attempts to measure the output of civil servants by allocating points to particular tasks such as writing official letters. Each civil servant and unit (section, division and office) is expected to accumulate a certain number of points during the year, and is rewarded or punished accordingly. Over-conformity in the observance of procedures and rules is, in some instances, also driven by a concern on the part of officials to remove any possibility that their actions could be misconstrued as improper or corrupt.

83. Source (BIR) requests anonymity.

84. Malaya, J., Assistant Secretary, Department of Education, Pasig City, September 27, 2007.

85. Ibid.

86. Taron, R., Chief (Collection Enforcement), Bureau of Internal Revenue, Quezon City, October 5, 2007.

87. Inocentes, A., Undersecretary, Department of Education, Pasig City, October 1, 2007.

88. Lorenzo, M., Assistant Commissioner, Bureau of Internal Revenue, Quezon City, October 5, 2007.

89. Source (Department of Education) requests anonymity.

90.   Mateo, J., OIC (Office of the Assistant Secretary, Educational Development Projects Implementing Taskforce), Department of Education, Pasig City, September 11, 2007.
91.   Source (BIR) given anonymity.
92.   Source (Senate) given anonymity.
93.   Ibid.
94.   Source (Department of Education) given anonymity.
95.   Source (Department of Education) given anonymity.
96.   Ibid.
97.   Source (CSC) given anonymity.
98.   Source (Department of Education) given anonymity.
99.   Source (Senate) given anonymity.
100.   Source (*Bangko Sentral Ng Filipinas*) given anonymity.
101.   Source (CSC) given anonymity.
102.   Ibid.
103.   Source (Senate) given anonymity.
104.   This is true even of the lowest ranking civil servants in local government and even when kinship obligations are involved: "...my brother is trying to get a job and asked me to secure a medical clearance from the city health department; but if I call on my friends to do that, then they might come back to me later on and say "Look, I helped you do this, can you help me do that?" So I've ... talked to my brother and ask him to do it on his own." Source (Quezon City Hall) requests anonymity.

4

Emotional and Technical Professionalism

Introduction

The weaknesses afflicting the civil service are not just those of politicians twisting the bureaucracy to suit their own particularistic interests, or of supine or complicit civil servants. They are also those of excessive formality and rigidity, and of ineffective and cumbersome arrangements of authority. This cycle of instrumentalism and authoritarianism is further energized by the sense of alienation that it foments. In reaction, however, another cycle emerges. It comprises a deepening sense that relationships are important in themselves, and a desire to distance social relationships conceptually from practice within the organization. With this distancing (emotional professionalism) relationships are (conceptually) washed out of the organization; and roles, rules and procedures—now bleached of relationships—are necessarily treated (in parallel with relationships in the social sphere) *as if* absolute (technical professionalism). In this way, the use to which relationships are put within the organization, and in fact *constitute* the organization, is masked; and the sense that relationships still rest within the social sphere and remain important in their own right is protected. Emotional and technical professionalism are consolidated and further encouraged by the practical benefits—such as sharpening hierarchy and authority, and greater precision, reliability, and flexibility in technical operations—which they bring to the organization. As this shift in perspective deepens—and the treatment of rules, roles and procedures *as if* absolute becomes second nature—explicitly social relationships are now admitted into the organization with confidence such that the social sphere loses geographical distinction. Thus compassion and empathy are introduced into the organization; friction and sensitivity to shame are reduced; resilience to criticism hardens; a willingness and a capacity to align representations and practices are enhanced; and coordination and cooperation are improved.

Emotional and technical professionalism, then, entail the reconfiguration of relationships and emotion as the organization's formal or official representations (its rules, roles and procedures). This reconfiguration or re-staging (of the "social" as the "official") is the ordinary, everyday, uncontroversial business of maintaining, renewing, and re-invigorating the organization and keeping it flexible and responsive. Rooted in the first cycle, however, are conditions or circumstances—personalistic and self-centered behavior, divisions in authority, over-conformity, and fundamental disagreements among politicians and civil servants over policy and functions—which (in so far as the first cycle retains its vigor) impede this constant renewal. That is to say, these circumstances erode the mystique surrounding rules, roles, and process, and reduce the efficacy of the organization. It is now increasingly without support of the organization's formal and partially ossified frameworks, and in opposition to the personalistic networks which hide behind them, that civil servants must work informally to fulfil what they hold to be their duties and responsibilities. Whilst essential to the organization, this positive informal behavior risks being viewed as illicit or semi-illicit or at least as improper. In this atmosphere, any informality is conflated with corruption, and personalistic networks mobilize official frameworks in their own interests: corruption is, in a word, politicized.

Emotional and Technical Professionalism

Emotional and technical professionalism emerge in order to defend the social sphere. They are also encouraged and deepened by the advantages they happen to bring to the organization. These benefits take a number of forms, the more significant of which are considered below.

1. The first is a demand to balance energy and time between the organization and social life (centered on the family). This more focused attention happens to sharpen hierarchy within the organization as superiors, juggling their time and efforts, find themselves increasingly distanced from their subordinates. "Before ... when I was not in this position, when I was a staff, and my kids had a baptism or birthday party, I used to invite my peers. But now, at my level, even if my staff ... have kids, will have birthday parties, and they would invite me, I won't go because of family commitments.... If I had the time I really would want to join them..."[1] Opportunities for those drinks after work also fade with the years. "When I was a bit younger, and I could spend more time with co-workers outside, then I would think that was the time that I was socially quite close to them. But as time goes on you have kids to think about, you have the pressure of things: somehow my social interactions ... going out after five with fellow workers ... has diminished."[2] A simple difference in age, too, plays its part: "When I was Division Chief of human resources and when I was Deputy for Administration, the members of my staff and myself were a lot closer [in] age ... and so we could relate better ... we were close, I could be very friendly with them, but they also knew that when it comes to work they have to remember what is required

in terms of integrity [and] training. Here, in Customs, it's a problem. They cannot mess up with me in that way ... [but] ... now that I am a Director ... the younger staff ... are ... not very comfortable with me any more.... I'm very far off from them already."[3] When rotation is rarely practiced and superiors emerge from the ranks of the very people they now manage, this sharpening of hierarchy and authority is especially significant. They may have worked with their staff for many years and know them very well, yet "my people ... know that I mean business.... I am very friendly to them, but when they really disobey the policies, I really oblige them to explain in writing ... so that will be part of their 201 file. I don't necessarily charge them outright, but I just bring a message that you have to be accountable for your actions. I am a friend, but these are the rules."[4]

2. This concentration of energy augments a second advantage brought by emotional and technical professionalism: greater precision, predictability and reliability in more specific and often vital operations. In decision making and policy formulation in the Central Bank, there is now

> ...less space for—I wouldn't call it politics—[but rather] more [room for working] on the basis of what the rules are, what [is] necessary to be able to carry out the job. I'll give you an example: I am head of monetary stability, so we are in charge of monetary policy. Now in the past—well, I was not the head of the sector then ... in the 70s and 80s...—monetary policy was more of an art ... than a science. Of course ... .models ... were formulated and implemented, but it was more of a ... you felt your way into it. But today under inflation targeting, we meet every six weeks: there is discipline. We explain to the general public what went behind any decision that we make. We hold ourselves accountable for the inflation forecast. We explain to them why we did this, or why we did not do that. And our decisions are basically driven by two things: one the inflation outlook; and two, the balance of risk. Both of which are driven by some quantitative models. But of course we exercise judgment: the models are very useful, but the models cannot capture everything in reality, so we have to make judgments. But judgment is limited to a certain place. Before, it [was] all judgment. Now, you have some judgment, but the model will have to be given its due weight. So, in other words, inflation targeting, to me, is constrained discretion: you still have discretion, but there are constraints. You have limits, you have boundaries.[5]

A further example is the allocation of collection targets to offices and officials of the BIR throughout the country. Under the attrition law these allocations have become extremely sensitive: the failure of officials to meet their target can mean dismissal from the service. "You just have to imagine the stigma of the family if that happens, though it's not your fault, because the target assigned to us is not fair. It's not fair, but that's the law, and you cannot ... question how the goals are assigned to us."[6] Consequently, those charged with setting targets

> ....have to consider all the data ... everything. Of course everybody would give you the data which would lower the goal.... Sometimes we find that they have hidden some data which would have an upward impact on their goal, but we discover [these data] in another region.... So we get data, [but] ... everybody expects that they have a relatively lower goal.... In fact, when we asked them ... "How much do you think it's reasonable for you to collect?" they of course have a conservative estimate ... and some of these [officials] are closer friends than the others. But you just have to stick to the data.[7]

An agency's procurement operation is another highly sensitive matter. After a run of corruption scandals, the Department of Education's new director of procurement (a political appointee) was determined to follow procedures strictly in accordance with the procurement law. When she took up her post there were those who "just took it for granted" that they would be allowed to bend the procurement process at will, and "there are still some who want to deviate, especially if the need is so urgent."[8]

> May be it's because that's the way they do things before.... But in my case ... I have only one [thing] in mind, [and that] is to implement and follow the laws ... the accountability and the processes are clear: there is no reason for you to deviate. So you only have to ... implement it, no matter what.... I just told [them] ... I said, "If it's not in accordance with the process, I just return it [the request]." Everything is included in the annual procurement plan, and if it is not there I just return it. Without anything personal in it, I just tell them that they should do this.[9]

Adherence to process, however, is only one aspect of greater predictability and stability brought by emotional and technical professionalism. Distancing relationships from the Department of Education's procurement machinery provides some measure of defense against the heat generated both among legislators (disappointed in their attempts to secure computers, books, tables and other equipment for schools in their districts) and among colleagues within the Department who would prefer to work quickly: "We hate that law ... oh my god, it gets on our nerves, and it stalls our programmes. Like, you just wanted to go to a seminar ... you have to post the seminar, you have to wait for two weeks so that hotels will be [booked].... We hate that law..."[10] As this last extract indicates, frustrations are directed more at the rules than at the person: "I wouldn't say it doesn't affect me, but I don't lose sleep over it.... I just say this is what the process requires ... that's all, nothing, it doesn't affect me. But people here in DepEd are so diplomatic; whether [or not] they ... like you ...when they see you, they still greet you and all these things.... And, in my case, if I say that this is not in accordance with the process and I return it, of course there's nothing personal about it: it's...merely because of the process." [11] At the same time, the treatment of rules, roles and procedures *as if* absolute permits a degree of flexibility. The law may be "very clear on ... the process—you cannot ... shortcut, because the moment you shortcut ... the rules and regulations, you will be accountable for deviating from the process." Yet there are "rules and regulations [that], I think, need to be looked at." For instance, "in the COA [Commission on Audit] rules and regulations, when you reimburse, there is a requirement that you submit the receipt, but when you ride jeepneys ... they don't issue receipts.... We cannot just simplify ... on our own, without waiting for the guidelines issued by the GPPB [Government Procurement Policy Board].... Unless a [new] guideline is issued, we cannot deviate from the processes as set out in the law." [12] But there is "...a continuous process of looking at the law, and its implementing rules and regulations. In fact, as a member of the technical working group of the GPPB we have already made a lot of revisions.... Because when that law was crafted, what was in the mind of the author of that law is to address corruption, and to address loopholes in account practices. So when it gets implemented, there are rules, there are regulations, that need to be simplified, and that's what we are doing." [13] With one eye on the criticisms which her office has had to endure, there is also an understanding of the need to align procurement operations more carefully with other processes within the agency: "We are looking now at how can we link timelines in procurement (because we are not allowed to shortcut the timelines) with ... other processes like planning and budgeting.... I think there [is] really is a need to link this process ... because it is not a "standalone." [14]

3. In their turn, greater predictability, reliability and stability reduce the need for constant supervision and referral and thus provide more opportunity for delegation. USECs and ASECs in particular (and third level staff more generally) put a deal of emphasis on delegation and often take pride in doing so:

> I try to let my subordinates think of the things they have to do rather than myself doing all the thinking in telling them what to do. I give them a lot of elbow room.... They know what their mandate is ... [and] ... given an appreciation of that mandate, they can think of what they have to do. I am not the type who will breathe down their necks just to check on them. [15]

Allowing subordinates to "exercise a lot of decision-making, and draw up their plans of things that have to be done" [16] is understood as a practical necessity in a strong and flexible organization: it prevents the leadership from becoming paralysed with minutiae and jaded by the routine; and it is a "part of developing these people."[17] It is also read by their subordinates as a mark of effective leadership and management:

> ...the authority given to them under the previous division chiefs—I have maintained ... they sign service records, they certify service records, they act on this, they act on [that] ...virtually everything has already been delegated to them.... I'm not saying that I do not have any more work to do ... but even if I'm [on] leave, even if I'm out of the office, attending to other important activities ... the division would run smoothly.... In fact I went to Japan—I was out [for] 14 days last August, and when I got back ... Jusef [Undersecretary Sangil] ... said: "Congratulations.... I see you're back, and so far when you were out, I've not heard of any, shall we say, shortfalls in functions in personnel. It's as if you were still there. So congratulations—I don't doubt that you've trained your people and you've delegated the required responsibilities." Of course ... I never delegate responsibilities [if] it's not going to be effective...[18]

Encouraging subordinates to take on these responsibilities, however, is not always easy: it takes time for them to develop, and become comfortable with, their own judgment. And when superiors feel the organization has become excessively hierarchical, then change must begin slowly: "They have to make certain minute decisions; and I just ... monitor them: you did this well, you did badly on this because ... and so on, and I explain to them why it's not good, why it's bad."[19] But if it is to be guidance rather than *diktat* and orthopraxy, then subordinates must be allowed room to experiment:

> There are some issues that I have had to send up the chain, up the ladder ... but as far as the authority that I exercise, my style of management is more—I think it is a more proactive style. I mean I give a lot of responsibility to my staff because I would rather empower them and have them feel responsible for their work, and I will review their work and if I find anything wrong I tell them and they can have an opportunity to correct it. I try not to impose my style. Different people have different styles of writing. I usually follow the principle of substance over form, so if the particular draft or communication conveys the substance that I would like, then I will adjust to that. So I give them a lot of leeway...[20]

And with greater freedom to make judgments comes greater responsibility. If they can make the case that their decisions are defensible, "then I'll go with them, because I am a risk-taker myself;" but if they cannot, they must also be prepared "to face the consequences of those decisions."[21]

It is, though, frustration with the gap between expectation and practice that bests conveys a desire to delegate and an understanding of its importance:

Subordinates seem to like the idea of giving a problem, and then it's for you to forward a solution. It's either they don't really have the solution or they're just testing you—if you can find the correct solution.... I've been telling the people that I work with, even until now, that as you go up the ladder it is ... the option of the person on top to give you the problem and for you to look for the solution, and not for you at the bottom or the lower end to give him the problem: you're wasting the time of the Commissioner. "So what you do," I tell them, "is if there's a problem you tell your superior your solutions, your recommendations, and leave it to your manager to choose the option, which one." So I've just talked to one of our consultants, and I have been able to convince him to conduct training—beginning perhaps with ... a hundred personnel—to change their mindset, of not telling the Commissioner that "This is the problem," [but] rather "Commissioner, this is a problem and these are our recommended solutions. It's up to you to choose".... You have to tell them that there is nothing to fear but fear itself. As long as you're honest, you have noble intention, you're pure in heart ... what's to fear? Nothing!"[22]

4. With deepening emotional and technical professionalism—and with a heightening in the sense that social relationships are, conceptually, put to one side selectively and temporarily in order to facilitate technical operations—it becomes easier to acknowledge overtly the presence of social and affective relationships within the organization. Thus, for instance, superiors "have to keep ... some image that you are not the same [as subordinates],"[23] but that "distance between you and your subordinates ... should not be too personal ... it should be just imaginary."[24] For when all is said and done, it is social relationships rather than the organization's frameworks that take priority:

> ...there has to be a balance with your relationship and with the work, but as much as possible I would say that, maybe, I would put the relationship a bit higher ... just a little bit higher ... because, after all, when you are gone ... no one will remember you that you have exceeded this goal, that you have done a lot of things for the Bureau. No. It is the people for whom you have done something good ... rather than "this person has collected so much." '[25]

This intrusion of affective relationships into the organization is such that the social sphere loses geographical distinction. That is to say, a conceptually bounded social sphere within the organization is now admitted. The pools and streams of affective relationships which gather and run through the organization sometimes make it more difficult to raise levels of technical proficiency. It is, for instance, clearly difficult on compassionate grounds to give a colleague with several children and a jobless husband a poor performance rating (two such ratings are sufficient cause for dismissal). And the leniency often shown by civil servants towards the performance of their colleagues is often a cause for exasperation. The disdain with which political appointees and many third-level career civil servants view security of tenure is a case in point (see chapter 2). Yet, for the most part, these explicitly social relationships co-exist quite happily alongside, and to the advantage of, the organization's frameworks. (The distinction between framework and relationships is, after all, only conceptual). More specifically, the intrusion of the affective brings to the organization four important qualities.

1. The first, compassion, lifts the weight of fear and the pressure this creates for over-conformity. Compassion may also be read as an aspect of integrity and as an opportunity for improvement.[26] Often, though by no means always, this takes on religious forms:

> You have to bring the church to the marketplace, and I think that spirituality is very important in the work of people. I think you get to have a firmer idea of what integrity is all about, what honesty is all about, if you have some spiritual armor.... I think I get to be...more flexible perhaps, more understanding of ... the weaknesses of people. I mean, not everyone ... can ... deliver all at the same time. People have some weaknesses and I think we have to have more room for, not really for tolerating, but understanding. Because first you have to identify what those weaknesses are, but you have to do something about those weaknesses. You just don't tolerate weaknesses and not do something about them. Once you have identified [them] ... you have to impress upon the person that he has to change, and he has to beef up on some of those weaknesses.[27]

Compassion alters not only the atmosphere for civil servants but also the tone of the service and government. An army of technocrats judged constantly, harshly, and solely on their technical proficiency, is unlikely to be either flexible enough in thought or sufficiently empathetic to deal with the mass of the people they are supposed to serve.

2. Second, the admission of affective relationships works to cool the friction generated by "official" representations—the arrangements of rules, roles, procedures, hierarchies and divisions of authority—which inform and constrain civil servants' actions. While the treatment of rules *as if* absolute helps (as noted earlier) to deflect frustration away from the person and towards the rules, the intrusion of affective relationships works to insulate "the person" still further. Civil servants may argue and vie with each because this is what the "harsh structure" in which they find themselves requires them to do; but they remain friends and are able to show "good judgment without favoring a friend and yet without hurting a friend,"[28] for each understands "it is just the job."[29]

> We've been together for so long and we know each other so deeply and personally that even if we have a little quarrel [over work] it doesn't really count any more because it [is] only ... work-related.... Like, in the case of the budget, demands from the budget, budget hearings, meeting deadlines.... One of the sources [of stress] that we can all agree [on] is running after all our bosses for their signature action, because they're all out, because they are too busy ... most of the time. And sometimes the delays ... you can pinpoint the delays because of that. After you've done your work on time, but because they are not available, because they are also attending urgent matters, official matters...[30]

The affective also allows supervisors to judge and manage subordinates more effectively: "It's really an advantage when you really know the person for a long time, you would understand her moods, you would understand how to deal with her.... Even my best friend would know that when it comes to work I mean work—so sometimes I scold her ... and she understands..."[31] It also easier "once you get to know people for a long time, you get to know the capability of that person very well ... to talk confidentially to that person to get them to improve their performance; and it'll be easier to know whether or not they are in fact performing badly."[32] And it allows subordinates "to know the person—not as a boss but as a person ... to know about the likes and dislikes of the person. What are the things that make him ... decide something ... What is important to him? [So you won't] do something that will somehow strain that relationship."[33]

3. Third, the intrusion of the affective encourages resilience to criticism. This is especially important when representations of self have become very tightly bound up with those of the organization:

> We love [X—an office in the Department of Education] because we became "beings" here, I mean—our family our children were educated because of this work, and we've been here for so many years, and this is our bread and butter. Me personally, I'm proud to be here at DepEd; and people in our neighborhood in our place look up to me; like, for instance, they have a problems dealing with DepEd, they will consult you—[such as] how to apply for a DepEd test—and I always help them. But, on the other hand, there are also people who have a bad image of ... DepEd because of ... corrupt[ion].... Corruption usually exists at the division, the regional [level], but here in Metro Manila not so much, especially at X.... Of course, we cannot always avoid those perceptions.... But we're not really affected ... because personally ... the true measure of your work is on your conscience...[34]

For third-level civil servants, too, an intrinsic interest in their work is no less important in the face of criticism and ridicule, and perhaps nowhere more so that in the BIR:

...the reputation of the Bureau definitely precedes us. The reputation is mostly from ... partly here [central office], but a big part also
is from the actions of our field officers—the people on the ground
talking to the taxpayers.... [It] is difficult for us from here to really
see [this] and catch [them]. But that does have an effect on us because ... when we introduce ourselves, or we meet people, we know
that at the back of their minds [they are thinking] "We are talking
to the Bureau so let's not be too open. These guys are like this or
like that." So that's a given that they might think that—there's a *very*
good chance they think that. For me, [I] just take it in my stride; it
is there, and the only way we can counter that is by showing good
actions, good examples.[35]

One further aspect to the admission of affective relationships—and one
that is intriguing and, possibly, highly significant—is the embarrassment and
shame felt about practices which not only infringe rules and laws but are also
held to be immoral in that they make use of colleagues and country for private
gain. And it is, perhaps, in those organizations where political interference
and money-making are prevalent that this shame is most keenly felt and most
obvious: in a strained and cautious atmosphere; in the shrines that decorate
offices, corridors and foyers; in the prayers read aloud across the office at
least once a day; and in other forms of demonstrative religious piety.

4. A deepening and less self-centered view of colleagues, organization,
government and wider world—combined with a sharpening and intrinsic
interest in ideas, techniques, processes, rules, and roles—bring to the organization a fourth quality: an openness and willingness to communicate and
exchange ideas, to enquire, to adjust, and to change altogether understandings of self within a much broader world.[36] There is, other words, a growing
desire to align representations and practices more carefully and effectively.
Indeed, the presence of these qualities within an organization is often seen
to depend not upon compulsion and instruction, but upon the recruitment
of the right people in the first instance. True, "not all people are interested
in a lot of things...there are people who are really made for specific things
... [but] I will expect good managers to have that [breadth]"[37] and to mesh
their subordinates together.

...For me, personally, I always say that I cannot claim to be better
than anyone in everything, meaning each person here has something
that they can [offer].... He may be a lowly employee, he may be a
clerk, but I'm sure that ... this person has something.... I may have
been given control over the functions in the office, but certainly
each one of them has something better [than me], and can offer
something better. And so, for me, I will have the humility to talk
and listen to them, as what they say may have the solution to problems in the office.... So, for me, in managing people, I look at them

as partners, I look at them as people who have their own gifts.... Some of these things may be in running their families which is not necessarily related to the office, some [are] working on computers which can help us.... Some [are] ... in looking at details.... I am only as good as their work. If they don't do their part, I don't think I'll be able to do mine.[38]

Staffs with a broad interest in the world and in other people are already well on the way to becoming effective managers and administrators. It is then just a matter of facilitating their predilection for alignment. There are four sets of activities important in this regard.

1. The first, and most obvious, is training. For organizations with the wherewithal, such as the Central Bank, training is partly about sending staff overseas to learn new techniques so that "we end up at least on a par with other Central Banks."[39] It is also about coordination within the organization and, hence, conveying to the nation a sense of the Bank's competency.

'When I came in as Deputy Governor in July 2005, we asked the institute together with our department heads to devise a three-part modular training programme for new hires....We have the elementary or basic, and we have the intermediate and advanced. And I told them to put in the curriculum, you know, risk management, monetary policy, monetary operations—all the important pillars of monetary stability. Not only that.... *I* made sure that everybody knows what monetary policy is all about, and how it is formulated—even on a more general level, not on a specialist level, so that anyone, whether is he is from the cash department or loans and credit, if he is asked *outside* the bank, he would know, and confidently answer, what [we] are doing in the bank as far as ensuring price stability, for example. I don't want people to appear stupid when they are asked outside, even if ... it's outside his own jurisdiction. So, through those three components of the training programme, by the time they finish the third component, they should be more confident, and more competent, to answer questions on monetary stability.[40]

2. A second activity is corporate planning. Started in the 1990s, it was only in 2001 with the establishment of a planning office that a more conscious effort was made to "have the managers working in one direction"[41] and to "pitch individual departments" work programmes to what we wanted to achieve in terms of the two pillars of central banking: price stability and financial system stability."[42]

3. Formal meetings comprise the third activity. Although Board Members—the governor (appointed by the President for a term of six years), a cabinet member, and five members from the private sector (and, occasion-

ally, the universities)—comprise the policy-making body of the Bank, they nevertheless require a working knowledge of the organization and processes of the Bank. They glean this from a series of briefings from sectoral and departmental heads during the first few weeks of their appointment, and from the Board meetings held once a week (every Thursday from 10.30 AM for much of the day and sometimes until late at night). More important, as far as coordination of the Bank's technical operations are concerned, are the Management Committee meetings held by heads of the Bank's three main sectors—monetary stability, supervision, and resource management—and chaired by the Governor.

4. A fourth activity is the periodic, and somewhat fitful, consolidation of laws, orders and memoranda—the written description of an agency, the scope of its authority, its functions, its rules, and procedures. These attempts to formulate more coherent representations with which to inform, align and integrate practice within the organization are no mean feat, especially in a large agency such as the Department of Education.

> When I reported for work I was really amazed with the volume of work, because there are only around seven lawyers here at the central office to cater or to serve around 570,000 employees. So all the legal problems, legal concerns, and legislative concerns are under my office.... It was a monumental task. So first thing, I tried to look [at] the pending cases.... What I did was to change the rules of procedure in administrative cases. So I ... proposed revised rules of procedure ... to expedite the proceedings ... at least that was the intention. And then ... I tried to revisit all the major education laws. So ... I prepared a codification of the education laws ... with some amendments [and, via the Secretary] submitted [these] to Congress...
>
> As for departmental orders, there are so many ... sometimes orders just repeat prior orders; or they change prior orders.... [But] what teachers or principals know are the prior orders [which] have already been changed.... So, to have a sense about all these things.... I prepared a quick index for the last 10 years,[and] tried to group these into ... different subjects.... I prepared a quick index ... for easy reference ... so that is 127 volumes.... And during the last election I prepared also the manual for the teachers who were on the board of election inspectors.... I am now trying to propose amendments to the *Magna Carta* for public schoolteachers.'[43]

Similar attempts at alignment are to be found within smaller, local government offices. One striking example is the Environmental Protection and Waste Management Department (EPWMD) at Quezon City Hall. As far as technical operations are concerned, "...it is important that we document, that we plan ahead, that we conceptualize within the group, and [that we take] ... the bottom-up approach: we plan it with the grassroots ... then we do the planning with our technical group, and implement with the grassroots."[44] However, planning and implementation are dependent upon more centralized modes of alignment codified as a set of "House Rules." These cover all kinds of matters from dress and uniforms (yellow for special occasions, green for everyday use, and a "washday" on Fridays) to monitoring attendance. These were drawn up and enforced by the assistant departmental head (who also doubles as Administrative head) who saw in the Department—as she saw in so many of her pupils when teaching, and in so much of local government—a need for a clearly stated and properly enforced guide for practice.

> When I moved here, I was shocked. This was a task force then. People would come, people would go, without any discipline, and it was allowed at the time. I was shocked. Some of them reported for work at nine o'clock and then, at 11 o'clock, they are gone. Others would come at one o'clock and after thirty minutes they were gone. I was shocked. It's not the kind of discipline that I like. So I made suggestions to the boss, to the director of the task force. So I said to the boss "Let's have discipline". In the government offices we have to render forty hours of service a week, so that's Monday to Friday. If the office hours are from eight o'clock to five o'clock, then they should be here from eight o'clock until five. And if their office hours from nine o'clock to six o'clock, they should be here from nine o'clock and leave at six o'clock. At first, I really had a hard time doing [this]. So we started with an office memorandum, and then later on I started to reprimand them—of course, with the approval of the Mayor. And then later on, up to now, all of them, I should say, are all disciplined.[45]

5. Implicit in the discussion so far is the suggestion that emotional and technical professionalism *happens* to bring advantages to the organization, and that these advantages are not the prime motive for professionalism. Nested within this suggestion is another: that it is the actors' interest in their work and in other people as matters of significance in their own right, rather than in any ulterior objectives, that best allows (albeit through a kind of happenstance) the effective realization of those objective. This affective or emotional approach to the organization and its tasks is especially strong in some quarters of the Central Bank— regarded widely by civil servants as one of the country's elite agencies. And it is an approach that has often been imported by those with long experience in the private sector— in this case as Senior Vice President of the Bank of Commerce:

> When you hire a person, you do not hire him as a clerk. You hire him for him to develop a career. I am not hiring you as a bank teller, I want you to be a banker. In the next five years you should be a banker.... What we need is that you have direction ... then we'll take

up training you. So there should be no dead-end positions.... I do not mind if, after three years ... they move out. I do not mind because during those three years we have benefited from their services.... We've trained people because we want to have good people not only in bank, but in the outside world as well ... I want people working for me because they are happy, not because they are bound by a written instrument. There was a time when the foreign banks were allowed to come in here, about ten years ago, and except for two, we lost twenty-three [staff]. All of them were pirated ... because there was no contract. Then the head of training, the human resources, was very depressed because we lost people that we [needed] for officer ranks.... [But] it means that we are training people well, and that's our contribution to the banking industry. We are training people not only for the bank, but for others also. What's the solution? ... train more people! Then we decided [on] an accelerated training programme ... and we solved our problem.[46]

His interest in the intrinsic significance of colleagues, work, and industry now permeates the Central Bank's legal department. At least, it is a frame of mind that he *expects* to find among his subordinates (who include thirty-five lawyers).

All the [other] departments are our clients, so if in one-day we receive fifteen requests for consultations, all of these are documented. I farm [these] out to my assistant, and he farms [them] out to our lawyers, with no instructions, it's just the name. Because you are supposed to think what is right.... The direction is [that] we should not [be] concern[ed] about the party or the amount. We decide on merits, we resolve based on merits; we should not let the amount of the transaction or the parties involved in the transaction affect our decision. So they prepare their study, comments, and these are elevated to me. If I agree, I sign it. If I disagree, I make my changes, and then if they are agreeable, they revise it and I sign it. But if they are not agreeable, they see me and then we discuss it [and] argue.... I like [this]!... Sometimes they reverse, sometimes I reverse.... We find fulfilment as lawyers here—because we *should* find fulfilment in the practice of law, in this office, because we are administrators of truth. We do not "wish facts" here, we do not suppress evidence here.... Of course we argue as best as we could ... so you feel you are doing the work honestly.... Even when you go to court, win or lose cases, it's based on the merit. Do not be afraid to lose cases because if it is a losing case we should lose.... I refuse to gauge our performance ... [by] ... the number of cases we lose or win—that should not be the standard. How well have we handled the cases—*that* should be the standard ... .if we win and you distort the facts [in order to win], we will not be happy that way. So our lawyers here—they are happy with that arrangement.[47]

It is thus that civil servants will produce, as a side effect, "a world-class legal group [that] can compete with the best law office or legal office, even from the UK"[48]— a legal office that is better placed to ensure that the actions taken by the bank's officers are legally valid and defensible, that the number of times they are called into court is minimized, and that they can focus their attentions and efforts on monetary and banking stability.

An understanding of this approach is by no means confined to the Central Bank: its importance is recognized elsewhere in the civil service, though perhaps more by its absence.

> One of the things that that has been forgotten is the mission of public servants.... Its own motivation for what you do, I think, has been lost.... My first year here—when my youngest daughter had been working for this ... multinational company—it just hit me in the face: how is it that this daughter of mine can be so committed to this company that sells soap and shampoo and toothpaste to the extent that she would react to the competitor's advertisements that we have to change all our usual products? How can someone be so dedicated, so loyal, so committed to a company that sells cosmetics? And why is it that [in] people who work in government [you] can hardly see that kind of commitment, that kind of fulfilment [in] a job that serves other people? *That* we are very far away from. It is the motivation of the service that needs to be engendered.... But I see it here, I see people sometimes sending text messages—people I don't know. They say "Ma'am, I saw somebody in this place doing this or doing that. This is against good public services. Please do something about it." So it is there ... I think if you look at the people in the career service, you really have pretty good people. In all honesty they may not be brilliant, but [for] a lot of them, at the professional level especially, it will take very little to make them really good public servants—the kind of people who stay on not because they cannot be hired but ... because they find fulfilment in the kind of work that they do.[49]

A sense of the importance of this approach becomes still more acute as a determination to monitor and measure the work of civil servants transforms their efforts into absolute targets which, as such, are now open to manipulation: "When you have a points system—this is my own opinion, because it's happening to me ... those under me are more conscious about attaining the points.... Somehow you lose your motivation because you're not really doing it out of the goodness of your heart any more.... You have to come up with a certain number of points but in reality, inside, you're not happy about it any more."[50]

Yet there is no question that an emotional approach is to be found in many parts of the civil service, such that "you can stir their passion; even without money they will do it; they can serve beyond office hours; they will deliver ... give it their best shot; and even though it is not their [role or responsibility] you can ask them 'Please help' and they will help, even without funds."[51] Even in what might appear to be the most unlikely places—such as in Customs—there are those, for whom the job "is not [about] doing [that] eight-to-five thing—that ... is not enough to get things done.... If you talk with them, [they] have this sense of importance [about their job] at the back of their [minds]..."[52] That the presence of this quality within the civil service is recognized by members of the legislature—where the bureaucracy's critics are among the most trenchant— is an indication of its extent and significance:

> You will find people who are there [in the civil service] because they believe that the institutions they belong to, house the capacity to actually do good. And they stay there because they see this and they would like to be part of that good.... Secretary X for Budget and Management: she was an accountant in the Department of Budget and Management; she was promoted; she rose through the ranks; and eventually [she was] appointed as the Secretary during Ramos's time and then [under] Arroyo.... When she was still the Secretary, and I was still working for social welfare, she would go to meetings with no notes, and she would say "I can realign so much from this agency to that. This is not allowed, this is allowed, [but] we can do this. I think we have whatever left from this fund." This was all in her head, and she was getting paid 30,000 pesos a month—gross. Who works that much for that much money?... How much does a middle range bureaucrat earn compared to someone in a private corporation? Don't even ask that—they are completely incomparable. [And] while the person in the corporation only worries about certain sectors or certain locations, this one is a bureaucrat [who] worries about the entire country. Like, the Social Welfare Department: social workers would ... ride in military choppers. A volcano has just erupted in Bicol? Go! No holiday! You have a real dedication and a willingness ... to work for the government.... Bureaucracy is not all lazy and corrupt...[53]

Deepening emotion is also reflected in a desire to move away from credentialism in the selection and promotion of civil servants; and, as a corollary, in a frustration with all those schools and universities which, rather than treat education and students as matters of intrinsic significance, "just give all these degrees so they can satisfy the standard [for appointment and promotion.... We have to recognize that there are [different rates of learners] ... there will be a slow learners in some aspects, but fast learners in some [other] aspects. So, having said that, the [kind of] teacher now that we have to develop is someone who can recognize the potential of every individual—so he or she may be good in, say, academics only but not good in arts and crafts and so on."[54] And it suggests that improvements in pay—if treated as a reward and an objective rather than as a condition that allows staff the freedom to concentrate on developing themselves, their colleagues, and their work as important endeavours in their own right—will not encourage lasting improvements in the quality of the civil service.

* * *

It is evident that professionalism is not synonymous with being "impersonal"; technical efficiency is not to be equated with a separation from, or denial of, social relationships. Quite the contrary: relationships and other aspects of representations and practice (and their alignment and integration) are the stuff of organizations. This sense if often carried by the word "harmony." "There must be harmony in our organization. Because each member of the team has a role to play and it's hard for that team to function if it's discordant. It's essential. So the challenge is also on the supervisors to make sure that everything is doing fine in terms of relationships within the organization. And not only within the department or unit, but in relation to the other departments as well."[55] The point is frequently acknowledged in the recruitment process:

> ...human resources go through...all the tests.... [But] before any employee is taken in, I'm the last to interview, so I will give the "go" signal. So when I interview I do not ask about their academics etcetera, etcetera, because all of this has been [established].... I start with questions like "How were you brought up? What household chores did you do? What are your saving habits? How are your relationships with your brothers and sisters? What type of discipline did your parents have on you? Who are your friends? How do you spend your leisure time? How do you spend Friday night?" And I ask a commitment from them ... that you will not be late for work. On a rainy day it's easy for employees to call sick. I don't want those type of employees. I want employees who ... will be willing to go through wet streets, and even through high traffic, and report because they have a responsibility to perform. [Though] I am not sure if I have hundred percent batting average![56]

The importance of technical competency, vigour, and ambition, and the effect which these qualities have on existing employees, should not be underestimated:

> I guess what's driving a lot of people, and this is something which I have observed over the last five years ... is the entry of the younger people, the new graduates.... Their entry has somehow challenged the old ones in the institution. So you have a level of performance that's driven both by the desire to excel, and [by] new blood ... posing a lot of challenges.... These young ones are simply the best. You

send them jobs and they...do it—fast.... That in itself is a mechanism which has improved ... performance also.'[57]

But with sharper competition and, inevitably, a stress on utilitarian objectives, comes a narrowing of thought and action: conceptually, relationships are marginalized or eradicated and the organization appears to become increasingly impersonal; and unless some way can be found of counteracting these qualities, the organization begins to weaken.

> You have a lot of professionals, and most of the professionals seem to forget that the relationship thing is big. In fact, one of the managers that I have spoken with has told me that in setting up, for instance, the early discounting system that they had, he realized later on that it is 90 percent relationships and 10 percent professional work. So he saw the value of relationships in that. The other thing that we have realized in the Central Bank of the Philippines is that we are hiring a lot of good examiners, good economists, very good professionals.... But when we promote them to become managers they lose the manager *and* the expert in them, because they end up being bad bosses and so they lose their credibility even as experts.... So we are now saying in the Central Bank we have to address two things. One is that we ... need training for experts to become managers. But we are also saying that, in the end, we have to realise that there are two kinds of people: the managers *and* the experts. Some of them may go up to become consultants, limited basically to their own studies.... So we may have [some]one who's very good in monetary policy, for example, and can go even up to the board to advise the board, and we will have to provide him some kind of a path as a professional. So we are now talking of dual track: some people who have to go as professionals because they are not able to manage; but for those who are trainable in terms of managing people, then we have to train them and let them manage people. So we are looking at tracks, we are looking at growth for each one, we are looking at growth for the best ones either as managers or as professionals.[58]

Informality

Threaded through much of what has been said is the suggestion that the organization's "official" framework is reconfigured by social relationships, emotions, and other representations and practices. This regeneration or replenishment of the official (formal) framework by the social (informal) is part of the organizations' constant, uncontroversial and often unnoticed business. New or altered formal arrangements are constantly emerging from informal social practice: "...that is how it evolves—informality first, before formality."[58] Indeed, for some officials the translation of informal into formal is a key principle of management:

> Again I have to talk from experience—whenever you [create] put people [in] a formal structure, there is a tendency for people to resist initially. I would rather have it evolve organically ... because then ... people ... feel that they are part of the decision-making itself, and it is not something imposed primarily because you have an expert or consultant who is supposed to know everything, who says this would be the best structure for you.... Sometimes it [the evolution] [takes] longer, but sometimes it's ... fast, because people see, "Yes we need to do that," so [they] form a committee, [then] a task force, [then] Let's make that now a permanent organization."[59]

A small illustration is provided by the near redundancy of older, formal procedures for handling grievances, and the emergence of new practices. While the older, formal machinery—that of written complaints, hearings and resolutions—still exist, it is, in many agencies, rarely used. In the CSC no cases have been taken to the committee for more than two years. And even where, in other agencies, disputes are elevated to USECs or ASECs, informal means are preferred: "I call their boss and I say "Okay, you better go and finish your conversation somewhere else..."[60] In the Central Bank the next obvious step has been taken: to encourage and regularize existing informal practice such that a new formal process is established—one of "dialogues" between parties or, in other words, "...making people understand that they are not actually in a contest here—they have just misunderstood each other. So it is a way of making people realize that there is a way of doing things where you need not really file cases against each other because there is really no case to speak about."[61]

Another small example is provided by the BIR where, ten to fifteen years ago, any member of staff who happened to be present in a district office when members of the public found their way into an office would find themselves having to deal with queries and requests for advice. An Officer-of-the-Day was therefore assigned to deal with these matters. As the traffic in queries grew, a small group of assistants to handle computations, supply the necessary forms, and to advise on their completion gathered around the Officer-of-the-Day. All of this was eventually institutionalized into a tax-payer assistance section.

A further illustration is the emergence of a semi-permanent corps within the Senate (separate from the Senate's secretariat) whose members are often passed on from one senator to the next as elections are lost or as terms of office expire. They provide a continuity of experience and legislation; they train, steer, and, in some cases, will have to carry new senators; and, critically, they are able to alleviate something of the tension during times of intense disagreements and personal disputes among senators.[62] During these periods, adherence to Senate protocols and conventions (most especially that of "being an honorable member") may allow Senators—through the rituals

179

of debate on the floor of the House—to distance their personal animosity from Senate business symbolically: to expect more than this would be to expect from them superhuman effort. But while some honorable members could not stand the sight of each other, their staff at least would be cordial and continue to operate behind the scenes. This at least was the atmosphere and practice before the Estrada and Arroyo presidencies.

> But with Erap and Gloria you could almost see the line of division, and it even came to a point that was pretty petty—that if you worked for an opposition senator, and you are administration, you were just civil, but that's all. It was that stupid. Osmena said that this is the first time that he felt that the chamber was so polarized, that there was this distinct line between opposition and administration.... It came to a point that you wouldn't choose somebody who worked with the opposing team. Before it was never a problem. It was only competence that mattered. It became silly.[63]

In the view of some, the Senate remains far from being collegial: "You can't really say: "he's my friend, I'll talk to him." I can say that in the [Lower] House, not with everybody, but with a good number. But I can't really say that in the Senate with regard to a single senator. For example you say "Look, this Senator he's been doing this and he's been doing that—he's been bothering me. But I am not in a position (I don't think anyone is in a position) to say, that's ok, I'll help, he's a good friend of mine, I'll take care of it."[64] For others, though, the atmosphere has improved more recently "to a point that now that they are no longer polarised by personality, but by issues, and they (the senators) will work together as a collegial body, whether opposition or administration. They are more ready to do it now than in the past."[65] Certainly Aquino's office was now taking "a lot of people from previous senators. It is very useful. I have never worked in the Senate before so I know absolutely nothing about the ins and outs in—who we talk to about this or that. So it is [good] to have that institutional knowledge."[66] Yet, even so, "they came from senators who are allied with us in the party so in terms of policy directions they are familiar with the stand."[67] And since the staff of the Senators is also the staff of the committees, and is always changing, "it deprives us of continuity; it deprives us of inherent knowledge with respect to the committees work in previous years. It ... [is] a hindrance, with respect to keeping track of records ... if the Senator leaves he takes with him all the files. We can't do anything about it."[68]

As this last example indicates, there are circumstances that may disrupt the translation of informality—in this case both personal and fundamental disagreements among politicians and civil servants over policy directions; over the functions, objectives, and philosophy of government and bureaucracy; and, therefore, over what is acceptable and what should be regularized and protected. Indeed, this is but one of four overlapping and mutually reinforcing conditions which interrupt translation. A second is personalism (such as interference in the civil service by politicians for their own financial gain) practiced to an extent and degree that it is difficult or impossible to establish formal and effective counter-measures, either because these will be blocked and subverted by existing placements, or because politicians will not pass the necessary legislation. A third is the presence (or perception) of complex division of authority that encourage circumvention. For instance, as part of their attempts to counter or increase their leverage over one another, legislators and the Office of the President will work to influence placements in the civil service. This third set of circumstances is closely related to the first and second in that these divisions (and especially, therefore, the issue of control) are the subject of intense disagreement, and may create a cellular administration in which divergent, insular and partisan perspectives emerge. Informal-formal translation is also disrupted by over-conformity and its underlying pressures. As noted in chapter 3, these pressures are very personal in that a failure to acquiesce may damage careers and livelihoods; and they are altruistic in that a failure to acquiesce may harm the efficacy of an organization or weaken the separation of powers. In either case, they are very strong.

Put another way, when personalism works to undermine rules and processes (such as those governing civil service appointments); when there are divergent representations of government, its functions and policies (and, therefore, sharp differences over which rules and processes are accepted and acceptable); when there is over-conformity (and, therefore, little or no possibility that rules and processes can evolve along with understandings about what civil servants believe to be important and needs to be done); and when authority is perceived to be misallocated such that divisions in authority conflict with the fulfilment of what are felt to be critical responsibilities and duties: under these circumstances existing sets of rules, processes and organizations lose psychological force, social practice is now exposed, and informality becomes more obvious. One consequence of this is that positive informal practice may whither. For instance, by creating an atmosphere in which all informality is de-legitimized, over-conformity may suppress creativity and experimentation while indirectly rewarding personalism: if one is to behave outside the constraints of formality, then why risk having one's behavior misinterpreted for the sake of a more effective organization rather than personal gain? More commonly, however, positive informal practice simply "goes it alone" and, indeed, a deal of such behavior is evident. It is indicative of selflessness, commitment, and an interest in the organization, the job, and the wider public good for their own sakes; and it is important in a number of other respects that are set out below.

Coordination, Communication, and Creativity

For reasons already set out, the Department of Education's Executive Committee meetings provide ASECs and USECs with only an uneven picture of what is happening elsewhere in the organization. The knowledge to complete this picture, and to improve coordination, has to be gleaned, and acted upon, by ASECs and USECs through their own informal arrangements as and when seems necessary.[69] For example, the undersecretary whose responsibility includes regional operations often finds himself working in this ad hoc manner with "the undersecretary for legal: a lot of problems that crop up in schools usually end up as formal complaints, which are handled by legal, and sometimes we try to ... look at ... ways of resolving the problems—informal, commonsense ways..."[70]

Among directors, too, informal communications are essential to overcome excessive formality. These emerge spontaneously and by design, though, as in the CSC, somewhat unevenly: "With some offices I happen to develop friendships with some of its officials as I moved from one position to the next, and therefore it is easier for me to coordinate and get in touch and talk with these people and easily get support—which happens with OPMIS and some other offices. With others it's really very formal even with people I have [known] for a long time ... via memo ... it's like talking to them formally."[71]

These differences in atmosphere, often quite marked, derive from staffs' understandings of their offices' particular mandates and technical features as well as from their own personalities. Second-level civil servants must also negotiate these differences. On the whole, staff from one department visiting another will first approach someone of the same rank. "...If there is nobody around, and the Assistant Director or Director is there, I go direct to them. Anyway I know them.... Because I have already been here fifteen years, I know most of the staff, most of the directors [and] assistant directors, so I'm familiar with them, [and] they are familiar with me.... Some of them were my directors before."[72] Better still is if "you [know a director] personally when he was still not the head of the office. It's easier to talk with him," since "if you don't know the person, then ... [it's] so formal—it's different because you don't know him and he doesn't know you"[73]

It also helps if a civil servant's backing and the reason for making the approach are suitably authoritative, though rarely is this a clear-cut matter. Officials in the CSC's Internal Audit unit who examine processes in other departments at central office answer directly to the Chair; and it is the Chair who determines which departments are to be audited, when, and how often. This direct line to the Chair makes it easier for its second-level officials to approach and gather information from other departments, but more difficult to report on them. Despite attempts to present the unit as a "partner in improving systems and procedures," "it's inevitable sometimes to have misunderstandings."[74] A critical report will cast a shadow over its authors' relationships and, in the minds of those whose departments have been censured, raise suspicions. Meanwhile, for those departments whose functions require them to maintain regular, even constant, interactions with most other departments, establishing and sustaining relationships is easier in that the fulfilment of those functions provides the justification and opportunity for deepening those relationships. In the case of personnel, fostering relationships is a matter of

> assuring them that we in personnel attend to *all* of their particular requirements. Also, if they have [matters] which need our support, such as if they request me to send X to assist them in a workshop.... I do not say no, I never say no, because I believe that being with them is part of the ... continued bonding, and the continued assurance.... [Moreover] X, whenever she assists, or one of us is going to assist them, then they tell us, "Oh, have lunch with us ... and we'll discuss ... we'll talk.... I have to update you with developments".... We are also on different committees.... Whenever I cannot [attend], I can delegate it—I send one of them to act as [our] member of [the] committee.... So I see to it that we have continuing communications ... especially [with] those who are in charge of their particular [departments].[75]

While internal audit's cachet and the nature of personnel's functions make it easier to cultivate relationships, staff (especially at second and first levels) from departments without those advantages must work especially hard to breach the walls within central office. The staffs of one department—formerly an independent body handling foreign-assisted projects— were brought administratively into Education's central office only to find that its denizens felt themselves to have

> a stature higher than [ours]. So ... we can [only] coordinate with them nicely, patiently ... we are under their mercy.[76] Even if you are already angry because, for instance, there is already so much delay, you cannot really express impatience.... You have to deal with them patiently, because otherwise they will not really work [through] your requirements. Sometimes we give out little tokens ... to expedite papers, or to be friends with them—a little chocolate ... to establish a rapport.[77]

The cultivation of relationships across departments within a central office is useful not only for communication and coordination, but also for developing solutions and sustaining the efficacy of particular operations. "Let's say there is a problem about special hardship allowances.... We get somebody from personnel, from finance, from the budget ... and also from the bureaux ... and form these [ad hoc] technical working groups to evaluate the pros and cons of the problem and to implement solutions, and that's being practiced right now.... Although it's not formal or based on the manual, it's really being practiced and it is very helpful..."[78]

Implicit in these informal communications is the breakdown of hierarchy. This is often complete (though again temporary) and fairly common within the boundaries of a single department. It does not always find expression in dress and manner, but it may often do so at third level and most especially among ASECs (Assistant Secretaries) and USECs (undersecretaries). The women (plainly turned out) and the men (with shabby clothing, ruffled hair, and scuffed shoes) work in simple, even Spartan, rooms. The unpretentious effect is intended. It is an expression of their style: to throw the emphasis on what is done, "on output rather than dress"[79]; and to emphasize competence, for "if you are good, you are good" and there is no need to separate yourself by rank.[80] They are accessible, and their doors open. They are addressed respectfully as *ma'am* or *sir* or perhaps by their title and their initials ("Director A.P.R."), but the delivery is familiar; the conversation is free, often joking; and subordinates will not hesitate to contradict their superiors.

The cultivation of this easy atmosphere is intended to encourage creativity and the exchange of ideas, and to improve the speed and quality of decisions. Policies, the analysis of problems, the solutions recommended, and mode of implementation are unlikely to be either imaginative or effective if formulated through a mechanical process and by staff who are reluctant to speak their minds. Indeed, it is perhaps when gatherings are primarily social, and when thinking is free and relaxed, that discussion are most creative.

> When ... we have informal discussions, sometimes we get ideas on what adjustments we need, what refinements to introduce, and so we institutionalize it. Over lunch ... aside from the meetings ... officials usually celebrate their birthdays and everybody's invited—that is a forum for those informal discussions. And also, let's say, we came from a budget hearing, or a Senate hearing or congressional hearing, and we spend hours sitting there waiting [to see] whether we'll be asked; and sometimes we get asked so many questions; and it's really so tiring and so stressful. So, we'll have a blowout, we'll treat ourselves. So that's where we get these things [ideas], and not just [from talk about official work]...[81]

The breakdown of hierarchy has other significant aspects and advantages. It is a way for superiors to stimulate and clarify their own thoughts: "In our sectoral meetings ... I barge in directly, I have managing directors, I have an assistant governor, and all the department heads. Now when we discuss issues I don't think rank is important.... [And] I encourage my people to speak, because sometimes the lower staff may have a better idea and therefore you have to listen before you make a judgment or you make your summary. [It's] the way you crystallize issues."[82] It is a way to bring on subordinates: "At times they really disagree, but they have to convince me why my position is wrong.... When I ... disagree with their recommendations ... I call the person. I don't immediately say that I don't agree with your position... I will ask them questions: 'Why did you say this and that? Why have you considered this and this and that?' So, in a way, when I present to him, process by process, the things that he has written here [in the recommendation], [then] at times the person himself will say, 'Oh, I did not see that.' So instead of telling him that I disagree with him, actually he will say 'Can I take back my draft and include this.'"[83] It allows superiors to work with their staff and assess them more effectively: "I treat them as my team, I don't treat them really as subordinates. In fact, I work with them.... I just don't give assignments or commands.... I work with them... I'm frank ... [and] ... I don't like people who don't tell me what's in their mind. I would like them to voice their opinion ... because that is the only occasion ... I can really evaluate or analyse what's inside them.... If they do not talk how can I tell what's in their mind? So I would rather they talk [and] voice their opinion..."[84] It also makes it more likely that a superior will know "immediately if there is a problem."[85] And, for some, airing opinions and criticisms makes for a healthier and more comfortable atmosphere: "I am a very frank person. If I don't like you, I will say I don't like you. Maybe I will tell you I don't like your idea. Of course different people have different ideas, different perspectives. Not all people will follow you, not all the people under you will say you are right. Some ... will say you are right in front [of you], but at [your] back say you are not right. But I appreciate people who are very, very frank—to tell me what he doesn't like.... There are people who [view] criticism [as] destructive; but for me I view criticism ... [as] constructive."[86] Direct and open debate does not mean that the superior will listen; and the subordinate must expect equally forthright responses. A director may encourage his subordinate to speak his mind, but "I will come in strongly as well ... call it passion!"[87]; so while there is, from a subordinate's perspective, "no problem ... discussing things with him ... sometimes, when I express views contrary to his, he cuts me short."[88]

There are, then, officials who will not permit familiarity or will do so only rarely; while others will encourage the breakdown of hierarchy such that they appear "very open [and] accommodating.... In my experience with X ... [who] ... is part of the collegiate commission, I [can] easily and quickly tell her what's on my mind, without limitations, without the thought that even if it is not accepted it's okay."[89] And subordinates are well able to "pinpoint the bosses that are very strict and very self-oriented or ... heads or chiefs or executives that are people-oriented ... [such that] we can always balance, we can always talk, we can always complain—in a nice way..."[90] Yet it would not be accurate to say that there is a clear distinction between those who encourage an informal atmosphere and those who do not. Much depends upon circumstance as well as upon the relationship between superior and subordinate. There are instances when a subordinate will tell her superior that

> ...she's wrong. Well, for example, she will ask me to stand in for her.... She's supposed to do a lecture on something, and she has a conflict, and she asks me to do it for her. [I say] "I'm not in a position to do that because I'm only a supervising personnel specialist. We have a division chief who is higher than me, we have an assistant director. Why not tell her to do it for you? Not me. I don't have the knowledge." And she says "No, I trust you, it's my way of training you—for you to become a director in the future. So I'm giving this assignment to you." So I tell her '"No ma'am, I'm sorry. I cannot." Of course I say that, but I end up doing it anyway.[91]

The line between debate and insubordination, though, remains clear: "[Our director] has this wall that all of us are aware of, [and] when she's like this you cannot joke around, and you have to follow her."[92] Superiors may also re-establish hierarchy unintentionally through sheer force of personality. The Head of the CSC may be open with her immediate staff and encourage them to call her "Karin," yet some could not quite bring themselves to do so; and whilst she was desperate to encourage civil servants to be more assured and more willing to show initiative and take responsibility, she

> comes in very strongly, she will dominate the conversation, the discussions, the debate—and she loves debates by the way—so it is ... like a platform built for the teacher who is on top of the platform and us students.... We can argue but almost always she wins, so at times it is better not to argue—*at times*.... Because of her style, many of us, including myself ... have the tendency ... not to say anything. Even if you know the topic authoritatively you shut your mouth.... You are rattled to the point of not saying anything.' [93]

And there are times when even those who are more relaxed with their subordinates, and who manage to get their subordinates to relax, may reassert hierarchy and protocol either because it is expected of them or because they sense that circumstances demand it. A director may feel able to disagree openly with a superior in private, but in front of their equal or subordinates careful phraseology is needed. "I will not tell you [the Director] that you are wrong, but I can tell you that, well, that the records show that actually there is this, when you said there is none." Moreover, once a decision is made it may be queried but not refused: "I could then be accused of insubordination. What I usually do is express my view and it's up to him whether or not to accept it; because for me it is enough that I am able to express my opposition, my view. After all, it will be he who is answerable for the decisions."[94] At the same time, it would not do (especially for high-ranking third-level civil servants) to appear pusillanimous when faced with their superiors.

> Since I'm with the management, if it is an executive committee meeting where only the assistant secretary, the undersecretary and secretaries are there, I can question the management; but if we are with the management committee where there are regional direc-tors, I cannot question. I sort of sanitise my remarks, like, "Perhaps I would like to clarify...." I have to do that. But in the executive committee [meeting] I am very vocal—I'm very open, I am not a typical Filipina who will sit there and sulk and cry.... I may cry, yes, but I definitely fight.[95]

Even a division chief faced with third-level appointees may find demonstra-tions of resolve and character necessary: "you have to be courteous ... [but] on my part, if I know that I am right, and what is being presented is wrong ... I will say so even if he is the Commissioner, [though] I will tell it in such a way as he will not be offended."[96]

Networks of Support

The breakdown of hierarchy is also associated, though not always so, with mentoring the emergence of clusters of staff within an office or bureau or group. The cultivation of these knots is often seen as a moral, rather than a formal, duty; but it is also a means of fashioning an effective and reliable staff who may well follow their mentor through the ranks and across offices and departments. "When I was in [Centre X] ... I sort of had a quality circle... I selected the best.... These ... people ... were my understudies. I had twenty-four in all when I was there. Unfortunately these people were all promoted ... but [Director X] is really my protégé—from the time that she became my Assistant Chief and then my Chief ... she practically followed my footsteps. Before her I was the Director and now she's the Director ... I hope that I when I [am no longer] Assistant Secretary, she will be Assistant Secretary."[97] And just as she brought on Director X, so Director X in her turn, when she was Division Chief, knew already

> ...who among [my] people have potential is become leaders. So in running a project, if there were extra responsibilities, I gave [these to] them, especially if they were younger than other people. So ... besides that, if there are scholarships then I will nominate those people for training and scholarships. But I do mentoring also in specific things ... like, if we are doing a project proposal then I will let them submit their ideas in draft and then later on we will sit down and say "What you think?" and ask questions ... about what you're doing and what else you will do? And, then, "How about this?" and "Perhaps it would be better if we do this?"...I spend a lot of effort and time on getting a person to learn on her own.[98]

187

Viewed from their own network, other circles often appear to be more exclusive and competitive than they should be: "There is a group here that appears to be ... they call it "the Limited." There is this Undersecretary: she has her own protégés—very, very obvious ... like [a Limited] Corporation. They are really very close, and it is very, very obvious.... There is competition for promotion.... It is not ... dog-eat-dog ... [but] while [I hear] 'Oh, I'm so happy for you,' of course, I don't believe that, because basically you're not happy when somebody is promoted and you know that you are promotable as well."[99] These tightly knitted relationships are occasionally nurtured by superiors in thanks for the support they received at some time in the past, as in the case of a division chief who took under her wing the niece of her former regional director who had done much to help her career.

> When I was with Region III ... I [was] afraid ... [I was] weak in communication—weak writing, written communication.... I was afraid to speak in public.... I trembled.... But by constant practice, [my Director] was able to overcome that.... He let me speak in front of him, and then [videoed me], and then after that he showed me. "Look at yourself, you are a division chief, and you are trembling, what's happening with you? You have the guts, but ... you don't believe in yourself, you don't trust [yourself], you have no confidence in yourself. The only thing that you can do to overcome that is to believe in yourself; but in believing yourself you have to prepare for yourself. For anything that you do you have to prepare it correctly and truthfully so that you can say what you want." I think it worked.[100]

As it was between herself and her Director, so it is between herself and the Director's niece who

> was only introduced to me when I attended the birthday of Y [Director in Region III]. And after eating, [Y] told me, "I've got M who is my niece. Can you do something, because I want her to be under you, or can you give her at least the chance to work with you ? " At that very moment I really did not say yes.... But ... it so happens that the volume of work here is already increasing, and besides I should get a person who is knowledgeable on the operation of the accounting side; and it so happened that [M] is an accounting graduate. Then I called her—she was working with Kenny Rogers [a fast-food company] when I got her. Formerly she was on contract of service.... Then I got a chance: there is one position in the department—it's the lowest position, accounting clerk.... And so I told her that "You better get this position. Time will come when there will be some promotion, [and] you will be on the rankings." Then after that, while we are working together, I see some potential in [M]. [M] is good in communications. Then I told her "Could you find a way to review for the board?" "Yes." So I gave her a chance: ... I arranged the kind

of work she will do; then we have reviewing during Saturdays and Sundays; and ... I found a way that [she could do her office work and] ... also study. She is my assistant, so there was a chance ... and luckily, [M] passed the board. So, we're just waiting for the rationalisation plan, because I want to give [M] an accountant position. And she is really good. It's not because I'm [re]paying [a debt] ... it is because she is really good. But also I don't like that [M] will be so conceited.... I treat her as an employee. But I'm also very careful with her personal life.... So I told her ... before ... I retire, I plan that she will be in the right position.... Of course ... she has three kids, so she is planning to send all her kids to college. But the salary in government during this time—you cannot really [do that] ... if you have no other income.... And, besides, the spaces of the kids are: twelve years old, X is grade 5, Y is 7, and Z is 10. So she will have to find a way [to pay for the children to go to college].[101]

Already unpopular because of her stand against un-reconciled cash advances, this relationship gave ammunition to her critics who accused her of favoritism. But she was adamant: "I have no favorites. [It's] just the same ... with my kids—no favorites. The problem will start if you have favorites. But there are ... staff who are close to you, very close to you, because ... you ... find something in him or her that you like.... I'm not a selfish person: once I know you have potential, I will watch you."[102]

Indeed, while it may be said more generally (and not without good reason) that patronage and attempts to secure a reliable base, find expression through informal mentoring, it is evident that relationships are also, and are often largely, about an interest in others, about affection, and about perpetuating the office, its competencies, its values and its direction. More extensive networks are also valuable in countering a common problem within many organizations, particularly the larger ones: delayed and distorted communications between central and regional offices through the memos and circulars that flow downwards, and the reports that flow upwards. One way to elicit more accurate information—and to forestall the need to issue memoranda, signed by an undersecretary, stating in painful detail the data to be provided by regional offices— is to place one's own people covertly in those offices "so that we can get the true situation."[103] Another is to establish a rapport with those offices. This is especially important when the information is sensitive. In Education, for instance, letters complaining about improper appointments or the distortion of an election by teachers are funneled through records at central office to the Secretary and back down to the Undersecretary concerned. The Undersecretary may deal with this directly through his own support networks—those "people within the organization who provide me with additional information aside from everything that is provided in formal reports: for instance, cases wherein a congressman wants to have the superintendent in his city or province replaced.... So I try to get information from certain people there or sometimes from the person who the congressman wants to replace.... I want his or her side on the matter. I also have ... people in the province or city who are not [staff] of the Department."[104] Or the case may be passed on to personnel where it lands eventually on the desk of a division chief or section chief with instructions to find out whether there is any substance to the allegations: "So what I do, or one of my staff will do, [is] call immediately, most often, the superintendent; if not, the assistant superintendent, the division administrative officer, [or] sometimes the personnel officer, and then ask them: 'You have an applicant for a principal position in the school who says that he was by-passed. What happened?' Straight questions like that. 'What is the side of the superintendent, of the official ... [about which the complaint is being made]?' "[105] Or they may turn to their own personal contacts—someone who they happen to know in the region "...especially if it is a question ... concerning a superintendent.... They [the contacts] are not there to do that job, [but] they *are* there and we *can* ask them...'Pwede ... can you give me information, between us only... And some of them readily give information: 'No, this is what happened,' they tell me. 'Ma'am, that's not the case, this is what happened actually.'"[106]

The emergence of these circles is often a matter of chance as it depends upon staff who, as part of their responsibilities, have opportunities over the years to build up relationships with regional officials.

> One of my staff, [X], she's been ... with the Association of Super-intendents; and so through the years she's was able ... to identify people who can really give classified information that I rely on. She ... has access to [these] people, who can [say] "No, she's not reliable, don't believe her. That person is a troublemaker in that division." That sort of information, [does] not exactly influence us, but guides us.... And can be used by the Secretary or the USEC to ... look deeper [into the question]. Is this information true? Like, there was ... information that one superintendent had been violating the rules on promoting [school] principals, and later on I learned that an investigating team from the legal department had been created; they proceeded to the [schools division in region] and came up with a report on whether the [allegation] was true ... but I don't know any more on what transpired.... So ... information—informal, side information—[is] used to, sort of, guide us here in coming up with our recommendations.[107]

Such relationships are also cultivated through various forums, though more with the intention of smoothing the way in the general conduct of business with the regions rather than of seeding informants. For instance,

> ...We conduct ... workshops, and we see to it that [regional officials] are invited. Also we have the HRM [Human Resource Management] plan.... The initial step taken [in making the plan] was to form the founder's group; and the founder's group is those who are considered expert in the field of human resource management; and they consist of ... regional directors ... superintendents ... chief administrative officers—those AOs [Administrative Officers] who head the entire regions in terms of administrative service ... records officers ... planning officers. So, you see ... it is a mix of people coming from different levels and positions.[108]

Another forum—though one used more often to select those regional directors through whom information and policies of the agency may be disseminated—is the Management Committee. For it is at this time, when the Committee convenes, that all the regional and bureau directors are gathered in one place:

> So what we do is, we call the meeting, we already see some leaders, some of those who are speaking but do not say anything or do not have any depth or meaning—[they] just want to hear their [own] voice. But you would also have some who can, when they talk, influence the others. So again, rather than trying to hit all of them, you will concentrate on those that can influence the others.... You ... explain it properly to them so they know what it is about and they get to push for it also ... that I have found to be useful.[109]

Modes of Resistance

As these examples show, networks established to ease communications and coordination are also a means through which political appointees as well as permanent civil servants can resist or deal with the aftermath of political interference. The CSC, under Constantino-David, is less susceptible to interference but here, too, informal resistance is needed and at all levels. "[When] the President fired [an] undersecretary at the Department of Education ... he came to us. Unfortunately, the President got to my two commissioners.... One commissioner had not yet been confirmed and so it was a question of the moment. Commissioner X went to pieces: "You are not going to be reappointed, if you don't toe the line." The other commissioner was in his last two months of his term and was promised another appointment." [110] The matter illustrated what the Chair at least viewed as a flaw in the Commission's collegiate leadership:

> You cannot run an organization with three heads. An organization has to have a line of command. So I [have] had four different combinations of Commissioners so far.... There are some who don't do

their work at all and just want to be kings or queens; there are some who keep on interfering; there are some who demand to be more involved; and there are [those] who say that it is beneath [them] to attend this or that meeting. So there is an inherent tension ... [but] I don't think I've had—except for one—major problems. To me, it's all a question of "Okay, as long as you set aside one day a week for us to meet I don't care what you do." I give them their respective office budgets and if you keep within that I am not going to pay attention to anything—your attendance [or] how you spend it. Because, as a collegial body, we are co-equal ... I can't tell them this is wrong or that is wrong. So you segregate the kingdoms; and that I'd planned, from the first year.[111]

Yet careful manoeuvring and a steady flow of information are also required by the Chair to keep ahead of the other commissioners' own personal and political agendas. Except for the traffic (paper and electronic) addressed directly to the two commissioners, incoming communications (no matter to whom they are addressed) pass across the Chair's desk where she spends an hour or so at the start of each day sifting through this material and re-directing it, aided by a computerized data tracking system.[112] This puts her in a position to see in detail: what is going on within the organization; and in what ways the Commissioners may be working through their subordinates, and to what ends. She also keeps an eye on the Commissioners more closely

...but informally, through the grapevine.... I have an ascendancy over most of the directors—the professional ones.... As for the useless ones (the two or three [useless ones]), I don't care about them anyway. But [through] the younger directors, who are really committed to the Commission, I get every single source of information ... everybody knows my cell number. So I get information, weird information, such as "Do you know that the staff of Commissioner [X] took the vehicle at 9 PM last night."[113]

Political appointees also establish networks to overcome permanent civil servants' attempts to resist their presence, decisions, and policies. Political appointees will often make a very conscious effort to bring permanent civil servants on board and to seek out allies within their ranks. In his attempts to reign in ill-discipline over cash disbursements, one undersecretary will

always talk to the ... division chiefs under me, especially accounting. So I talked to the Chief Accountant and say "I will delegate this to you," and "Make sure this is being followed," and "If you have problems with a particular employee, then just tell me." So I put them onto my side, and they are very receptive, and very happy to see some changes. Because that has been a perennial findings of the

Commission on Audit—our level of un-liquidated cash advances [which were] not really decreasing but increasing.... But when I came in, after a year, it was being controlled and is going down. And they are very happy about it.[114]

This targeting of allies is accompanied by methods intended more generally to draw staff closer to them:

You just to live each day.... You always allow them to participate in management meetings, like the management committee meetings on a monthly basis. We allow them to have time with us .... to seek an audience with us.... It's about avoiding confrontation and, in fact, we are also supporting them ... when they go out around the whole country ... support their travel ... we have this sports programme, we have sports activities, we have family day programme, Xmas parties, all this sort of thing.... We even have on a monthly basis the birthday celebrants for a particular month...[115]

Appointees must also learn to tread carefully:

...here in the Department [Education], the culture ... is incremental change. So, you're not supposed to make some changes or else the bureaucracy will resist. If you want to survive in this department, you have to imbibe the issue of incremental change.... If you want change done, it cannot be imposed immediately. There has to be a system, it has to be justified, it has to be accepted, it has to be done in a slow manner.[116]

And they must be sure of their brief, and must be *seen* to be sure of it.

...it's really a big challenge—*really*. I have to do my homework, because I don't want to appear [as if] I don't understand what's being discussed, because I'm sure there will be people—there *have* been people—who were trying to test me, about my knowledge about the Department. What's weird about me is that before I got here I came from here already but for less than a year, so I did know something about how the Department works; and my mother was a superintendent and public school teacher, so I also know something about the situation in the schools as well. So I'm not totally zero [in my knowledge] so far as DepEd is concerned. But I did need to read ... because it would be weird for me to ask questions, stupid questions, to my subordinates. So I had to read the manual, I had to read the reform agenda, I had to read a lot of stuff. I also need to know more, because when I go to the field people expect me to know everything. Sometimes they would ask questions about teachers' benefits, they would ask questions about operations which are not normally within my field or jurisdiction. So I really took it upon myself to study.[117]

For this sense of being tried by one's subordinates is entirely justified:

> At first, we will test that person,[to see] if that person is really worth the position.... We will have an experience dealing with him or her, and some discussions with him or her.... It's a matter of testing that person. And then, after that, we will know whether he is difficult to deal with [or] he doesn't seem to know.... But, definitely, if he needs something ... as long as it is within our duties and responsibilities, we will entertain that person ... unless he will create a situation...[118]

However, finding allies, encouraging a more convivial atmosphere, and meeting expectations, goes only so far. The networks established by permanent civil servants in order to resist political appointees merge with a general defensiveness (see chapter 3) and are difficult to counter or dislodge: "...they have groups that have been there quite a time and they are very close. So if you make some mention against a particular person you spur the whole [network]..."[119] It is also nigh impossible to neutralize all the various motivations fuelling resistance. Subordinates may object to an appointee's ideas, ideals, or personal interests (as in the case of cash disbursements); or it may be that their priorities and responsibilities (as in the case of the inflexible application of procurement procedures) clash. Or they may be critical of an appointee's appetite for work: "If that person is ... worth the appointment, if that person is really performing, it really doesn't matter whether he was referred by the Commissioner or whosoever—as long as he performs well. There will be an issue if that person, referred by somebody or a politician, and occupies a higher position receiving a higher salary, and is not performing.... *That* is an issue within X. Because all of us here are very dynamic, I think, and we work very hard..." [120] Or they may object to one or other aspect of their personality and the simple fact that their boss is a political appointee:

> We won't like that person if he is too boastful of his connections; probably he might be referred by the director, or might be hired by the Director, [but] you don't have to boast, use your connection.... Rather, what you can give us? What can you perform?... That's one thing that we can really admire—if you really perform very well and show ... traits of a public servant. That's what we will like about him. But [if he is] *mayabang* [boastful] about ... [being] a rich person, or ... very intelligent, or he knows the Director or he knows somebody else in the DepEd Central Office, and he keeps telling us that ... that's something that we will not like. But even [if] he has got all these traits—like being rich, being intelligent, being connect[ed]—it's okay

with us, as long as you are very kind, you've been [working] with us gently, and you perform.[121]

Appointees may also find that permanent civil servants will call on their political godfathers:

> I think the very reason why I have so many enemies right now in the Department is because I won't budge to the request of the politicians, even [to] those people [civil servants] who believe that they [the politicians] can prop them up. Like, for example ... I won't sign [something] ... they go straight on another person of higher rank than me ... and that person will talk to me. But I keep on saying .... If you want to remove me from my office, just remove me, but I'm not going to sign it.[122]

Permanent civil servants are well versed in a number of other techniques with which to make life difficult for political appointees (and some of these are also used to defend their interests more generally[123]). One is the use of "white papers"[124] which "can really hit you hard with all their statements.... You don't know who they are, and they say ... you're not performing your job...."[125] A second is to withdraw cooperation, reducing the efficacy of the political appointee and adding to their workload.

> ...When I came here ... I was used to working in private organizations. Most people there are really very efficient in submitting a particular report that you need. When I came here, well ... they are supposed to be doing a pre-audit; but it turned out [it wasn't being done] and that I'm the one doing all these things ... and I should not be doing that. I should be looking at the big picture rather than at all these little things. So I sent notes: "Please correct this etc." And they are offended.... I tried to get across to them that this is a positive sign on my part: they should be learning from my notes so that next time they submit a report the same mistakes won't be made. You should be submitting something that is really perfect. But ... they take it against you. I was surprised. I make corrections ... [but] the same mistakes keep on happening almost every day.... So I make some more notes, and again they get offended. "When will you learn?!" And there was this time I had this book about misconstruing or misconceiving a particular work ... and I photocopied it and I gave it to them.... And then after two or three days I was expecting them to thank me for that, but I never got any "thank you" from them, because they were offended. "How can you be offended ? I was doing a favor for you, so that when you make a memo.... I don't have much to change or to check".... I call them up, and I set up standards for preparing a memo.... But that is supervisors' work.... [And] still it's a continuous bombardment of notes...[126]

195

A third is to circumvent the authority of the appointee altogether:

> Like, for example, one specific [and] very sensitive issue—it's about un-liquidated cash advances.... When I came here.... I found that [liquidations] were two or three years behind.... So I have to put an end to that. So the next time they travel, I got from them ... a promissory note on when they were going to pay for it. So if they have a promissory note, I will allow them to travel. But the next time they travel, and if there is no movement in their previous account, I will not let them travel. And what they do is to bypass me and go straight to another office...[127]

A fourth technique is to encourage a sense of exclusion in political appointees through a studied coldness:

> I had a big problem. Personally, I had a big problem because ... by DepEd's standards I am really, really young.... So when I came in there was an adjustment period.... They had a tendency ... of saying, "Oh this guy doesn't know anything; and he'll just be here for a short while." I even heard someone say—not really heard myself, but someone told me—"Anyway, he will be gone soon," and another guy was saying, "We've been here far longer than he's been alive." So that personally was my problem. I was having difficulty calling my directors.... They are mostly in their sixties, they are the age of my parents. So I had some difficulties. I had to call them "ma'am," and had to call them "sir".... So in that sense I ... had to adjust. I also had to adjust to ... the pace of the work. The pace of the work is slow. I've worked in government mostly at the top.... In [the] three government agencies I've been in, I've always worked with the Secretary. And, when you work with a Secretary, everybody follows. So when ... I was Chief of Staff, which was my former position, whatever I say everybody follows. Now that I'm one of the top bureaucrats it's a different thing altogether. I will have to establish myself now as the person in authority as opposed to ... working for the Secretary [when] I was a reflection of his authority and no one can question it. So I ... had a difficult time getting people to believe that I was serious, that I knew something, that I had expertise, that I had something to contribute.[128]

A fifth method is prevarication:

> I will not bluntly tell you no ... I will first of course consider that you are the top [my superior].... Bluntly? No? That cannot be! [Instead, I'll say] "I will look into that, sir; I will see it if we will not be violating something; I will study it first, I will review it first, then I will just talk to you, sir."[129]

But a civil servant faced with repeated interventions by a political appointee or a politician will then have to be more creative. When regional directors and field officers come under daily pressure from politicians—as in the case of the CSC whose function is to review and approve (or disapprove) appointments throughout the bureaucracy— civil servants begin to manoeuver in a way that allow them to retain their integrity and the politician to keep face. "Even if our budget is on the line [they say] "This is the practice of our officials here" [and they will say] "I will take your request and go back to the office, and I will see what is taking so long to facilitate it, but without making of any promises…"[130] It may even be possible to string out a decision until the politicians' term of office expires or an election is lost. Civil servants can then rule as they would want to, while politicians may claim they are no longer in any position to influence the decision. And if, despite these tactics, a politician continues to insist that, say, a particular person is given an appointment

> …you could just tell him "Okay. But the problem, Mr. Mayor, is that she is not even qualified. Perhaps you could recommend someone else, and we'll see about it." It's just give and take. It's not totally "Oh, I'm sorry. You are interfering in DepEd matters." That will never work. The Mayor will resent it and shut down funding to the school, or cut the electricity, because sometimes the schools are paid for, the electricity is paid for, by the local government. The way to do it is to engage the politician. Not totally… [but] you have to give him [the politician] a way out: "If I can't take this person, then perhaps the Mayor can recommend this person because he is in the ranking list and then you can claim … "Here, we have that person."[131]

Open and direct confrontation is not preferred, but it is not uncommon; for another and important method of resistance is to establish a reputation for resilience, and this is so even in the Central Bank: "If the board members will approach me and tell me, 'I'm not quite familiar with these issues. Can you send somebody to orient me on this, to familiarize me on this…', I don't mind that. But for them to be going directly to my department heads and ask them to do things without my knowledge, I mind it and I tell them that, because I should know what's happening."[132] Direct and external political coercion may, in particular, demand robust treatment if politicians are to be dissuaded from future attempts to browbeat the civil servant.

> When I was still a field director a former mayor who was a known actor … was pressuring me to get information on [and rule on] an opponent [who was involved in disciplinary case]…. On several occasions we were, like, in a shouting [match] … and I was just initially referring to the law as my shield and justifying my action for not

providing [the information]. What I did ... I just had to finish the case swiftly and never budge and never surrender.... I had to face the guy and on several occasions had to point out the limits of our [freedom for] action, that I cannot just do as he pleased.... I had to be firm and level with him.... It was one of the experiences I had as a field director and was new at the third level. It was a baptism of fire.[133]

Very similar strategies are also adopted by political appointees faced with unwanted external interference. Again, inventiveness is best when dealing with a tenacious politician:

[the] congressman was so persistent ... there was ... a vacancy.... Deputy Collector for Operations.... I was also in and out of the Commissioner's office ... the special assistants were there.... So he [the Commissioner of Customs] was talking to the congressman, [and the congressman] was telling him, "You appoint my guy, you designate my guy, Deputy Collector for Operations".... [But] the Commissioner tells the congressman: "I am so sorry... I have designated another fellow."

"Who is he?" He could not think of anybody, and then he saw Attorney [X]—one of the trusted guys of the Commissioner—come to the door.... "Oh, it's Attorney [X]" [even though] there was no designation yet.... That's how things get done in the Commission.

But some are also prepared to confront:

The first few years, you really have angry congressmen demanding. Well, I meet arrogance with arrogance. If you want to talk to me like you're my boss, I will answer you like I am *your* boss, and to hell! There are more than 200 congressmen, why do I have to bow to one?... X, one of the dirtiest congressmen and one of the most arrogant of congressmen ... came to me first, acting as though he owned the world; and I said, "Congressman X, you have your work, I have mine. You are a lawyer, I am not, so you must understand the law more than me. From my understanding this is the way things are." But then he said, "I want." But I said, "We cannot operate on the basis of *I want*." I don't know why people lose all their self-respect in front of congressmen—you are just a representative of one district.[134]

The willingness of an agency head to show their mettle is important not only because it may forestall further attempts at intimidation. The morale of subordinates is also lifted by a secretary who cannot be "bullied around (because some members of congress feel *they* are Secretary for Education)"[135] or by "a very strong and really hard-working Chair who's even got balls to say no to the President—and that to me is a source of pride and inspiration because you get less and less of that as you move up."[136] How far such inspiration goes when civil servant themselves, rather than their leader, comes face to face with raw threat is another matter. There are, as already noted, times when they will manoeuvre or confront. But

> if the ... career officials know that ultimately their careers are dependent upon one person, then they tend to tread very lightly ... [to avoid] stepping on the toes of anyone who has contact now, or in the future, with the President. [This] leads to timidity, which leads to an officiousness or to saying "Yes" to everything, which leads ... to their brains rusting away.... I always tell the career servant, when your Secretary is asking you to do something [illicit], there is no shame is telling your Secretary: "Sir, please can you ask someone else. I'm part of the career service, I will stay here." But you know, they are so timid. Some of the career civil servants that I respected, all of a sudden I found that...
> "What the hell were you doing!?"
> "I was told I couldn't say no": that is their reply; and that is the most tragic of all when career public servants tell me to my face that they have no choice. I tell them you always have a choice, and your choices are not limited to staying or leaving.[137]

Lack of resolve is understandable, for resistance may well bring consequences:

> I stick to policies.... I can bend a little but I won't break it. [But] I find some [colleagues] who actually and practically ... [perform] more violations than compliance.. I don't do anything about it because I did once and the Undersecretary was mad at me.... I went to him and said "This is a violation, it's wrong ... [the person involved is] supposed to be dismissed ... it was dishonesty".... And I brought the evidence. He [the Undersecretary] didn't do anything about it and, on top of that, he didn't talk to me for one year.[138]

And the pressure to buckle may soon become intolerable.

> I tell one of my guys, "You make a profile of this company and submit this to the Commission." It gets done. And then when the company is notified as being audited, one by one all [its] godfathers begin to show and then tell you: "Oh ...we didn't know it was going to be hit. Oh, he's a good friend of the Commissioner, he's a good friend of the Senator, he is a friend of the President." What do you do? So the next time around if you want to profile [a company], one of the considerations is, is this company politically connected? How come his declaration is so ... [low]? Does he have any political godfathers?

So, that is one of the basic considerations. It's useless, no? You want to audit somebody; you see 50 million pesos that can be collected; and you can't collect—not even a centavo. [They] just hire a lawyer ... give one million to the lawyer, and then delay the case.... And then suddenly you get transferred ...."Oh, assign him to Mindanao."[139]

The damage done to self-esteem and self-confidence by these constant threats is palpable. The point is well made by one senior civil servant in the BIR who, during the course of this passage, was moved close to tears:

...Here, even promotions, transfers, everything could be subject to political pressure. The commissioners, the district officers, those who manage the districts—they are subject to political pressure. It could be a congressman calling up, or it could be the Commissioner calling up the district officer because the Commissioner was pressured politically. It happens. It happens every day. Even in the assignment of cases—some would prefer that this guy they know in the BIR would be given better cases. It happens. It happens also to me personally. A congressman would talk to me—there are certain cases ... [to be left alone], or favors for people in this office.... If I know that I won't be transferred because of resisting political pressure, I won't give in to the pressure. But you see, we can be transferred any time. As I said, we are used to change, we are used to that; and of course we want to stay ... in a certain office because we become familiar with the work, we become more efficient; and it's near my house. So whenever there is pressure I would say, "I don't want to be transferred." So if it is not illegal, [if] it is a matter of giving favors to a particular subordinate, I would say "Why not? Give it to him. It's not illegal".... If it's illegal I say, "Sir, I would be charged" and then the person would understand. I believe he would not push because he would understand...[140]

Inter-Agency and Inter-Branch Communication

Informal modes of communication and coordination also exist between: (1) executive agencies (and commissions); (2) executive agencies and the legislature; (3) the legislature and the palace; (4) executive agencies and the private sector.

1. Without informal connexions, coordination among executive agencies is otherwise formalized and sclerotic and, as Constantino-David puts it, "really predominantly useless because—apart from a few heads who are professionals [and] who will themselves attend the meetings—most of these meetings are representatives of the representatives of the representatives. Nobody can make any decisions; they meet, but nothing happens."[141] As among directors within an agency, much depends upon the development

of personal relationships built around some point of commonality. In the case of the CSC and the Department of Budget and Management, the initial kernel of association was professional status and behavior as opposed to political partisanship.

> Relations between the Department of Budget [and Management] and the CSC remained excellent because the first Cabinet Secretary of the DBM was not really a friend but was a professional who knew what she wanted to do. She knew the organization, because she came from within the organization, and a lot of things could be done. None of us was cutting ribbons and flying [in] to give welcome remarks.... That is why my first order, when I came here, was that I am not going to give invocations or welcome remarks or closing remarks or inspirational talks, or cut ribbons. "You want me to give a lecture? [Okay], but don't waste my time ... handing out certificates."[142]

Heads of organization, even the most well-connected, must also rely on their subordinates' inter-organizational relationships. Political appointees—most especially those who are appointed for their experience of working within numerous other agencies and professions—are well aware that they bring with them vital contacts: "...the Secretary recognizes also that, because I have been moving around, I am able to informally ask or get certain things immediately from people in the other organizations, like the DPWH [Department of Public Works and Highways] ... I can ask somebody in the DPWH what's going on with this construction ... and sometimes any informal complaints, [I am] able to fix it up; I do the same thing for DNR [Department of National Defence] and DILG..."[143] And because contacts in other agencies also move around from one organization to the next during their careers, there builds up an extensive, complex and informal network of relationships through which inter-agency business is conducted, jobs are secured, and new political appointments are made.

Informal relationships among agencies, then, provide an important sense of cohesion and means of coordination. Such connexions can be stable and reliable, but they can also prove to be very fragile. One example is that of a covenant established between the Office of the Ombudsman, the CSC, and the Commission of Audit (COA) with the intention of avoiding overlaps of responsibilities and consequent problems. The covenant was created from, and operated through, informal relationships among the heads of these agencies.

> When X came in, on his own he came to me and said "Look you've got to tell me what to look out for." He is purely private sector. We didn't know each other, though we went to the same university. And so we worked out a Memorandum of Agreement. He told me what his plans were, [and] I told him my plans. We looked at the overlaps,

201

and we took on functions that were cluttering up the Ombuds-man—the small, the less-than-P100,000 cases. So they were turned over to the CSC, and we subdivided the work, [and] said there would be no overlap. Despite the fact that this was a lot of work for us, we were happy to see cases being won. We were co-operating with each other on many corruption cases. There did not seem to be a problem until, of course, he resigned; and the new Ombudsman couldn't care less. And so I revoked the Memorandum of Agreement. Why should I continue when there is a different trajectory?[144]

The broader, and deeper, tensions underlying this rift included what was widely held to be the President's politicization of the Ombudsman and its use to undermine political opponents and intimidate civil servants. But one specific matter of concern was jurisdiction over sexual harassment cases. Under the covenant the CSC had agreed to handle these cases, until "one day we saw in the newspaper that the Office of the Ombudsman was taking on [the] sexual harass-ment cases of the Department of Education. So the Chair thought, why all of a sudden...? That is one of the reasons for terminating the agreement..."[145]

2. Presidential-Legislative Liaison Officers (PLLO) and the Legislative-Executive Development Advisory Council (LEDAC) provide formal channels (routed through the Palace) between executive agencies and commissions on the one hand, and the Legislature on the other. But unless the legislation required by an agency falls within the President's policy agenda, or an agency head can argue their case (or find a champion) in cabinet, then agency heads and their USECs and ASECs are on their own and must deal with the Legis-lature directly. At third-level, civil servants (career and political appointees) often have direct access to legislators: these connexions are developed over the years; or, in some cases, present themselves in the form of kinship; or are initiated by politicians for whom the department may be of some interest.

Securing the support of one politician, however, by no means guarantees that the support of many others will follow (as if they are connected by unseen webs). Other politicians may neither know nor care that, say, the CSC or Department of Education has managed to persuade one or other representative to author or support a bill. Work must, therefore, go on at lower levels to garner support, chivvy, and shepherd efforts and votes in the right direction. Some agencies (such as the CSC) have set up special-ized offices to liaise with Congress, while others (such as the Department of Education[146]) have not. In either case, the liaison officers[147] who tread the corridors of the House and Senate are to some extent expected to function on their own. They must also work informal relationships established with the legislators' staff, or find themselves pushed to the back of a very long queue of officials and private lobbyists who are hoping to catch a legislator's eye. The manner in which these relationships are established and sustained varies. Members of the Lower House rely on around three or four technical people and a lawyer, and it is these staffs that the civil servant will approach first. For the experienced liaison officer the initial contact is likely to be an old friend; and she will take with her a small gift—perhaps a box of doughnuts, enough for the politician's entire staff. It is then a matter of pleading for support and, if necessary, arranging an appointment with the politician. In the right circumstances it is also quite possible simply to approach the politician when alone:

> It amuses me to try with people like the President's son, who is a congressman. He is a very new congressman, and I was told he is a good person. But in the end he is still the President's son, and people don't trust him very much. And so, he was seated there, no one was paying attention to him, and I took the chance and introduced myself and said, "Sir, we need your help." And it really appealed to him to help.
> And he said, "Thank you."
> And I said, "For what?"
> "For actually coming over and talking to me."[148]

Wringing support out of Senators, however, is no easy thing. They are surrounded by a larger number of staff; they will also hire additional specialists—lawyers from the best law schools and those experienced in, say, working the media. These staffs are, for the most part, both competent and powerful: "When we talk to the staff of the Senators, we treat them with respect, because they really determine how their bosses will look at you.... When I talk to their staff I give that staff member my respect and ask, "Please help us.'"[149] It is, therefore, more difficult to secure an audience with a Senator: "that door is not as open as it is with Congress [the Lower House]; in Congress you actually wave to them; but Senators are gods."[150] Nevertheless, personality has a big part to play here too, and there are senators who are more approachable.

> For example, if you give Bong Revilla something shocking and it's showbiz chizmiz [gossip]—and it's *really* from showbiz—he likes that. Once I was pushing for an antidiscrimination bill ... so I told him "Do you know, Sir ... X was attacked by congressman Y, and they fought and they rolled on the floor."
> And he said, "Oh, is that what happened?"
> "Yes sir, so you better do something about your bill".... And he asked for a committee hearing. You don't do that with somebody like Senator Enrile, who is so formidable.[151]

3. Between the Legislature and Palace, there exists, as noted above, various formal organizational arrangements and procedures (LEDAC, PLLO,

and oversight committees) through which communications and coordination are supposed to be realized. The extent to which these formal arrangements work as they should, however, depends upon the goodwill of Palace and legislators. At the best of times there are so many competing interests that communication with the Palace is slow and uncertain. During times of political tension—when the executive may choose simply to withdraw cooperation and refuse to attend hearings—it becomes well-nigh impossible for opposition politicians to obtain information, let alone support, from the executive. Informal connexions with the Palace, necessarily developed over many years, are therefore invaluable.

> I was in the Palace before, so there are still people there who owe me favors and who I owe favors to; and they are still there and we are friends. Supposing I need to get something from the Palace for my boss: I tend to seek out the people that I once worked for, not necessarily the person I need to see. For instance, I need to see this guy. I don't go directly to him. I know someone below him. I will go and see that person and he can endorse me. That's how I work, because usually if somebody endorses as you, it kind of breaks the ice a little. But if I have to deal with somebody directly, and I don't know anybody, it is usually professional, very professional, although usually I get better service if I course it through a friend.[152]

4. There is also an important place for informal connexions between executive departments and the private sector. For example, such is the experience and knowledge offered by working in the Bureau of Internal Revenue (BIR) that a stint in the Bureau, until one reaches a respectable rank, is a useful career strategy for the young lawyer or accountant with an eye on a lucrative job in, say, a private accountancy firm. The steady loss of personnel that follows from this undoubtedly weakens the Bureau; yet this movement also has its advantages. This is especially so given that a relatively small number of tax payers account for a disproportionately large share of total revenues whose collection is the responsibility of a small, specialized unit within the Bureau: that is, the working of a small number of informal relationships can have a significant impact on collections. These connexions with former colleagues now working in, say, accountancy firms are also useful to bureau officials because it means that the private sector has a better understanding of the bureau and a rapport with its officials. They

> ...know where we're coming from. They won't blame us if we say you have to pay so much.... And it's easier to explain to them why we have to collect this amount from the taxpayer because, having been exposed to taxation, they readily understand the accounting basis, the tax code basis for this collection. It is easier to deal with them.... The person who recruited me [into the BIR] is now a partner

in SGV. And when we discuss, it is easier to discuss. Aside from the personal relationship ... when I say "these are the points" it is easier for him to understand; and if he has a point.... "Okay, *sige*, we can reduce this to this amount because you have a good reason here." Or "this is the amount payable, you cannot refute that, you have to pay this".... It's easier.[153]

Less common are officials who have worked in the private sector and have a good sense of how businesses think. In the BIR this is especially useful if they have worked with auditors: "I worked for X.... I got to see the perspective of the external auditors ... how these financial statements are prepared ... the process they have to go through.... It helps me in my work here because, in our case, you usually look at the tax consequence of the financial statements."[154]

These kinds of connections also enable the Central Bank to be more responsive:

> ...We are not an ... island ... we are partners with private industry, so we need them also for evolution.... We act as policeman only when you violate the rules but otherwise we are partners.... And so we attend meetings, socials, cocktails, with them; we mix; I know many bankers; we are comfortable with each other.
>
> [And] in my experience, what happens is this: they discuss issues with me.... "Okay, how do you interpret this law? Is this bank covered by this prohibition or not?" They may have some valid points and in some cases they are right, so I should not be closed to discussion with them. But it's not: "Please, please accommodate us on this." It's not like that—never, never. [What I say is] "Okay if you think that way, present me [with] your legal paper, present your authorities, and then address it to me, and then I'll study it. I'll not decide on my own, I'll consult another sector. So that has been the arrangement. I think that's okay. I don't think that's bad. So we see lawyers from banks, even bank presidents, [asking] "Is this allowable under the rules?" Then [we say] "Please submit a paper on that and then we'll study it and if it is okay then we'll recommend it." And we have amended regulations on that basis, because we saw the benefit to the banking industry.... Because banks should be global, because it's a reality that practices evolve ahead of regulations. Because ... you [are] creative, you are resourceful, you are a banker, [you] should have new products.... It's okay, it's just natural that the practices evolve ahead of the regulations. So we just follow. It cannot be the other way around: [that] there are no practices yet and you regulate [that].... You cannot reverse it. So it's a perpetual change between bank practices and regulations.... Our role is to keep the margin as narrow as possible—that margin represents the exposure of the public to risk [and the regulatory burden on the banks].[155]

205

Relationships between bureaucracy and private sector also provide crucial intelligence as in Customs where, as far as post-entry audit operations are concerned,

> ...my experience has been that the most reliable intelligence comes from the brokers themselves. It's a matter of broker A, broker B. You have the importer as your client who then transfers to the other broker. And then you [the broker] talk to me [customs] and tell me "Look, he stole my client and he's doing this thing".... And since you [the broker] have the past reports you can easily give it to me and I can use it and check.... This is the number one source of information that we have.[156]

Constructive Political Intervention

It is suggested above that positive informality becomes marked when the everyday translation of the social into the official is disrupted by the presence of particular circumstances: negative informality (when social practice is worked for the benefit of individuals or groups at the expense of organization, government and constituents); over-conformity; the misallocation of authority; and fundamental disagreements over what is accepted and acceptable. For instance, political interference—one expression of negative informality—undermines and circumvents the appointments' process such that civil servants must rely on social practice unsupported by formal rules and regulations in order to resist political appointees.

However, political interference (in so far as it is a response to divisions in authority which disrupt the translation of social relationships into a cabinet whose political bases would reach deep into agencies) may also be said to have a beneficial influence if only from the perspective of the executive. It is also possible to make a broader case for political interference as an expression of positive informality.

(a) First, the displacement of personnel within an agency when a new head brings in a slew of new people may ruffle feathers (especially if career civil servants find their promotions blocked), but it is also a necessary part of well-intentioned change. There is no question that politicians do place high-quality political appointees because they are high-quality; and that among political appointees, and those who appoint them, there are those who want the best for the nation and who genuinely believe that their authority to overcome inertia and entrenched habits within a department is woefully inadequate, most especially given the short time they have to turn a department around and set it on a new course. They must ease out old staff and appoint new staff—especially those who they already know and trust[157]. The contrasts experienced by the Chair of the CSC illustrate this point nicely:

When I came here I was entitled to more than a dozen primarily confidential staff, and I came in here with my two drivers—that's it—because of loyalty to them. But apart from them I got everyone from the inside: because the Commission was not known to be all that corrupt ... so I could deal with the career people. But before I came to the Commission, I was Secretary of Housing and I could not work only with the career people. I knew the extent of corruption. I knew the history behind all those corporations, and I needed to bring in people. I needed people who knew law and who knew housing finance; and so I got good people.[158]

It would also be churlish to deny that there are also members of the House who are concerned to serve constituents and nation because they are of the view that public service is in itself worthwhile; and who genuinely believe that the varied demands made of them—and the legal, procedural, organizational and political framework in which they operate—leaves them unable to meet the needs of their constituents. They, too, must attempt to influence appointments in the bureaucracy and in other ways adopt practices (such as switching parties) which they would prefer to shun.

It is also the case that politicians will support civil servants vying for promotion, and candidates hoping to enter the bureaucracy, for a host of other reasons largely free of ulterior motives. Competition for posts, the interests of politicians, and the belief that every other candidate has their supporters, inevitably create an atmosphere in which most civil servants feel compelled to seek political endorsements. Members of both Houses are therefore inundated with requests for references. These are often agreed to, and signed, by politicians as a matter of course, usually out of courtesy. For instance, a Senator may offer backing simply because the candidate is from his or her province[159] and it would seem rude and mean-spirited not to play to the candidate's expectation that this is a good enough reason. Or a Senator may offer support because the candidate is an underdog and the Senator happens to like underdogs. In these cases, formal endorsements are usually *just* that, and the politician makes no attempt to follow up the application. The point is often corroborated by low-level officials involved in the administration of selection procedures (and who read the traffic in letters) and by high-level officials involved in decision-making. From their perspective there is no question that while many applications are accompanied by references from politicians, these letters are indeed commonly treated only as recommendations by both civil servants[160] and politicians. Occasionally, a politician may go a little further and try to lift a jobless constituent with children into a position in local government and, strictly speaking, this is improper. But, they argue, would it be acceptable morally to sacrifice the well being of this particular family for the sake of a rule?

(b) Secondly, political appointees, whose selection is unconstrained by the processes, criteria and detailed standards which govern the selection of permanent civil servants, are drawn from a very wide range of backgrounds and walks of life and bring with them a deal of varied experience. This breadth is clear when viewed across the piece and even across the span a single officer's career. They are often generalists and self-consciously so:

> I felt it was better, especially on certain levels, [to move around] ... I can work in any sector—public or private or government. At a certain level you do not need the expertise of the area. I do not have to be a teacher at my level, as undersecretary.... It is a different type of experience. You have to be a manager, an administrator, a supervisor, and so on. So it's different skills and I feel that the civil service may be in a better position, or would have a better pool of resources, if you had [permanent civil servants] being moved around.... [But] what has happened is [that] the civil service has been static ... [and,] in terms of intellectual awareness, I do think that to be static [is] to be dead.[161]

Commonly, they began their working lives in the civil service but quickly moved into the private sector. For instance, one undersecretary (Education), started with the Board of Investments where he reviewed investment priority stamps.

> After that I moved ... to another government agency which was the Department of Labour and Employment. So from investments, from capital, I went to Labour [to] work on the social economic surveys of sugar workers here in the Philippines, and also mining workers here in the Philippines. And I was part of the team that did the market research for overseas recruitment at that time. So I spent about a month in the Middle East going from one country to another talking to government officials and also private chambers [of commerce] and private enterprises ... checking out investment projects.... So it was primarily more infrastructure. So that was the start of the boom in the Middle East. I left government about 1979, I joined PLDT [the Philippine Long-Distance Telephone Company. I did manpower recruitment and planning for PLDT. At that time, PLDT was undergoing an expansion programme, and because of the overseas market at that time, we were losing a lot of experienced personnel in telecommunications.... So I did manpower recruitment and planning for them. But once I had completed the programme I left.... At that time PLDT was, unlike now, a closed family corporation and in order to move up your boss had to retire or die.... I was the youngest department manager at that time, I was a little ambitious... I said I would not stay ten years doing the same thing here. [So] I joined a company which did international overseas

recruitment.... It was a joint-venture [with] ...a training company from Australia. And again, since I was familiar [with] the Middle East, since I knew a number of people already who were there.... I stayed with the company for ... five years.... I left because I did not want to stay in the Middle East—it wasn't as pleasant as it is now. So I joined ... the Employers' Confederation of the Philippines, which was related to my work in the Department of Labour ... [but] now the employers' side. So from the Department of Labour which is primarily from the workers' point of view, I now moved to the employers' point of view, and I would also represent the IOE [The International Organisation for Employers]. I was there, again for a couple of years, and [then] I left for the United States for a while. And ... when I came back I was invited by President Ramos to join again the government. So I worked with the Metro Manila Development Authority as the assistant general manager for finance. From the MMDA I was invited to join the Subic Bay [development authority], and then with the Department of Public Works and Highways until last year. Last year I was appointed here [at DepEd].[162]

Other political appointees may have remained in government but have been shunted between branches, as in the following example (again from Education):

After UP [University of the Philippines] I went straight to the government. I first worked at the House of Representatives, I worked with the Chairman of the Committee on Higher Education, and then Basic Education, and then [the] Committee on Constitutional Amendments, and then ... I spent six years there at the House of Representatives. And then I transferred to the Senate because my boss who was a congressman lost the election, so I had to look for a job elsewhere. It was good that one of the Senators took me in. Senator Roxas, my boss, took me in as his director for his legislative unit in his office. So I stayed there for a while. Then I went to the Department of Education—I was Chief of Staff to the Secretary. But then the Secretary ... joined the ... cabinet members who resigned *en masse* from the cabinet. So I found myself out of a job. But it was a good thing then that my [former] boss, the former congressman, was then appointed Presidential Legal Adviser. So I was appointed as Assistant Secretary in the Office of the President, [and] I worked in *Malacañang*. Afterwards I went to the Office of the Solicitor General, I was Chief of Staff to the Solicitor General in the Department of Justice, and then I transferred to here [Education].[163]

(c) Drawn from a pool of men and women who have come to know each other over many years as they move among sectors, branches, and agencies, political appointees bring not only a range of perspectives and experience into government[164] but also greater cohesion and better coordination than might otherwise be the case. This is especially valuable given frequent changes in policy and the comparative brevity of political life. This pool also allows a degree of vertical integration in that political appointees are occasionally seconded *from* the permanent service and to all intents and purposes become "permanent" political appointees in a single agency where they may spend a large part of their career. They are, therefore, able to marry an intimate knowledge of the upper circles of government with an unparalleled knowledge of the agency. The experience of one undersecretary in the Department of Education is fairly typical. While working for NEDA,

> ...one of the Deputy Ministers at that time...was also then concurrently a Deputy Minister in the Department of Budget and Management. And later on he became the Minister of the Department of Budget Management, and he invited me to go over to the Department. I worked there from more than five years.... When one of the Assistant Secretaries in Education decided to retire....there was that opening.... I don't know if I should say "apply," not really "apply," but I expressed interest... I had some friends who were working here and they put in some good words to me. And then, at that time, there was an Undersecretary who came from the same school that I went to; and that person knew my brothers—who were very good ... and he told the Minister at that time.... So I guess he also influenced the decision of the Secretary.... And I was asked to—well, I had a brief talk with a Minister at that time, though I had not really made up my mind—and she asked me to join the Education Department.[165]

(d) The informal selection of political appointees may also admit qualities and personalities that a more technical process might well exclude or leave unrecognized, but which have their time and place. Indeed, as the following instance seem to illustrate, it is possible that within the same official less desirable traits (in this case the search for a sinecure) usually assigned to political appointees rest alongside more noble facets (passion and commitment) more usually ascribed to permanent civil servants. The Undersecretary in question began his career teaching economics at the University of the East while studying law in the University of the Philippines. In 1978, he became a lawyer and immediately went into private practice when, in 1979, the results of the bar examination became known. Shortly after, he left the University and became a full-time trial lawyer. But "...after twenty-six years ... in active private practice, I wanted to have some rest.... I heard that the X Commissioner will ... retire from the service, [and] I heard that in the X Commission there is no work there—you just travel from one place to another. So I got interested in that position to become an X Commissioner.... There was one congresswoman who was introduced to me by my good friend ... Congressmen [Y], and that congresswoman made a recommendation to the President that I be appointed as X Commissioner." As the appointment was about to be announced, however,

> the Finance Secretary at the time [who] was newly appointed ... asked the President that, instead of appointing me, another person be appointed because, according to the Secretary, he must have his team, his own people. So I was not appointed, so that was it. I was not looking for another job anyway.. So when I received an appointment from the President as Assistant Secretary for the Department of Agrarian Reform, I thank[ed] the President ... but I rejected it.... I [then] received a call from the Office of the Secretary of Transportation and Communication asking me whether I am interested about the position to be the head of the Transport Co-operative. Then ... my friend Congressmen X, asked me ... if I'm interested about this position [Z] to be Undersecretary. I told him I'm not interested because ... because of the work ... I know that there is a lot of work here. Then ... I received [another] call from my friend, Congressman X.... He had had dinner with President [and] the President was already visibly angry, according to him. Why I was not accepting positions? So it was an ultimatum whether I accepted that position as Undersecretary. So I don't want to antagonize the President, so I told my friend, OK...[166]

His political connection had arisen from his legal work; from meetings which he and Congressman X had had with the husband of the President "with respect to ... a case... I cannot mention about the case.... I met the husband ... five or six times..."; and his work on drafting De Venecia's revised constitution[167]... into which he was bounced by X:

> got a call from him, and then he told me that "I told the President that you are drafting a constitution." But I said "That's not true, I'm not drafting a constitution" ... but he told me that he will be going to, I think, Paris at the time because he is President of the Chess Association here in the Philippines. So he was going to Europe ... for that; but after two weeks he will be coming back, and [he told me] "I told the President that it [the constitution] would be finished in two weeks time." So what I did ... because I had to submit something.... I got twenty constitutions at random from different countries ... plus the 1935 constitution that we had, the 1973 constitution and the 1987 constitution ... [as my models]. So I started with the preamble.... I got the meaning, the essence of the preambles [from my models] and made my own preamble ... a very simple one.... Then I went to the "National Territory" and looked at the twenty constitutions ... [but] it's only in the Philippines that we have a definition of the "National Territory." So I simplified my definition of what the

"National Territory" is. Then I went to the Bill of Rights.... I got one from here, one from there.... I just copied from here, I copied from there, I copied from everywhere.... I think that is how they make laws also.... Then, it was finished. So when Congressmen X came [back], I submitted it to him, and then I think with the approval of the President ... 194 congressmen signed that.[168]

The casual and breezy manner which this account reveals—and which also describes how decisions are so often made at high levels— also masks a passion for what he had *hoped* would be a sinecure but had ended up as a cause. Faced with a backlog of cases in Education, he attempted to expedite procedures for their disposal. He attempted codify and bring some coherence to Departmental orders; to amend the *Magna Carta*; to improve pay and conditions (especially the working hours of teachers); to re-examine the Roxas Law; to increase the number of teachers; and to clarify guidance on their role in elections (with the intention of having them removed from the process altogether). He was also prepared to stray outside his brief and talk critically about the curriculum.

What is being taught ... should be overhauled—the entire curriculum system ... [changed].... Like, for example, yesterday ... I went to the high school...and they don't have any textbooks.... I asked who is the best student in the English class? Then I asked the student to recite any poem that he knows. He can't recite a single poem—supposedly the best student. So what they are teaching? They were telling me about functional English.... They just inject a portion ... a sonnet from William Shakespeare, but that is all.... They will not ask the students to read Hamlet, for example. Personally I believe that ... you teach them, first, grammar—they should master that.... They should master Philippine literature.... And then ... they should master English literature. As of now they don't have any mastery of anything because they are more concerned about "functions." I really don't understand that: functional literature—they get a portion here and a portion there.... The students don't have a mastery of anything ... it's very fragmented. [169]

And he was clear in his disdain for the politicization of education.

Actually I have certain principles—I studied in the seminary ... St. Peter's seminary, we were under ... Belgian priests ... so I have some principles in life, some moral [principles] that cannot be altered by anybody at this stage in my life. I always believe that when one is in an organisation he has to be a team player; but if your principles will already be affected by that, then that's another thing. I can work within the system here, with a Secretary, so long as it does not compromise my principles—that's it. So long as what is being asked of me is in accordance with the law, no problem.... I just do my thing ['though], at least to a certain extent, I want to be also a team player; but when I see something and I want to pursue that, I really pursue it. I don't care about ... what the politicians think ... I'm not afraid of anybody here!... If they kick me out or [I'm] thrown in the river, OK!... I'll be happier if I will get out, so I don't care![170]

(d) This particular instance also reveals an understanding of patronage and obligation that is more complex than is perhaps usually assigned to civil servants. Political appointees may often feel obliged to the appointing authority, or at least to those who recommended them to the President. But this is by no means always the case. To an extent, the sheer number of political appointees means that, except for those with the highest profiles, most are hardly likely to be at the forefront of the President's mind; and some positions have fixed terms that reach beyond the President's term of office. Political appointees may also take on a post knowing that their life-expectancy is limited and, therefore, do what they feel is best regardless of what the politicians think of them or want them to do. Still others are of the view that the choice they face is not between subservience and resistance, but between being idealistic and realistic. How is the job best done in the circumstances?

I kind of mentally do a cost benefit analysis, because for me if you want to push for something, you do not say that everything is constant, you have to consider that there are realities, and that the realities are this: if you do something which you know will not be in line with policies of the government, you know it's not going to push through. So for me, from my own experience, I know what the policies of the government are and I know what the directions of the Secretary are: his priorities will be ICT, will be textbooks, will be teachers. Then these are the areas which I feel would be best to promote. So these are the things that I look at. Again, because with so many areas, I would think that you would also have to try to zero-in on certain things rather than having a shotgun effect. I would rather concentrate on the areas which I know are the policies: this is the direction that has been set by the President ... this is what we have as an Agency Development Programme, these are the things that we have under the Basic Education Reform Agenda.... Why go out that area which is not a priority; and to me, those are already more than enough—just taking one of those already has a large effect on education itself.[171]

Conclusions

Philippine political and bureaucratic organizations are usually presented as weak, permeable, distorted and corrupted and, as such, lie some way from a proper condition of formality. There is no question that informal behavior can and does have a deleterious effect on the civil service and the organizations it staffs, and that such behavior and its damaging effects are prevalent in the Philippines. Yet, of greater significance is the positive quality of informality—a direct expression of deepening emotion. This is more than just a support to—or an additional quality to be considered alongside—formal, impersonal, legal-rational frameworks. It provides the room and atmosphere for creative thought, discussions, and decisions; it compensates for the inadequacies which stem from highly formal arrangements; and it overcomes negative informality when it is not possible, for political considerations, to establish open and effective counter-procedures (as in the case of resisting political interference in the bureaucracy). It also constitutes the core of new practices around which organizations may be reformed, improved, and developed: it is the source of innovation, and the base material from which the formal—the temporary regularization of informal innovations— is shaped.

Notes

1. Lorenzo, M., Assistant Commissioner, Bureau of Internal Revenue, Quezon City, October 5, 2007.
2. Duncano, D., Deputy Commissioner, Bureau of Internal Revenue, Quezon City, October 9, 2007.
3. Azana, M.C., Director, Bureau of Customs, Manila, May 3, 2007.
4. de la Fuente, C., Director, Civil Service Commission, Quezon City, December 4, 2007.
5. Guinigundo, D., Deputy Governor, *Bangko Sentral Ng Pilipinas*, Malate, September 28, 2007.
6. Duncano, D., Deputy Commissioner, Bureau of Internal Revenue, Quezon City, October 9, 2007.
7. Source (BIR) requests anonymity.
8. Carpentero, A., Director, Office of Procurement, Department of Education, Pasig City, October 8, 2007.
9. Ibid.
10. Inciong, T., Assistant Secretary, Department of Education, Pasig City, September 25, 2007. Close observance of the procurement law is no less frustrating for those responsibility it is to keep the physical infrastructure of the CSC throughout the Philippines in a good state of repair: "...with the procurement law it takes a number of bids before you can procure what you want. In the private sector it is much quicker—you provide the memorandum to the higher officials, say you want this, and they get it. Here it may take seven days, fifteen days, it depends.... We have to abide by the existing rules and regulations of the procurement law—for transparency ... but maybe there are ways of making improvements.... There must be technology and processes which will lessen the procurement times.' (Formilleza, I., Division Chief, Civil Service Commission, Quezon City, December 4, 2007).
11. Carpentero, A., Director, Department of Education, Pasig City, October 8, 2007.
12. Ibid.

13. Ibid.
14. Ibid.
15. Bacani, R.C., Undersecretary, Department of Education, Pasig City, September 24, 2007.
16. Ibid.
17. Ibid.
18. Joson, L.G., OIC (HRMD, Planning), Department of Education, Pasig City, September 10, 2007.
19. Mateo, J., OIC (Office of the Assistant Secretary, Educational Development Projects Implementing Taskforce), Department of Education, Pasig City, September 11, 2007.
20. Roldan, J., Assistant Commissioner, Bureau of Internal Revenue, Quezon City, October 9, 2007.
21. Mateo, J., OIC (Office of the Assistant Secretary, Educational Development Projects Implementing Taskforce), Department of Education, Pasig City, September 11, 2007.
22. Duncano, D., Deputy Commissioner, Bureau of Internal Revenue, Quezon City, October 9, 2007.
23. Ibid.
24. Porio, F., Director, Civil Service Commission, Quezon City, November 21, 2007.
25. Duncano, D., Deputy Commissioner, Bureau of Internal Revenue, Quezon City, October 9, 2007.
26. And it is often regarded quite explicitly by the lower, as well as upper, ranks as "the most important quality for a manager.... A former ... director and former supervisor in exam records were the best people I have worked for: they were compassionate. They treated me as an equal, they asked for my opinions, they let me work independently, and they always look after the welfare of their staff; we had a good working relationship. This motivated me to do my work." (Badiola-Causing, M.T., Administrative Assistant VI, Civil Service Commission, Quezon City, November 22, 2007).
27. Guinigundo, D., Deputy Governor, *Bangko Sentral Ng Pilipinas*, Malate, 28 September, 2007.
28. Agamata, L., Director, Civil Service Commission, Quezon City, December 6, 2007.
29. Ibid.
30. Sources (three interviewees) request anonymity (Department of Education).
31. Source (BIR) requests anonymity.
32. Formilleza, I., Division Chief, Civil Service Commission, Quezon City, December 4, 2007.
33. Galvan, J.G., Assistant Secretary, Department of Education, Pasig City, October 8, 2007.
34. Source (Department of Education) requests anonymity.
35. Source (BIR) requests anonymity.
36. Thus it is not unusual to find that first and second-level employees "can say anything ... [to] our ... directors ... you can make suggestions. In an office where there are so many people, it is not easy to manage ... but ... we are professional and we know what our jobs are, so when there are things to

which we cannot come to an agreement, we talk, we compromise and we explain why we are doing the things we are doing and why certain things were not done; and our director is understanding and very positive." (Judan, R., Administrative Assistant VI, Civil Service Commission, December 4, 2007).

37. Dulce, V.H., Deputy Director, *Bangko Sentral Ng Pilipinas*, Malate, September 18, 2007.

38. Ibid.

39. Guinigundo, D., Deputy Governor, *Bangko Sentral Ng Pilipinas*, Malate, 28 September, 2007.

40. Ibid.

41. Dulce, V.H., Deputy Director, *Bangko Sentral Ng Pilipinas*, Malate, September 18, 2007.

42. Guinigundo, D., Deputy Governor, *Bangko Sentral Ng Pilipinas*, Malate, 28 September, 2007.

43. Sunga, F.C., Undersecretary, Department of Education, Pasig City, September 27, 2007.

44. Mercado, S.S., Project Evaluation Officer IV, Quezon City Hall, May 3, 2007.

45. Dela Cruz, G. R. F., OIC (Administrative Division, Environmental Protection and Waste Management Department), Quezon City Hall, Quezon, May 3, 2007.

46. de Zuniga, J., Assistant Governor, *Bangko Sentral Ng Pilipinas*, Malate, September 21, 2007.

47. Ibid.

48. Ibid.

49. Constantino-David, K., Chair, Civil Service Commission, Quezon City, December 27, 2007.

50. Lopez-Espejo, C., Supervising Personnel Specialist, Civil Service Commission, Quezon City, December 6, 2007.

51. Agamata, L., Director, Civil Service Commission, Quezon City, December 6, 2007.

52. Anquilan, R., Director, Bureau of Customs, Manila, September 7, 2007.

53. Abad, J., Chief of Staff, Senator Aquino, B., The Philippine Senate, Pasay City, December 19, 2007.

54. Mateo, J., OIC (Office of the Assistant Secretary, Educational Development Projects Implementing Taskforce), Department of Education, Pasig City, September 11, 2007.

55. De Zuniga, J., Assistant Governor, *Bangko Sentral Ng Pilipinas*, Malate, September 21, 2007.

56. Ibid.

57. Dulce, V., Assistant Director, *Bangko Sentral Ng Pilipinas*, Malate, September 18, 2007.

58. de Zuniga, J., Assistant Governor, *Bangko Sentral Ng Pilipinas*, Malate, September 21, 2007.

59. Inocentes, A., Undersecretary, Department of Education, Pasig City, October 1, 2007.

60. Inciong, T., Assistant Secretary, Department of Education, Pasig City, September 25, 2007.

61. Dulce, V., Assistant Director, Bangko Sentral Ng Pilipinas, Malate, September 18, 2007.

62. Urquilo, P., Chief of Staff, Senator Honasan, G., The Philippine Senate, Pasay City, December 12, 2007; Abad, J., Chief of Staff, Senator Aquino, B., The Philippine Senate, Pasay City, December 19, 2007.

63. Urquilo, P., Chief of Staff, Senator Honasan, G., Philippine Senate, Pasay City, December 12, 2007.

64. Escudero, F., Senator, Philippine Senate, Pasay City, 19 December 2007.

65. Urquilo, P., Chief of Staff, Senator Honasan, G., Philippine Senate, Pasay City, December 12, 2007.

66. Abad, J., Chief of Staff, Senator Aquino, B., Philippine Senate, Pasay City, December 19, 2007.

67. Ibid.

68. Escudero, F., Senator, Philippine Senate, Pasay City, 19 December 2007.

69. Malaya, J., Special Assistant, Department of Education, Pasig City, September 27, 2007.

70. Bacani, R.C., Undersecretary, Department of Education, Pasig City, September 24, 2007.

71. Porio, F., Director, Civil Service Commission, Quezon City, November 21, 2007.

72. Silubrico, I., Supervising Specialist II, Civil Service Commission, Quezon City, November 27, 2007. These relationships are enough to overcome even the barriers surrounding the CSC's Office of Legal Affairs. "You cannot just go there and approach a lawyer ... because their work is totally different from the other departments. They work with highly confidential papers. You have to stay in their receiving areas, and you cannot even talk directly to the lawyers. But I can go there anytime I like because I came from office, and I worked for them for ten years." (Costes, V.C., Chief Personnel Specialist, Civil Service Commission, November 22, 2007).

73. Taron, R., Chief (Collection Enforcement), Bureau of Internal Revenue, Quezon City, October 5, 2007.

74. Silubrico, I., Civil Service Commission, Quezon City, November 27, 2007.

75. Joson, L.G., OIC (HRMD, Planning), Department of Education, Pasig City, September 10, 2007.

76. There was much laughter at this point from two other interviewees then present.

77. Source (Department of Education) requests anonymity.

78. Galvan, J.G., Assistant Secretary, Department of Education, Pasig City, October 8, 2007.

79. Sunga, F.C., Undersecretary, Department of Education, Pasig City, September 27, 2007.

80. Inciong, T., Assistant Secretary, Department of Education, Pasig City, September 25, 2007.

81. Lorenzo, M., Assistant Commissioner, Bureau of Internal Revenue, Quezon City, October 5, 2007.

82. Guinigundo, D., Deputy Governor, *Bangko Sentral Ng Pilipinas*, Malate, September 28, 2007.

83. Tabino, A., Director, Civil Service Commission, Quezon City, December 18, 2007.

84. dela Fuente, C., Director, Civil Service Commission, Quezon City, December 4, 2007.

85. Roldan, J., Assistant Commissioner, Bureau of Internal Revenue, Quezon City, October 9, 2007.

86. Source (Department of Education) requests anonymity.

87. Porio, F., Director, Civil Service Commission, Quezon City, November 21, 2007.

88. Source (CSC) requests anonymity.

89. Porio, F., Director, Civil Service Commission, Quezon City, November 21, 2007.

90. Source (Department of Education) requests anonymity.

91. Lopez-Espejo, C., Supervising Personnel Specialist, Civil Service Commission, Quezon City, December 6, 2007.

92. Ibid.

93. Porio, F., Director, Civil Service Commission, Quezon City, November 21, 2007. The warm respect, and real trepidation, with which directors (especially the younger ones) viewed the Chair is also nicely captured by another director's comment that "...the ... chair is also open—we can easily go to her office. There are not many restrictions—just as long as you're ready to be scolded ... that's just a joke!" (Fernandez, M.C., Director, Civil Service Commission, Quezon City, November 22, 2007).

94. Barba, M.C., Chief Personnel Specialist, Civil Service Commission, Quezon City, November 27, 2007.

95. Inciong, T., Assistant Secretary, Department of Education, Pasig City, September 25, 2007.

96. Taron, R., Chief (Collection Enforcement), Bureau of Internal Revenue, Quezon City, October 5, 2007.

97. Inciong, T., Assistant Secretary, Department of Education, Pasig City, September 25, 2007.

98. Quijano, Y., Director, Department of Education, Pasig City, September 25, 2007.

99. Inciong, T., Assistant Secretary, Department of Education, Pasig City, September 25, 2007.

100. Source (Department of Education) requests anonymity.

101. Ibid.

102. Ibid.

103. Lim, C., Atty., Assistant Commissioner, Bureau of Internal Revenue, Quezon City, October 10, 2007. Securing reliable information from the Bureau's regional offices has, in some areas of activity, become "...our main problem.... Because of the attrition law [which compels collection officers to meet targets or face dismissal] they [the revenue districts] don't want us [Central Office Enforcement Services] to conduct ... fraud investigations [into taxpayers] ... in their jurisdictions.... According to them, if the [fraud] audit will not be conducted by their district it may lessen their authority over these taxpayers ... [and] that may affect the [future] compliance of the taxpayers.' (King, C., Atty., Assistant Commissioner, Bureau of Internal Revenue, Quezon City, October 4, 2007).

104. Bacani, R.C., Undersecretary, Department of Education, Pasig City, September 24, 2007.

105. Source (Department of Education) requests anonymity.
106. Ibid.
107. Source (Department of Education) requests anonymity.
108. Joson, L.G., OIC (HRMD, Planning), Department of Education, Pasig City, September 10, 2007.
109. Inocentes, A., Undersecretary, Department of Education, Pasig City, October 1, 2007.
110. Constantino-David, K., Chair, Civil Service Commission, Quezon City, December 27, 2007.
111. Ibid.
112. Communications are passed direct to the Chair from a low-level official in Information and Records Management Office who is responsible for all the incoming communications: "Complaints, queries, appeals, miscellaneous letters, allegations, confidential letters ... [from] the whole bureaucracy ... the Office of the Ombudsman, the Supreme Court, the Court of Appeals ... come to me—for my eyes only. I encode them on the tracking system, I give [them] to the Office of the Chair ... and then the Office of the Chair will take charge of all that..." Cajucom, F., Data Controller IV, Civil Service Commission, November 29, 2007.
113. Ibid.
114. Galvan, J.G., Assistant Secretary, Department of Education, Pasig City, October 8, 2007.
115. Source (Department of Education) requests anonymity.
116. Malaya, J., Assistant Secretary, Department of Education, Pasig City, September 27, 2007.
117. Ibid.
118. Source (Department of Education) requests anonymity.
119. Source (Department of Education) requests anonymity.
120. Source (Department of Education) requests anonymity.
121. Ibid.
122. Source (Department of Education) requests anonymity.
123. And these issues—from the appointment of unqualified staff to pay, conditions and benefits—are the meat of unions who represent rank-and-file (second and first-level civil servants) and who regard themselves "as the watchdog of the proper implementation of the [civil service] system" (Costes, V.C., Chief Personnel Specialist, Civil Service Commission, November 22, 2007). The unions, however, are very fluid affairs. An agency is permitted a maximum of three unions (as each union needs 30 percent of the agency's workforce to be accredited by the CSC) and their memberships range from several thousand to around twenty or so (as in the case of the Bureau of Communications under the Office of the President). Abella, R.C., Clerk III, Civil Service Commission, Quezon City, November 22, 2007.
124. Anonymous written allegations circulated among colleagues.
125. Source (Department of Education) requests anonymity.
126. Source (Department of Education) requests anonymity.
127. Galvan, J.G., Assistant Secretary, Department of Education, Pasig City, October 8, 2007.
128. Source (Department of Education) requests anonymity.

129. Source (Department of Education) requests anonymity. A very similar approach—prevarication and the offer the compromise—is taken by civil servants in response to requests from legislators to re-direct agency spending into their districts: "'I have just received a letter from Congressman X and he is requesting for the feeding program to be expanded in his district, but utilizing our funds. So what I said is we can cover some of his constituents but if he wants to have a wider coverage of the program he will have to fund it.... There is also ... one congressman from Lanao del Norte, who is advocating milk feeding ... [from our funds].... I have yet to see a letter from a congressman saying, 'Can you please give me data because I'm going to use my funds for a program.' Because these funds—the pork barrel—[they] use mostly for infrastructure" (Santos, T., Director, Department of Education, Pasig City. September 24, 2007).

130. Umbac, S., Chief (Legislative Liaison) Civil Service Commission, Quezon City, December 7, 2007.

131. Source (Department of Education) requests anonymity. As alluded to earlier, mayors "have a great deal of influence.... Because the resources are so wanting ... the schools, if they want ... school buildings, they go to the mayors, they go to the school board, they go to the governors; and whatever they [the schools] get, they [the politicians] say [in return], 'You hire this, you hire this, you hire this.'" (Santos, T., Director, Department of Education, Pasig City. September 24, 2007).

132. Guinigundo, D., Deputy Governor, *Bangko Sentral Ng Pilipinas*, Malate, September 28, 2007.

133. Source (CSC) requests anonymity.

134. Constantino-David, K., Chair, Civil Service Commission, Quezon City, December 27, 2007.

135. Malaya, J., Assistant Secretary, Department of Education, Pasig City, September 27, 2007.

136. Porio, F., Director, Civil Service Commission, Quezon City, November 21, 2007.

137. Constantino-David, K., Chair, Civil Service Commission, Quezon City, December 27, 2007.

138. Inciong, T., Assistant Secretary, Department of Education, Pasig City, September 25, 2007.

139. Source (Bureau of Customs) requests anonymity.

140. Source (Bureau of Internal Revenue) requests anonymity.

141. Constantino-David, K., Chair, Civil Service Commission, Quezon City, December 27, 2007.

142. Ibid.

143. Inocentes, A., Undersecretary, Department of Education, Pasig City, October 1, 2007.

144. Constantino-David, K., Chair, Civil Service Commission, Quezon City, December 27, 2007.

145. Tabino, A., Director, Civil Service Commission, Quezon City, December 18, 2007.

146. In Education, third-level civil servants (career and non-career) work independently and together to lobby not only and local government but also other central offices to finance new programs in the Department. "...There

is a tendency for us just to submit [for incorporations into the following year's budget] whatever program we have now ... and just add five or ten percent.... But if there *is* a new program ... and they say that you don't have any [new] money... [then] we go to the Department of Interior and Local Government, we go to the mayors, to the Department of Health, for support." (Santos, T., Director, Department of Education, Pasig City. September 24, 2007). International aid organizations are another source that directors will tap as in the case of the Bureau of Alternative Learning: "The percentage share of the DepEd budget of the Bureau is 0.17 percent. Before I came it was 0.068 percent. Last year it was increased to 0.17 percent.... So... I have my own money here which is small ... so ... I have a shopping list, my wish list ... and [when] ...US aid and AUS aid ... come and say 'Can we help?' I say. 'Yes, here is my shopping list, please choose ... we need a national workshop we need this we need that...'; and we share the outputs with them, and pilot for them, and sometimes we use part of our small funds jointly." (Guerrero, C.S., Director, Department of Education, Pasig City, September 21, 2007). Staffs at lower levels at Education's central office and in the regions are also urged to press local government and legislators. Indeed, "we have trained our health personnel in social mobilization. And during that social mobilization training ... we train health personnel, such as doctors, to prepare their project plans. We say 'If you go to the mayor you will have to answer questions: What is that, and how much?'" So you just have to have a one-page paper with the title of the program, the rationale and justification. The data should be specific and area specific: 'That in your town the children have these kinds of diseases and we can have interventions like this and that, and [this] is how much it will cost.' You know...the provincial governors and the congressmen - they are so parochial, [so] you have to tell them that 'In your area you have this number who are undernourished and this is the kind of intervention, how many days [it will take], and this is the cost, and these are the benefits'; and then you have to follow it up. And there was even a time when we wrote to all congressmen, and I had to go to Congress and to give them a position paper. [So] we get [the funds] from there... from their districts, from their own funds, their pork barrel." (Santos, T., Director, Department of Education, Pasig City. September 24, 2007). As Santos acknowledges, "social mobilization" by civil servants only encourages further unsolicited requests (noted earlier in this chapter) from legislators to re-direct the Department's spending into their districts. Civil servants may also petition legislators indirectly through "our NGO partners... It's not so much my line, my expertise to do that; of course I can, but I don't know .... I'm a little bit embarrassed, because I may not .... I am not that familiar with them, and I recognize that there are people who can do this better than me along that line." (Guerrero, C.S., Director, Department of Education, Pasig City, September 21, 2007).

147. These officers are quite separate from the PLLO (who work for the Palace in the legislature).
148. Source (CSC) requests anonymity.
149. Umbac, S., Chief (Legislative Liaison Division), Civil Service Commission, Quezon City, December 7, 2007.

150. Source (CSC) requests anonymity.
151. Source (CSC) requests anonymity.
152. Source (Senate) requests anonymity.
153. Source (Large Taxpayers Service, Bureau of Internal Revenue, Quezon City) requests anonymity. A similar point is frequently made by revenue officers and auditors about the relative compliance of larger businesses who "will look for technicalities but otherwise ... are more or less good taxpayers," and the smaller businesses who "are the problem." Source (National Investigation Division, BIR, Quezon City) requests anonymity.
154. Lim, C., Atty., Assistant Commissioner, Bureau of Internal Revenue, Quezon City, October 10, 2007.
155. de Zuniga, J., Assistant Governor, *Bangko Sentral Ng Pilipinas*, Malate, September 21, 2007.
156. Source (Bureau of Customs) requests anonymity. For the BIR's auditors and investigators, too, "'outsiders' are an important well of information. Nowadays there are plenty of informants.... Some ... were previously employees of [those businesses under investigation]; some were accountants; some were their external auditors. Because they can no longer stomach the tax evading practices of their employers ... [and because they may be rewarded] 10 percent of the amount collected [up to 1 million pesos] ... so they come in and generate the information." And, as one official makes plain, this is despite receiving little or no effective protection: "...we have the so-called affidavit ... in the affidavit form there is only aliases. However, [employers] can work out the real identity of the informer—that's why sometimes ... informers [are] receiving death threats." Source (National Investigation Division, BIR, Quezon City) requests anonymity.
157. Inocentes, A., Undersecretary, Department of Education, Pasig City, October 1, 2007; Constantino-David, C. Chair, Civil Service Commission, Quezon City, December 27, 2007; Pawid, L. , Legislative Staff Officer, Office of Senator Gordon, The Philippine Senate, Pasay City, September 17, 2007.
158. Constantino-David, C., Chair, Civil Service Commission, Quezon City, December 27, 2007.
159. The consideration here on the part of the politician is not votes. The Senator's constituency is national and, unlike House Representatives the Senatorial staff will coldly dismiss potential voters who turn up in their offices looking for, say, money to travel back their hometown.
160. Sebastian, M.C.A., Administrative Assistant III, Civil Service Commission, Quezon City, December 10, 2007. Even in the BIR, civil servants will let these written endorsements "go to file for future reference. Because if you are technically equipped and good enough, why would you ask for endorsements from Congressman and Senators?" (Cosca, E., Head Revenue Executive Assistant to Assistant Commissioner, Bureau of Internal Revenue, Quezon City, October 2, 2007).
161. Inocentes, A., Undersecretary, Department of Education, Pasig City, October 1, 2007.
162. Ibid.
163. Malaya, J., Assistant Secretary, Department of Education, Pasig City, September 27, 2007.

164. The point is often recognized by career civil servants—even those most committed to limiting or eradicating political interference. "Actually, in fairness, there are a lot of cases where the people from the private sector enter government, and the government agencies to which they have been assigned greatly benefit ... that's why we are very much against, very much against, intrusion into appointments to ... third level positions (Fernandez, M.T.C., Director, Civil Service Commission, Quezon City, November 22, 2007).
165. Bacani, R.C., Undersecretary, Department of Education, Pasig City, September 24, 2007.
166. Source requests anonymity.
167. This was one of several draft constitutions drawn up by various actors both as justification for invoking a Constitutional Assembly, and as a kernel for debate in that Assembly.
168. Source requests anonymity.
169. Ibid.
170. Ibid.
171. Inocentes, A., Undersecretary, Department of Education, Pasig City, October 1, 2007.

Conclusions

Although not its original intention, this book has sought to draw attention to, and find a way of accommodating, the dimensions of practice and thought. It suggests that scholars' analyses and conceptual devices should be accorded a status equal to that enjoyed by the representations of those actors whose behavior they purport to explain. As such, actors' representations are assumed to be no less accurate than those of scholars; no less functional in the extent to which they make it possible for actors to operate within the social world; and, when drawn upon to inform practice, no less concrete and unpredictable in their effects.

Given their equal status, analysis is necessarily focused on the strings of practice and representation that constitute the social world's *surface* features. Dimension and interaction rather than "deep" structures and their classification (as, say, "economic," "social," "political," "Eastern" or "Western") are now of interest; distinctions and divisions among categories of phenomena—such as "structure," "individual," "culture," "society," "formal," "informal," "modern," "traditional," "developed," "underdeveloped," "historical," and "contemporary"—are brought into question; and the "imagined," too, may inform practice and thus have effects no less concrete and unpredictable than the "real".

From this view, the general is a way of arranging and fitting together the details and dimensions of a social world that is extraordinarily fuzzy. Yet patterns, imprecise and uncertain though they may be, can be made out. Described as gyres of instrumentalism, deepening emotion, and Puritanism, they are neither deterministic nor self-reproducing; the details through which they find expression are always changing; and the meaning of these fuzzy practices, and their bearing upon subsequent representations and events, are unpredictable. These patterns appear and re-appear again and again and at all scales because their details are manifestations of practical compromise and the shared experiences of being human—commonalities rooted ultimately in interactions with other people and the natural world. Both detail and pattern, then, are expressions of being and doing—experiences rooted in the public. Thus it becomes possible to reconcile contradiction, ambiguity, the

225

unexpected and the muddle so apparent in everyday life with the patterns formed beyond the realm of each actor's immediate world.

Does this approach, and this particular study, offer any practical guidance to attempts to improve Philippine bureaucracy? Advice without responsibility is an easy thing to give. And there are many civil servants and politicians who are well aware of the problems that surround them and how these might be dealt with, and who have an intimate understanding of those solutions' implications. It is with them, rather than with any outside experts, that advice is best sought. Nevertheless, a study that accommodates the accounts of actors in this fragmented bureaucracy may provide an intriguing and perhaps helpful "take" on these matters.

1. One immediate objective to which efforts might be directed is the reconfiguration and alignment of actors' representations of government and bureaucracy. This would require a simplification and clarification of divisions in authority across government and bureaucracy, and would involve a number of technical changes in practice.

The first is the centralization of civil service recruitment, training, and placement by a larger and more powerful Civil Service Commission; and the extension of probation from 6 months to at least three years. For practical purposes, training would need to be undertaken by affiliates of a Central College attached to agencies; though the training of selected officials—especially those at, or destined for, the higher ranks—would be focused in the Central College itself through which around 5-10 percent of the Service would pass at some stage in their careers. These arrangements would also apply to civil servants staffing local government offices. At the national level, however, a layer of political appointees would be retained. This, potentially at least, offers: greater breadth of experience; broader views of government, society, and the Philippines' place in the world; and political sensitivity. And, since many of its members are well known to each other, it may also bring more coherence to policy and the conduct of business across government. The formalization or semi-formalization of their selection, and the creation of a pool of ready candidates from which politicians could draw, might allow both politicians and permanent civil servants to have more faith in them. For instance, entry into this pool could be vetted by an independent panel, comprising members of the Civil Service Commission, the Judicial and Bar Council, the Church, business, universities, and (as silent members) legislators. Their decisions would be made with reference to a wide set of criteria including experience, vision, leadership, competence, and character. Career civil servants could also apply or be recommended for entry. An agency's upper echelon would be drawn either from this pool, or directly from the career service, or from both. The admission of career civil servants in this way, and the placement of various grades of directors and commissioners in the career service on the same salary scale as assistant secretaries and undersecretaries, would also help to reduce friction between permanent and political staffs.

The second change is to hand to legislators in the Lower House more direct authority over development efforts in their districts; to reduce the legislative burden associated with these efforts; and to provide for the automatic release of fair subventions (perhaps though an equalization fund).

The third is to peel away the layers of local government. Aside from congressional districts, a single layer of local government is envisaged: city governments with extended geographical jurisdictions. Their activities would be coordinated through membership of interregional development authorities on whose boards would also sit congressional representatives and members of NEDA [National Economic Development Authority]. In these city regions, elected politicians (Mayors, Vice-Mayors and councillors) would depend upon civil servants whose recruitment, training and placement would be determined centrally by the CSC. Whilst their geographical jurisdiction will have increased, the functions of local government would focus more narrowly on coordinating with national line agencies in the provision of basic urban and rural services to congressional districts.

A fourth change is to place initiative for the Budget with the Executive. The assent of the Senate for this particular item of legislation would no longer be required; and whilst the Finance Bill would still need to pass though the Lower House, the scope and length of debate would be curtailed. The strong presumption would be that, as an initiative of the President, this Bill should receive the consent of the House as a matter of course. But there would be two important constraints with which the executive would have to live. One is that the ground rules according to which annual budgets are drawn up, shaped, and finalized would have to be agreed by the Senate and the Lower House (though these would not need to be renegotiated each year). These rules would include, for instance, the automatic release of subventions to congressional districts and schools, and the formula by which those funds are calculated; and the identification of categories and levels of increase in tax, or exceptional items of expenditure, that would require separate legislation and the acquiescence of both Houses. The other is provided by the Senate whose authority to examine and investigate the executive's *subsequent* management of the country's finances, economy, foreign policy, and wider social and civil development—and, therefore, to compel civil servants and elected members of the executive to provide information and appear before its committees—would be strengthened by unambiguous and automatic legal sanctions.

As a consequence of these measures, the civil service would be far better placed to cultivate officers whose understanding of government and their own roles is more coherent and aligned, less likely to suffer interference, and more able to resist. The retention of a layer of closely vetted political appointees leaves politicians with confidants and career civil servants with colleagues rather than interlopers and competitors. Meanwhile, with its legitimate control over the Budget strengthened, the executive is now released from a need to circumvent and engage in such intense political bargaining (at least as far the Budget's preparation is concerned), and is given more time and space to consider its policies and proposed legislation more thoroughly. With a thinning in the flow of local bills and with their independence reinforced, the Senate and Lower House would also have more time to consider, introduce, and scrutinize legislation more carefully. At the same time, the responsibilities of civil service, executive and legis-lature are defined more sharply. With more room to cultivate its staff and more authority over them, the civil service will find it more difficult to shift its own failings on to politicians. By the same token, the executive may now have more authority over the Budget, but President and cabinet are solely responsible for the subsequent performance of the economy—a responsibility that will sooner or later work in favor of the political opposition. Members of the Lower House, too, are likely to have their abilities or inabilities to manage their districts exposed, as are local government politicians. They, like heads of agencies and President, are now caught between the template of a robust civil service and the electorate's verdict on their abilities to bring about tangible improvements in the lives of their constituents. With greater freedom comes greater responsibility.

It must be acknowledged that these reforms amount to something of wish list in that many of them require constitutional change. But in one shape or another they have been raised by politicians and civil servants.[1] Moreover, it is not so much these precise changes which are needed, as it is admission of the general principles they reflect—a reconfiguration, simplification and clarification of representations of government and bureaucracy.

2. Another objective suggested by this study is to stimulate a more affective state of mind within the civil service and throughout society more generally. This is far less difficult politically, and more important, in that the efficacy of any technical changes, including those outlined above, will ultimately depend on it. Again, it is not so much the implementation of specific measures as it is admission of the objective that is of critical importance; but there may be three measures of some note.

The first is to identify and encourage those positive informal practices that already occur within the polity and civil service. In this way, as civil servants cultivate innovations, ideas, and social relationships as if they are important in their own right, the bureaucracy is loosened up; it begins to operate more effectively, and room for deepening emotion and its expression is opened up still further. Many of these informal practices (such as admission of compas-sion, resolution of grievances, and breakdown of hierarchy) are best left as informal practices (though encouraged), for their significance and efficacy lies in tension with those formal arrangements they are attempting to compensate for. Other informal practices, however, might be usefully regularised, such as: *ad hoc* groupings of heads of agencies to discuss the coordination of their respective functions or complex policies; or the selection of high-level political appointees. A further, and related, practice is the circulation of non-career staffs within the Senate. A fourth is welfare provision by offices of members of the Lower House. Large numbers of constituents who visit their Representatives' offices (in their districts and occasionally in Congress) are seeking help with the cost of medicines and doctors' fees or with other similar matters (such as a job for someone down on his luck). And often they receive either small payments from their Representative's pork barrel or a letter guaranteeing payments by the Representative; or a conversation will be had on the constituent's behalf calling in a past favour or pledging a favour from the Representative at some point in the future. These kinds of exchanges can make a crucial difference to the lives of constituents. A dedicated adjunct to Representative's distinct offices could take on a useful role directing and advising constituents, continuing to meet emergency payments or (in so far welfare is available from agencies or through the SSS) laying out clear paths through the bureaucracy.

A second measure is to encourage—through schools, universities, academies, Churches, civil associations, exhibitions, and the provision of scholarships and tax allowances—the pursuit of education, art, music, literature, and science as matters of interest and significance in their own right. Given the association between deepening emotion and the development of organizations, support for small—and especially family-owned—businesses through taxation, banks, credit unions, and micro-finance might also prove to be extremely beneficial (and this is quite apart from any immediate economic rewards).

A third is to encourage civil servants to engage in organizational life outside the civil service including small family businesses and larger corporations; and to pursue further education as well as artistic, musical and literary endeavours. This would require the introduction of regular sabbaticals which are, at present, are ruled out[2] by a somewhat phobic attitude towards anything that might be construed as a conflict of interest.

***

While this study and the notion of emotional bureaucracy has clear implications for how "developing" bureaucracies and their features may be understood, it also speaks to the "developed" world and, more especially, to highly formalised societies in the west. Here, it suggests, actors have become so inured to the affective and its pervasiveness that relationships, rules, processes and organizations treated *as if* absolute are losing their significance and meaning and are being replaced by fixed, autonomous, and corporeal versions. Informality, creativity, initiative, and social convention weaken and crumble in the wake of this new Puritanism; and into the spaces left increasingly detailed and formal rules and procedures are moving to restore order and direction. The more tightly this mesh is drawn, the more quickly informality, creativity, and convention wither and die. A point is reached, however, when the repression of self demanded by all this prompts a return to instrumentalism and circumvention; the mesh itself begins to corrode; and the corruption that it contains breaks through.

As citizens and their politicians and civil servants in the Philippines look to the future, they might consider the experience of these "developed" societies. Instrumentalism, personalism, informality and corruption bring imperfection and hurt; but they also stimulate deepening emotion and serve as critical reminders of its importance. Effective, stable, flexible and creative organizations depend for their constant renewal and reinvigoration upon the presence of those very imperfections. Rather than accept the developed world's formalism and Puritanism, Filipinos may do better to walk their own, and necessarily uncertain, path and keep emotion at the heart of mind.

Notes

1. For instance a Civil Service Academy, funded in part by the Japanese government, is likely to be established, though it may offer training only to personnel officers.
2. Except in those rare cases where scholarships to study overseas are awarded.

Appendices

Appendix I
Government Employees

Government Employees	Career & non-career	Contractual	Elected	Total
Congress Of The Philippines	4826	753	259	5838
National Executive Agencies				
Department Of Education	497767	3184		500951
Department Of Interior And Local Government	149234	58		149292
State Universities And Colleges	54835	5078		59913
Department Of Health	26307	423		26730
Department Of Environment And Natural Resources	20550	2040		22590
Department Of Finance	19075	117		19192
Department Of Public Works And Highways	18140	9130		27270
Department Of Justice	16137	876		17013
Other Executive Offices	15380	1877	1	17258
Department Of Agrarian Reform	13905	631		14536
Department Of Transportation And Communications	12416	1877		14293
Department Of Agriculture	12043	542		12585
Department Of National Defense	9082	3208		12290
Department Of Labor And Employment	7272	272		7544
Department Of Science And Technology	4405	66		4471
National Economic And Development Authority	4233	370		4603
Department Of Trade And Industry	3191	192		3383
Office Of The Press Secretary	2319	71		2390
Department Of Social Welfare And Development	2263	80		2343
Department Of Foreign Affairs	1881	509		2390
Department Of Tourism	1322	163		1485
Office Of The President	1084	266		1350
Department Of Budget And Management	865	145		1010
Department Of Energy	621			621
Office Of The Vice-President	89	20	1	110
Local Government Units				
Municipal Governments	114635	25071	17656	157362
City Governments	88736	34619	1735	125090
Provincial Governments	73622	1303	1123	87775
Constitutional Offices	17255	351		17606
The Judiciary	26878	53		26931
Government Owned / Controlled Corporations	88923	15054		103977
Autonomous Regions In Muslim Mindanao	24961	519	27	25507
TOTAL GOVERNMENT EMPLOYEES	**1334252**	**120645**	**20802**	**1475699**

Source: compiled from materials provided by the CSC, 2007.

Appendix II
Political Appointees in Provincial Governments

	PA	PA%		PA	PA%
Abra	9	1.28	Lanao del Norte	17	3.18
Agusan del Norte	39	5.21	Lanao del Sur	89	16.64
Agusan del Sur	37	3.85	Leyte	1	0.07
Aklan	7	0.86	Maguindanao	6	85.71
Albay	12	1.20	Maguindanao	35	4.48
Antique	23	1.41	Marinduque	8	1.18
Apayao	9	1.79	Masbate	19	1.89
Aurora	4	1.17	Misamis Occidental	1	0.12
Basilan	24	4.08	Misamis Oriental	4	0.38
Bataan	18	2.19	Mt. Province	4	0.57
Batanes	3	0.98	Negros Occidental	3	0.16
Batangas	85	4.37	Negros Oriental	17	1.15
Benguet	7	0.86	Northern Samar	10	0.96
Biliran	18	5.81	Nueva Ecija	20	1.03
Bohol	9	0.65	Nueva Vizcaya	25	3.40
Bukidnon	1	0.21	Occidental Mindoro	3	0.38
Bulacan	138	9.17	Oriental Mindoro	10	1.21
Cagayan	15	1.10	Palawan	44	4.01
Camarines Norte	11	1.61	Pampanga	4	0.28
Camarines Sur	11	0.85	Pangasinan	38	2.01
Camiguin	7	2.62	Quezon	3	0.23
Capiz	22	2.36	Quirino	18	2.34
Catanduanes	8	1.19	Rizal	27	2.06
Cavite	77	4.81	Romblon	29	3.50
Cebu	9	0.60	Samar	2	0.19
Compostela Valley	37	9.54	Sarangani	46	7.40
Cotabato	21	2.22	Siquijor	2	0.48
Davao Del Norte	36	4.92	Sorsogon	12	1.19
Davao Del Sur	3	0.34	South Cotabato	11	1.21
Davao Oriental	11	1.68	Southern Leyte	2	0.28
Eastern Samar	16	1.43	Sultan Kudarat	12	1.96
Guimaras	16	3.86	Sulu	16	6.72
Ifugao	15	2.33	Surigao del Norte	22	2.55
Ilocos Norte	4	0.51	Surigao del Sur		0.00
Ilocos Sur	4	0.28	Tarlac	11	1.38
Iloilo	73	3.65	Tawi-Tawi	2	6.06
Isabela	14	1.34	Zambales	1	0.16
Kalinga	7	0.89	Zamboanga del Norte	13	1.34
La Union	43	6.53	Zamboanga del Sur	131	18.99
Laguna	30	1.87	Zamboanga Sibugay	23	3.61
			TOTAL	**1674**	**2.33**

Source: compiled from materials provided by the CSC, 2007.

PA Political Appointees. See table 2 and text for more details.

Appendix III
Political Appointees in City Governments

		PA	PA%			PA	PA%			PA	PA%
Alaminos City	NT	3	1.38	Iriga	NT	10	2.17	Sagay	NT	2	0.42
Angeles	NT	13	1.48	Isabela	NT	2	0.71	San Carlos	NT	12	2.27
Antipolo	NT	104	22.81	Kabankalan	NT	3	0.71	San Carlos City,			
Bacolod	NT	4	0.32	Kidapawan	NT	28	7.51	Pangasinan	NT	8	1.13
Bago	NT	6	0.67	Koronadal	NT	6	2.87	San Fernando,			
Baguio	NT	57	4.68	La Carlota	NT	5	1.03	Pampanga	NT	33	6.76
Bais	NT	10	1.89	Laoag	NT	9	1.45	San Fernando,			
Balanga	NT	4	1.11	Lapu-Lapu	NT	66	9.40	La Union	NT	25	5.14
Batangas	NT	17	1.35	Las Piñas	NT	2	0.74	San Jose	NT	14	3.08
Bayawan	NT	5	1.18	Legazpi City	NT	9	1.74	San Jose Del Monte	NT	14	3.65
Bislig	NT	21	6.16	Ligao City	NT	7	3.55	San Pablo	NT	35	3.93
Butuan	NT	14	1.46	Lingayen, Pangasinan	NT	7	4.58	Santiago	NT	5	1.28
Cabanatuan	NT	42	5.02	Lucena	NT	20	4.31	Silay	NT	5	0.85
Cadiz	NT	17	2.44	Maasin	NT	5	3.05	Sipalay	NT	3	2.13
Cagayan De Oro	NT	17	0.69	Makati	NT	146	3.85	Sorsogon	NT	3	1.31
Calamba	NT	41	8.06	Malabon	NT	78	9.73	Surigao	NT	4	0.82
Calapan	NT	3	0.74	Malaybalay City	NT	4	1.10	Tabaco City	NT	5	3.36
Calbayog	NT		0.00	Malolos	NT	4	1.16	Tacloban	NT	6	0.86
Caloocan	NT	88	4.56	Mandaluyong	NT	2	0.23	Tacurong	NT	9	3.50
Candon	NT	9	3.49	Mandaue	NT	15	2.99	Tagaytay	NT	9	1.65
Canlaon	NT	9	2.87	Manila	NT	457	5.09	Tagbilaran	NT	1	0.21
Cauayan	NT	8	2.19	Marawi	NT	34	10.00	Taguig	NT	25	6.14
Cavite	NT	3	0.88	Marikina	NT	7	1.36	Tagum	NT	7	2.30
Cebu	NT	2	0.13	Masbate	NT	15	6.15	Talisay (Cebu)	NT	88	30.34
Cotabato	NT	38	5.50	Muntinlupa	NT	2	0.42	Talisay,			
Cotabato	T	38	33.04	Naga	NT	1	0.24	(Negros Occidental)	NT	4	1.68
Dagupan City	NT	12	2.13	Olongapo	NT	20	2.49	Tanauan	NT	17	1.79
Danao	NT	9	1.89	Ormoc	NT	1	0.19	Tangub	NT	3	0.84
Dapitan	NT	21	3.84	Oroquieta	NT	1	0.19	Tanjay	NT	5	2.20
Davao	NT	333	11.79	Ozamiz	NT	22	2.78	Tarlac	NT	15	2.57
Digos	NT	6	2.35	Pagadian	NT	56	8.37	Toledo	NT	5	0.87
Dipolog	NT	4	0.77	Palayan	NT	13	3.66	Trece Martires	NT	19	5.21
Dumaguete	NT	1	0.18	Panabo	NT	27	13.71	Tuguegarao	NT	6	1.83
Escalante	NT	2	0.76	Parañaque	NT	55	6.56	Urdaneta	NT	12	3.87
Gapan	NT	17	5.50	Pasay	NT	102	6.36	Valencia City	NT	1	0.57
General Santos	NT	66	4.48	Pasig	NT	6	0.62	Valenzuela	NT	25	3.42
Gingoog	NT	2	0.56	Passi	NT	17	2.80	Victorias	NT	6	2.07
Himamaylan	NT	3	1.94	Puerto Princesa	NT	53	6.88	Vigan	NT	16	4.68
Iligan	NT	5	0.36	Quezon	NT	30	0.60	Zamboanga	NT	26	1.62
Iloilo	NT	8	0.47	Roxas	NT	3	0.45	**Total**		**2885**	**3.25**

Source: compiled from materials provided by the CSC, 2007.

PA   Political Appointees. See table 2 and text for more details.
NT   Non-teaching staff
T   Teaching staff

Appendix IV
Political Appointees in Municipalities by Region

	PA	PA%
REGION 4	769	3.61
REGION 3	400	3.55
REGION 6	278	2.69
REGION 5	253	3.02
REGION 10	248	4.44
ARMM	248	6.87
REGION 1	238	3.24
REGION 12	218	4.72
REGION 11	197	4.49
REGION 8	184	2.21
REGION 2	149	2.02
CARAGA	145	2.79
REGION 9	137	2.74
REGION 7	113	1.61
CAR	83	1.97
NCR	34	3.92
TOTAL	**3694**	**3.20**

Source: compiled from materials provided by the CSC, 2007.

PA   Political Appointees. See table 2 and text for more details.

Appendix V a
Political Appointees by Branch/Agency – National Executive

		PA	PA%
OFFICE OF THE PRESIDENT			
Office of the President		265	24.95
Mindanao Economic Development Council			
North Luzon Growth Quadrangle		1	100.00
Office of the Presidential Adviser on the Peace Process		21	100.00
Presidential Anti-Graft Commission			
OFFICE OF THE PRESIDENT		**287**	**26.48**
OFFICE OF THE VICE-PRESIDENT		**20**	**22.47**
DEPARTMENT OF AGRARIAN REFORM		33	0.26
National Commission on Indigenous Peoples		7	0.50
DEPARTMENT OF AGRARIAN REFORM		**40**	**0.29**
DEPARTMENT OF AGRICULTURE		170	3.18
Agricultural Training Institute			
Bureau of Agricultural Research			
Bureau of Agricultural Statistics			
Bureau of Animal Industry			
Bureau of Plant Industry			
Bureau of Soils and WaterManagement			
Agricultural Credit Policy Council		1	2.63
Bureau of Fisheries and Aquatic Resources		2	0.14
Bureau of Post Harvest Research and Extension		2	1.32
Cotton Development Authority			0.00
Fertilizer and Pesticide Authority		1	1.10
Fiber Industry Development Authority			
Livestock Development Council			
National Agricultural and Fishery Council			
National Meat Inspection Service			
National Nutrition Council			
Philippine Carabao Center			
DEPARTMENT OF AGRICULTURE		**176**	**1.46**
DEPARTMENT OF BUDGET AND MANAGEMENT		**3**	**0.35**
DEPARTMENT OF EDUCATION			
Department of Education	NT	768	1.15
Department of Education	T	193	0.04
National Book Development Board		12	27.27
Philippine High School for the Arts	NT		
Philippine HighSchool for the Arts	T		
DEPARTMENT OF EDUCATION		**973**	**0.20**
STATE UNIVERSITIES AND COLLEGES		**171**	**0.31**
DEPARTMENT OF ENERGY		**20**	**3.22**
DEPARTMENT OF ENVIRONMENT AND NATURAL RESOURCES		60	0.35
Ecosystems Research and Development Bureau			
Forest Management Bureau			

Appendix V b

		PA	PA%
Ecosystems Research and Development Bureau			
Forest Management Bureau			
Land Management Bureau		13	5.68
Protected Areas and Wildlife Bureau			
Environmental Management Bureau			
Mines and Geosciences Bureau			
National Mapping and Resource Information Authority	NU	22	4.32
National Mapping and Resource Information Authority	U		0.00
DEPARTMENT OF ENVIRONMENT AND NATURAL RESOURCES		**95**	**0.46**
DEPARTMENT OF FINANCE		21	4.72
Board of Liquidators		7	5.65
Bureau of Customs		4	0.08
Bureau of Internal Revenue		6	0.05
Bureau of LocalGovernment Finance			
Bureau of the Treasury			
Central Board of Assessment Appeal		5	17.24
Cooperative Development Authority		4	0.61
Insurance Commission			
National Tax Research Center			
Privatization and Management Office		67	94.37
DEPARTMENT OF FINANCE		**114**	**0.60**
DEPARTMENT OF FOREIGN AFFAIRS		12	0.67
Foreign Service Institute			
Technical Cooperation Council of the Philippines			
UNESCO National Commission of the Philippines		1	7.69
DEPARTMENT OF FOREIGN AFFAIRS		**13**	**0.69**
DEPARTMENT OF HEALTH		7	0.11
Government Hospitals		3	0.02
Commission on Population			
DEPARTMENT OF HEALTH		**10**	**0.04**
DEPARTMENT OF INTERIOR AND LOCAL GOVERNMENT		39	0.77
National Council for Civil Aviation Security			
Bureau of Fire Protection	NU		
Bureau of Fire Protection	U		
Bureau of Jail Management and Penology	NU		
Bureau of Jail Management and Penology	U		
Local Government Academy			
National Police Commission		15	1.29
Philippine National Police	NU		
Philippine National Police	U		
Philippine Public Safety College	NT	4	2.37
Philippine Public Safety College	T		
DEPARTMENT OF INTERIOR AND LOCAL GOVERNMENT		**58**	**0.04**
DEPARTMENT OF JUSTICE		29	0.67
Bureau of Corrections	NT		
Bureau of Corrections	T		
Bureau of Immigration		24	2.40

Appendix V c

		PA	PA%
Commission on the Settlement of Land Problems		5	5.95
Land Registration Authority		2	0.06
Land Registration Authority - CARP			
National Bureau of Investigation		13	0.75
Office of the Government Corporate Counsel		4	3.60
Office of the Solicitor General		2	0.52
Parole and Probation Administration			
Public Attorney's Office		21	1.19
DEPARTMENT OF JUSTICE		**100**	**0.62**
DEPARTMENT OF LABOR AND EMPLOYMENT		19	1.12
Institute for Labor Studies			
National Conciliation and Mediation Board		1	0.49
National Labor Relations Commission		29	3.03
National Maritime Polytechnic	NT		
National Maritime Polytechnic	T		
National Wages and Productivity Commission - CO		5	5.49
Regional Tripartite Wages and Productivity Board			
Philippine OverseasEmployment Administration		2	0.44
Technical Education and Skills Development Authority	NT	58	2.15
Technical Education and Skills Development Authority	T	2	0.22
DEPARTMENT OF LABOR AND EMPLOYMENT		**116**	**1.60**
DEPARTMENT OF NATIONAL DEFENSE		32	10.19
General Headquarters & Logistics Command			
Philippine Air Force	NU		
Philippine Army	NU		
Philippine Military Academy	NU	34	11.76
Philippine Military Academy	T		
Philippine Navy	NU		
AFP Medical Center			
Government Arsenal			
National Defense College of the Philippines	NT	1	1.72
National Defense College of the Philippines	T		
Office of the Civil Defense			
Philippine Veterans Affairs Office			
Military Shrine Services			
Veterans Memorial Medical Center			
DEPARTMENT OF NATIONAL DEFENSE		**67**	**0.74**
DEPARTMENT OF PUBLIC WORKS AND HIGHWAYS		**482**	**2.66**
DEPARTMENT OF SCIENCE AND TECHNOLOGY		11	2.22
Advance Science and Technology Institute			
Food and Nutrition Research Institute			
Forest Product and Research Development Institute		1	0.42
Industrial Technology Development Institute			
Metals Industry Research and Development Center			
National Academy of Science and Technology			
National Research Council of the Philippines			
Philippine Atmospheric Geophysical and Astronomical Services Admin.			
Philippine Council for Advanced Science and Technology R&D		8	20.00

Appendix V d

		PA	PA%
Philippine Council for Agriculture, Forestry Natural Resources R&D			
Philippine Council for Aquatic and Marine R & D			
Philippine Council for Health R & D			
Philippine Council for Industry and Energy R & D			
Philippine Institute of Volcanology and Seismology			
Philippine Nuclear Research Institute			
Philippine Science High School	NT		
Philippine Science High School	T		
Philippine Textile Research Institute			
Science and Technology Information Institute			
Science Education Institute			
Technology Application and Promotion Institute			
DEPARTMENT OF SCIENCE AND TECHNOLOGY		**20**	**0.45**
DEPARTMENT OF SOCIAL WELFARE AND DEVELOPMENT		23	1.07
Inter-Country Adoption Board		7	31.82
National Council for the Welfare of Children		1	3.03
National Council for the Welfare of Disabled Persons		1	1.75
DEPARTMENT OF SOCIAL WELFARE AND DEVELOPMENT		**32**	**1.41**
DEPARTMENT OF TOURISM		13	2.09
Intramuros Administration			
National Parks Development Committee		1	0.16
DEPARTMENT OF TOURISM		**14**	**1.06**
DEPARTMENT OF TRADE AND INDUSTRY		68	2.91
Board of Investments		3	1.01
Construction Industry Authority of the Philippines			
ConstructionManpower Development Foundation			
Intellectual Property Office		6	2.01
Philippine Trade Training Center			
Product Development and Design Center of the Philippines			
DEPARTMENT OF TRADE AND INDUSTRY		**77**	**2.41**
DEPARTMENT OF TRANSPORTATION AND COMMUNICATIONS		206	23.07
Air Transportation Office		4	0.14
Land Transportation Franchising and Regulatory Board		12	3.70
Land Transportation Office			
Philippine Coast Guard	NU	21	5.00
Philippine Coast Guard	U		
Civil Aeronautics Board			
Maritime Industry Authority		13	2.76
National Telecommunications Commission		7	1.40
Office of Transport Cooperatives		2	5.13
Toll Regulatory Board			
DEPARTMENT OF TRANSPORTATION & COMMUNICATIONS		**265**	**2.13**
NATIONAL ECONOMIC AND DEVELOPMENT AUTHORITY		7	0.59
National Statistical Coordination Board			
National Statistics Office		2	0.07
Philippine National Volunteer Service Coordinating Agency			
Statistical Research and Training Center			
Tariff Commission		4	3.77

Appendix V e

		PA	PA%
NATIONAL ECONOMIC AND DEVELOPMENT AUTHORITY		13	0.31
OFFICE OF THE PRESS SECRETARY		15	17.65
Bureau of Broadcast Services			
Bureau of Communications Services			
National Printing Office			
News and Information Bureau		1	0.44
Philippine Information Agency			
Presidential Broadcast Staff- RTVM		1	0.78
OFFICE OF THE PRESS SECRETARY		**17**	**0.73**
OTHER EXECUTIVE OFFICES			
Commission on Filipinos Overseas		2	3.23
Commission on Higher Education	NT	27	4.55
Commission on Higher Education	T		
Commission on Information and Communications Technology			
National Computer Center			
Telecommunications Office		2	0.05
Commission on the Filipino Language		3	4.69
Dangerous Drugs Board		4	3.13
Energy Regulatory Commission		21	8.90
Games and Amusement Board		7	3.83
Housing and Land Use Regulatory Board		6	1.29
Housing and Urban Development Coordinating Council		33	32.35
Metro Manila Development Authority		6	0.13
Movie and Television Review and Classification Board		31	38.75
National Anti-Poverty Commission		11	34.38
National Commission for Culture and the Arts			
National Commission for Culture and the Arts (Proper)		1	3.13
National Historical Institute		7	3.10
National Library			
National Museum			
Records Management and Archives Office			
National Commission on the Role of Filipino Women		3	4.55
National Security Council		22	27.85
National Water Resources Board			
National Youth Commission		23	26.14
Office on Muslim Affairs		7	0.86
Optical Media Board			
Palawan Council for Sustainable Development Staff		5	20.00
Pasig River Rehabilitation Commission		31	100.00
Philippine Racing Commission		9	9.89
Philippine Sports Commission		13	9.49
Presidential Commission for the Urban Poor		7	4.86
Presidential Commission on Good Government		22	24.18
Presidential Legislative Liaison Office		6	17.14
Presidential Management Staff		3	0.85
Professional Regulation Commission		7	1.65
Securities and Exchange Commission		29	8.08
OTHER EXECUTIVE OFFICES		**348**	**2.26**
TOTAL NATIONAL EXECUTIVE		**3531**	**0.39**

Source: compiled from material provided by the CSC, 2007.

Note: T - Teaching staff, U - Uniformed staff, NT - Non-teaching staff, NU - Non-uniformed staff

Appendix VI
Political Appointees by Branch/Agency - Legislature

CONGRESS OF THE PHILIPPINES	PA	PA%
Senate	774	52.02
Senate Electoral Tribunal	47	41.59
Congressional Oversight Committee on Agriculture and Fisheries Modernization		
Congressional Oversight Committee on Labor and Employment	1	100.00
Legislative Oversight Committee on the Visiting Forces Agreement	2	100.00
Joint Congressional Power Commission	1	3.13
Commission on Appointments	87	43.94
House of Representatives	1558	54.29
House of Representatives Electoral Tribunal	39	31.97
CONGRESS OF THE PHILIPPINES	**2509**	**51.99**

Source: compiled from materials provided by the CSC, 2007.

PA   Political Appointees. See table 2 and text for more details.

Appendix VII
Political Appointees by Branch/Agency –
Judiciary and Constitutional Offices

	PA	PA%
THE JUDICIARY		
Supreme Court of the Philippines and the Lower Courts	515	2.05
Court of Appeals	545	38.16
Court of Tax Appeals	19	25
Sandiganbayan	65	19.23
Judiciary Total	**1144**	**4.25**
CONSTITUTIONAL OFFICES		
Civil Service Commission	31	2.40
Career Executive Service Board	1	2
Commission on Audit	23	0.24
Commission on Elections - CO	111	2.20
Commission on Human Rights	41	7.20
Ombudsman	44	5.80
Constitutional Offices Total	**251**	**1.45**

Source: compiled from materials provided by the CSC, 2007.

PA   Political Appointees. See table 2 and text for more details.

Appendix VIII

Scores for Machiavellianism, Self, Others, and Alienation among staff in the Civil Service Commission

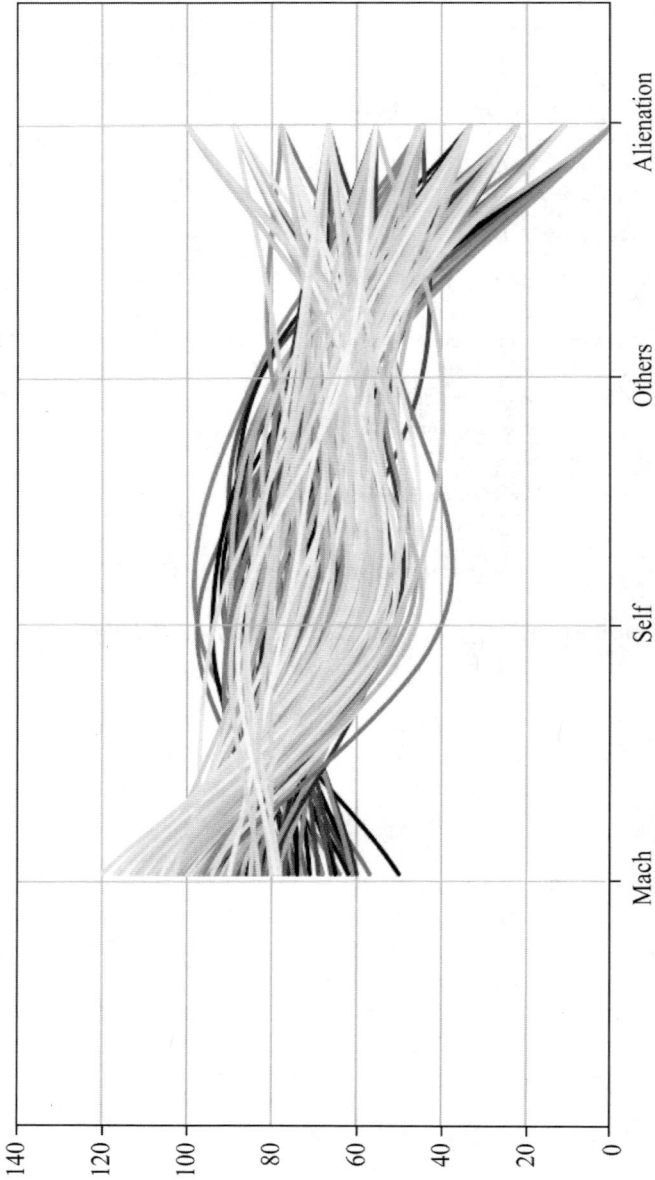

Source: compiled from surveys conducted by the author in 2007.

Appendix IX
Correlations Amongst Scores for Machiavellianism, Self, Others, and Alienation (Shift 1) by Agency

	mach	self	others	alienation	
mach	1	-.586**	-.428**	.550**	
self	-.586**	1	.597**	-.638	**BIR**
others	-.428**	.597**	1	-.501	**(N183)**
alienation	.550**	-.638**	-.501**	1	
mach	1	-.649**	-.582**	.539**	
self	-.649**	1	.753**	-.675**	**BOC**
others	-.582**	.753**	1	-.554**	**(N103)**
alienation	.539**	-.675**	-.554**	1	
mach	1	-.524**	-.496**	.360**	
self	-.524**	1	.642**	-.549**	**BRG**
others	-.496**	.642**	1	-.416**	**(N177)**
alienation	.360**	-.549**	-.416**	1	
mach	1	-.595**	-.565**	.525**	
self	-.595**	1	.737**	-.654**	**CB**
others	-.565**	.737**	1	-.605**	**(N65)**
alienation	.525**	-.654**	-.605**	1	
mach	1	-.714**	-.660**	.449**	
self	-.714**	1	.808**	-.471**	**CSC**
others	-.660**	.808**	1	-.398**	**(112)**
alienation	.449**	-.471**	-.398**	1	
mach	1	-.542**	-.445**(0.002)	.410** (0.004)	
self	-.542**	1	.837**	-.567**	**CGR**
others	-.445**(0.002)	.837**	1	-.375** (0.009)	**(N48)**
alienation	.410** (0.004)	-.567**	-.375**(0.009)	1	
mach	1	-.708**	-.716**	.554**	
self	-.708**	1	.844**	-.730**	**DepEd**
others	-.716**	.844**	1	-.615**	**(N50)**
alienation	.554**	-.730**	-.615**	1	
mach	1	-.420*	-.480**	0.247	
self	-.420*	1	.408*	-0.226	**MMDA**
others	-.480**	.408*	1	-0.231	**(N31)**
alienation	0.247	-0.226	-0.231	1	
mach	1	-.473**	-.513**	.219	
self	-.473**	1	.739**	-.568**	**QCH**
others	-.513**	.739**	1	-.488**	**(N97)**
alienation	.219*	-.568**	-.488**	1	

** Correlation is significant at the 0.01 level (2-tailed)
* Correlation is significant at the 0.05 level (2-tailed)

Source: compiled from surveys conducted by the author in 2007.

Appendix X
Correlations Amongst Scores for Machiavellianism, Self, Others, and Alienation (Shift 2) by Agency

	mach	self	others	alienation	
mach	1	-.575**	-.489**	.653**	
self	-.575**	1	.578**	-.522**	BIR
others	-.489**	.578**	1	-.413**	(N170)
alienation	.653**	-.522**	-.413**	1	
mach	1	-.533**	-.500**	.701**	
self	-.533**	1	.779**	-.611**	BOC
others	-.500**	.779**	1	-.458**	(N111)
alienation	.701**	-.611**	-.458**	1	
mach	1	-.526**	-.586**	.745**	
self	-.526**	1	.638**	-.643**	BRG
others	-.586**	.638**	1	-.498**	(N139)
alienation	.745**	-.643**	-.498**	1	
mach	1	-.662**	-.687**	.748**	
self	-.662**	1	.732**	-.705**	CB
others	-.687**	.732**	1	-.609**	(N53)
alienation	.748**	-.705**	-.609**	1	
mach	1	-.648**	-.525**	.761**	
self	-.648**	1	.725**	-.638**	CSC
others	-.525**	.725**	1	-.482**	(N87)
alienation	.761**	-.638**	-.482**	1	
mach	1	-.421**	-.541**	.753**	
self	-.421**	1	.810**	-.608**	CGR
others	-.541**	.810**	1	-.678**	(N38)
alienation	.753**	-.608**	-.678**	1	
mach	1	-.804**	-.744**	.781**	
self	-.804**	1	.844**	-.733**	DepEd
others	-.744**	.844**	1	-.616**	(N38)
alienation	.781**	-.733**	-.616**	1	
mach	1	-.545**	-.528**	.634**	
self	-.545**	1	.725**	-.602**	QCH
others	-.528**	.725**	1	-.563**	(N84)
alienation	.634**	-.602**	-.563**	1	
mach	1	-.407* (0.035)	-.533** (0.004)	.782**	
self	-.407* (0.035)	1	.527** (0.005)	-0.078 (0.0698)	MMDA
others	-.533** (0.004)	.527** (0.005)	1	-.414*	(N27)
alienation	.782**	-0.078 (0.698)	-.414*	1	

** Correlation is significant at the 0.01 level (2-tailed)
* Correlation is significant at the 0.05 level (2-tailed)

Source: compiled from surveys conducted by the author in 2007.

Appendix XI
Correlations Amongst Scores for Machiavellianism, Self, Others, and Alienation (Shift 3) by Agency

	mach	self	others	alienation	
mach	1.000	-.586**	-.428**	.550**	
self	-.586**	1.000	.597**	-.638**	**BIR**
others	-.428**	.597**	1.000	-.501**	**(N205)**
alienation	.550**	-.638**	-.501**	1.000	
mach	1	-.674**	-.598**	.552**	
self	-.674**	1	.743**	-.686**	**BOC**
others	-.598**	.743**	1	-.486**	**(N112)**
alienation	.552**	-.686**	-.486**	1	
mach	1	-.584**	-.465**	.524**	
self	-.584**	1	.563**	-.697**	**BRG**
others	-.465**	.563**	1	-.339**	**(N144)**
alienation	.524**	-.697**	-.339**	1	
mach	1	-.562**	-.566**	.562**	
self	-.562**	1	.732**	-.636**	**CB**
others	-.566**	.732**	1	-.499**	**(N73)**
alienation	.562**	-.636**	-.499**	1	
mach	1	-.711**	-.555**	.578**	
self	-.711**	1	.766**	-.644**	**CSC**
others	-.555**	.766**	1	-.574**	**(N92)**
alienation	.578**	-.644**	-.574**	1	
mach	1	-.714**	-.673**	.575**	
self	-.714**	1	.789**	-.684**	**CGR**
others	-.673**	.789**	1	-.616**	**(N35)**
alienation	.575**	-.684**	-.616**	1	
mach	1	-.806**	-.853**	.645**	
self	-.806**	1	.875**	-.839**	**DepEd**
others	-.853**	.875**	1	-.797**	**(N36)**
alienation	.645**	-.839**	-.797**	1	
mach	1	-.620**	-.569**	.356**	
self	-.620**	1	.760**	-.509**	**QCH**
others	-.569**	.760**	1	-.503**	**(N110)**
alienation	.356**	-.509**	-.503**	1	
mach	1	-0.337	-.428*(0.02)	0.221	
self	-0.337	1	.826**	-0.128	**MMDA**
others	-.428* (0.02)	.826**	1	-0.07	**(N29)**
alienation	0.221	-0.128	-0.07	1	

* Correlation is significant at the 0.05 level (2-tailed)
** Correlation is significant at the 0.01 level (2-tailed)

Source: compiled from surveys conducted by the author in 2007.

Appendix XII
Correlations Amongst Scores for Machiavellianism, Self, Others, and Alienation (Shift 4) by Agency

	mach	self	others	alienation	
mach	1	-.714**	-.600**	.730**	
self	-.714**	1	.683**	-.686**	**BIR**
others	-.600**	.683**	1	-.526**	**(N156)**
alienation	.730**	-.686**	-.526**	1	
mach	1	-.653**	-.594**	.758**	
self	-.653**	1	.781**	-.648**	**BOC**
others	-.594**	.781**	1	-.487**	**(N94)**
alienation	.758**	-.648**	-.487**	1	
mach	1	-.470**	-.401**	.642**	
self	-.470**	1	.590**	-.550**	**BRG**
others	-.401**	.590**	1	-.371**	**(N136)**
alienation	.642**	-.550**	-.371**	1	
mach	1	-.684**	-.683**	.806**	
self	-.684**	1	.748**	-.745**	**CB**
others	-.683**	.748**	1	-.664**	**(N53)**
alienation	.806**	-.745**	-.664**	1	
mach	1	-.703**	-.556**	.703**	
self	-.703**	1	.763**	-.599**	**CSC**
others	-.556**	.763**	1	-.453**	**(N81)**
alienation	.703**	-.599**	-.453**	1	
mach	1	-.592**	-.360*	.748**	
self	-.592**	1	.636**	-.731**	**CGR**
others	-.360*	.636**	1	-.528**	**(N41)**
alienation	.748**	-.731**	-.528**	1	
mach	1	-.819**	-.857**	.750**	
self	-.819**	1	.839**	-.868**	**DepEd**
others	-.857**	.839**	1	-.826**	**(N36)**
alienation	.750**	-.868**	-.826**	1	
mach	1	-.529**	-.564**	.621**	
self	-.529**	1	.738**	-.504**	**QCH**
others	-.564**	.738**	1	-.418**	**(N82)**
alienation	.621**	-.504**	-.418**	1	
mach	1	-.523* (0.031)	-.604* (0.01)	.798**	
self	-.523* (0.031)	1	.625**(0.007)	-.323	**MMDA**
others	-.604*(0.01)	.625**(0.007)	1	-.365	**(N17)**
alienation	.798**	-.323	-.365	1	

* Correlation is significant at the 0.05 level (2-tailed)
** Correlation is significant at the 0.01 level (2-tailed)

Source: compiled from surveys conducted by the author in 2007.

Appendix XIII

The Association Between Machiavellianism and Authoritarianism

(all agencies)

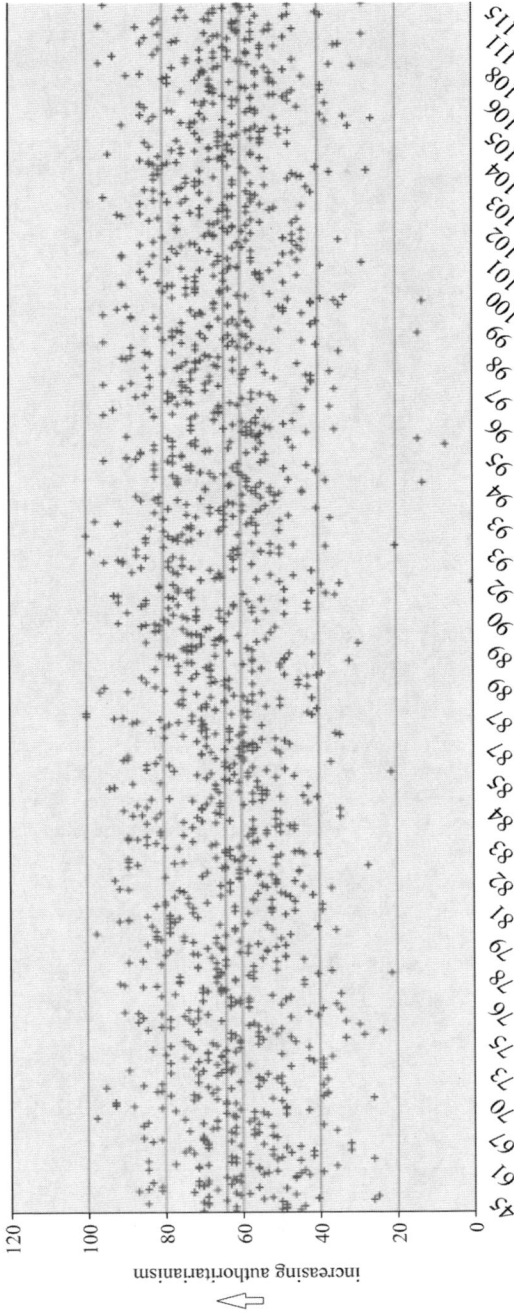

Source: compiled from surveys conducted by the author in 2007.

247

Appendix XIV

The Association Between Machiavellianism and the Perceived Quality of Organizations (all agencies)

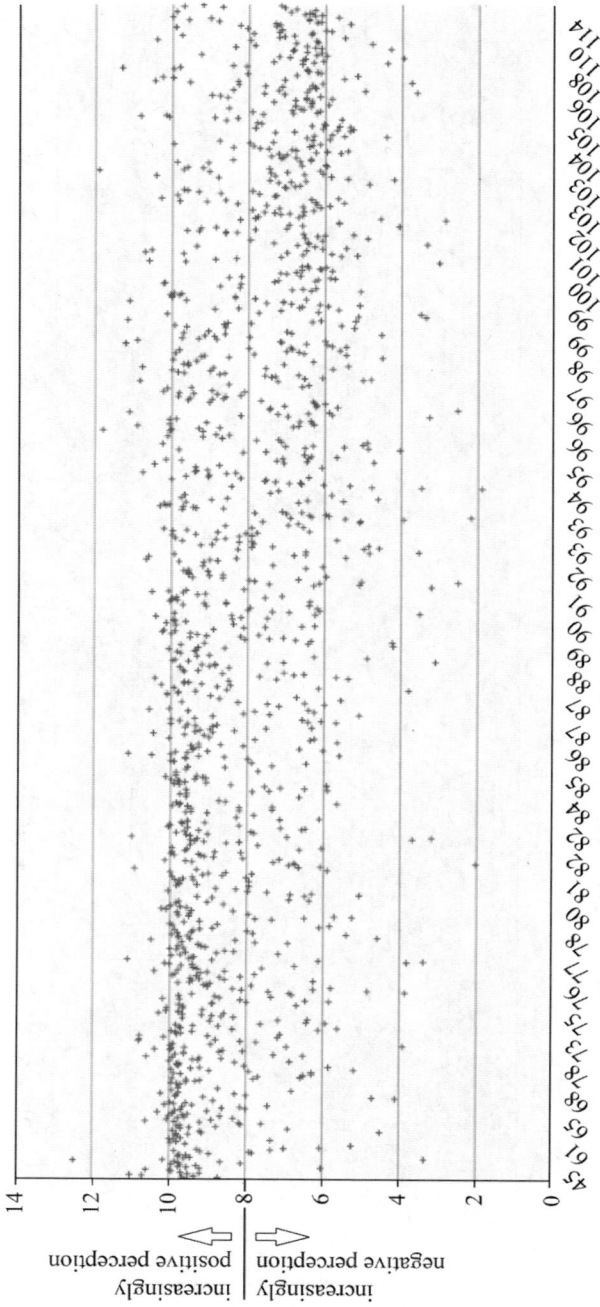

Source: compiled from surveys conducted by the author in 2007.

Appendix XV
Number of Offences and Amounts Involved: DECS

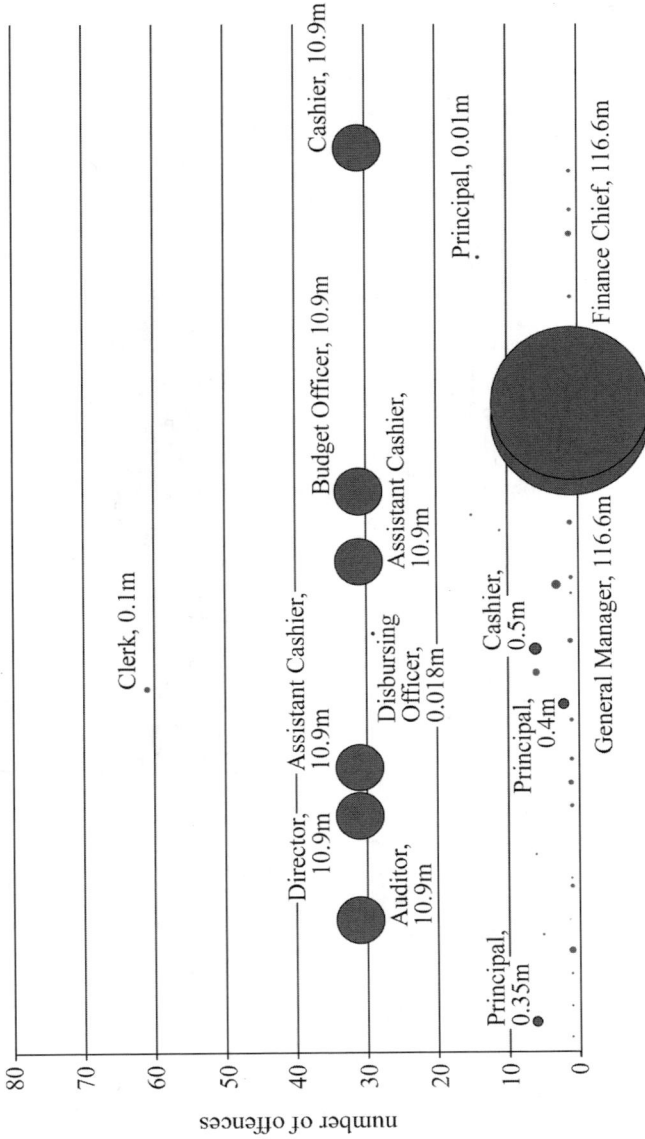

Source: compiled from materials provided by the Sandiganbayan, 2007.

Note: each bubble represents one official

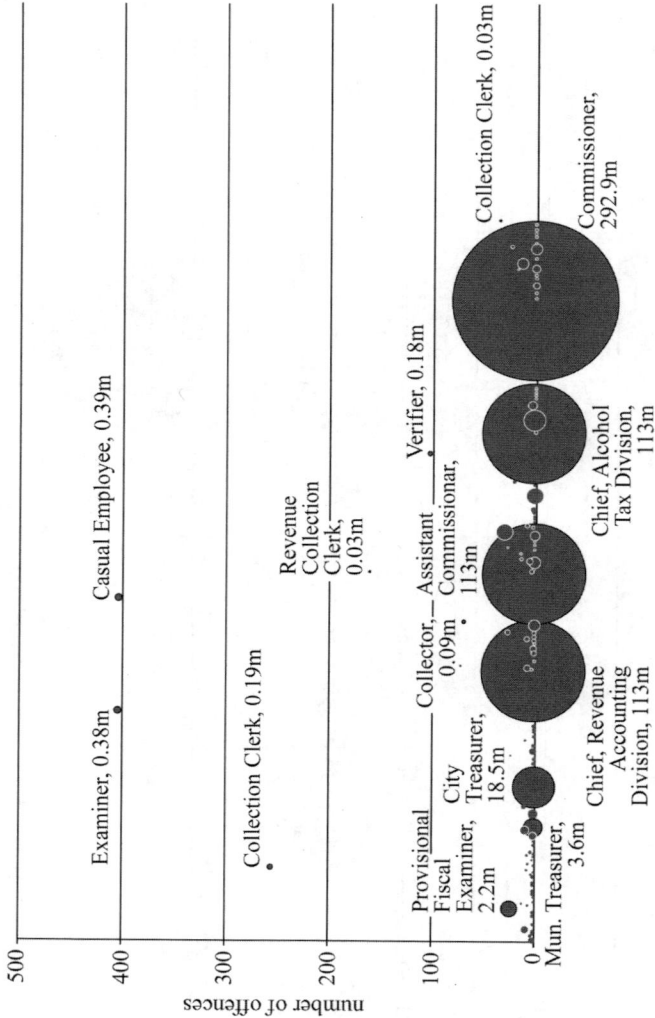

Appendix XVI
Number of Offences and Amounts Involved: DOF

Source: compiled from materials provided by the Sandiganbayan, 2007.

Note: each bubble represents one official

Bibliography

Abric, J.C. 1993. "Central system, peripheral system: Their functions and roles in the dynamics of social representations." *Papers of Social Representations* 2: 75-78.

Abueva, J. V. 1965. "Social background and recruitment of legislators and administrators in the Philippines." *Philippine Journal of Public Administration* 9: 10-29.

Abueva, J. V. 1970a. "Administrative culture and behavior and middle civil servants in the Philippines," in E. W. Weidner (ed.) *Development Administration in Asia.* Durham NC: Duke University Press, pp. 132-186.

Abueva, J. V. 1970b. "The contribution of nepotism, spoils and graft to political development," in A. J. Heidenheimer (ed.) *Political Corruption.* New York: Holt, Rinehart and Winston, pp. 534-539.

Alfiler, M. C. P. 1979. "Administrative measures against bureaucratic corruption: The Philippine experience." *Philippine Journal of Public Administration* 23: 321-349.

Alfiler, M. C. P. 1985. "Corruption control measures in the Philippines." *Philippine Journal of Public Administration* 29: 180-220.

Araral, E., Jr. 2005. "Bureaucratic incentives, path dependence, and foreign aid: An empirical institutional analysis of irrigation in the Philippines." *Policy Sciences* 8: 131-157.

Arce, W. T. and Poblador, N. S. 1981. "Formal organisations in the Philippines: Motivation, behavior, structure and change," *Philippine Studies* 25: 5-29.

Aron, R. 1935. *La Sociologie Allemande.* Paris: Alcan.

Asian Development Bank. 1998. *Anticorruption Policy.* Manila

Azurin, A. M. 2002. "Orientalism? Privileged vistas most probably." *Philippine Political Science Journal* 23: 139-150.

Bailey, F.G. 1983. *The Tactical Uses of Passion: An Essay on Power, Reason and Reality.* Ithaca, NY: Cornell University Press.

Balogh, T. 1966. *The Economics of Poverty.* London: Macmillan.

Banfield, E.C. 1970. "The moral basis of a backward society," in *Political Corruption,* A. J. Heidenheimer (ed.). New York: Holt, Rinehart and Winston, pp. 129-31.

251

Banfield, E.C. 1975. "Corruption as a feature of governmental organisation." *Journal of Law and Economics* XVIII: 587-605.

Banfield, E.C. 1958. *The Moral Basis of a Backward Society*. New York: Free Press.

Bardhan, P. 1997. "Corruption and development: A review of issues." *Journal of Economic Perspectives* XXXV: 1320-1346.

Bardhan, P. 2002. "Decentralisation of governance and development." *Journal of Economic Perspectives* 16: 185-205.

Bauer, P. and Yamey, B. 1957. *The Economies of Underdeveloped Countries*. Cambridge: Cambridge University Press.

Bautista, V. A. 1982. "Nature, causes and extent of corruption: A review of the literature." *Philippine Journal of Public Administration* 26: 235-270.

Bayley, D.H. 1966. "The effects of corruption in a developing nation." *Western Political Quarterly* XIX: 719-732.

Bell, D. 1976. *Cultural Contradictions of Capitalism*. New York: Basic Books.

Berger, E. 1952. "The relation between expressed acceptance of self and expressed acceptance of others." *Journal of Abnormal Social Psychology* 47: 778-782.

Berger, P. and Luckmann, T. 1966. *The Social Construction of Reality*. Garden City, NY: Anchor Books.

Bhargava V. and Bolongaita E. 2004. *Challenging Corruption in Asia: Case Studies and a Framework for Action*. Washington, DC: World Bank.

Bicchieri, C. and Duffy, J. 1997. "Corruption cycles." *Political Studies* XLV: 477-495.

Blau, P. 1973. *The Dynamics of Bureaucracy: A Study of Interpersonal Relations in Two Government Agencies*, revised edition. Chicago and London: University of Chicago Press.

Bourdieu, P. 1980. *The Logic of Practice*. Cambridge: Cambridge University Press.

Bourdieu, P. 1990 *In Other Words*. Cambridge: Cambridge University Press.

Brentano, F. 1973. *Psychology from an Empirical Standpoint*, volume 1. O. Kraus (ed.), L. McAlister et al. (trans.). London: Routledge and Kegan Paul.

Brilliantes, A. B. and Mangahas, J. V. 2006. "Philippines: Restructuring, reorganization and implementation," in Ho Khai Leong (ed.) *Rethinking Administrative Reforms in Southeast Asia*. Singapore: Marshall Cavendish Academic.

Brilliantes, A. B. and Pancho, A. 1988. "The Bureaucracy," in R. P. de Guzman and M. A. Reforma (eds.) *Government and Politics of the Philippines*. New York: Oxford University Press, pp. 180-206.

Briones, L. M. 1979. "Negative bureaucratic behavior and development: The case of the BIR." *Philippine Journal of Public Administration* 23: 255-278.

Brooks, R.C. 1910. *Corruption in American Politics and Life*. New York: Dodd, Mead, and Co. r"," ". New York: Holt, Rinehart and Winston.

Brown, D. E. 1991. *Human Universals.* Philadelphia: Temple University Press.

Business Week. 1993. "The destructive costs of greasing palms." December 6.

Callaghy, T.M. 1989. "Toward state capability and embedded liberalism in the Third World: Lessons for adjustment," in J.M. Nelson (ed.), *Fragile Coalitions: The Politics of Economic Adjustment.* New Brunswick, NJ: Transaction Publishers.

Campos J.E., Lien D., and Pradhan S. 1999. "The impact of corruption on investment: Predictability matters." *World Development* 27: 1059-1067.

Cariño L. V. 1975. "Bureaucratic norms, corruption and development." *Philippine Journal of Public Administration* 19: 278-292.

Cariño L. V. 1979. "The definition of graft and corruption and the conflict of ethics and law." *Philippine Journal of Public Administration* 23: 221-240.

Cariño L. V. 1985. "The politicization of the Philippine bureaucracy: Corruption or commitment?" *International Review of Administrative Sciences* 51: 13-18.

Cariño L. V. 1986. *Bureaucratic Corruption in Asia: Causes, Consequences and Controls.* Manila: JMC Press and UP College of Public Administration.

Cariño L. V. 1992. *Bureaucracy for Democracy.* Manila: Philippine Institute for Development Studies.

Cariño L. V. 1994. "Enhancing accountability in the Philippines: The continuing quest," in J. Burns (ed.), *Asian Civil Service Systems: Improving Efficiency and Productivity.* Singapore: Times Academic Press, pp. 106-125.

Cariño L.V. 1990. "Philippine public administration: A westernized system in an authoritarian Asian setting." In V. Subramaniam (ed.) *Public Administration in the Third World: An International Handbook.* New York: Greenwood Press, pp. 102-127.

Cariño L.V. 1983. "Administrative accountability: A review of the evolution, meaning and operationalisation of a key concept in public administration." *Philippine Journal of Public Administration* 27: 118-148.

Cariño, L. V. and de Guzman, R. P. 1979. "Negative bureaucratic behavior in the Philippines: The final report of the IDRC Philippine Team." *Philippine Journal of Public Administration* 23: 350-385.

Cartier-Bresson, J. 1997. "Corruption networks, transaction security and illegal social exchange." *Political Studies* XLV: 463-476.

Chen, A. H. Y. 1999. "Rational law, economic development, and the case of China." *Social and Legal Studies* 8: 97-120.

Cheng, T. J., Haggard, S. and Kang, D. 1998. "Institutions and growth in Korea and Taiwan: The bureaucracy." *Journal of Development Studies* 34: 87-111.

Chew, D. C. E. 1993. "Civil service pay in the Asia-Pacific region." *Asia-Pacific Economic Literature* 7: 28-52.

Christie, R.T. and Geis, F.L. 1970. *Studies in Machiavellianism.* New York: Academic Press.

Cohen, A. 1974. *Two-Dimensional Man: An Essay on the Anthropology of Power and Symbolism in Complex Society.* California: University of California Press.

Collingwood, R.G. 1946. *The Idea of History.* Oxford: Oxford University Press.

Cooley, C.H. 1964. *Human Nature and the Social Order.* New York: Charles Scribner's Sons.

Cooley, C.H. 1962 *Social Organization.* New York: Schocken Books.

Corpuz, O. D. 1989. *The Roots of the Filipino Nation.* Quezon City: Aklahi Foundation.

Corpuz, O. D. 1957. *The Bureaucracy in the Philippines.* Manila: Institute of Public Administration.

Crouch, H. 1985. *Economic Change, Social Structure, and Political Systems in Southeast Asia: Philippine Development Compared with Other ASEAN Countries.* Singapore: Institute of Southeast Asian Studies.

Crouch, H. 1979. "Patrimonialism and military rule in Indonesia." *World Politics* 31: 571-87.

Dans, A. M. 1977. "The Philippine Civil Service: Structure and policies." *Philippine Journal of Public Administration* 21: 283-302.

Dasgupta, P. 2000. "Economic progress and the idea of social capital," in P.Dasgupta and I. Serageldon (eds.). *Social Capital: A Multifaceted Perspective.* Washington, DC: World Bank, pp. 325-424.

De Guzman, R. P. 2003. "Is there a Philippine Public Administration?" in V. A. Bautista, Afiler, M. C. P., Reyes, D. R. and Tapales, P. D. (eds.) *Introduction to Public Administration in the Philippines.* NCPAG, University of the Philippines, pp. 3-11.

De Guzman, R.P. 1979. "Bureaucratic behavior and development: A case study of supply management in a Philippine government agency." *Philippine Journal of Public Administration* 23: 279-295.

de Sardan, Olivier J.P. 1999. "A moral economy of corruption in Africa?" *Journal of Modern African Studies* 37: 25-52.

Deaux, K. and Philogène, G. 2001. *Representations of the Social.* Oxford: Oxford University Press.

Department of Budget and Management. 1995. *Re-engineering the Bureaucracy for Better Governance: Principles and Parameters.* Manila: DBM.

Derrida, J. 1976. *Of Grammatology.* Baltimore, MD: Johns Hopkins University Press.

Derrida, J. 1978. *Writing and Difference.* London: Routledge.

Dia, M. 1996. *Africa's Management in the 1990s and Beyond: Reconciling Indigenous and Transplanted Institutions.* Washington, DC: World Bank.

Dilthey, W. 1976. *Selected Writings.* H. Rickman (ed. and trans.). Cambridge: Cambridge University Press.

Dittmer, L. 1995. "Chinese informal politics reconsidered." *China Journal* 34: 193-205.

Dittmer, L. 1995. "Chinese informal politics." *China Journal* 34: 1-34

Dobel, J.P. 1978. "The corruption of a state." *American Political Science Review* 72: 958-73.

Doise, W., Clémence, A. and Lorenzi-Cioldi, F. 1993. *The Quantitative Analysis of Social Representations.* London: Taylor and Francis.

Downs, A. 1967. *Inside Bureaucracy.* Boston: Little, Brown and Company.

Dunleavy, P. 1991. *Democracy, Bureaucracy and Public Choice: Economic Explanations in Political Science.* London: Harvester Wheatsheaf.

Durkheim, E. 1984. *The Division of Labour in Society.* Basingstoke: Macmillan.

Duveen, G. and Lloyd, B. 1993. "An ethnographic approach to social representations," in G. M. Breakwell and D.V. Canter (eds.), *Empirical Approaches to Social Representations.* Oxford: Oxford University Press, pp. 90-109.

Eckstein, H. 1966. *Division and Cohesion in Democracy: Study of Norway.* Princeton, NJ: Princeton University Press.

Elias, N. 1994. *The Civilizing Process.* Edmund Jephcott (trans.). Oxford: Oxford University Press.

Endriga, J. N. 1979. "Historical notes on graft and corruption in the Philippines." *Philippine Journal of Public Administration* 23: 241-254.

Endriga, J. N. 1985. "Stability and social change in the Philippines." *Philippine Journal of Public Administration* 29: 12-54.

Endriga, J. N. 2001. "The National Civil service System in the Philippines," in J. Burns and B. Bowornwathana (eds.) *Civil Service System in Asia.* Cheltenham: Edward Elgar Publishing.

Evans, P. 1992. "The state as problem and solution: predation, embedded autonomy, and structural change," in S. Haggard and R.R. Kaufman (eds.), *The Politics of Economic Adjustment.* Princeton, NJ: Princeton University Press, pp. 139-180.

Evans, P. B. 1995. *Embedded Autonomy: States and Industrial Transformation.* Princeton, NJ: Princeton University Press.

Evans, P. B. 1989. "Predatory, developmental and other apparatuses: A comparative political economy perspective on the third world state." *Sociological Forum* 4: 233-246.

Farr, R., and Moscovici, S. (eds.) 1984. *Social Representations.* Cambridge: Cambridge University Press.

Fineman, S. (ed.) 1993. *Emotion in Organizations.* London: Sage.

Fiorina, M. and Noll, R. 1978. "Voters, bureaucrats and legislators: A rational choice perspective on the growth of bureaucracy." *Journal of Public Economics* 9: 239-254.

Firth, R. 1951 *The Elements of Social Organisation.* London: Watts and Co.

Fisman R. and Gatti R. 2002. "Decentralisation and corruption: Evidence across countries." *Journal of Public Economics* 83: 325-345.

Flatters F. and Macleod M. 1995. "Administrative corruption and taxation." *International Tax and Public Finance* 2: 397-417.

Fodor, J. 1987. *Psychosemantics: The Problem of Meaning in the Philosophy of Mind.* Cambridge, MA: Harvard University Press.

Foucault, M. 1980. *Power-Knowledge.* Brighton: Harvester.

Francisco, G. A. 1960. "Higher civil servants in the Philippines." Unpublished Ph.D. thesis. UP College of Public Administration.

Friedrich, C.J. 1963. *Man and His Government.* New York: McGraw-Hill.

Fritzen, S. A. 2007. "Discipline and democratize: Patterns of bureaucratic accountability in Southeast Asia." *International Journal of Public Administration* 30: 1435-1457.

Fukuyama, F. 1999. *The Great Disruption: Human Nature and the Social Order.* Simon and Schuster: New York.

Galtung, F. 1998. "Criteria for sustainable corruption control," in M. Robinson (ed.), *Corruption and Development.* London: Frank Cass, pp. 105-128.

Geach, P. and Black, M. (eds.) 1960. *Philosophical Writings of Gottlob Frege.* Oxford: Blackwell.

Geertz, C. 1965. "The impact of the concept of culture on the concept of man," in J. R. Platt (ed.), *New Views of the Nature of Man.* Chicago: University of Chicago Press.

Gerth, H. H. and Wright Mills, C. (eds. and trans.) 1977. *From Max Weber: Essays in Sociology.* London: Routledge and Kegan Paul.

Giddens, A. 1984. *The Constitution of Society.* Cambridge: Polity.

Giddens, A. 1992. *The Transformation of Intimacy.* Cambridge: Polity.

Girling, J. 1997. *Corruption, Capitalism and Democracy.* London: Routledge.

Goetz, A. 2007. "Manoeuvering past clientelism: Institutions and incentives to generate constituencies in support of governance reforms." *Commonwealth and Comparative Politics* 45: 403-424.

Goffman, E. 1956 (a). *The Presentation of Self in Everyday Life.* Edinburgh: University of Edinburgh Press.

Goffman, E. 1956 (b). "Embarrassment and social organization." *American Journal of Sociology* 62: 264-271.

Goffman, E. 1963. *Behaviour in Public Places.* Glencoe, IL: Free Press.

Golden, M. 2003. "Electoral connections: The effects of the personal vote on political patronage, bureaucracy and legislation in postwar Italy." *British Journal of Political Science* 33: 189-212.

Goudie, A.W. and Stasavage, D. 1998. "A framework for the analysis of corruption." *Crime, Law and Social Change* 29: 113-159.

Graham, M. 2003. "Emotional bureaucracies: Emotions, civil servants, and immigrants in the Swedish Welfare State." *Ethos* 30: 199-226.

Granovetter, M. 1985. "Economic action and social structure: The problem of embeddedness." *American Journal of Sociology* 91: 481-510.

Gray, C. 1979. "Civil service compensation in Indonesia." *Bulletin of Indonesian Economic Studies* 15: 85-113.

Guelke, L. 1974. "An idealist alternative in human geography." *Annals of the Association of American Geographers* 64: 193-202.

Gupta, A. 1995. "Blurred boundaries: The discourses of corruption, the culture of politics, and the imagined state." *American Ethnologist* 22: 375-402.

Haggard, S. 2000. *The Political Economy of the Asian Economic Crisis.* Washington, DC: Institute of International Economics.

Haller D. and Shore C. (eds.) 2005. *Corruption: Anthropological perspectives.* London: Pluto Press.

Haque, M. S. 1997. "Incongruity between bureaucracy and society in developing countries: A critique." *Peace and Change* 22: 432-462.

Haque, M. S. 2007. "Theory and practice of public administration in Southeast Asia: Traditions, directions and impacts." *International Journal of Public Administration* 30: 1297-1327.

Harris, C. 1978. "The historical mind and the practice of geography." In Ley, D. and Samuels, M. (eds.), *Humanistic Geography.* London:

Harris, R. 2003. *Political Corruption: In and Beyond the Nation State.* London: Routledge.

Hayami, Y. 1998. Community, market and state. In A. Maunder and A. Valdes (eds.). *Agriculture and Governments in an Independent World.* Amherst, MA: Gower, pp.3-14.

Heady, F. 1957. "The Philippine administrative system: A fusion of East and West." *Philippine Journal of Public Administration* 1: 27-45.

Heclo, H. and Wildavsky, A. 1974. *The Private Government of Public Money.* London: Macmillan.

Heidenheimer, A.J. (ed.) 1970. *Political Corruption.* New Brunswick, NJ: Transaction Publishers.

Heidenheimer, A.J. 1970 a. "The context of analysis," in A.J. Heidenheimer (ed.), *Political Corruption.* New Brunswick, NJ: Transaction Publishers.

Herzfeld, M. 1992. *The Social Production of Indifference: Exploring the Symbolic Roots of Western Bureaucracy.* Chicago: University of Chicago Press.

Heywood, P. 1997. "Political corruption: Problems and perspectives." *Political Studies* XLV: 417-435.

Hochschild, A. 1983. *The Managed Heart: The Commercialisation of Human Feeling.* Berkeley: University of California Press.

Hodder, R. 1996. *Merchant Princes of the East.* Chichester: Wiley.

Hodder, R. 2006. *Overseas Chinese and Trade Between the Philippines and China.* Lewiston: Mellen.

Huntington, S. 1968. *Political Order in Changing Societies.* New Haven, CT: Yale University Press.

Huntington, S. 1970. "Modernization and Corruption," in *Political Corruption,* A.J. Heidenheimer (ed.). New Brunswick, NJ: Transaction Publishers.

Hutchcroft, P. 1991. "Oligarchies and cronies in the Philippine state: The politics of patrimonial plunder." *World Politics* 43:216-243.

Hutchcroft, P. 1994. "Booty Capitalism: Business-government relations in the Philippines," in A. MacIntrye (ed.), *Business and Government in Industrialising Asia.* St. Leonards: Allen and Unwin, pp. 216-243.

Hutchcroft, P. 1997. "The politics of privilege: Assessing the impacts of rents, corruption and clientelism on Third World development." *Political Studies* XLV: 639-658.

Hutchcroft, P. 1998. *Booty Capitalism: The Politics of Banking in the Philippines.* Ithaca, NY: Cornell University Press.

Hutchcroft, P. 2001. "Centralisation and decentralisation in administration and politics: Assessing territorial dimensions of authority and power." *Governance* 14: 23-53.

Hwang, K. K. 1996. "South Korea's bureaucracy and the informal politics of economic development." *Asian Survey* 36: 306-319.

Ileto, R. C. 1999. *Knowing America's Colony: A Hundred Years from the Philippine War*. Honolulu: Center for Philippine Studies, School of Hawaiian, Asia and Pacific Studies, University of Hawai'i at Manoa.

Ileto, R. C. 2001. "Orientalism and the study of Philippine politics." *Philippine Political Science Journal* 22: 1-32.

Ileto, R. C. 2002. "On Sidel's response and bossism in the Philippines." *Philippine Political Science Journal* 23: 151-174.

James, N. 1993. "Divisions of emotional labour," in Stephen Fineman (ed.), *Emotions in Organizations*. London: Sage, pp. 94-117.

Jodelet, D. 1991. *Madness and Social Representations*. London: Harvester Wheatsheaf.

Johnston, M. 1998. "Fighting systemic corruption: Social foundations for institutional reform," in M. Robinson (ed.), *Corruption and Development*. London: Frank Cass, pp.85-104.

Johnston, R.J. 1992. *Philosophy and Human Geography*. London: Edward Arnold.

Jomo, K.S. 2000. "Comment: Crisis and the developmental state in East Asia," in R. Robinson, M. Beeson., K. Jayasuriya and H. Kim (eds.) . *Politics and Markets in the Wake of the Asian Crisis*. London: Routledge, pp.25-33.

Katz, D. and Kahn, R. L. 1967. *The Social Psychology of Organizations*. New York: John Wiley and Sons.

Keehan, E. B. 1990. "Managing interests in the Japanese bureaucracy." *Asian Survey* 11: 1021-1037.

Kelley, I.B. 1934. "Construction and validation of a scale to measure attitude towards any institution." *Purdue University Study of Higher Education* 35:18-36.

Kerkvliet, B. J. 1995. "Toward a more comprehensive analysis of Philippine politics: Beyond the patron-client, factional framework." *Journal of Southeast Asian Studies* 26: 401-19.

Khan, M.H. 1996. "The efficiency implications of corruption." *Journal of International Development* 8: 683-696.

Khan, M.H. 1998. "Patron-client networks and the economic effects of corruption in Asia," in M. Robinson (ed.), *Corruption and Development*. London: Frank Cass, pp. 15-29.

Klitgaard, R. 1991. *Controlling Corruption*. Berkeley: University of California Press.

Landé, C. H. 1965. *Leaders, Factions and Parties: The Structure of Philippine Politics*. Monograph 6. New Haven, CT: Yale University, Centre for Southeast Asian Studies.

Landé, C. H. 2001. "The return of 'people power' in the Philippines." *Journal of Democracy* 12: 88-102.

Landé, C. H. 1996. *Post-Marcos Politics: A Geographical and Statistical Analysis of the 1992 Presidential Election*. New York: St. Martin's Press.

Landé, C. H. 2002. "Political clientelism, developmentalism and post-colonial theory." *Philippine Political Science Journal* 23: 119-128.

Leach, E.R. 1954. *Political Systems of Highland Burma*. Cambridge, MA: Harvard University Press.

Lee, S. and Rhyu, S. 2008. "The political dynamics of informal networks in South Korea: The case of parachute appointment." *Pacific Review* 21: 45-66.

Leff, N.H. 1964. "Economic development through bureaucratic corruption." *American Behavioral Scientist* VIII: 8-14.

Levinson, D. and Huffman, O., 1955. "Traditional family ideology and its relation to personality," *Journal of Personality* 23: 251-273.

Leys, C. 1965. "What is the problem about corruption?" *Journal of Modern African Studies* 3: 215-230.

Li, J. S. 2003. "Relation-based versus rule-based governance: An explanation of the East Asian miracle and Asian crisis." *Review of International Economics* 11: 651-673.

Linz, J. J. and Chehabi, H.E. 1990. "Sultanistic Regimes." Paper presented at the Conference on Sultanism, Harvard University Center for International Affairs, November 2-3.

Magadia, Jose J. 2003. *State-Society Dynamics.* Quezon: Alteneo de Manila University Press.

Malcolm, N. 1966. "Knowledge of other minds," in G.. Pitcher (ed.), *Wittgenstein: The Philosophical Investigations: A Collection of Critical Essays.* Garden City, NY: Anchor, pp.371-383.

Mangahas, J. V. 1993. "A study of size, growth and nationalization of the bureaucracy." *Philippine Journal of Public Administration* 37: 201-238.

Masa, E. M. 1976. "The Higher Civil Service in the Philippines." Ph.D. thesis. UP College of Public Administration.

Mauro, P. 1995. "Corruption and growth." *Quarterly Journal of Economics* CX: 681-712.

Mauro, P. 1998. "Corruption and the composition of government expenditure." *Journal of Public Economics* 69: 263-279.

McClosky, H. and Schaar, J.H. 1965. "Psychological dimensions of anomy." *American Sociological Review* 30: 14-40.

McCoy, A. W. (ed.) 1993. *An Anarchy of Families: State and Family in the Philippines.* Madison: University of Wisconsin Press.

McMullan, M. 1961. "A theory of corruption: Based on a consideration of corruption in the public services and governments of British colonies and ex-colonies in West Africa." *Sociological Review:* 181-201

Michels, R. 1962. *Political Parties.* New York: Collier Books.

Moore, M.P. 1998. "Death without taxes: Democracy, state capacity, and aid dependence in the fourth world." in M. Robinson and G.. White (eds.), *The Democratic Developmental State: Political and Institutional Design.* Oxford: Oxford University Press, pp.84-121.

Mosca, G. 1939. *The Ruling Class.* New York: McGraw-Hill.

Moscovici, S. 1973. "Foreword," In C. Herzlich (ed.) *Health and Illness.* New York: Academic Press, pp. ix-xiv.

Moscovici, S. 1981. "On social representations," in J.P. Forgas (ed.) *Social Cognition: perspectives on Everyday Understanding.* London: Academic Press, pp. 181-209.

Moscovici, S. 1982. "The coming era of representations," in J.P. Codol and J.J. Leyens (eds.) *Cognitive Approaches to Social Behaviour.* La Haye: M. Nijhoff, pp. 115-150.

Moscovici, S. 1984. "The phenomenon of social representations," in R. Farr and S. Moscovici (eds.) *Social Representations.* Cambridge: Cambridge University Press, pp.3-70.

Mumby, D. And Putnam, L. 1992. "The politics of emotion: a feminist reading of bounded rationality." *Academy of Management Review* 17: 465-485.

Myrdal, G.. 1968. *Asian Drama: An Inquiry into the Poverty of Nation.* London: Penguin.

Nakata, T. 1978. "Corruption and the Thai bureaucracy: Who gets what, how and why in its public expenditures." *Thai Journal of Public Administration* 18: 102-28.

Nathan, A.J. and Tsai, K.S. 1995. "Factionalism: A new institutionalist restatement." *China Journal* 34: 157-192.

Niskasen, W. 1971. *Bureaucracy and Representative Government.* Chicago: Aldine-Atherton.

Noble, T. 2000. *Social Theory and Social Change.* Basingstoke: Macmillan.

North, D. 2004. *Institutions, Institutional Change, and Economic Performance.* Cambridge: Cambridge University Press.

Nye, J.S. 1967. "Corruption and political development: A cost benefit analysis." *American Political Science Review* LXI: 417-427.

Olson, M. 1982. *The Rise and Decline of Nations.* New Haven, CT: Yale University Press.

Parsons, T. 1949. *The Structure of Social Action.* Glencoe, IL: Free Press.

Parsons, T. 1951. *The Social System.* New York: Free Press.

Parsons, T. and Shils, E.A. 1951. *Toward a General Theory of Action.* Cambridge, MA: Harvard University Press.

Parsons, T. and Smelser, N. 1956. *Economy and Society.* London: Routledge and Kegan Paul.

Pedersen, P.E. 1996. "The search for the smoking gun." *Euromoney.* September: 49.

Perinbanayagam, R.S. 1985. *Signifying Acts.* Carbondale: Southern Illinois University Press.

Peters, B. G. 1995. "Bureaucracy in a divided regime: The United States," in J. Pierre (ed.) *Bureaucracy in the Modern State.* Cheltenham: Edward Elgar, pp. 18-38.

Philp. M. 1997. "Defining political corruption." *Political Studies* XLV: 436-462.

Polanyi, K. 1944. *The Great Transformation.* New York: Farrar and Rinehart.

Putnam, R. 1993. *Making Democracy Work.* Princeton, NJ: Princeton University Press.

Putnam, R. 1995. "Bowling alone: America's declining social capital." *Journal of Democracy* 6: 65-78.

Putnam, R. 2000. *Bowling Alone: The Collapse and Revival of American Community.* Simon and Schuster: New York.

Putzel, J. 1999. "Survival of an imperfect democracy in the Philippines." *Democratization* 6: 198-223.

Pye, L. 1995. "Factions and the politics of guanxi: Paradoxes in Chinese administrative behavior." *China Journal* 34: 35-54.

Quibria, M.G. 2003. "The puzzle of social capital: a critical review." *Asian Development Review* 20: 19-39.

Radcliffe-Brown, A.R. 1930. "Applied anthropology." *Australian and New Zealand Association for the Advancement of Science.* Brisbane Meeting.

Radcliffe-Brown, A.R. 1959. *Structure and Function in Primitive Society.* London: Cohen and West.

Rebullida, M.L. and Serrano, C. 2006. *Philippine Politics and Governance.* Manila: Ateneo de Manila University Press.

Rebullida, M.L. 2003. "Politics of the urban poor housing need: Civil society-state dynamics." *Philippine Political Science Journal* 24: 237-68.

Reuters Newswire. 1997. "Philippines corruption a nightmare" – Ramos. January 11.

Reyes, D. R. 1982. "Control processes and red tape in Philippine bureaucracy: Notes on administrative inefficiency." *Philippine Journal of Public Administration* 26: 271-285.

Reyes, D. R. 1990. *Bureaucracy in Action: Case Studies in Executive Leadership in Philippine Government.* Quezon City: College of Public Administration.

Reyes, D. R. 1994. "Reinventing government and bureaucracy in the Philippines: Old themes and new image." *Philippine Journal of Public Administration* 38: 77-87.

Reyes, D. R. 1999. "Public administration in the Philippines: History, heritage and hubris," in V. A. Miralao (ed.) *The Philippine Social Sciences in the Life of the Nation*, vol. I. Quezon City: The Philippine Social Science Council, pp. 243-260.

Ritzer, G. 2004. *The McDonaldization of Society.* Thousand Oaks, CA: Sage.

Ritzer, G. 2006. *McDonaldization: The Reader.* Thousand Oaks, CA: Pine Forge Press.

Robinson, J.P and Shaver, P.R. 1973. *Measures of Social Psychological Attitudes.* Survey Research Center, Institute for Social Research, University of Michigan: Ann Arbor.

Robinson, J.P., Shaver, P.R., and Wrightsman, L.S. (eds.) 1991. *Measures of Personality and Social Psychological Attitudes.* Academic Press: London.

Robinson, M. 1998. "Corruption and development: an Introduction," in M. Robinson (ed.) *Corruption and Development.* London: Frank Cass, pp.1-14.

Rogow, A.A. and Lasswell, H.D. 1970. "The definition of corruption," in A.J. Heidenheimer (ed.) *Political Corruption.* New York: Holt, Rinehart and Winston, pp.54-55.

Rose, R. 1980. "Government against sub-governments: a European perspective on Washington," in R. Rose and E. N. Suleiman (eds.) *Presidents and Prime Ministers.* Washington, DC: American Enterprise Institute, pp. 47-82.

Rose-Ackerman, S. 1999. *Corruption and Government: Causes, Consequences and Reform.* Cambridge: Cambridge University Press.

Sampson, S. 1983. "Bureaucracy and corruption as anthropological problems: A case study from Romania." *Folk* 25: 63-96.

Schutz, A. 1932 [1967]. *Phenomenology of the Social World*, G. Walsh and F. Lehnert (trans.). Evanston, IL: Northwestern University Press.

Scott, J.C. 1969a. "Corruption, machine politics, and social change." *American Political Science Review* 63: 1142-1159.

Scott, J.C. 1969b). "The analysis of corruption in developing nations." *Comparative Studies in Society and History* 11: 315-341.

Scruton, R. 1997. *Modern Philosophy: An Introduction and Survey.* London: Arrow Books.

Shaw, M. E. and Wright, J.M. 1967. *Scales for the Measurement of Attitude.* New York: McGraw-Hill.

Sidel, J. T. 1997. "Philippines politics in town, district and province: bossism in Cavite and Cebu." *Journal of Asian Studies* 56: 947-966.

Sidel, J. T. 1998. "The underside of progress: land, labor and violence in two Philippine growth zones, 1985-95." *Bulletin of Concerned Asian Scholars* 30: 3-12.

Sidel, J. T. 1999. *Capital, Coercion and Crime: Bossism in the Philippines.* Stanford, CA: Stanford University Press.

Sidel, J. T. 2002. "Response to Ileto. Or, why I am not an orientalist." *Philippine Political Science Journal* 23: 129-138.

Singh, G. 1997. "Understanding political corruption in contemporary Indian politics." *Political Studies* XLV: 626-638.

Sobel, J. 2002. "Can we trust social capital?" *Journal of Economic Literature* 40: 139-154.

Sta. Ana, F. III. 1996. "Re-engineering the bureaucracy, Philippine-style." *Philippine Journal of Public Administration* 40: 271-280.

Stencross, B. and Kleinman, S. 1989. "The highs and lows of emotional labor: detectives' encounters with criminals and victims." *Journal of Contemporary Ethnography* 17: 435-475.

Sto. Tomas, P. A. 1995. "Client satisfaction as a performance measure in the Philippine civil service." *Asian Review of Public Administration* 7: 597-608.

Stryker, S. 1962. "Conditions of accurate role-taking in Mead's theory," in A. Rose (ed.) *Human Behavior and Social Processes.* Boston: Houghton Mifflin, pp. 41-62.

Stryker, S. 1980. *Symbolic Interactionism: A Social Structural Version.* Menlo Park, CA: Benjamin/Cummings Publishing Co.

Tanzi, V. 1998. "Corruption around the world." *IMF Staff Papers* 45: 559-594.

Tapales, D., Enriquez, V. G. and Trinidad, O. S. 1995. "Value profile and corruption propensity: Correlates among employees in two types of government agencies." *Philippine Journal of Public Administration* 39: 407-433.

Tapales, P. D. 1984. "Socioeconomic Backgrounds of Higher Civil Servants in the Philippines c. 1983." *Philippine Journal of Public Administration* 28: 297-320.

Theobald, R. 1990. *Corruption, Development and Underdevelopment*. Durham, NC: Duke University Press.

Theobald, R. 1999. "So what really is the problem about corruption?" *Third World Quarterly* 20: 491-502.

Thompson, J. 1995. "Participatory approaches in government bureaucracies: Facilitating the process of institutional change." *World Development* 23: 1521-1554.

Thompson, M. R. 1995. *The Anti-Marcos Struggle: Personalistic Rule and Democratic Transition in the Philippines*. New Haven, CT: Yale University Press.

Tilman, R.O. 1968. "Emergence of black-market bureaucracy: Administration, development, and corruption in new states." *Public Administration Review* 28: 440-442.

Ting Gong. 1997. "Forms and characteristics of China's corruption in the 1990s: Change with continuity." *Communist and Post-Communist Studies* 30: 277-288.

Toye, J. and Moore, M. 1998. "Taxation, corruption and reform," in M. Robinson (ed.), *Corruption and Development*. London: Frank Cass, pp. 60-84.

Treisman, D. 2000. "The causes of corruption: A cross-national study." *Journal of Public Economics* 76: 399-457.

Tuan, Y.F. 1974. *Topophilia*. Englewood Cliffs, NJ: Prentice-Hall.

Valdeavilla, E. V. 1995. "Breakthroughs and challenges of making the Philippine government work for gender equality." *IDS Bulletin* 26: 94-101.

van Klarvan, J. 1970. Die historische Erscheinung der Korruption, in ihrem Zusammenhang mit der Staata- unde Gesellschaftsstrukur betrachet, *Vierteljahresschrift für Sozial- und Wirtschaftschichte* 44: 289-94. Reprinted as "The concept of corruption," P. Hofmann and K. Kurtz (trans.) in A.J. Heidenheimer (ed.) *Political Corruption*. New Brunswick, NJ: Transaction Publishers.

Varela, A. P. 1990. "Identifying Administrative culture in the Philippine Bureaucracy. Quezon City." UP College of Public Administration and Ford Foundation, Research Report.

Varela, A. P. 1995. "Different faces of Filipino administrative culture," in P. D. Tapales and N. N. Pilar (eds.) *Public Administration in the Year 2000: Looking Back into the Future*. Quezon City: UP College of Public Administration and UP Press, pp. 161-177.

Varela, A. P. 1996. *Administrative culture and political change*. Quezon City: UP College of Public Administration and UP Press.

Varela, A.P. 1992. "Personnel management reform in the Philippines: The strategy of professionalisation." *Governance* 5: 402-422.

Veneracion, J. B. 1988. *Merit or Patronage? A History of the Philippine Civil Service*. Quezon City: Great Books Trading.

Vivanathan S. and Sethi H. 1998. "By way of a beginning," in S. Vivanathan and H. Sethi, (eds.), *Foul Play: Chronicles of Corruption 1947-97*. New Dehli: Banyan Books, pp.1-14.

von Mises, L. 1944. *Bureaucracy*. New Haven, CT: Yale University Press.

Wade, R. 1982. "The system of administrative and political corruption: Canal irrigation in India." *Journal of Development Studies* 18: 287-328.

Wade, R. 1990. *Governing the Market.* Princeton, NJ: Princeton University Press.

Waterbury, J. 1973. "Endemic and planned corruption in a monarchical regime." *World Politics* XXV: 533-555.

Weber, M. 1997. "Bureaucracy," in H. H. Gerth and C. Wright Mills (eds. and trans.), *From Max Weber: Essays in Sociology.* London: Routledge, pp. 196-244.

Wei, S.J. 1997. "How taxing is corruption on international investors?" *Working Paper 6030.* National Bureau of Economic Research: Cambridge, MA.

Weiss, L. 1998. *The Myth of the Powerless State.* Ithaca, NY: Cornell University Press.

Weiss, L. 2000. "Developmental states in transition: adapting, dismantling, innovating, not normalizing." *Pacific Review* 13: 21-55.

Williams, R. 1999. "New concepts for old?" *Third World Quarterly* 20: 503-513.

Williams, R.J. 1976. "The problem of corruption: A conceptual and comparative analysis." *PAC Bulletin* 22: 41-53.

Wilson, G. and Wilson, M. 1945. *The Analysis of Social Change.* Cambridge: Cambridge University Press.

Woolgar, S. (ed.) 1988. *Knowledge and Reflexivity.* Sage: London.

World Bank. 1997. *World Development Report.* Washington, D.C.

Wui, M.A. and Lopez, G.S. (eds.) 1997. *State-Civil Society Relations in Policy Making.* Quezon City: Third World Studies Center.

Wurfel, D. 1988. *Filipino Politics: Development and Decay.* Ithaca, NY: Cornell University Press.

Yang, D. 2008. "Can enforcement backfire? Crime displacement in the context of customs reform in the Philippines." *Review of Economics and Statistics* 90: 1-14.

Yang, Mayfair. 1994. *Gifts, Favors and Banquets: The Art of Social Relationships in China.* Ithaca, NY: Cornell University Press.

Yang, Mayfair. 2000. "Putting global capitalism in its place: Economic hybridity, bataille and ritual expenditure." *Current Anthropology* 41: 477-509.

Yang, Mayfair. 2002. "The resilience of *guanxi* and its new deployments: A critique of some new *guanxi* scholarship." *China Quarterly* 170: 459-476.

Zinn, D. 2001. *La Racconandazzione: clientelismo vecchio e nouvo.* Donzelli: Roma.

Index